Here are my PSP, iPod, ring, ballpoint pen and the work gloves my mother made me that I wear whenever I draw. I always have all these things with me.

　—**Katsura Hoshino**

Shiga Prefecture native Katsura Hoshino's hit manga series *D.Gray-man* has been serialized in *Weekly Shonen Jump* since 2004. Katsura's debut manga, "Continue," appeared for the first time in *Weekly Shonen Jump* in 2003.

Katsura adores cats.

D.GRAY-MAN
VOL. 13
The SHONEN JUMP ADVANCED Manga Edition

STORY AND ART BY
KATSURA HOSHINO

English Adaptation/Lance Caselman
Translation/John Werry
Touch-up Art & Lettering/HudsonYards
Design/Matt Hinrichs
Editor/Gary Leach

Editor in Chief, Books/Alvin Lu
Editor in Chief, Magazines/Marc Weidenbaum
VP, Publishing Licensing/Rika Inouye
VP, Sales & Product Marketing/Gonzalo Ferreyra
VP, Creative/Linda Espinosa
Publisher/Hyoe Narita

Printed in the U.S.A.

Published by VIZ Media, LLC
P.O. Box 77010
San Francisco, CA 94107

SHONEN JUMP ADVANCED Manga Edition
10 9 8 7 6 5 4 3 2 1
First printing, May 2009

THE WORLD'S MOST CUTTING-EDGE MANGA

SHONEN JUMP ADVANCED

www.viz.com

www.shonenjump.com

RATED T+ FOR OLDER TEEN

PARENTAL ADVISORY
D.GRAY-MAN is rated T+ for Older Teen and is recommended for ages 16 and up. This volume contains fantasy violence.

ratings.viz.com

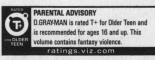

SHONEN JUMP ADVANCED MANGA EDITION

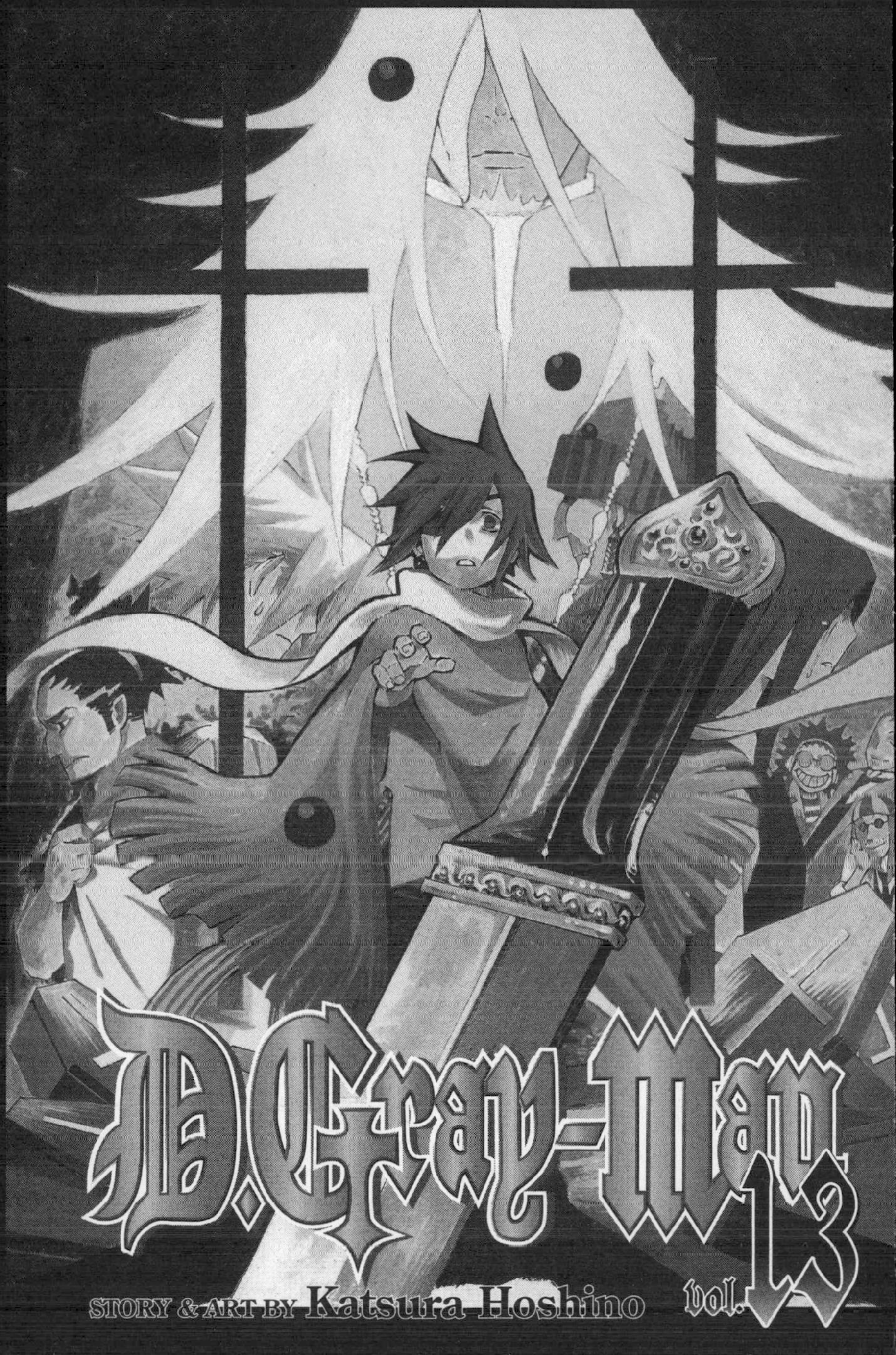
D.Gray-man
vol. 13
STORY & ART BY Katsura Hoshino

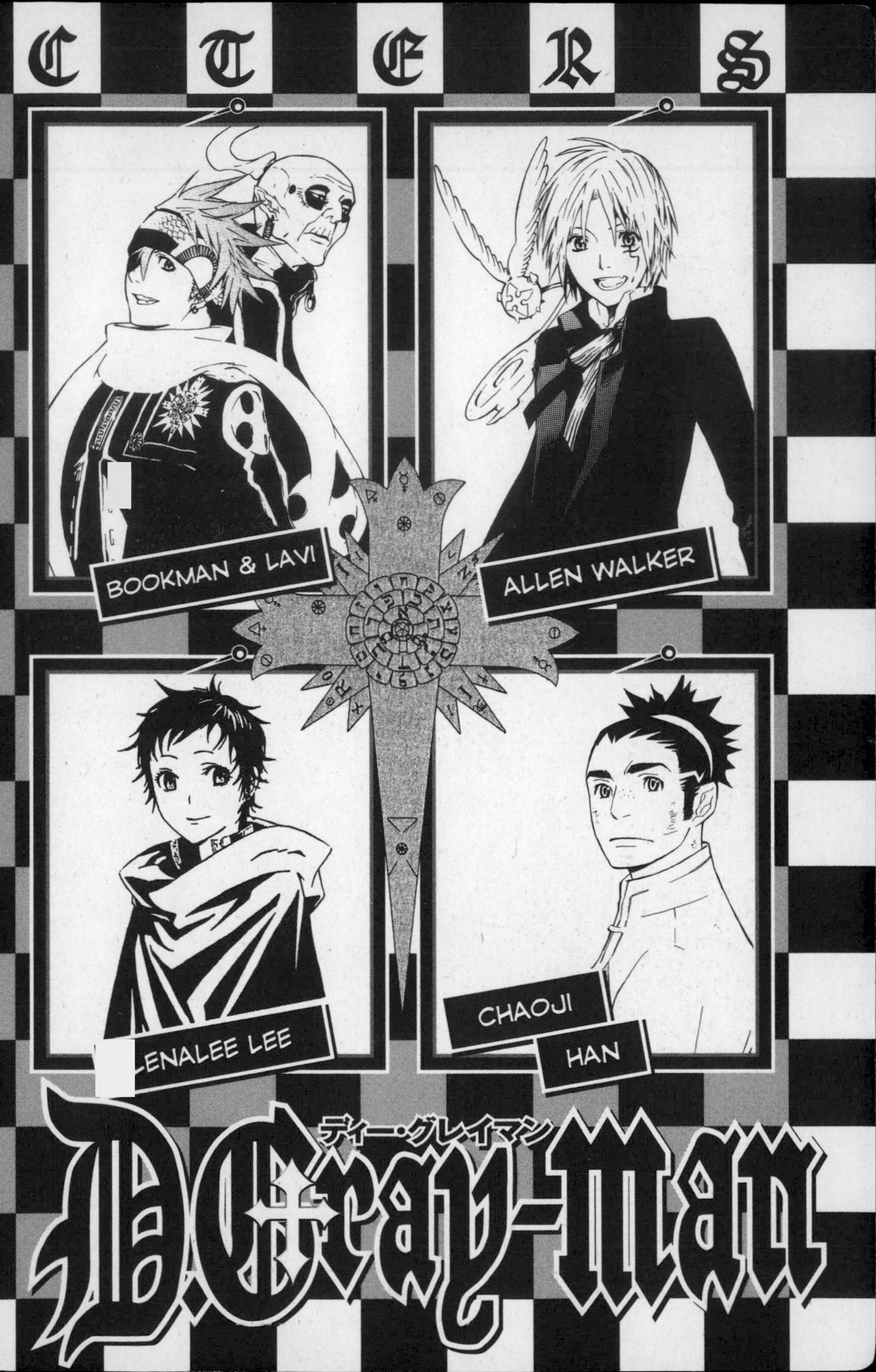
C T E R S
ALLEN WALKER
BOOKMAN & LAVI
CHAOJI
HAN
LENALEE LEE
ディー・グレイマン
D.Gray-man

CHARA

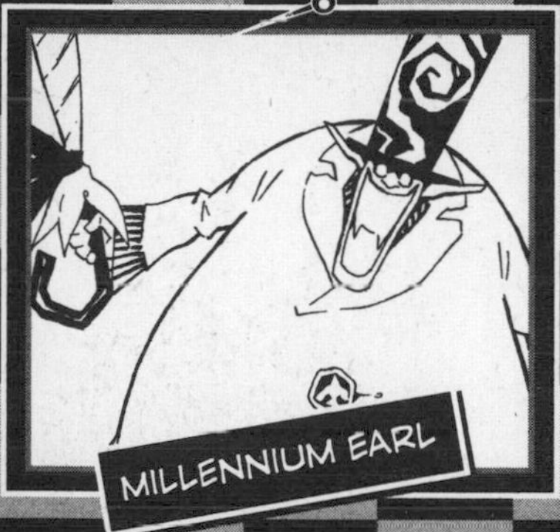
MILLENNIUM EARL

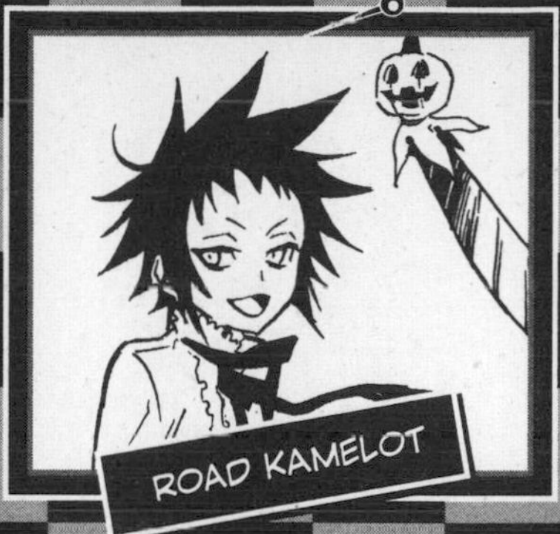
ROAD KAMELOT

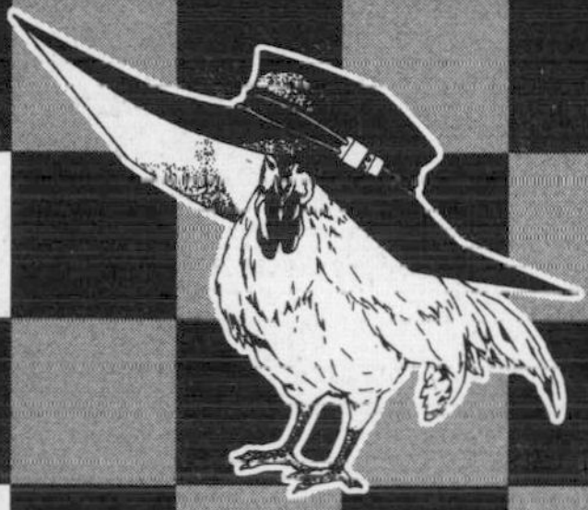

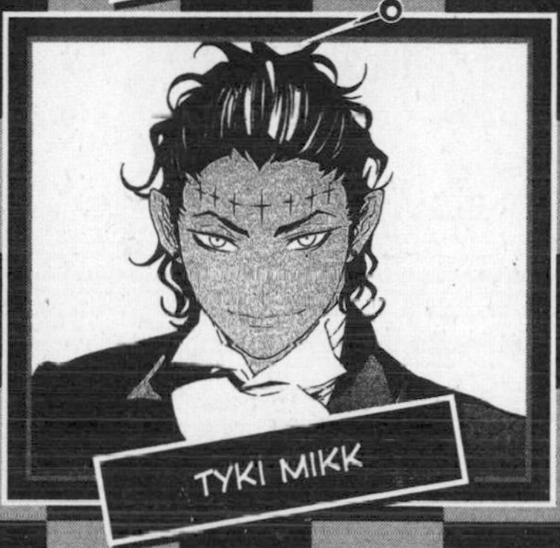
TYKI MIKK

STORY

IT ALL BEGAN CENTURIES AGO WITH THE DISCOVERY OF A CUBE CONTAINING AN APOCALYPTIC PROPHECY FROM AN ANCIENT CIVILIZATION AND INSTRUCTIONS IN THE USE OF INNOCENCE, A CRYSTALLINE SUBSTANCE OF WONDROUS SUPERNATURAL POWER. THE CREATORS OF THE CUBE CLAIMED TO HAVE DEFEATED AN EVIL KNOWN AS THE MILLENNIUM EARL BY USING THE INNOCENCE. NEVERTHELESS, THE WORLD WAS DESTROYED BY THE GREAT FLOOD OF THE OLD TESTAMENT. NOW, TO AVERT A SECOND END OF THE WORLD, A GROUP OF EXORCISTS WIELDING WEAPONS MADE OF INNOCENCE MUST BATTLE THE MILLENNIUM EARL AND HIS TERRIBLE MINIONS, THE AKUMA.

THE EXORCISTS FIGHT FOR THEIR LIVES AS THE ARK DISINTEGRATES AROUND THEM. ALLEN DEFEATS TYKI BY DESTROYING HIS INNER NOAH, AND IN RETALIATION, ROAD ATTEMPTS TO PIERCE LAVI'S HEART!

D.GRAY-MAN
Vol. 13

CONTENTS

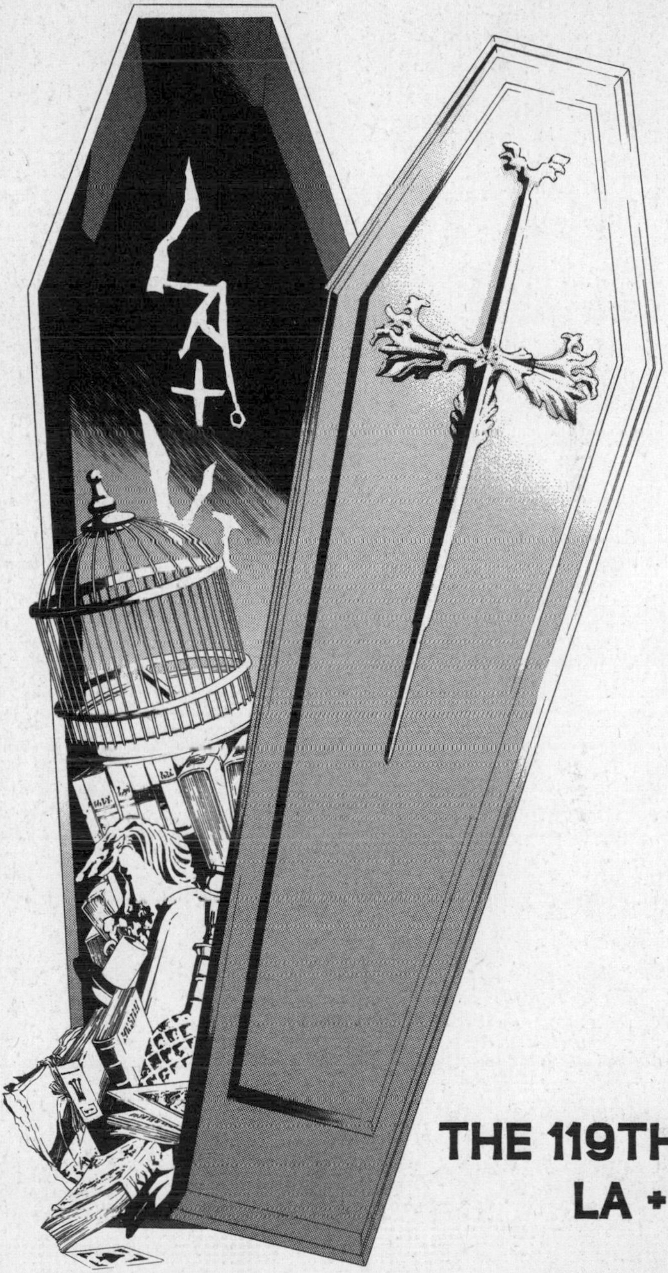
LA+VI

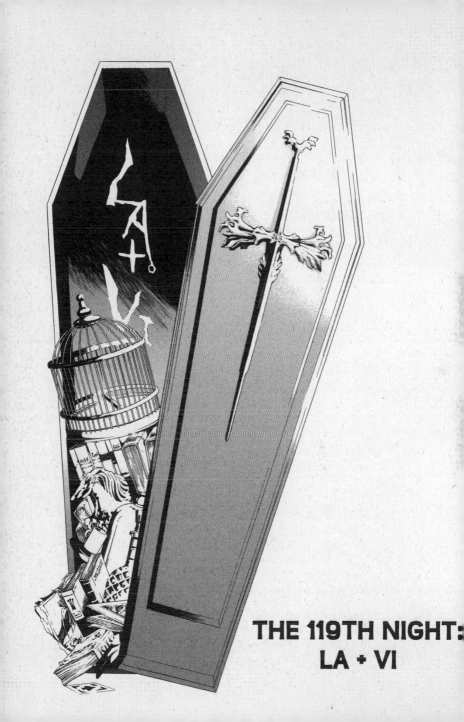

THE 119TH NIGHT: LA + VI

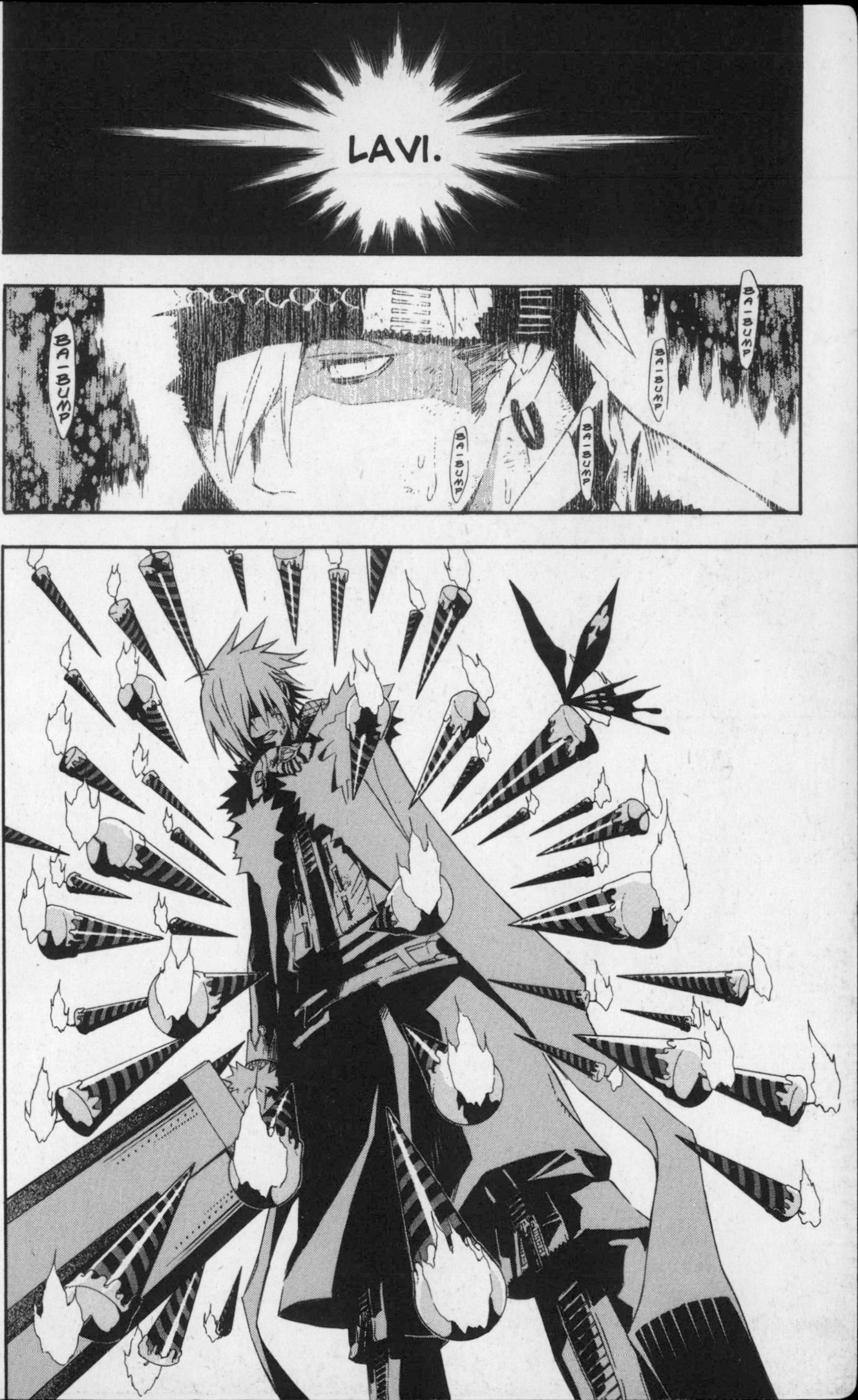
LAVI.
BA-BUMP
BA-BUMP
BA-BUMP
BA-BUMP
BA-BUMP

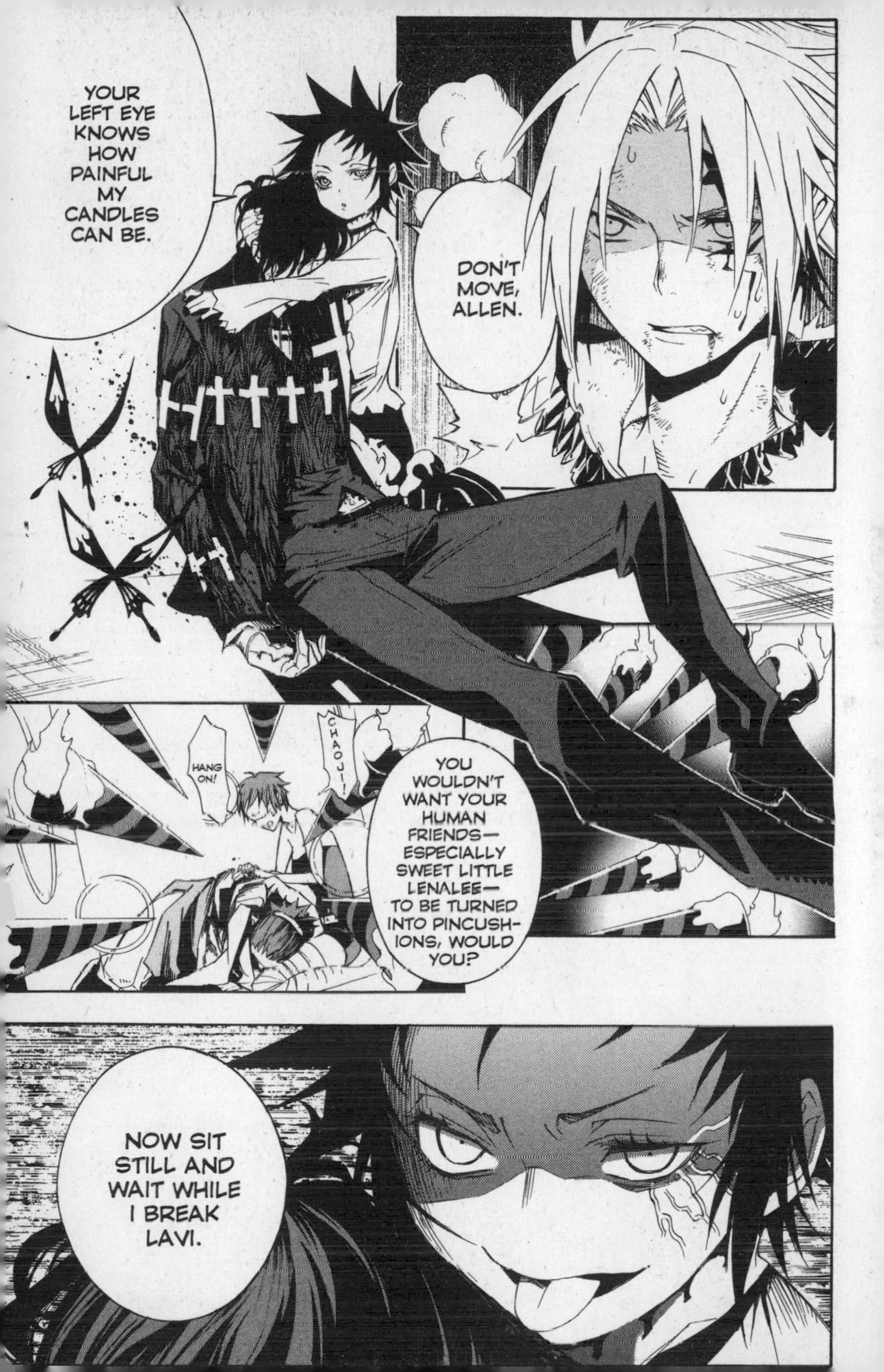
DON'T MOVE, ALLEN.
YOUR LEFT EYE KNOWS HOW PAINFUL MY CANDLES CAN BE.
YOU WOULDN'T WANT YOUR HUMAN FRIENDS— ESPECIALLY SWEET LITTLE LENALEE— TO BE TURNED INTO PINCUSHIONS, WOULD YOU?
CHAOJI!
HANG ON!
NOW SIT STILL AND WAIT WHILE I BREAK LAVI.

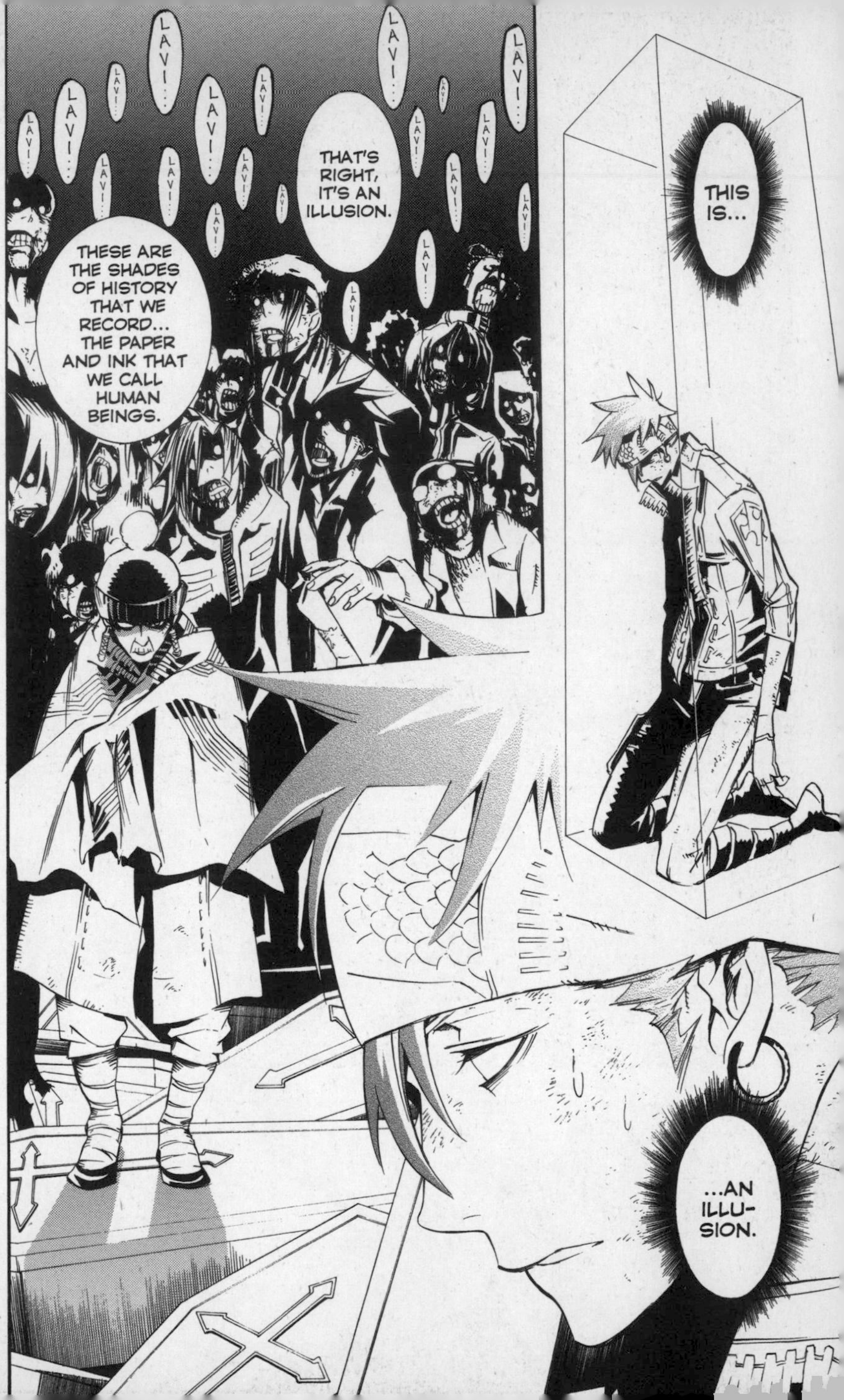
THIS IS...
...AN ILLUSION.
LAVI...
LAVI...
LAVI...
LAVI...
LAVI...
LAVI...
LAVI...
LAVI...
LAVI...
THAT'S RIGHT, IT'S AN ILLUSION.
LAVI...
LAVI...
LAVI...
LAVI...
LAVI...
LAVI...
LAVI...
LAVI...
LAVI...
LAVI...
THESE ARE THE SHADES OF HISTORY THAT WE RECORD... THE PAPER AND INK THAT WE CALL HUMAN BEINGS.

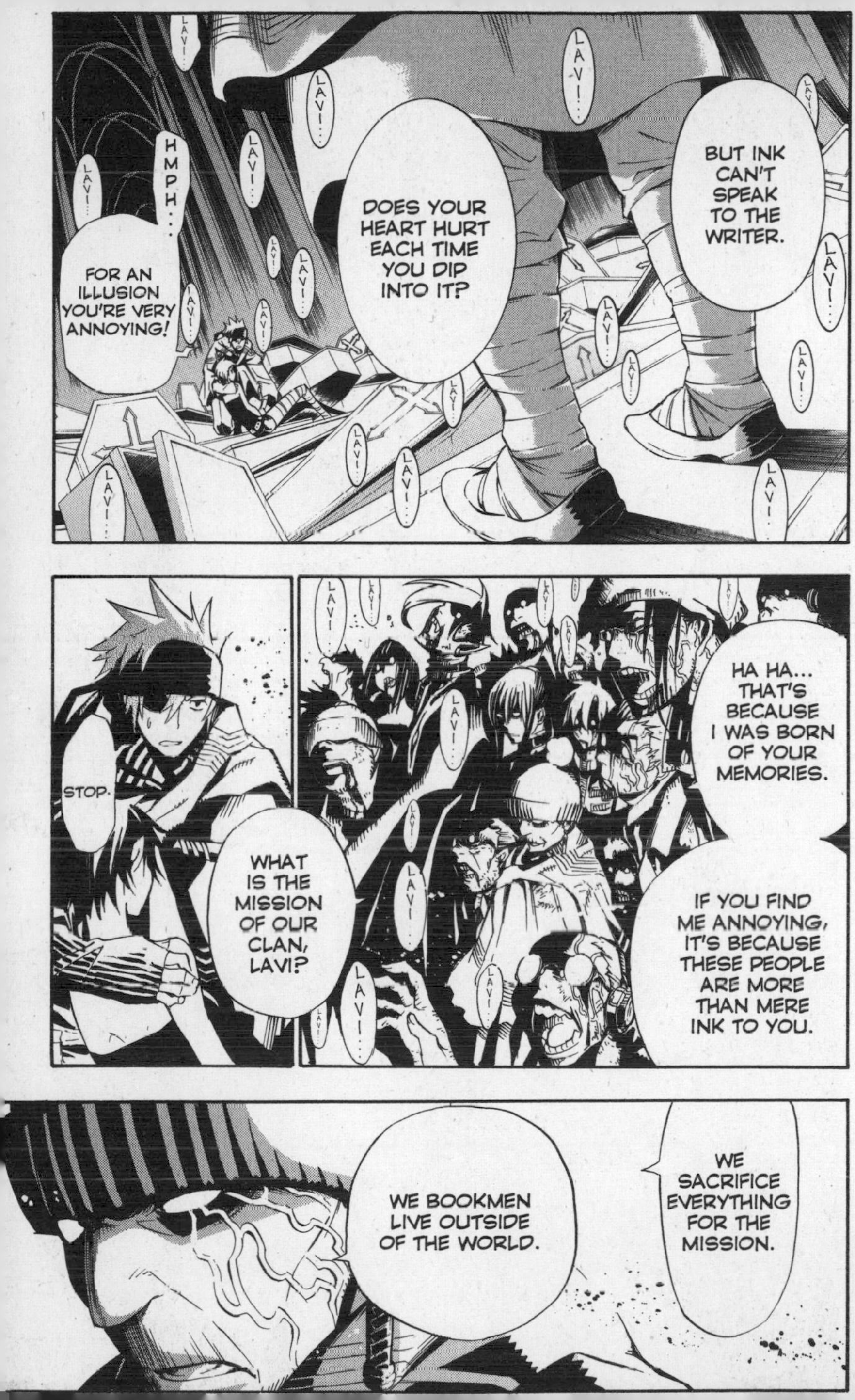
LAVI...
LAVI...
BUT INK CAN'T SPEAK TO THE WRITER.
LAVI...
LAVI...
LAVI...
LAVI...
DOES YOUR HEART HURT EACH TIME YOU DIP INTO IT?
LAVI...
LAVI...
LAVI...
LAVI...
LAVI...
LAVI...
LAVI...
LAVI...
HMPH...
LAVI...
LAVI...
FOR AN ILLUSION YOU'RE VERY ANNOYING!
LAVI...
LAVI...
HA HA... THAT'S BECAUSE I WAS BORN OF YOUR MEMORIES.
LAVI...
LAVI...
LAVI...
LAVI...
IF YOU FIND ME ANNOYING, IT'S BECAUSE THESE PEOPLE ARE MORE THAN MERE INK TO YOU.
LAVI...
LAVI...
LAVI...
LAVI...
LAVI...
WHAT IS THE MISSION OF OUR CLAN, LAVI?
LAVI...
STOP.
WE SACRIFICE EVERYTHING FOR THE MISSION.
WE BOOKMEN LIVE OUTSIDE OF THE WORLD.

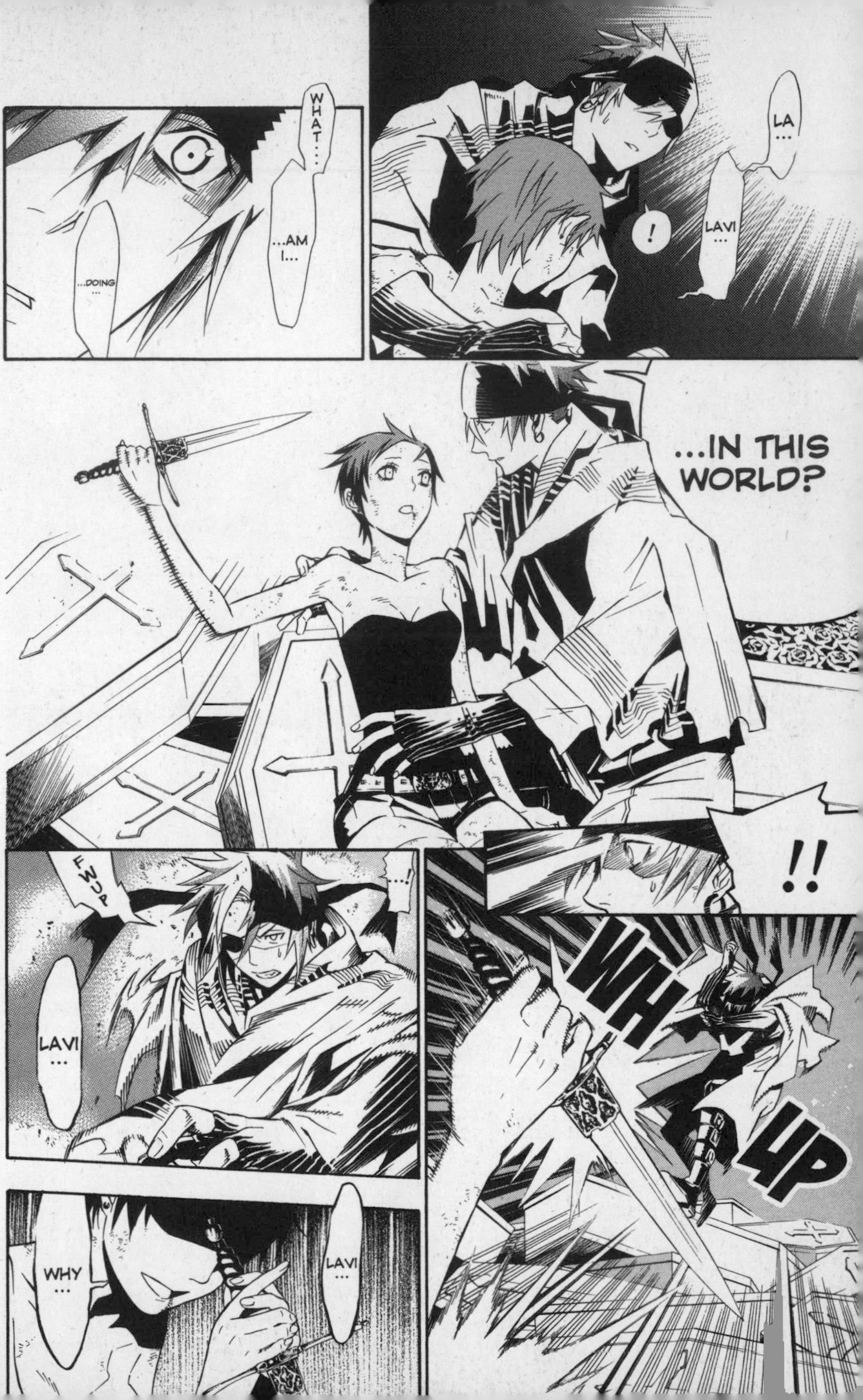
LA...
!
LAVI...
WHAT...
...AM I...
...DOING...
...IN THIS WORLD?
!!
WHUP
FWUP
...!
LAVI...
LAVI...
WHY...

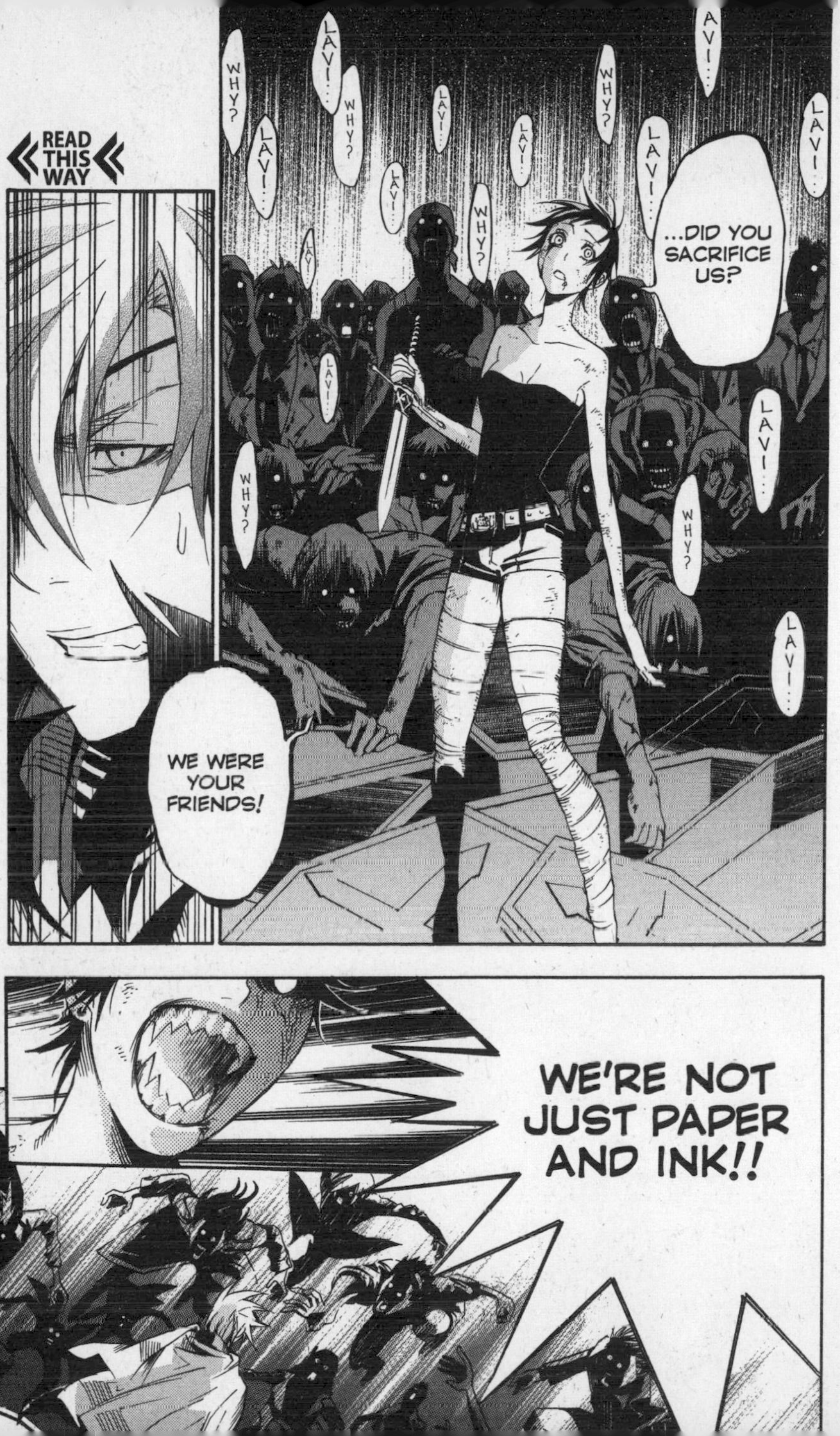
READ THIS WAY
LAVI...
LAVI...
WHY?
LAVI...
...DID YOU SACRIFICE US?
LAVI...
LAVI...
WHY?
LAVI...
LAVI...
WHY?
LAVI!...
LAVI!...
WHY?
LAVI
LAVI...
LAVI...
WHY?
LAVI...
WHY?
WE WERE YOUR FRIENDS!
WE'RE NOT JUST PAPER AND INK!!

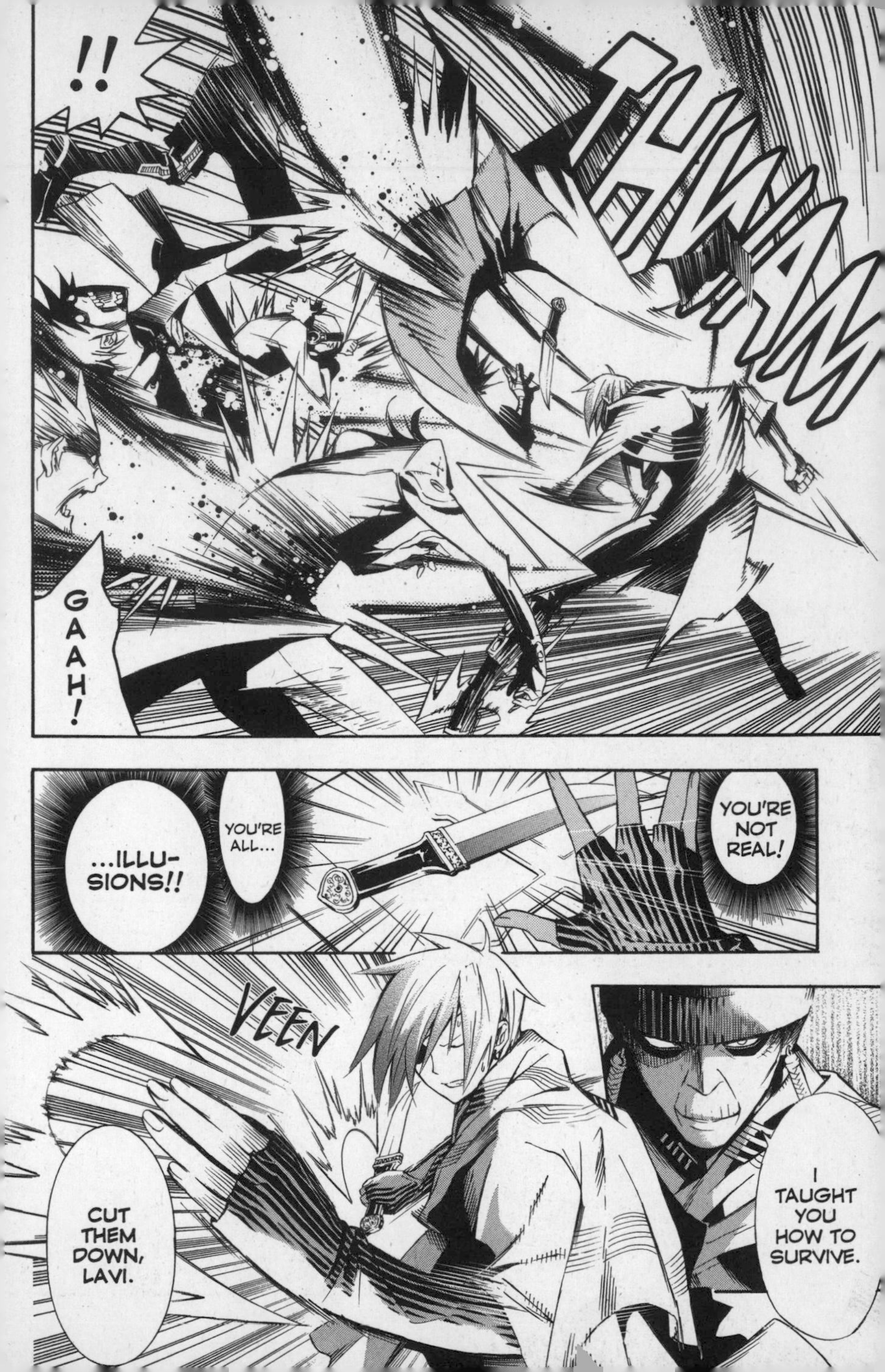
THWAM
!!
GAAH!
YOU'RE NOT REAL!
YOU'RE ALL...
...ILLUSIONS!!
I TAUGHT YOU HOW TO SURVIVE.
VEEN
CUT THEM DOWN, LAVI.

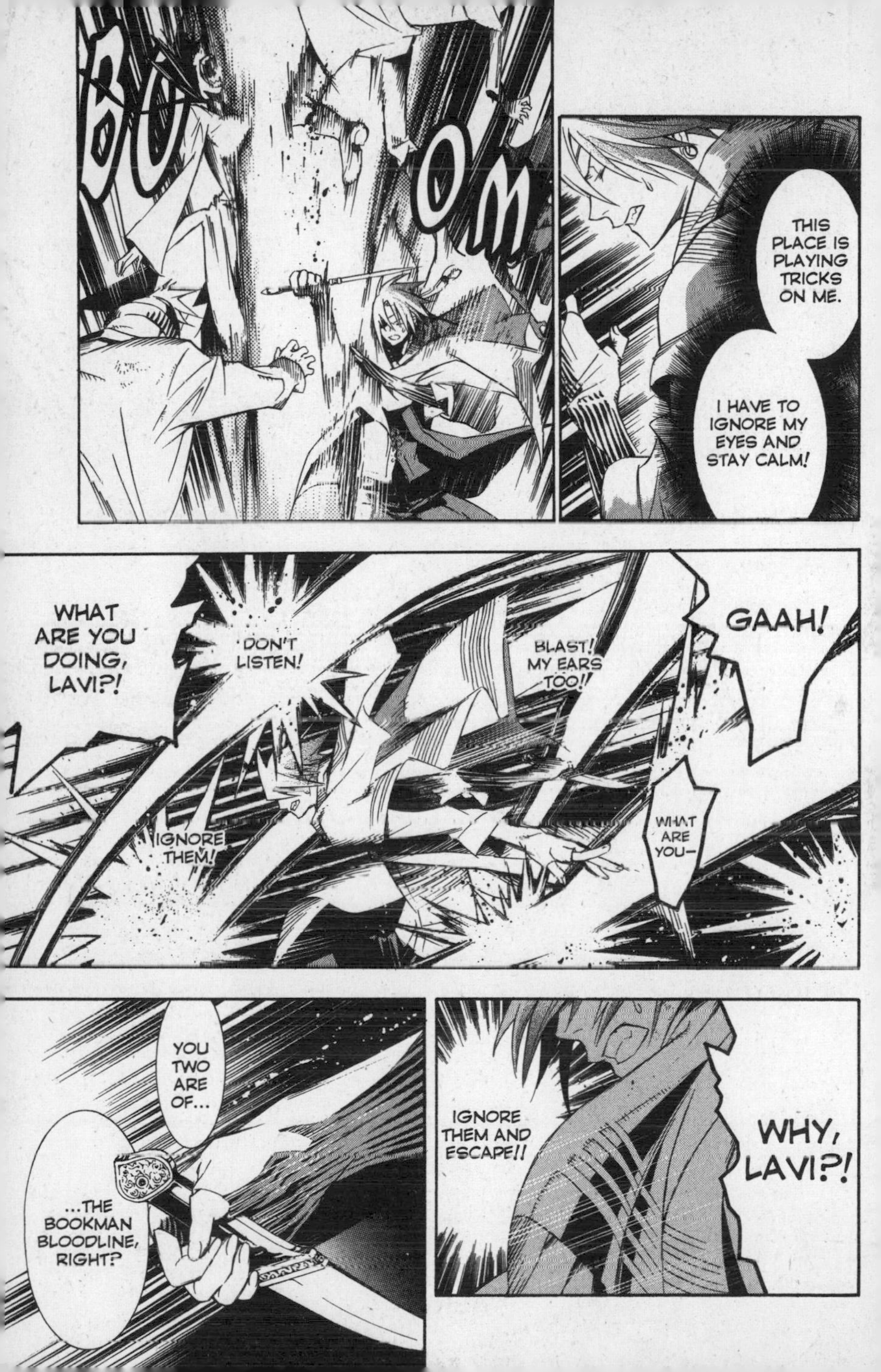
THIS PLACE IS PLAYING TRICKS ON ME.
I HAVE TO IGNORE MY EYES AND STAY CALM!
BOOM
GAAH!
BLAST! MY EARS TOO!!
DON'T LISTEN!
WHAT ARE YOU DOING, LAVI?!
WHAT ARE YOU—
IGNORE THEM!
WHY, LAVI?!
IGNORE THEM AND ESCAPE!!
YOU TWO ARE OF...
...THE BOOKMAN BLOODLINE, RIGHT?

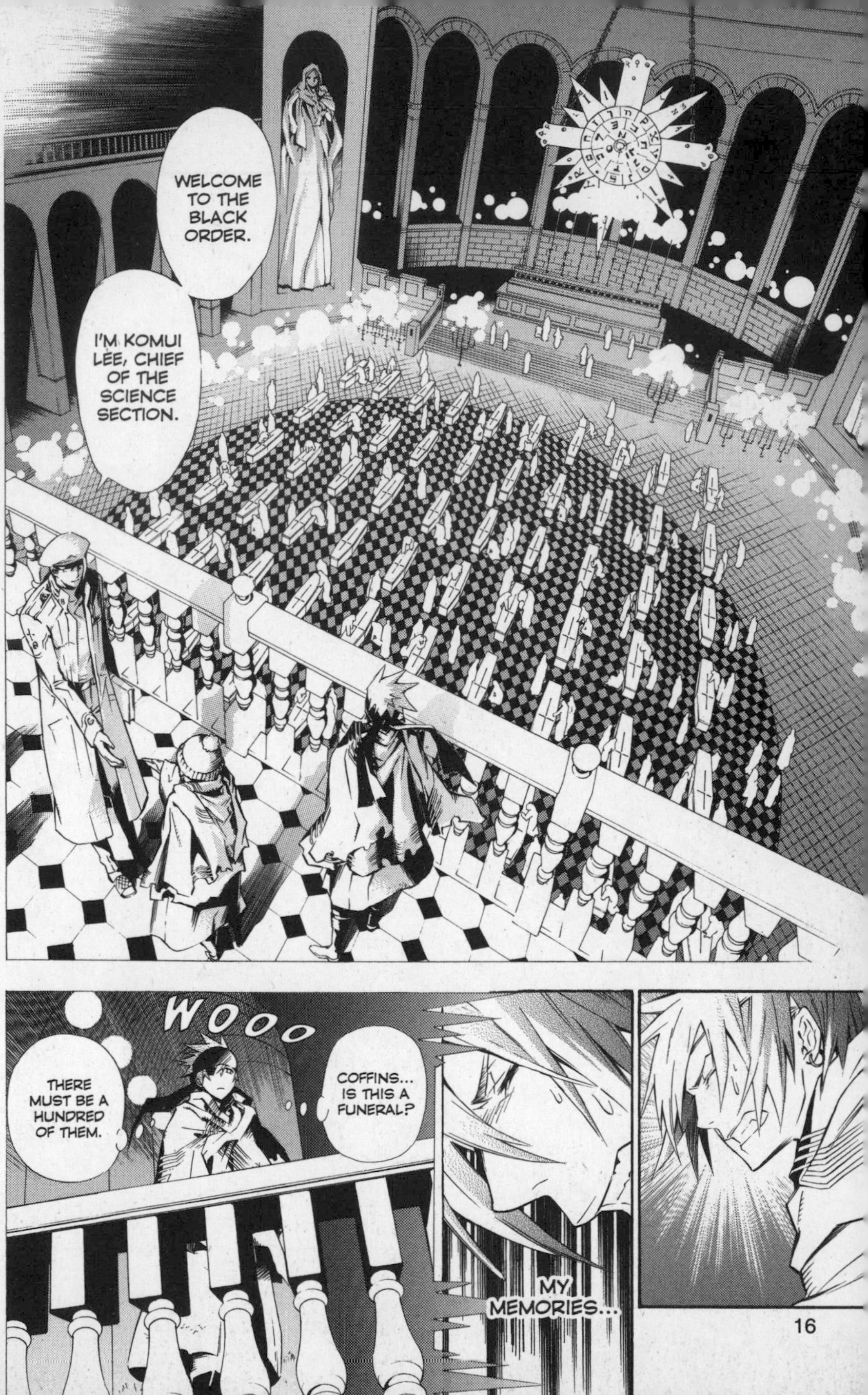
WELCOME TO THE BLACK ORDER.
I'M KOMUI LEE, CHIEF OF THE SCIENCE SECTION.
MY MEMORIES...
WOOO
COFFINS... IS THIS A FUNERAL?
THERE MUST BE A HUNDRED OF THEM.

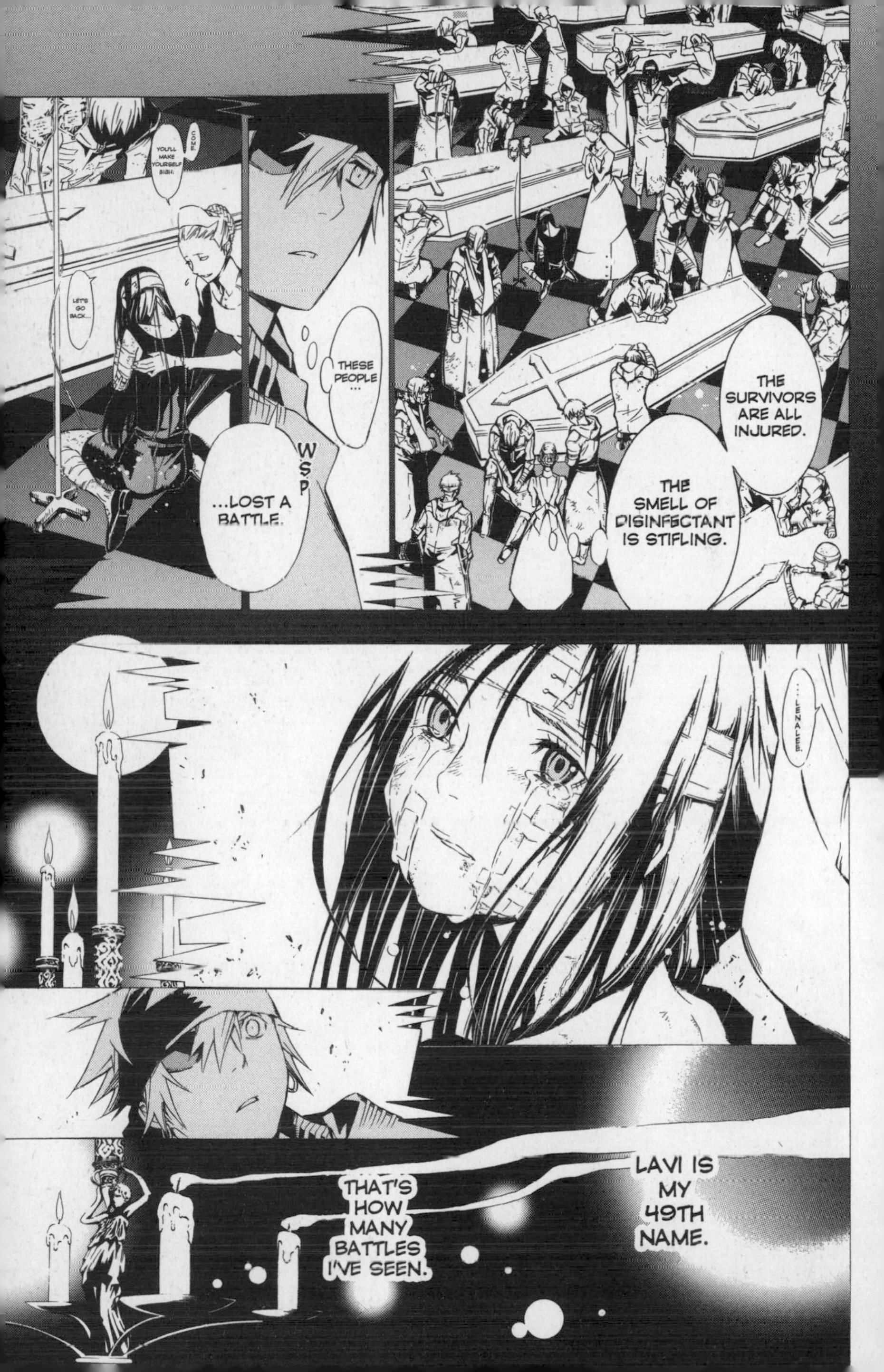

THE SURVIVORS ARE ALL INJURED.
THE SMELL OF DISINFECTANT IS STIFLING.
THESE PEOPLE...
W.S.P
...LOST A BATTLE.
COME.
YOU'LL MAKE YOURSELF SICK!
LET'S GO BACK...
...LENALEE.
LAVI IS MY 49TH NAME.
THAT'S HOW MANY BATTLES I'VE SEEN.

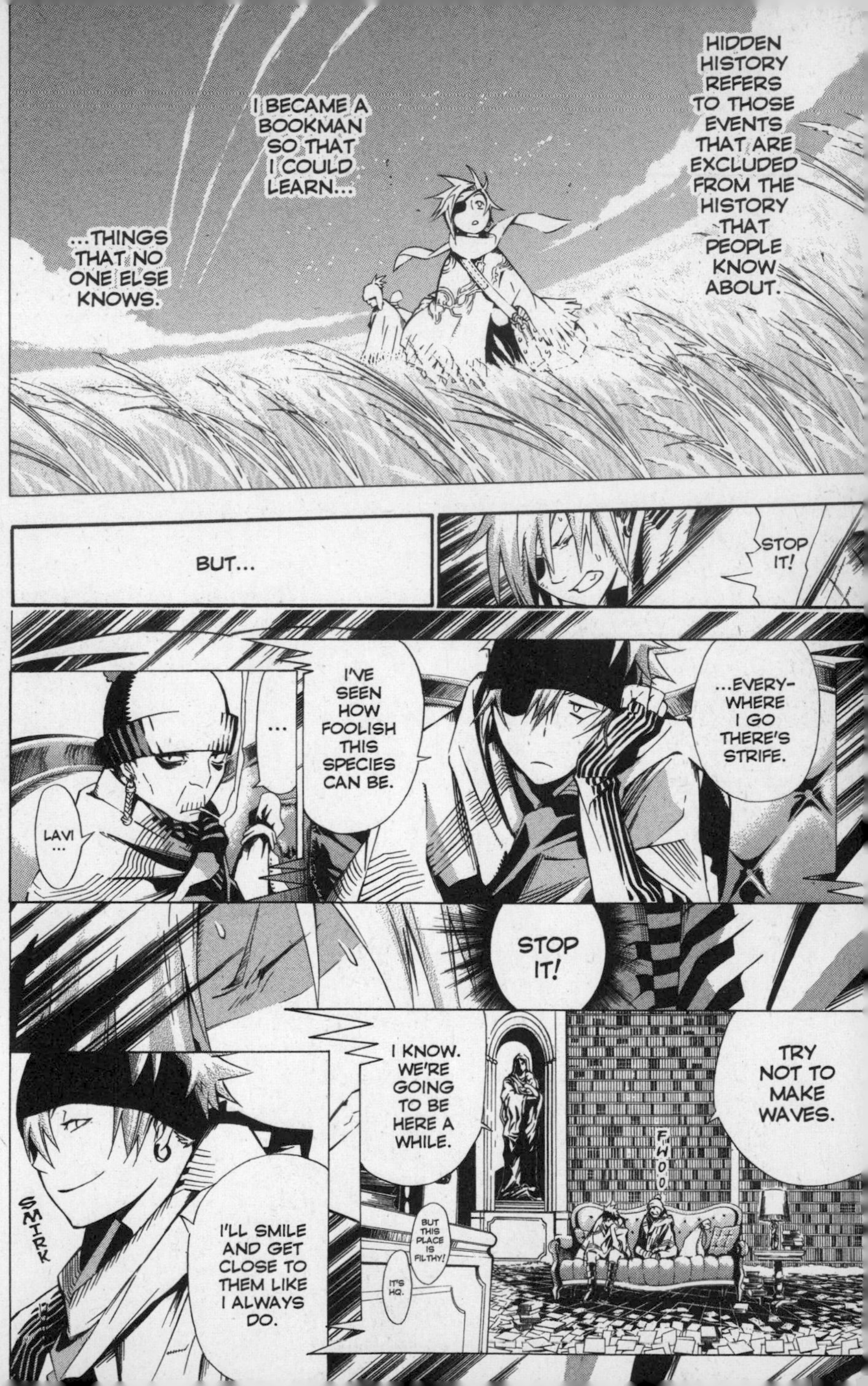
HIDDEN HISTORY REFERS TO THOSE EVENTS THAT ARE EXCLUDED FROM THE HISTORY THAT PEOPLE KNOW ABOUT.
I BECAME A BOOKMAN SO THAT I COULD LEARN...
...THINGS THAT NO ONE ELSE KNOWS.
STOP IT!
BUT...
...EVERY-WHERE I GO THERE'S STRIFE.
I'VE SEEN HOW FOOLISH THIS SPECIES CAN BE.
...
LAVI...
STOP IT!
TRY NOT TO MAKE WAVES.
FWOO
I KNOW. WE'RE GOING TO BE HERE A WHILE.
BUT THIS PLACE IS FILTHY!
IT'S HQ.
I'LL SMILE AND GET CLOSE TO THEM LIKE I ALWAYS DO.
SMIRK

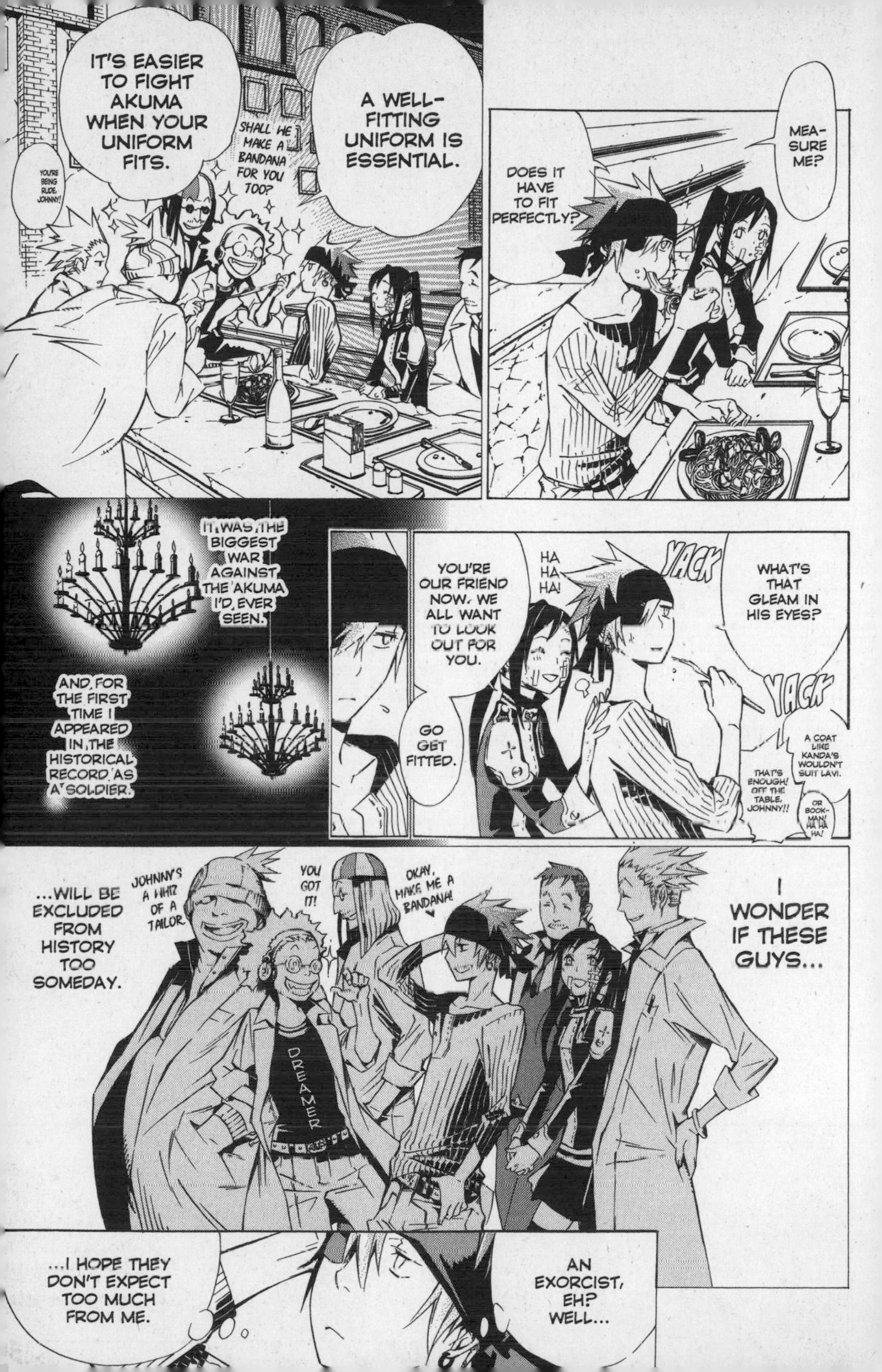
MEA-SURE ME?
DOES IT HAVE TO FIT PERFECTLY?
A WELL-FITTING UNIFORM IS ESSENTIAL.
IT'S EASIER TO FIGHT AKUMA WHEN YOUR UNIFORM FITS.
SHALL WE MAKE A BANDANA FOR YOU TOO?
YOU'RE BEING RUDE, JOHNNY!
WHAT'S THAT GLEAM IN HIS EYES?
YACK
YACK
HA HA HA!
YOU'RE OUR FRIEND NOW. WE ALL WANT TO LOOK OUT FOR YOU.
GO GET FITTED.
A COAT LIKE KANDA'S WOULDN'T SUIT LAVI.
OR BOOKMAN! HA HA HA!
THAT'S ENOUGH! OFF THE TABLE, JOHNNY!!
IT WAS THE BIGGEST WAR AGAINST THE AKUMA I'D EVER SEEN.
AND FOR THE FIRST TIME I APPEARED IN THE HISTORICAL RECORD AS A SOLDIER.
I WONDER IF THESE GUYS...
OKAY, MAKE ME A BANDANA!
YOU GOT IT!
JOHNNY'S A WHIZ OF A TAILOR.
...WILL BE EXCLUDED FROM HISTORY TOO SOMEDAY.
DREAMER
AN EXORCIST, EH? WELL...
...I HOPE THEY DON'T EXPECT TOO MUCH FROM ME.

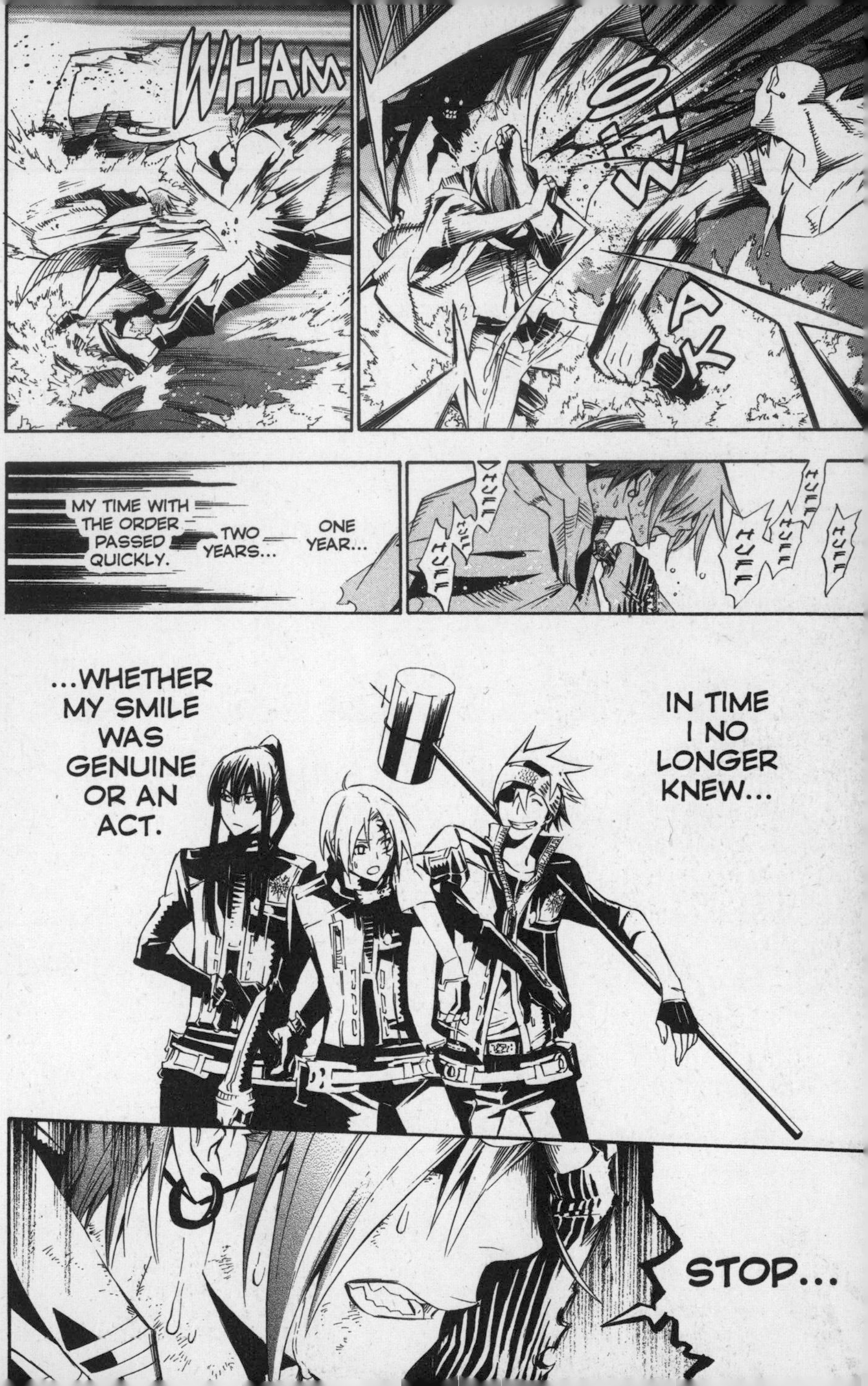
SWAK
WHAM
HUFF
HUFF
HUFF
HUFF
HUFF
HUFF
HUFF
ONE YEAR...
TWO YEARS...
MY TIME WITH THE ORDER PASSED QUICKLY.
IN TIME I NO LONGER KNEW...
...WHETHER MY SMILE WAS GENUINE OR AN ACT.
STOP...

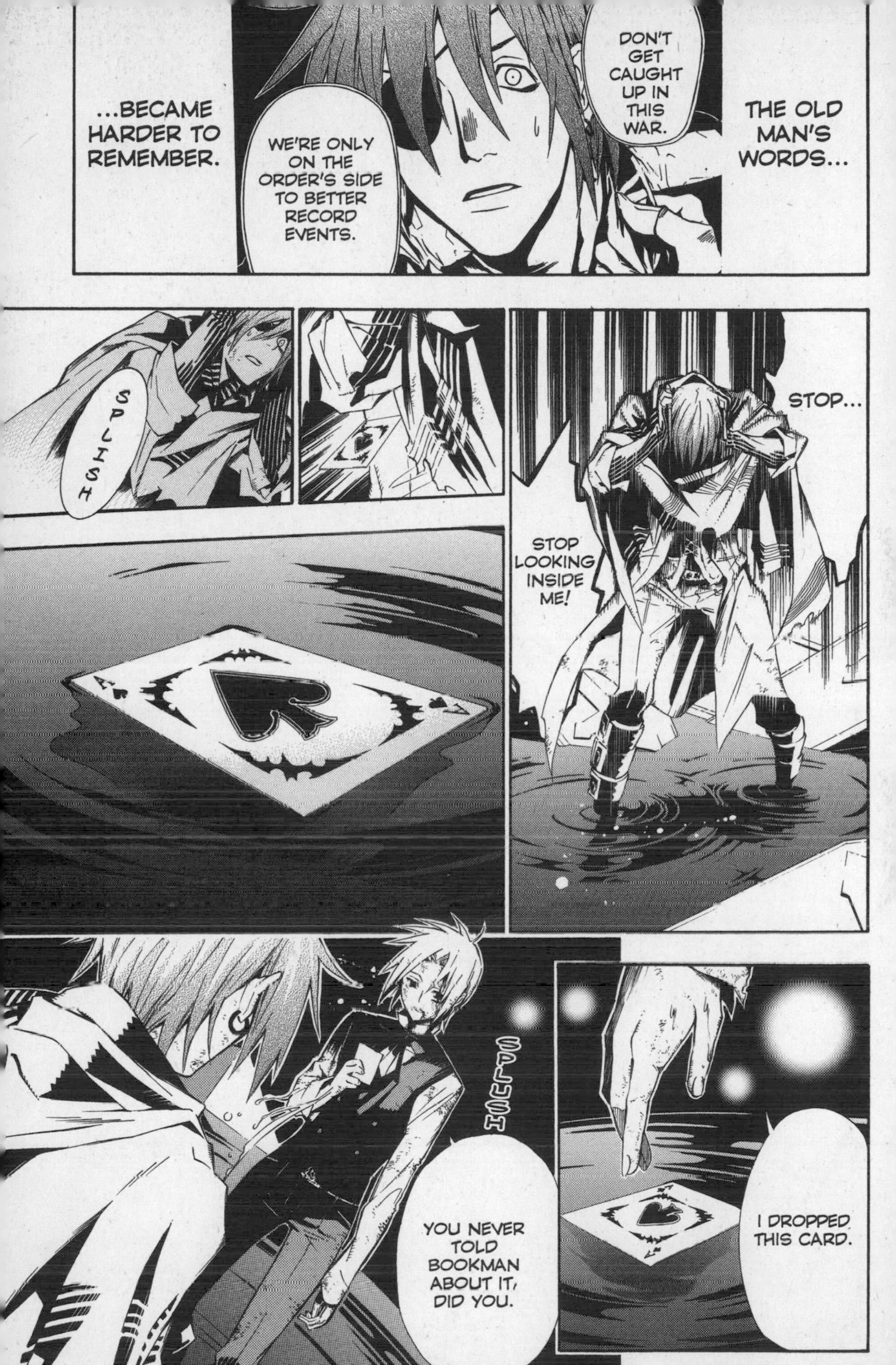
THE OLD MAN'S WORDS...
DON'T GET CAUGHT UP IN THIS WAR.
WE'RE ONLY ON THE ORDER'S SIDE TO BETTER RECORD EVENTS.
...BECAME HARDER TO REMEMBER.
STOP...
STOP LOOKING INSIDE ME!
SPLISH
I DROPPED THIS CARD.
SPLISH
YOU NEVER TOLD BOOKMAN ABOUT IT, DID YOU.

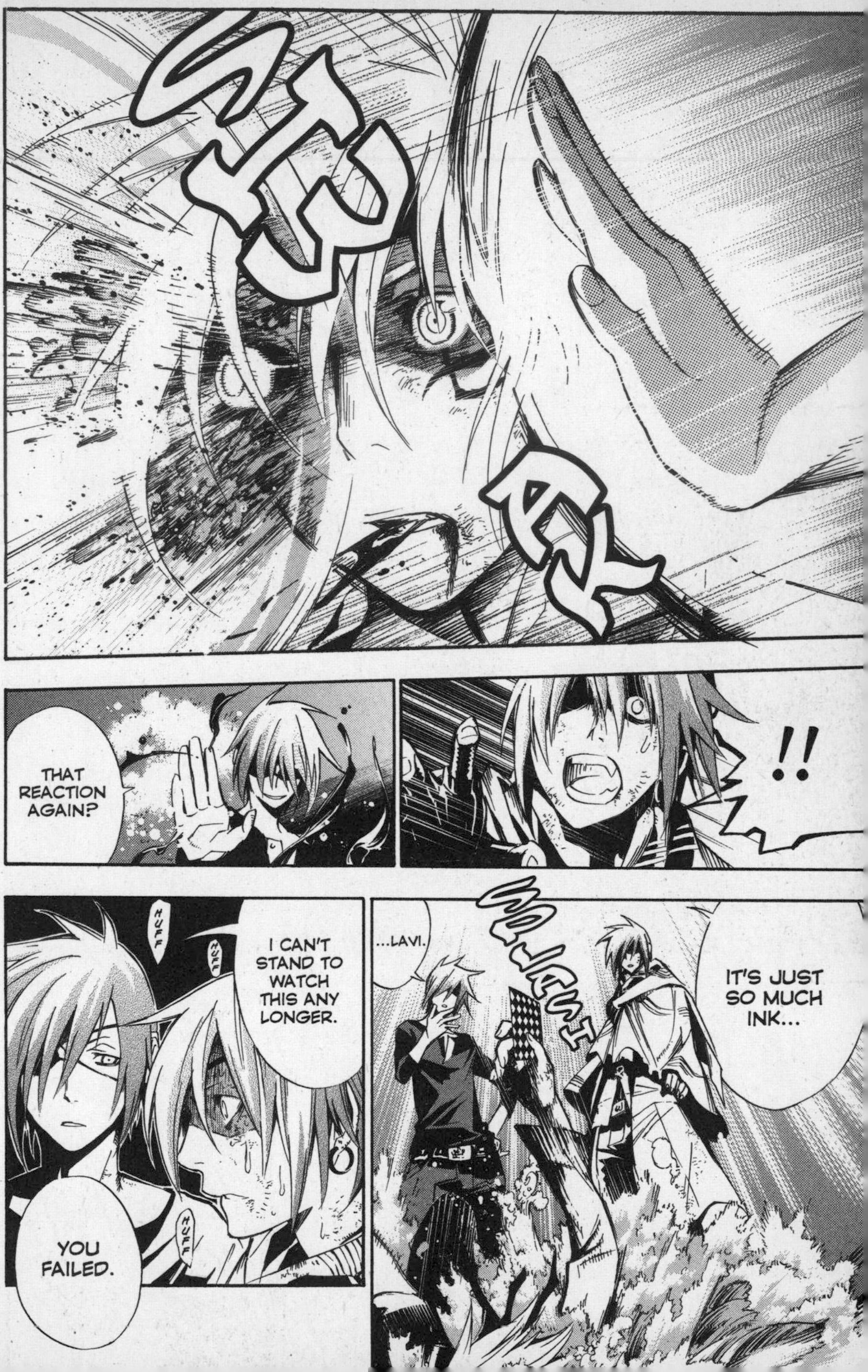
!!
THAT REACTION AGAIN?
IT'S JUST SO MUCH INK...
SPLAT
...LAVI.
HUFF
HUFF
I CAN'T STAND TO WATCH THIS ANY LONGER.
HUFF
YOU FAILED.

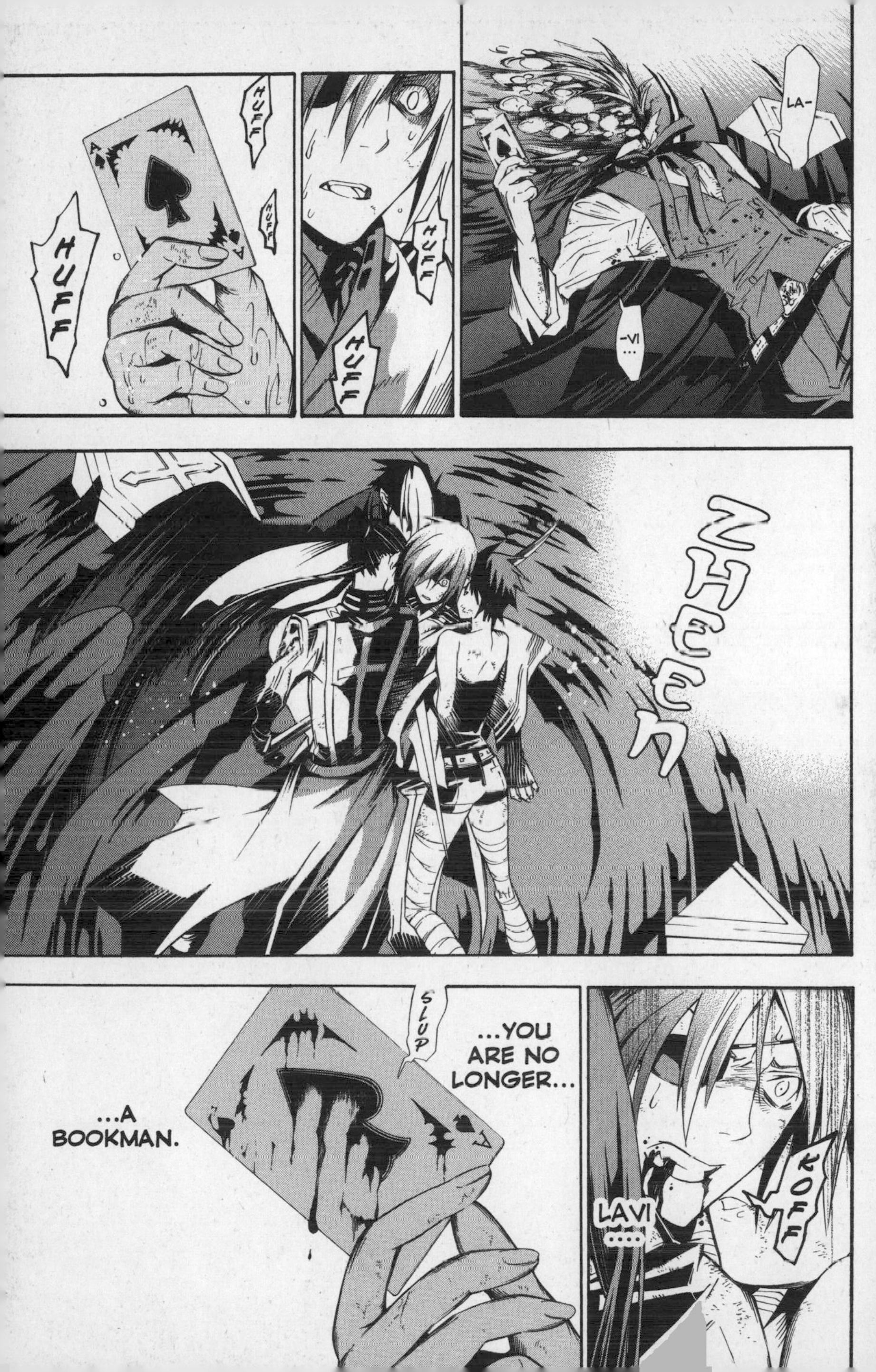
LA-
-VI ...
HUFF
HUFF
HUFF
HUFF
HUFF
HUFF
ZHEEN
KOFF
LAVI ....
SLUP
...YOU ARE NO LONGER...
...A BOOKMAN.

IN VOLUME 2, I NOTICED THAT ALLEN ORDERED 20 STICKS OF RICE FLOUR DUMPLINGS FROM JERRY. HOW MANY *DANGO* CAN HE EAT AT ONE SITTING? (HARUNA MATSUMOTO, KAGAWA PREFECTURE)

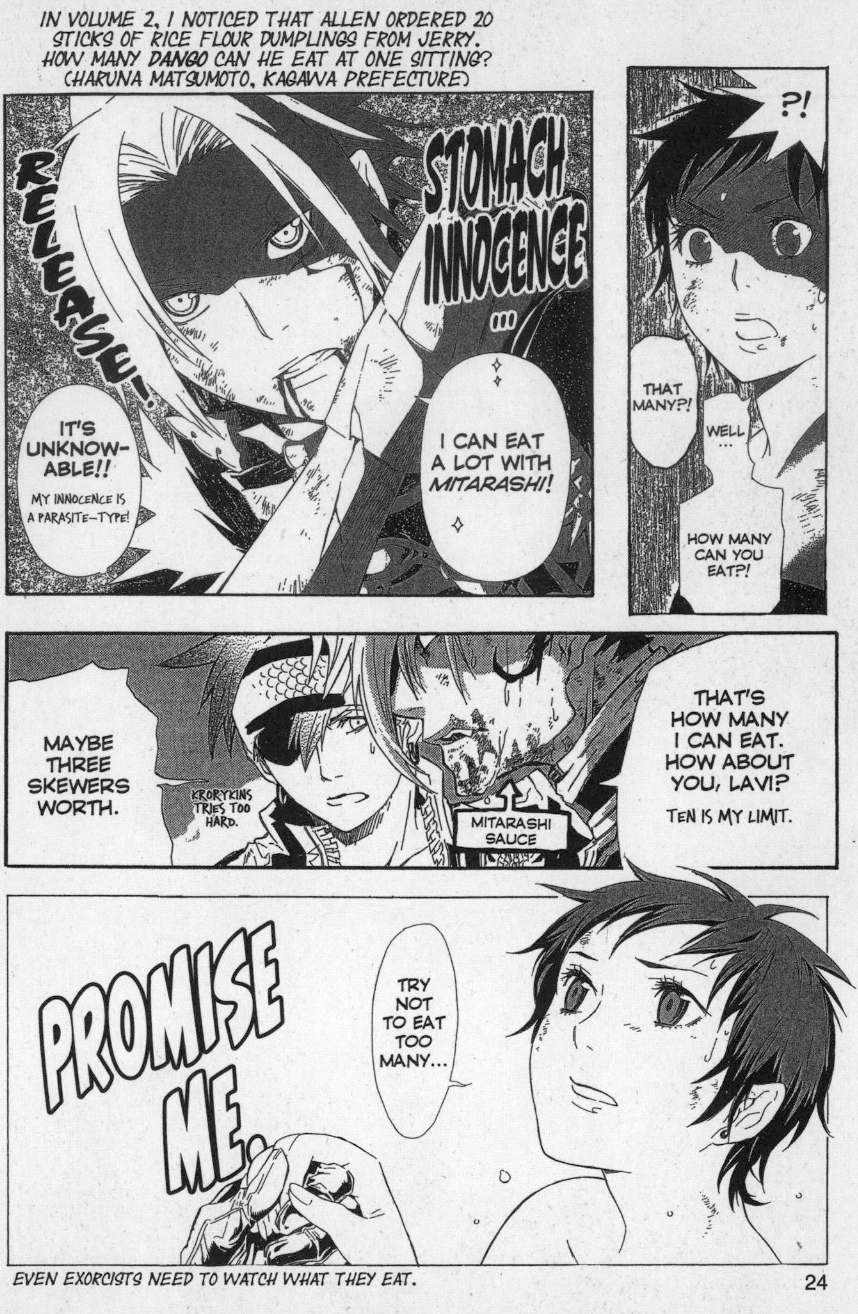
?!
THAT MANY?!
WELL...
HOW MANY CAN YOU EAT?!
STOMACH INNOCENCE...
RELEASE!
I CAN EAT A LOT WITH *MITARASHI*!
IT'S UNKNOWABLE!!
MY INNOCENCE IS A PARASITE-TYPE!
THAT'S HOW MANY I CAN EAT. HOW ABOUT YOU, LAVI?
TEN IS MY LIMIT.
MITARASHI SAUCE
KRORYKINS TRIES TOO HARD.
MAYBE THREE SKEWERS WORTH.
TRY NOT TO EAT TOO MANY...
PROMISE ME.

EVEN EXORCISTS NEED TO WATCH WHAT THEY EAT.

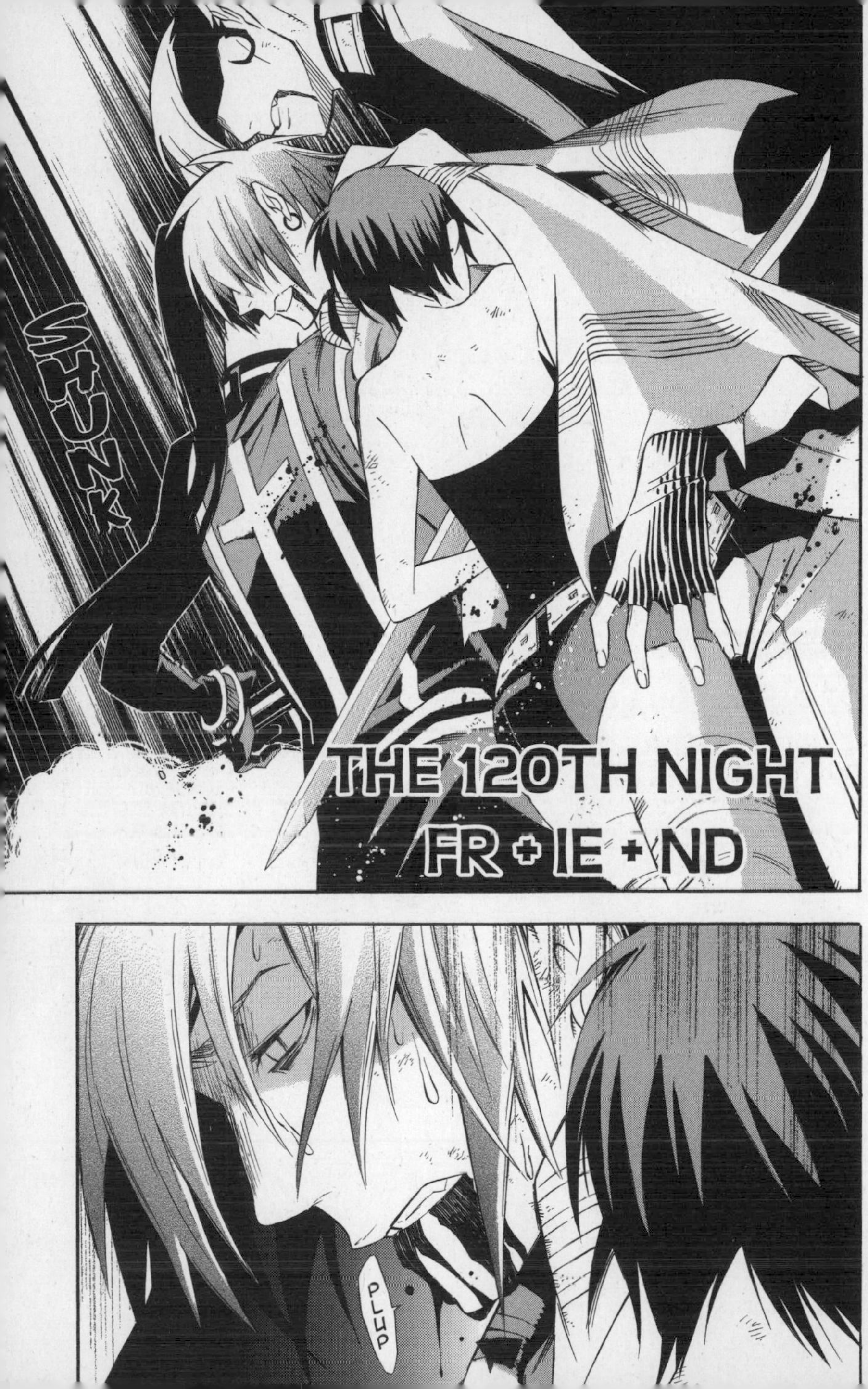
SHUNK
THE 120TH NIGHT
FR + IE + ND
PLUP

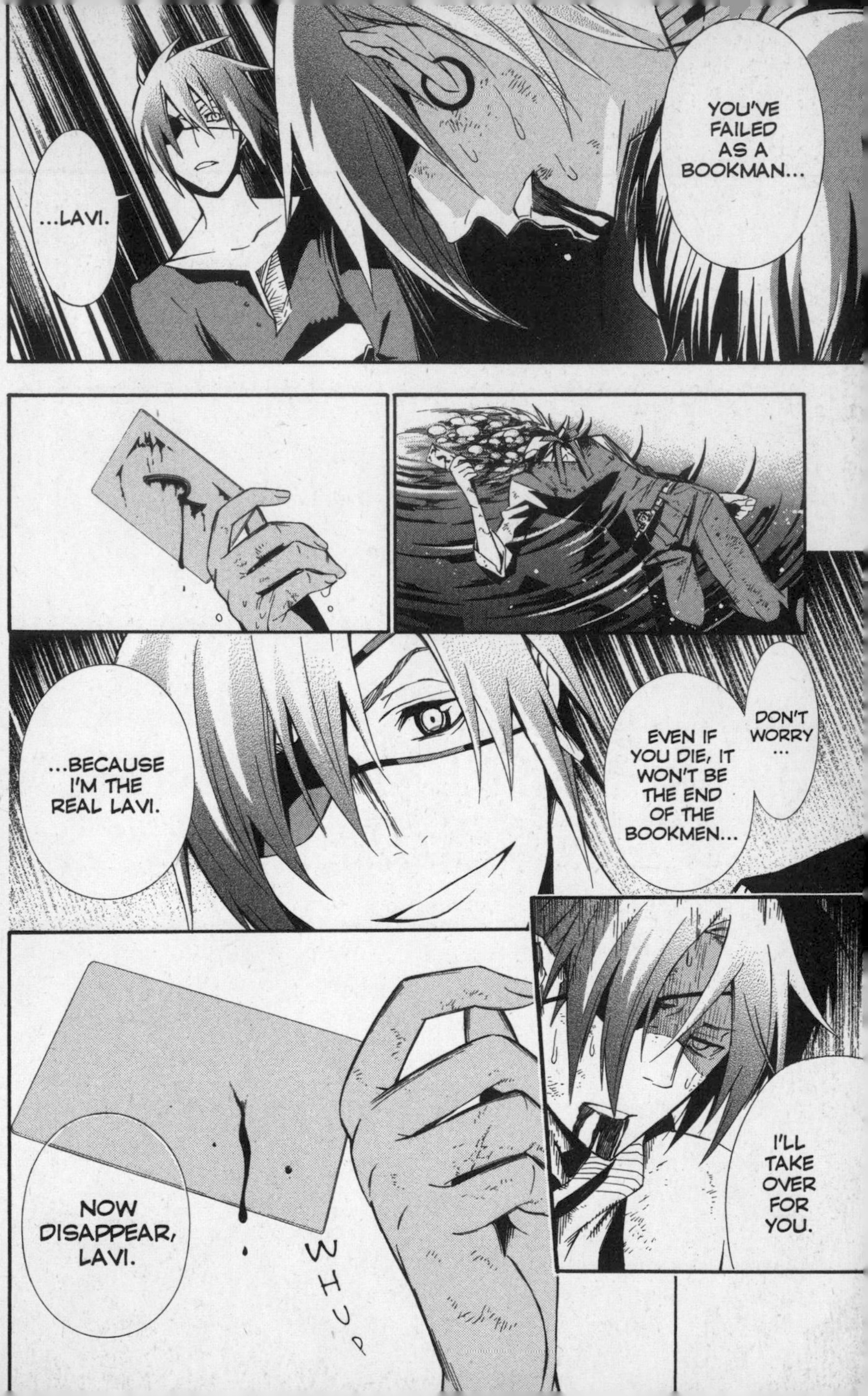
YOU'VE FAILED AS A BOOKMAN...
...LAVI.
DON'T WORRY...
EVEN IF YOU DIE, IT WON'T BE THE END OF THE BOOKMEN...
...BECAUSE I'M THE REAL LAVI.
I'LL TAKE OVER FOR YOU.
NOW DISAPPEAR, LAVI.
WHUP

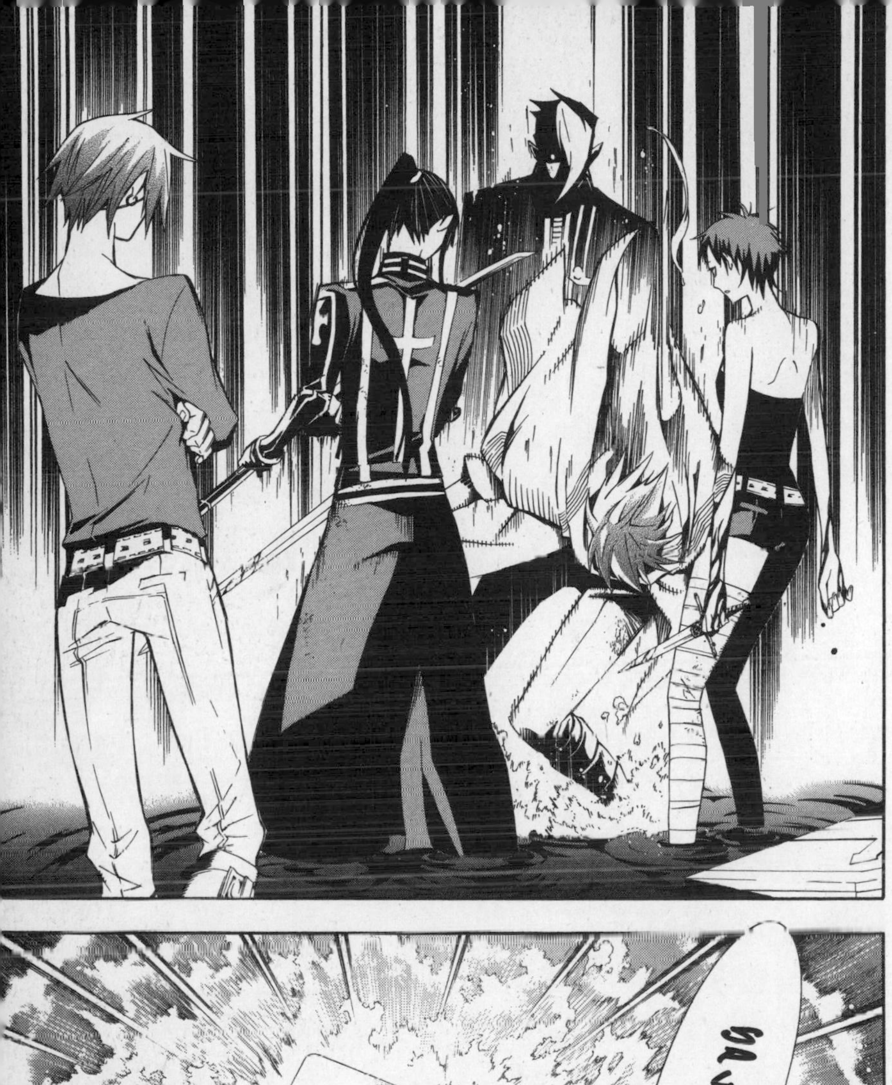

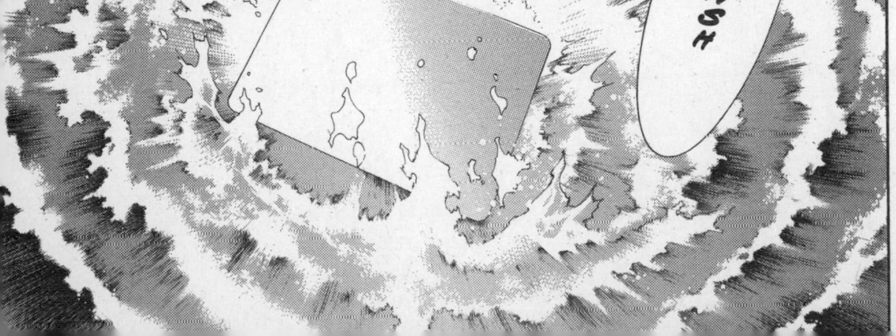
SPLASH

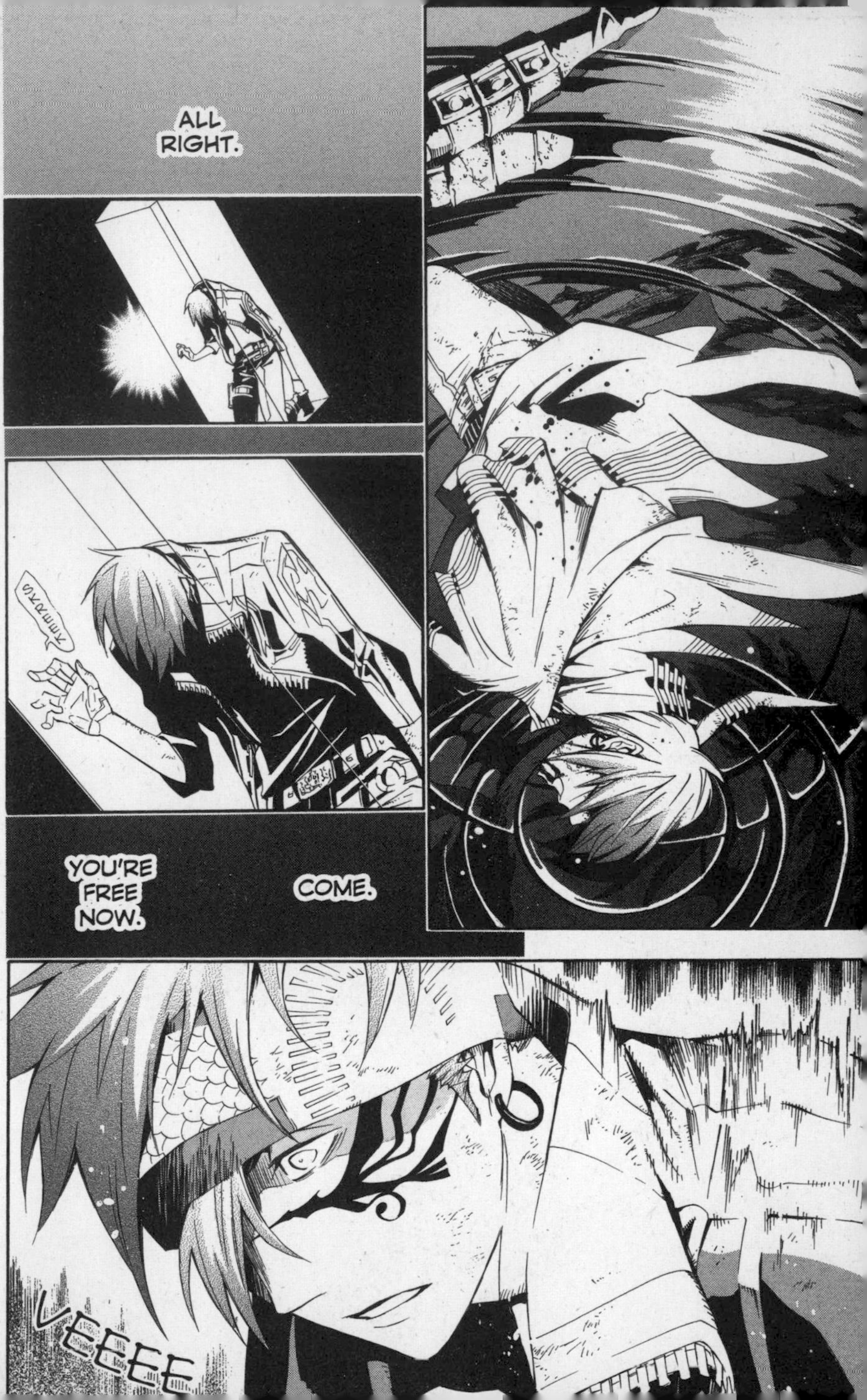
ALL RIGHT.
SKREEK
COME.
YOU'RE FREE NOW.
VEEEE

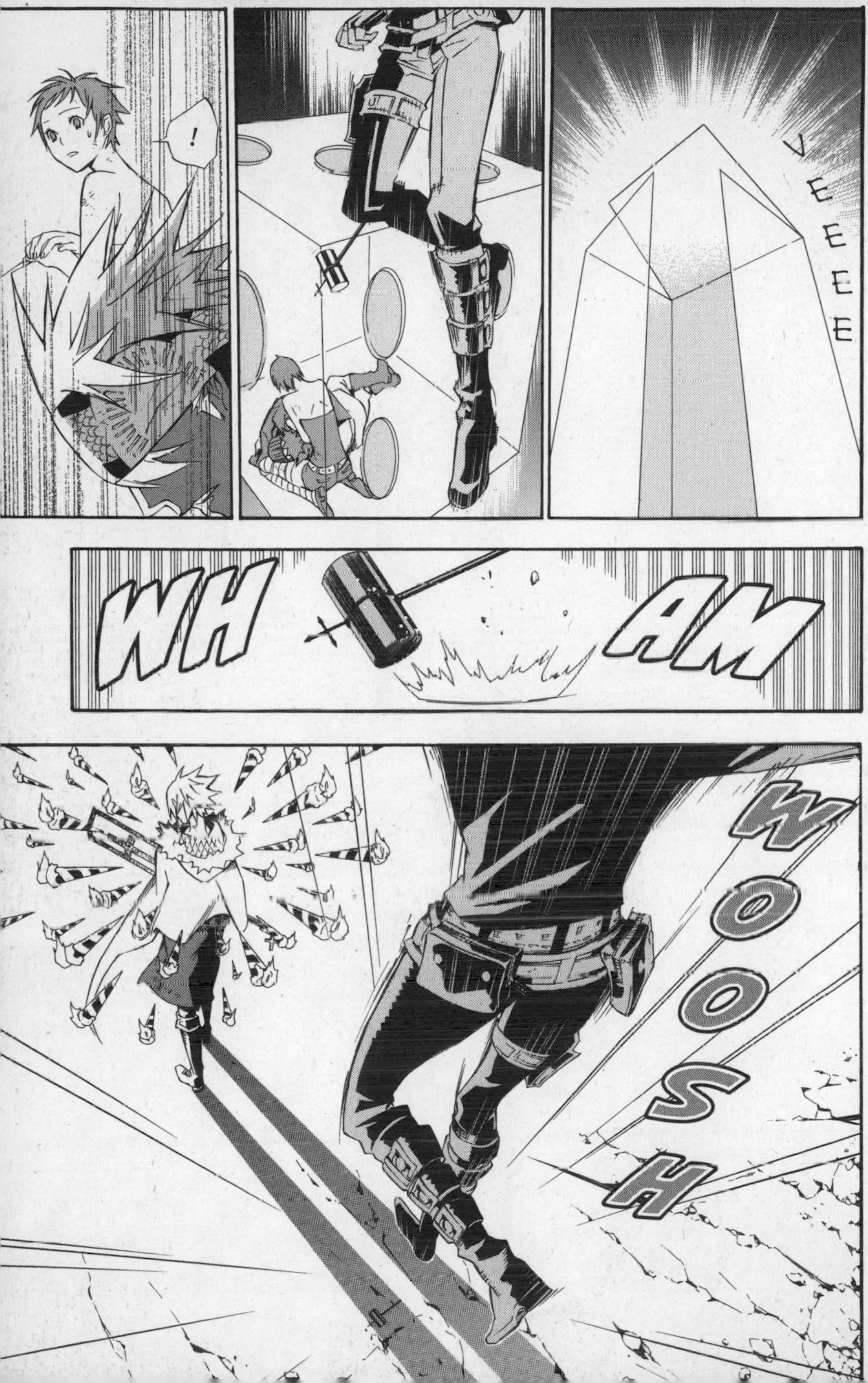
VEEEE
!
WHAM
WOOOSH

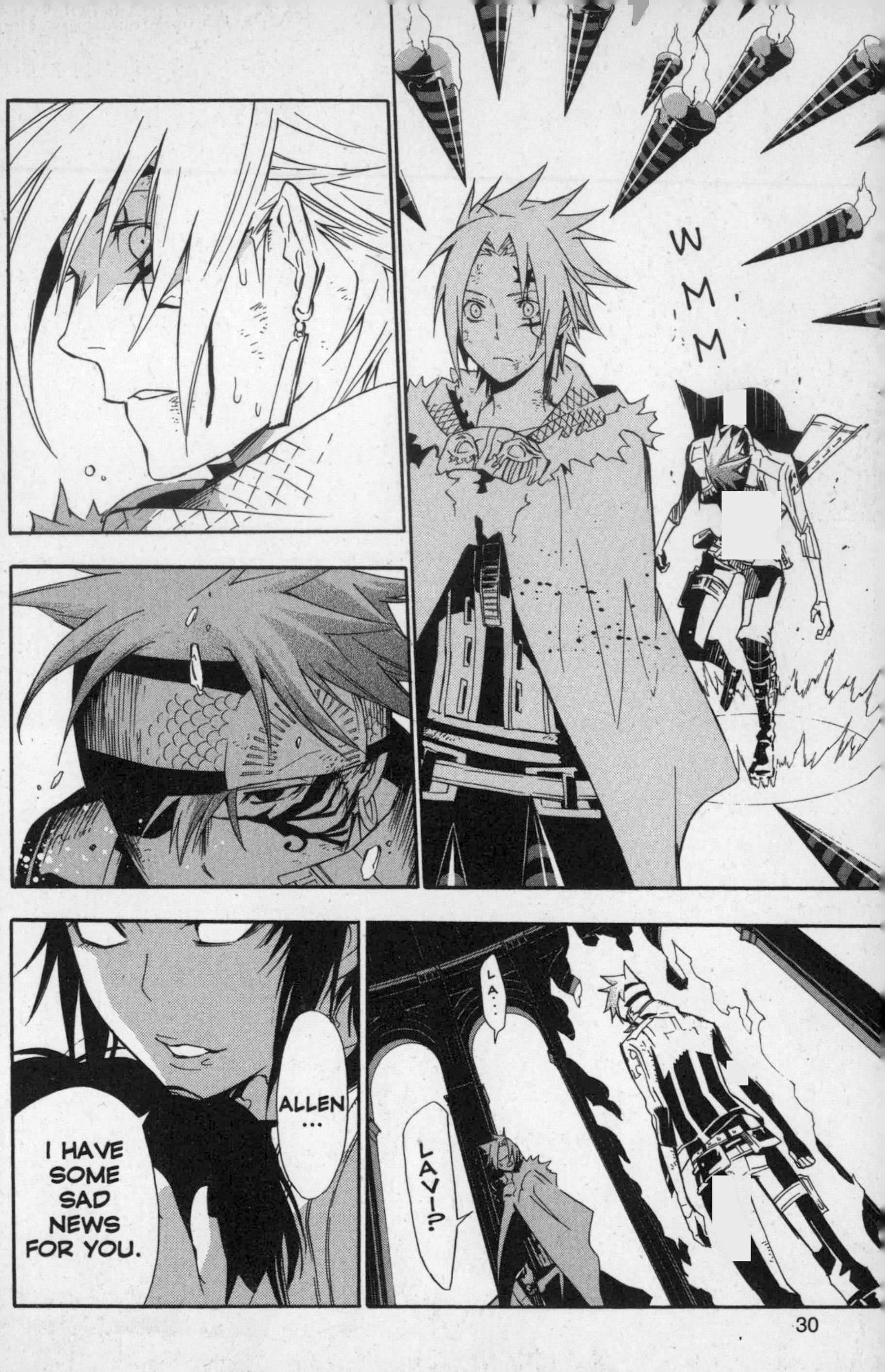
WMM
LA...
LAVI?
ALLEN...
I HAVE SOME SAD NEWS FOR YOU.

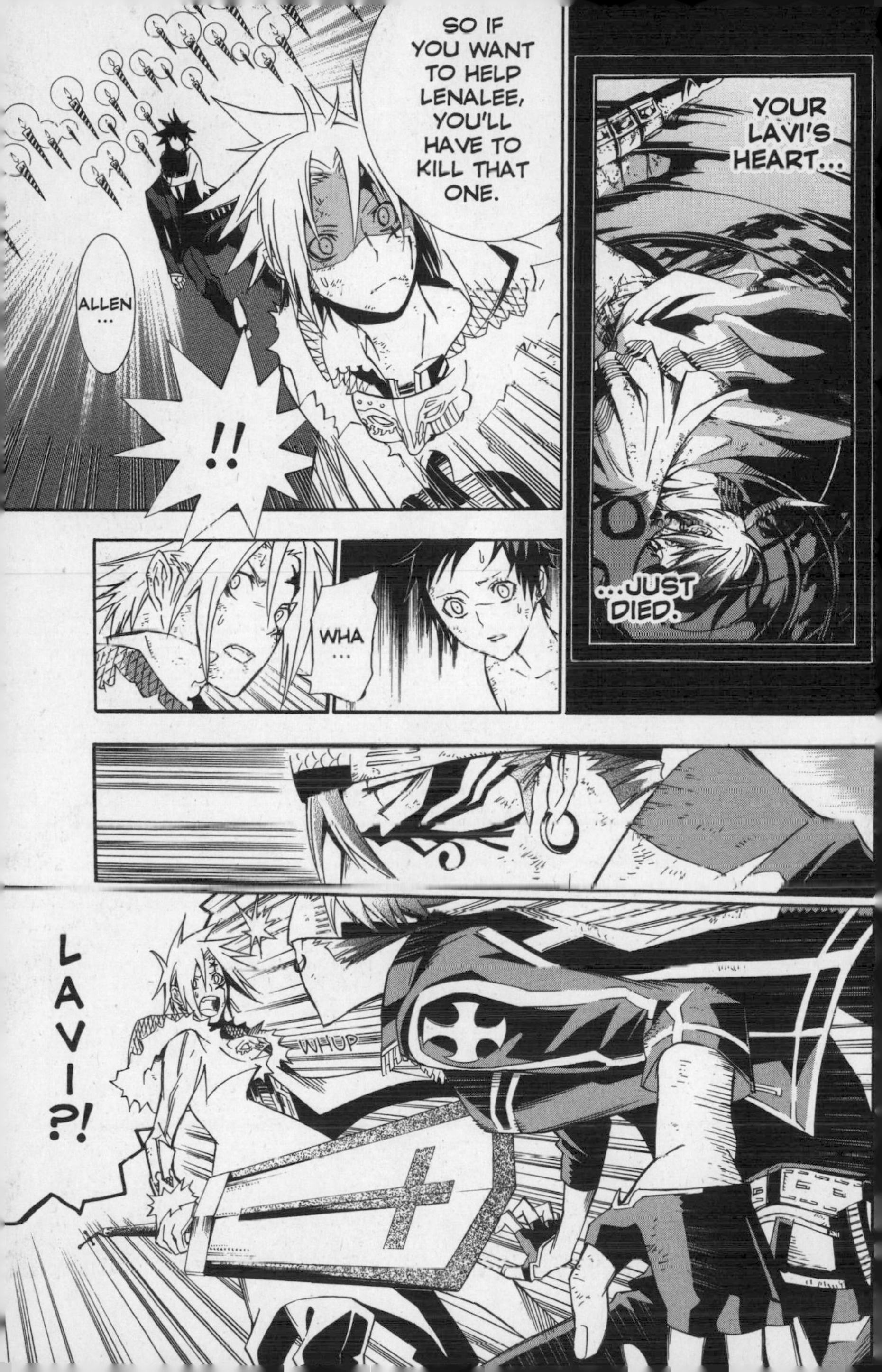
YOUR LAVI'S HEART...
...JUST DIED.
SO IF YOU WANT TO HELP LENALEE, YOU'LL HAVE TO KILL THAT ONE.
ALLEN ...
!!
WHA ...
WHUP
LAVI?!

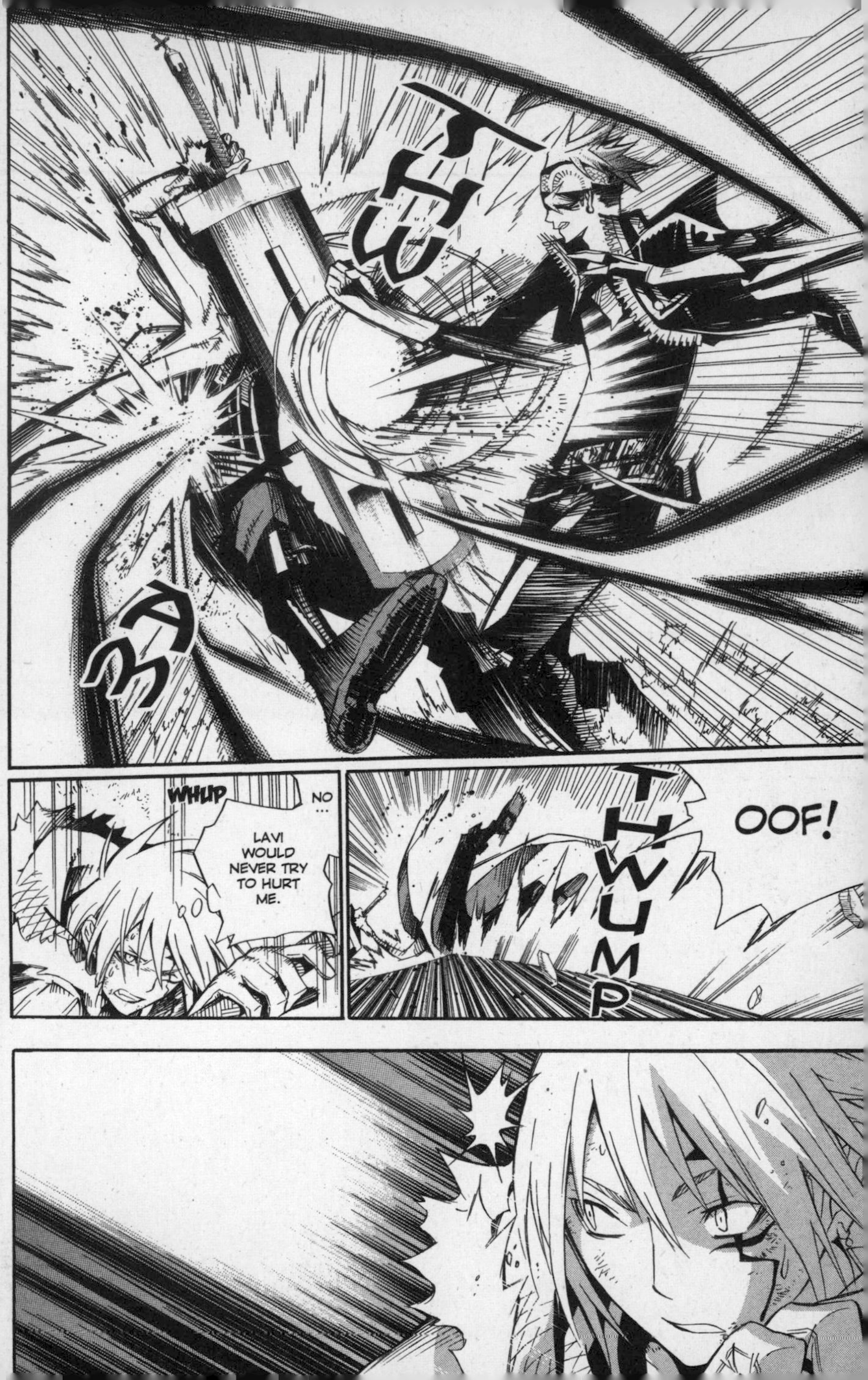
THWUMP
OOF!
WHUP
NO ...
LAVI WOULD NEVER TRY TO HURT ME.

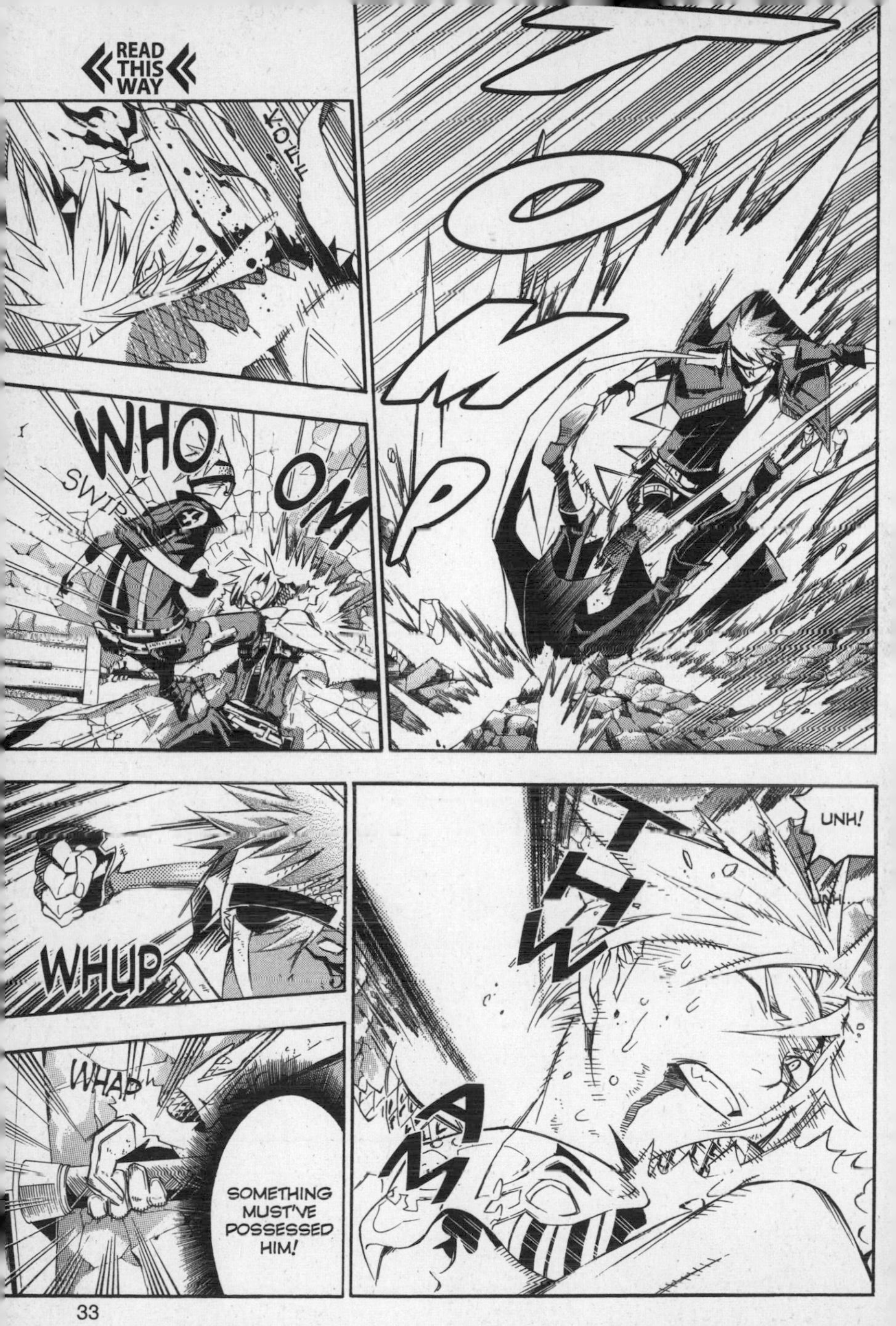
READ THIS WAY
KOFF
WHOOM
SWIP
UNH!
UNH...
WHUP
WHAP
SOMETHING MUST'VE POSSESSED HIM!

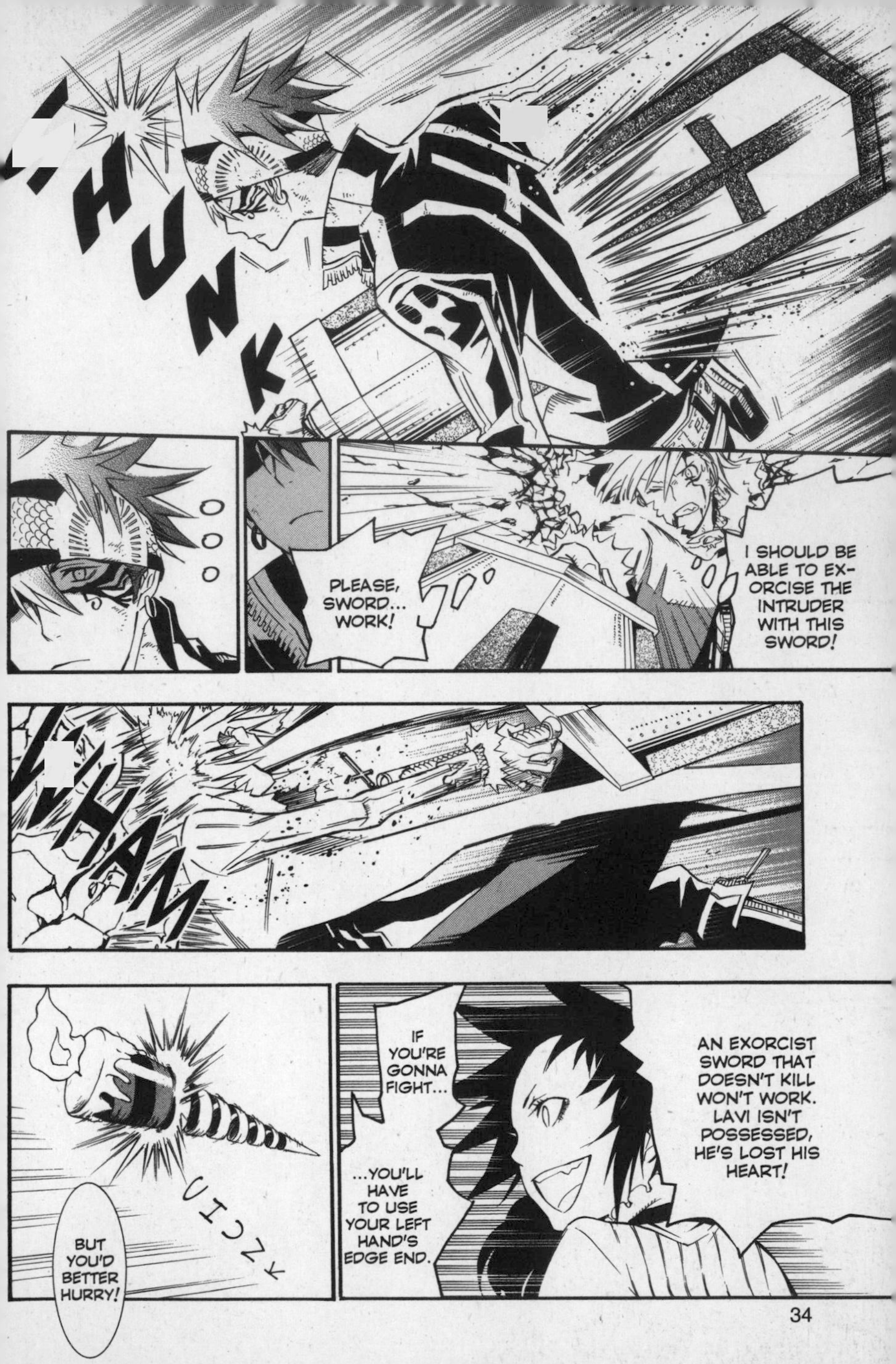
HUNK
I SHOULD BE ABLE TO EX-ORCISE THE INTRUDER WITH THIS SWORD!
PLEASE, SWORD... WORK!
WHAM
AN EXORCIST SWORD THAT DOESN'T KILL WON'T WORK. LAVI ISN'T POSSESSED, HE'S LOST HIS HEART!
IF YOU'RE GONNA FIGHT...
...YOU'LL HAVE TO USE YOUR LEFT HAND'S EDGE END.
BUT YOU'D BETTER HURRY!

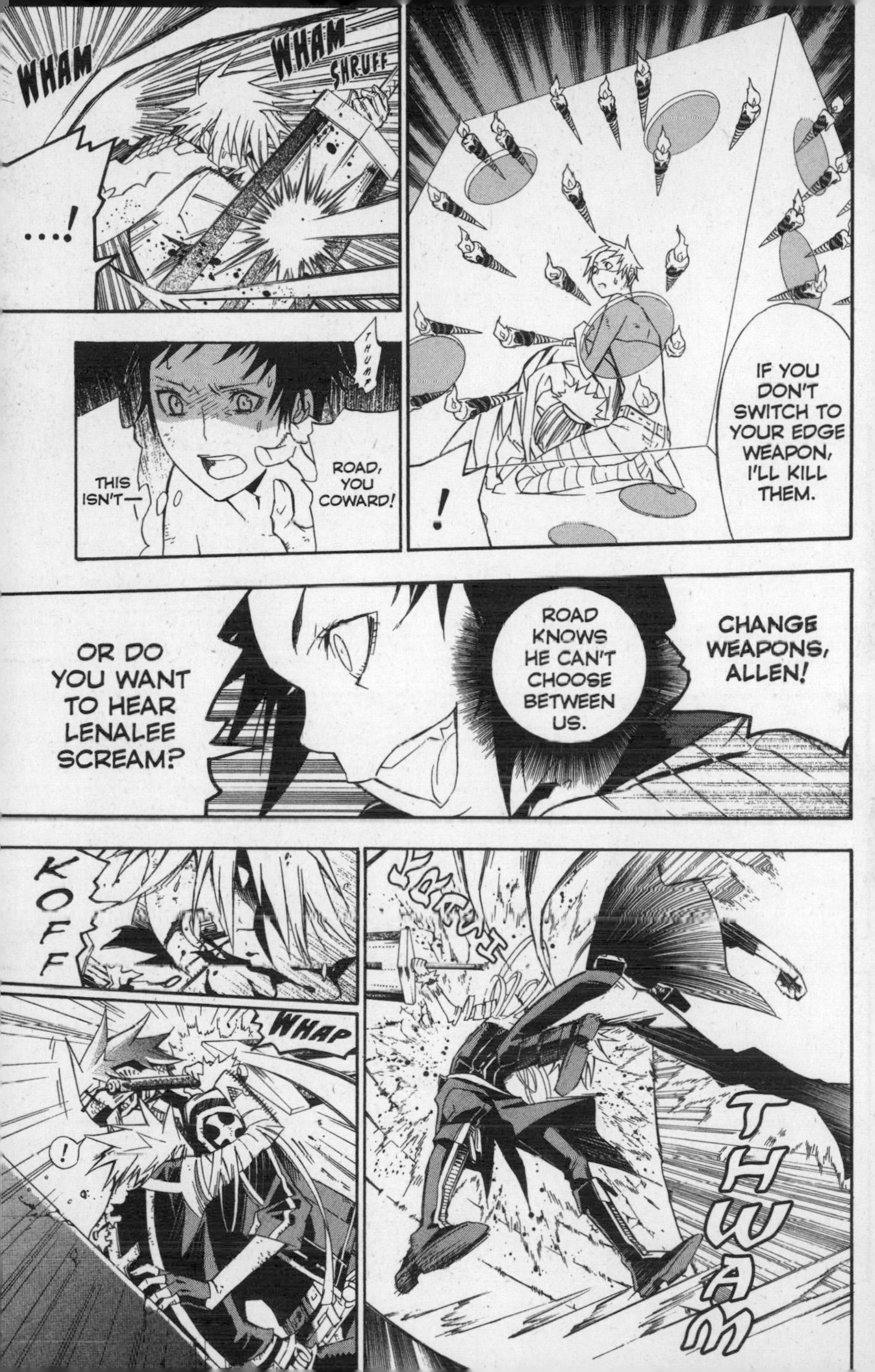
IF YOU DON'T SWITCH TO YOUR EDGE WEAPON, I'LL KILL THEM.
!
WHAM
WHAM
SHRUFF
...!
THUMP
ROAD, YOU COWARD!
THIS ISN'T—
CHANGE WEAPONS, ALLEN!
ROAD KNOWS HE CAN'T CHOOSE BETWEEN US.
OR DO YOU WANT TO HEAR LENALEE SCREAM?
THWAM
KOFF
WHAP
!

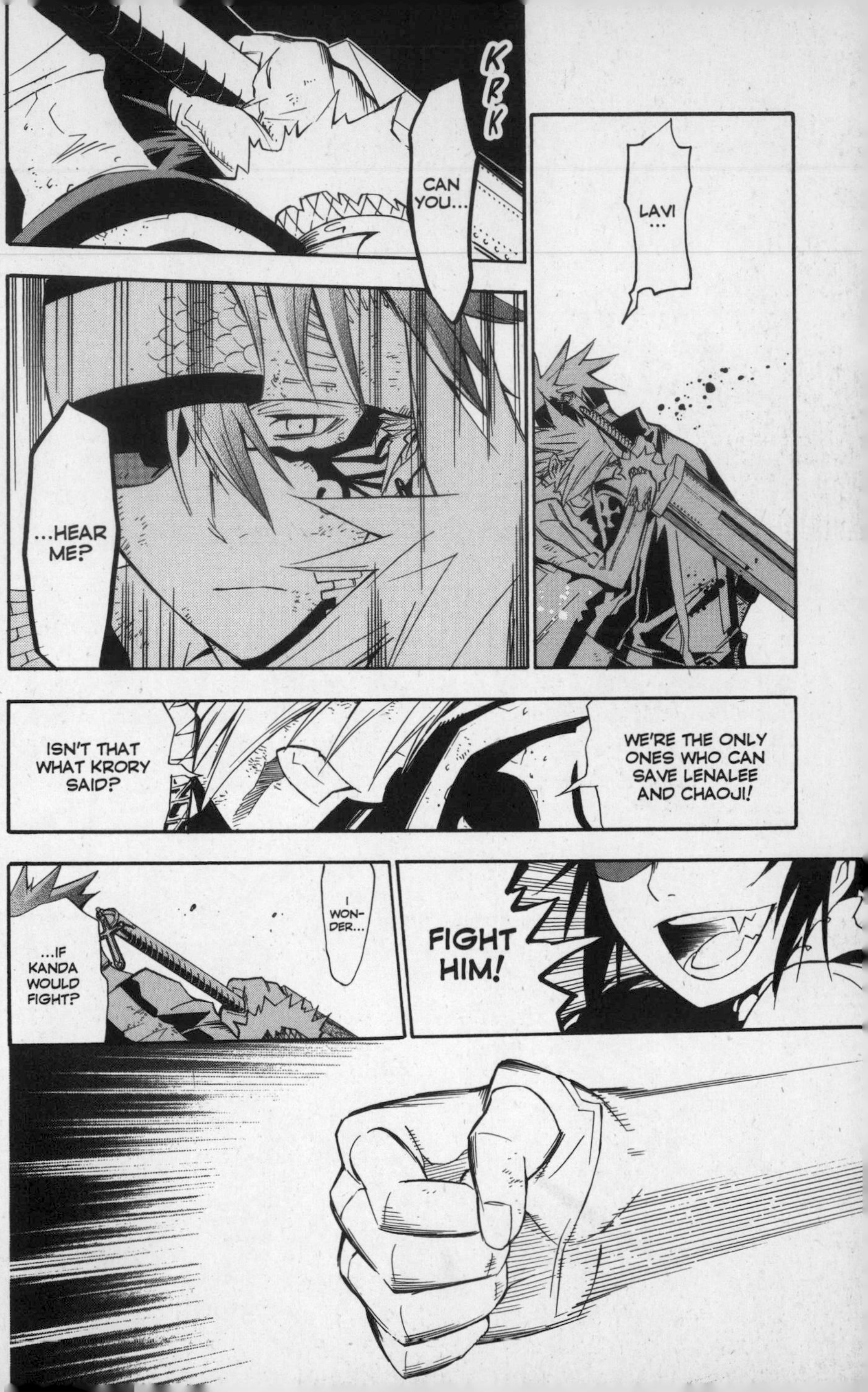
LAVI ...
KRK
CAN YOU...
...HEAR ME?
WE'RE THE ONLY ONES WHO CAN SAVE LENALEE AND CHAOJI!
ISN'T THAT WHAT KRORY SAID?
FIGHT HIM!
I WONDER...
...IF KANDA WOULD FIGHT?

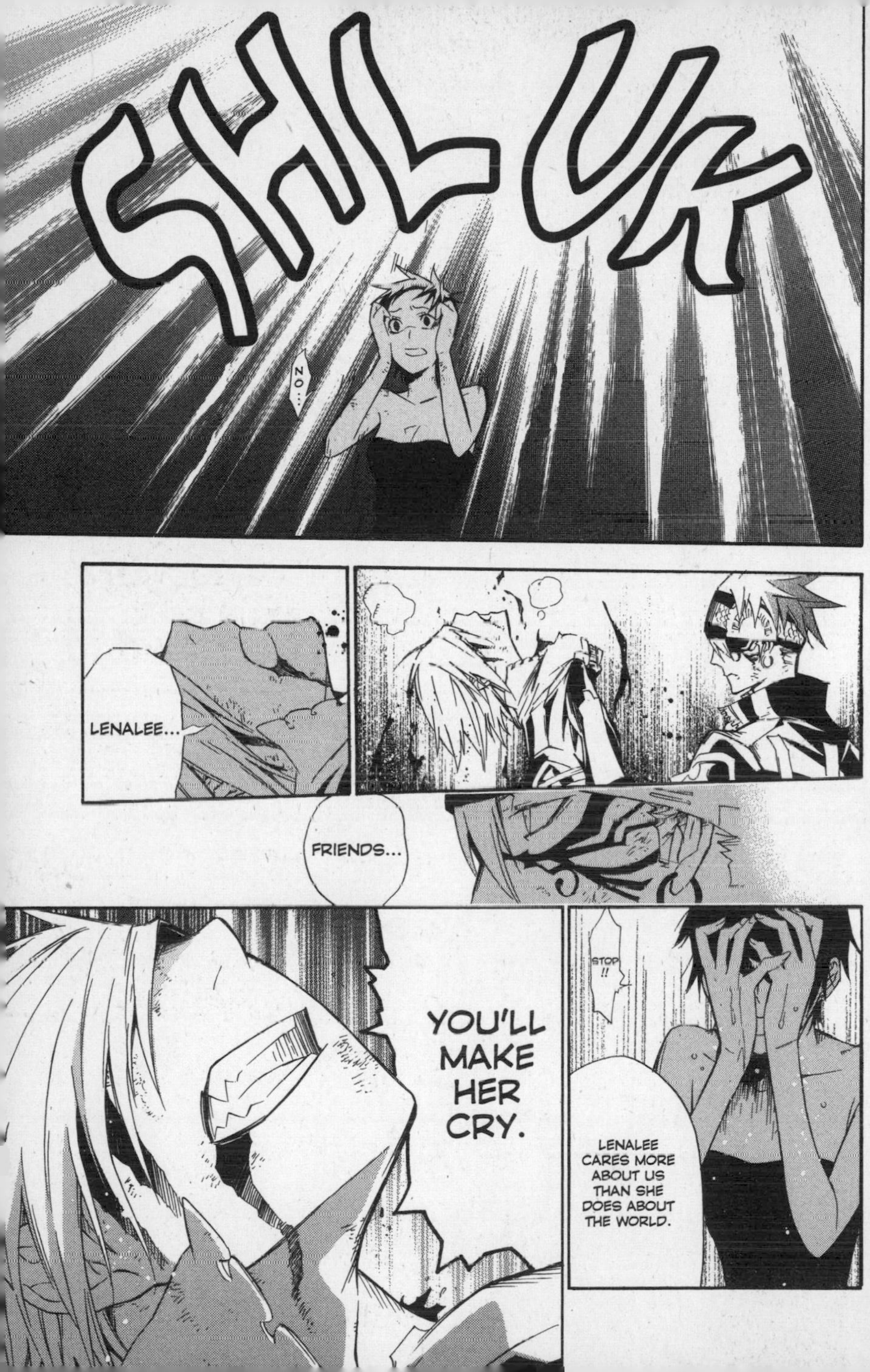
SHLUK
NO...
LENALEE...
FRIENDS...
STOP!!
LENALEE CARES MORE ABOUT US THAN SHE DOES ABOUT THE WORLD.
YOU'LL MAKE HER CRY.

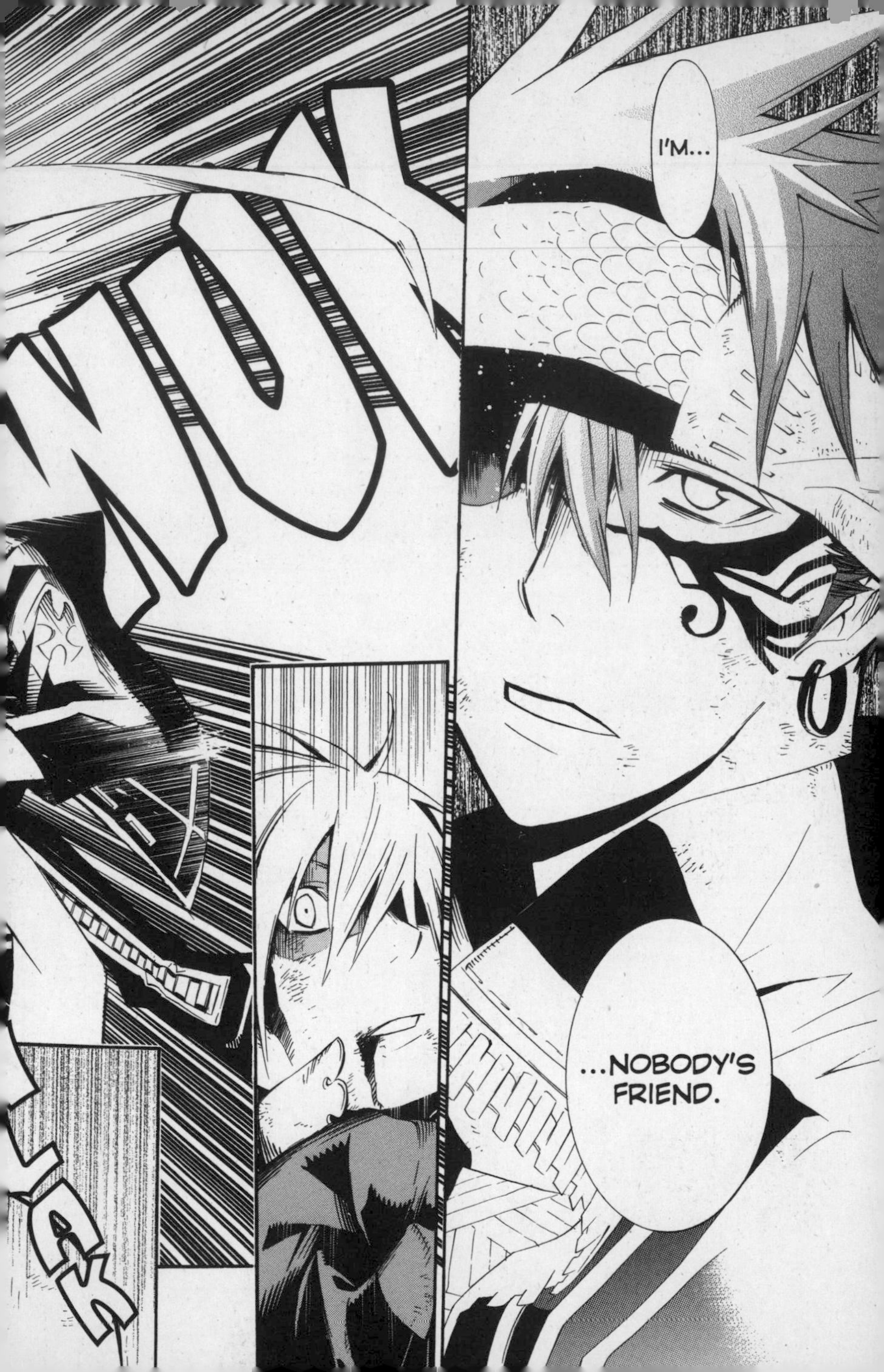
I'M...
...NOBODY'S FRIEND.

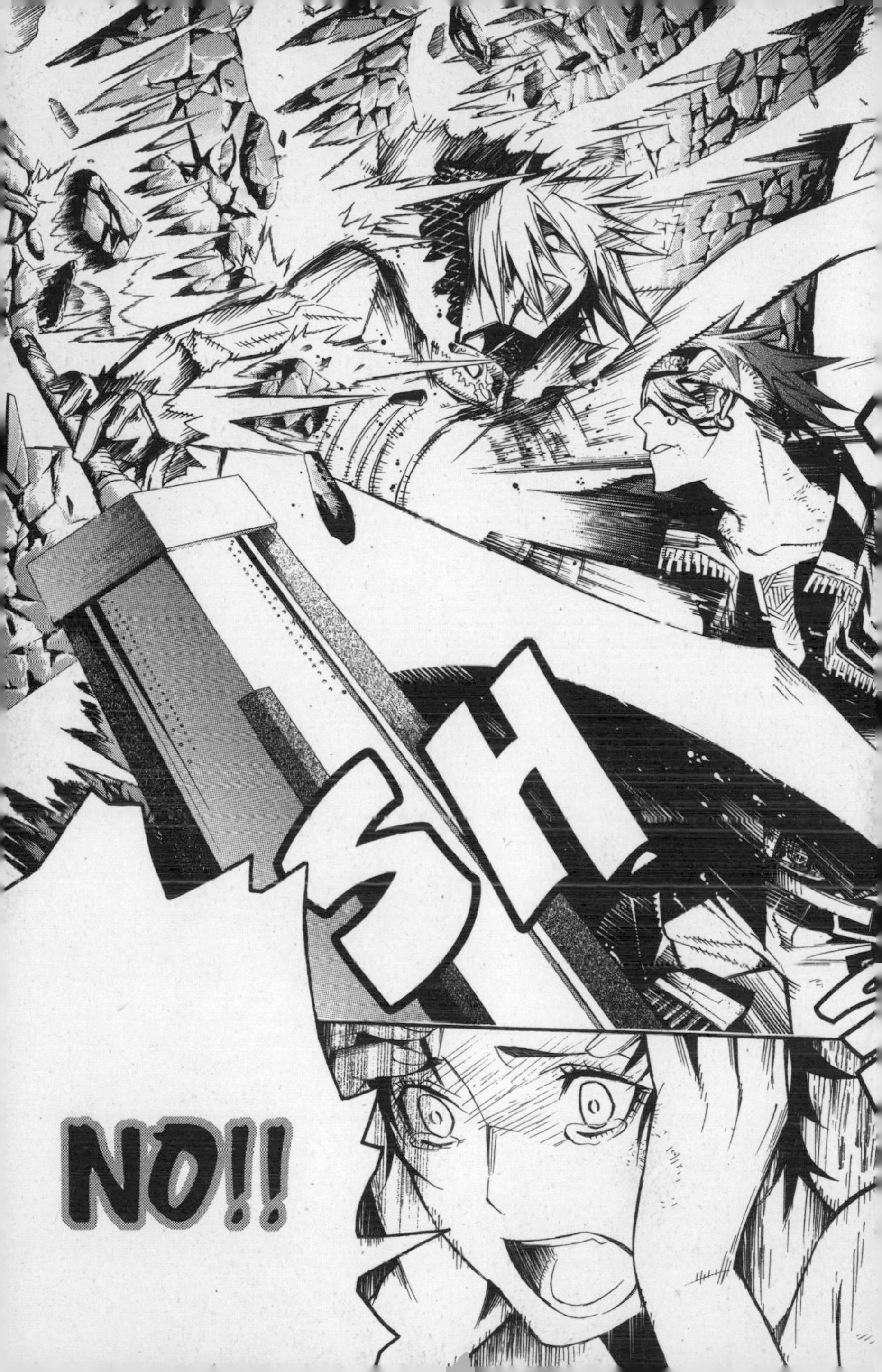
SH
NO!!

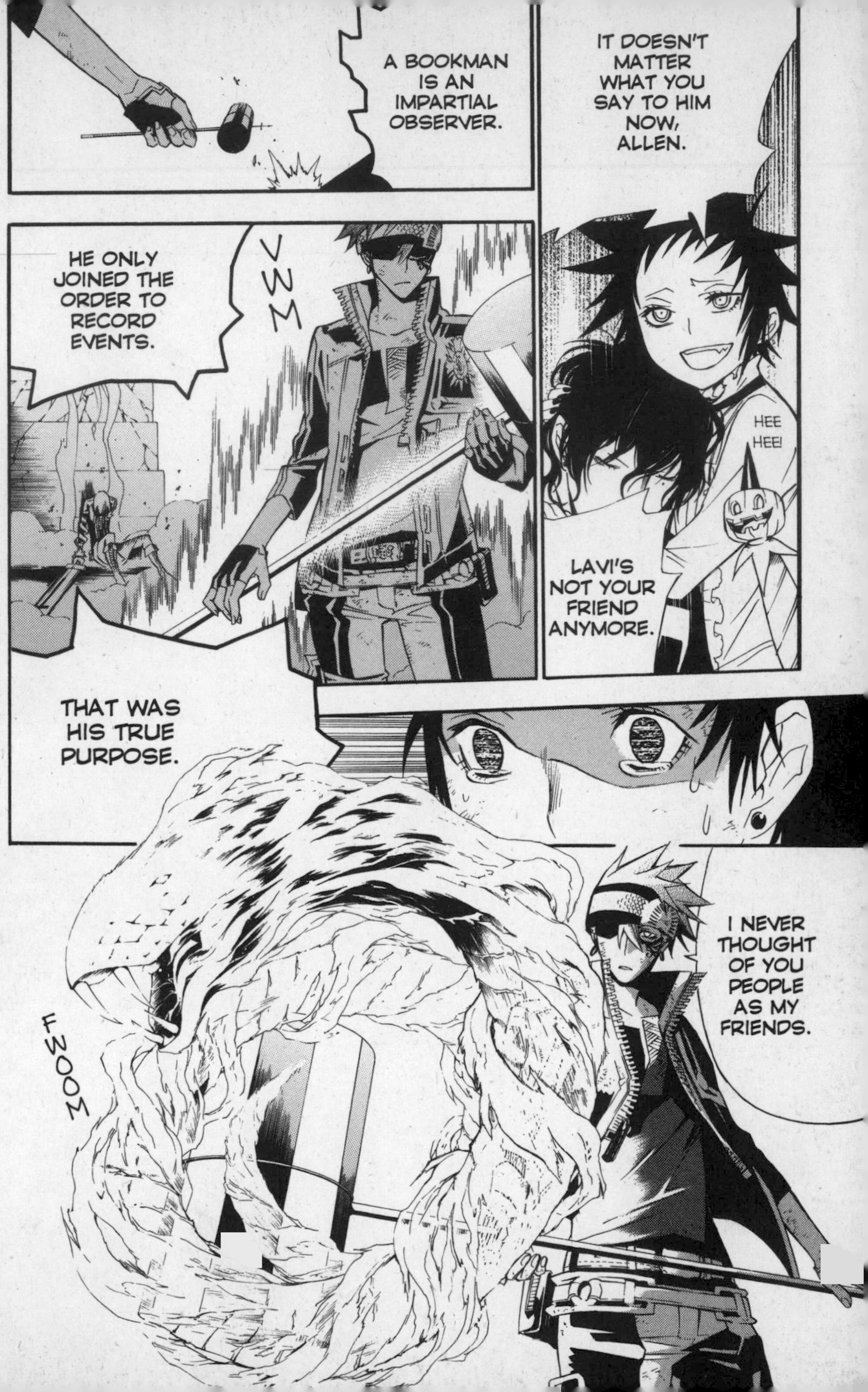
IT DOESN'T MATTER WHAT YOU SAY TO HIM NOW, ALLEN.
HEE HEE!
LAVI'S NOT YOUR FRIEND ANYMORE.
A BOOKMAN IS AN IMPARTIAL OBSERVER.
HE ONLY JOINED THE ORDER TO RECORD EVENTS.
VWM
THAT WAS HIS TRUE PURPOSE.
I NEVER THOUGHT OF YOU PEOPLE AS MY FRIENDS.
FWOOM

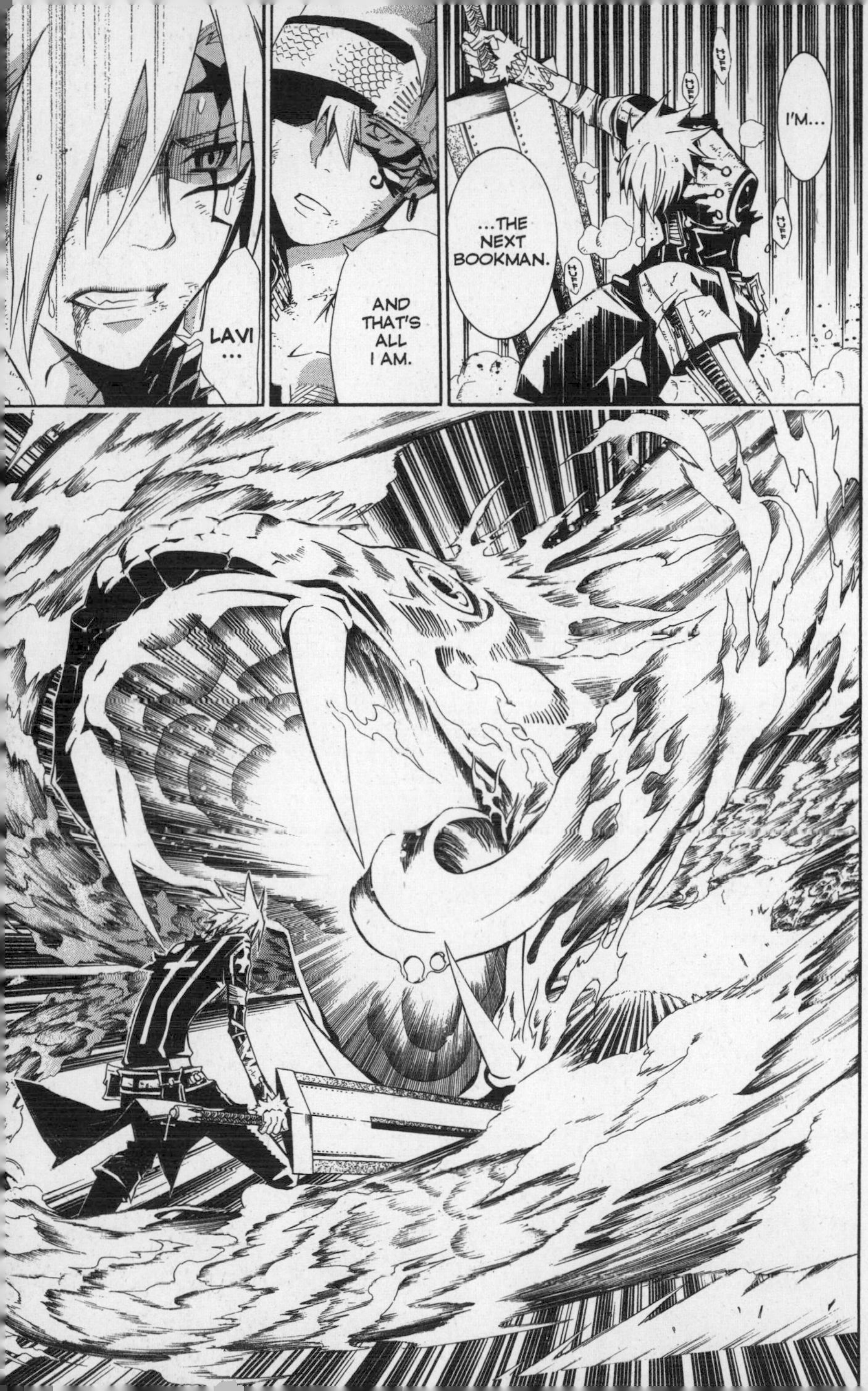
I'M...
HUFF
HUFF
HUFF
...THE NEXT BOOKMAN.
HUFF
AND THAT'S ALL I AM.
LAVI ...

D.GRAY-MAN INVESTIGATION SERIES (?)

FAVORITE FOODS ♡

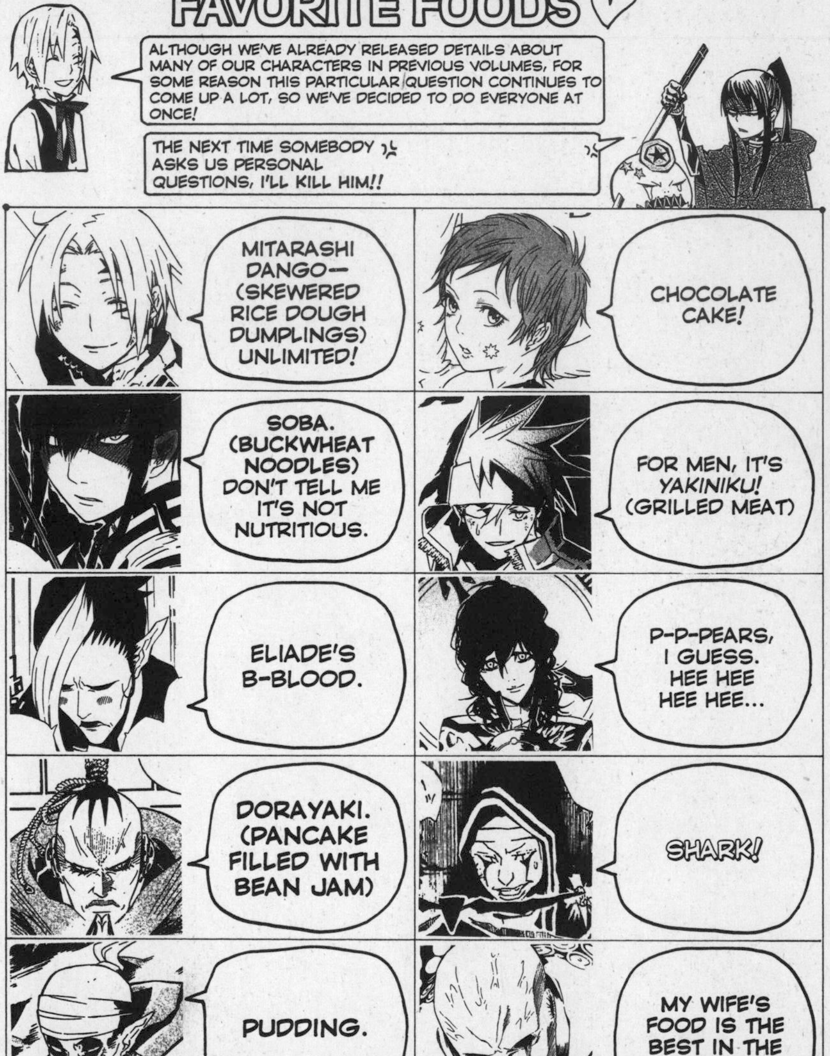
ALTHOUGH WE'VE ALREADY RELEASED DETAILS ABOUT MANY OF OUR CHARACTERS IN PREVIOUS VOLUMES, FOR SOME REASON THIS PARTICULAR QUESTION CONTINUES TO COME UP A LOT, SO WE'VE DECIDED TO DO EVERYONE AT ONCE!
THE NEXT TIME SOMEBODY ASKS US PERSONAL QUESTIONS, I'LL KILL HIM!!
CHOCOLATE CAKE!
MITARASHI DANGO— (SKEWERED RICE DOUGH DUMPLINGS) UNLIMITED!
FOR MEN, IT'S YAKINIKU! (GRILLED MEAT)
SOBA. (BUCKWHEAT NOODLES) DON'T TELL ME IT'S NOT NUTRITIOUS.
P-P-PEARS, I GUESS. HEE HEE HEE HEE...
ELIADE'S B-BLOOD.
SHARK!
DORAYAKI. (PANCAKE FILLED WITH BEAN JAM)
MY WIFE'S FOOD IS THE BEST IN THE WORLD!!
PUDDING.

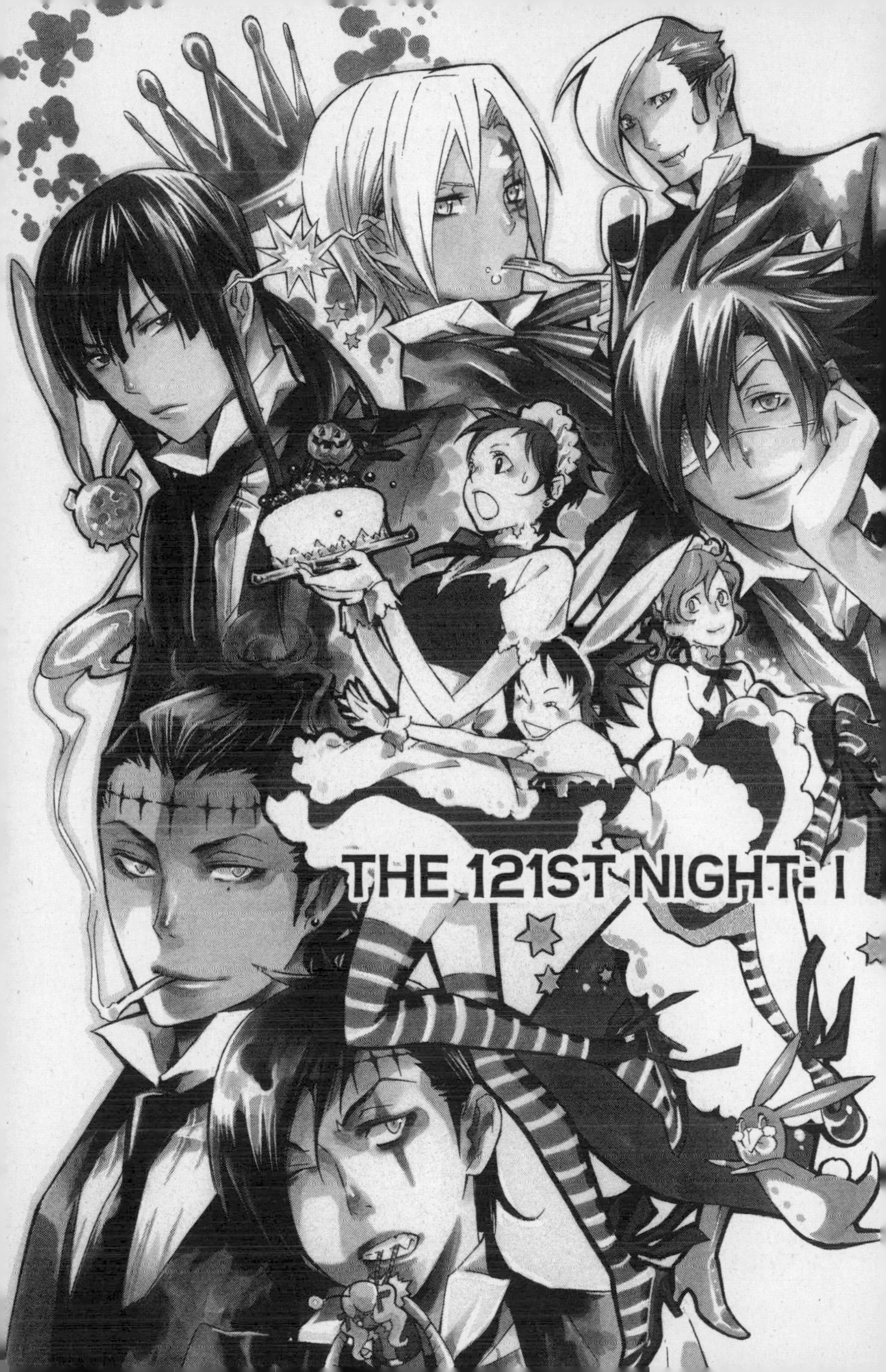
THE 121ST NIGHT: I

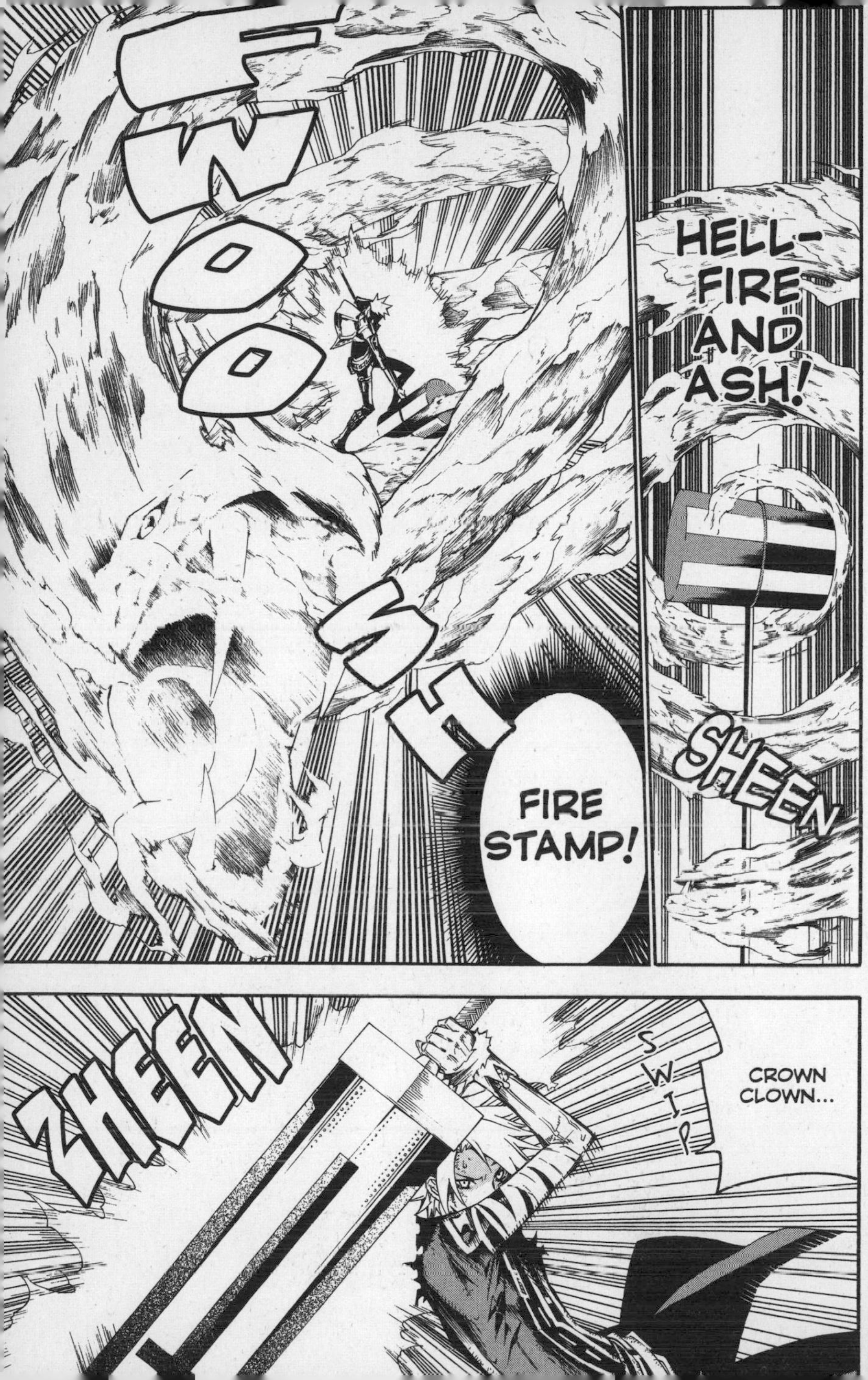
HELL-FIRE AND ASH!
SHEEN
FWOOSH
FIRE STAMP!
CROWN CLOWN...
SWIP
ZHEEN

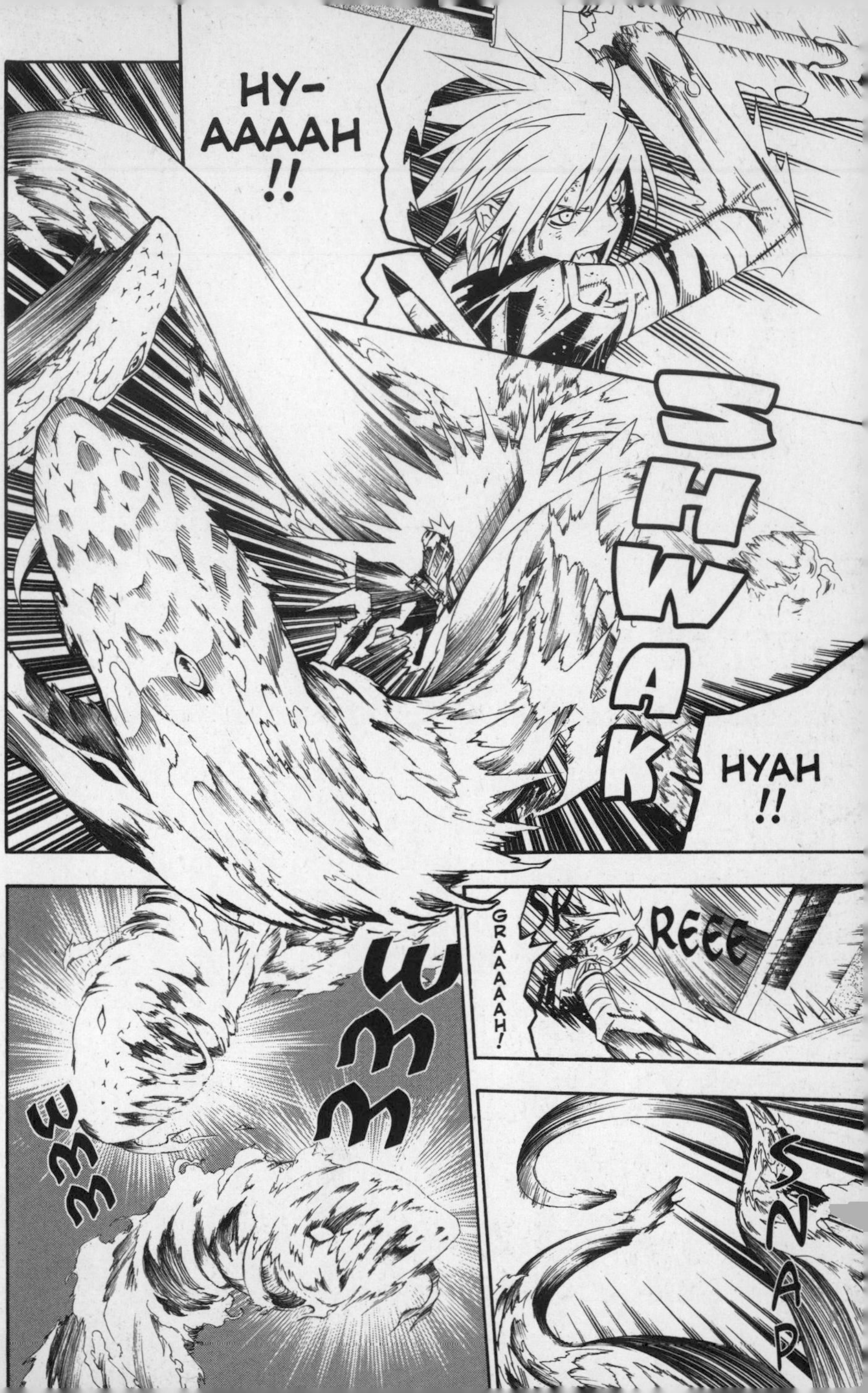
HY-AAAAH!!
SHWAK
HYAH!!
SKREEE
GRAAAAAAH!
SNAP

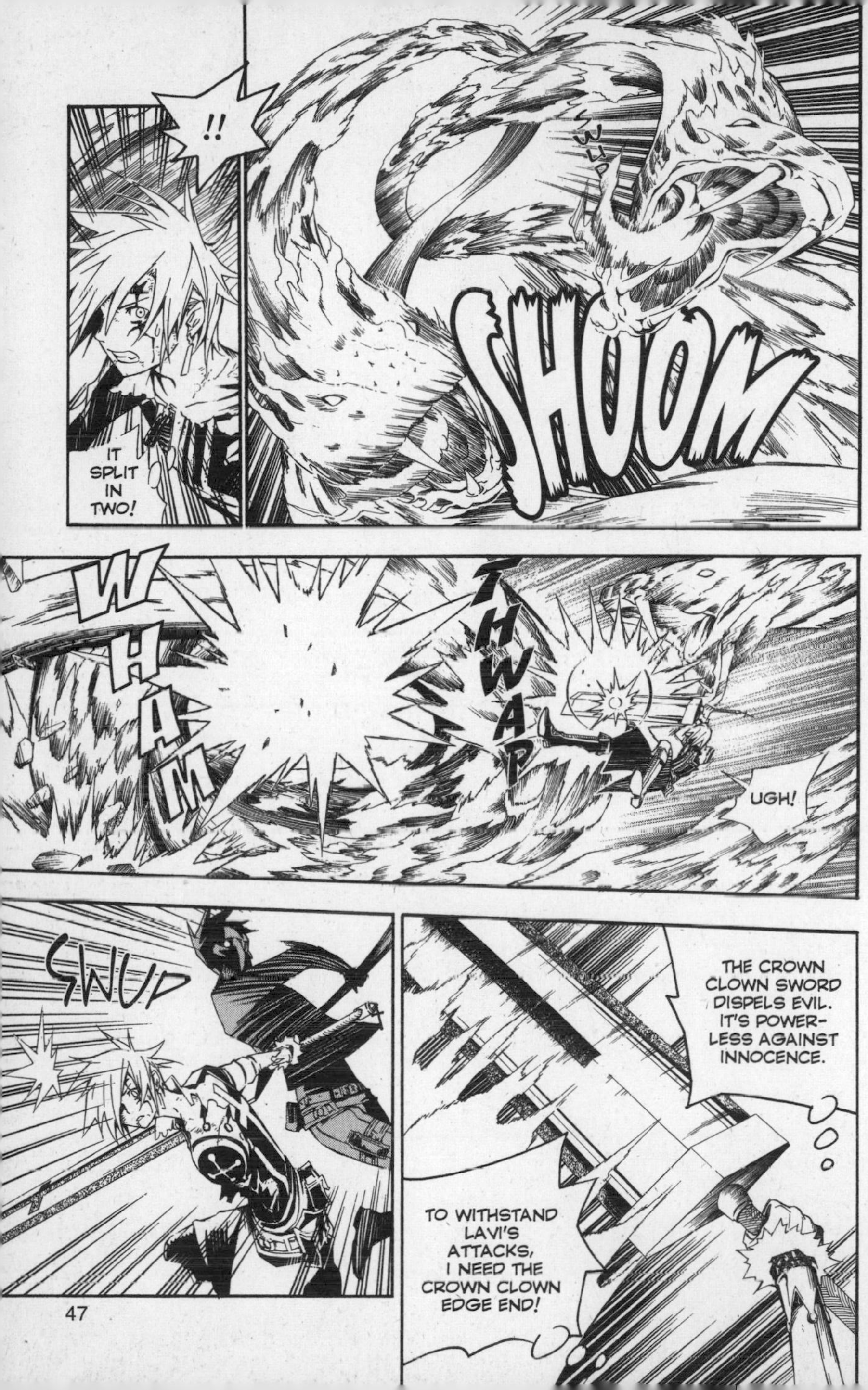
SWUP
SHOOM
!!
IT SPLIT IN TWO!
THWAP
UGH!
WHAM
THE CROWN CLOWN SWORD DISPELS EVIL. IT'S POWERLESS AGAINST INNOCENCE.
TO WITHSTAND LAVI'S ATTACKS, I NEED THE CROWN CLOWN EDGE END!
SWUP

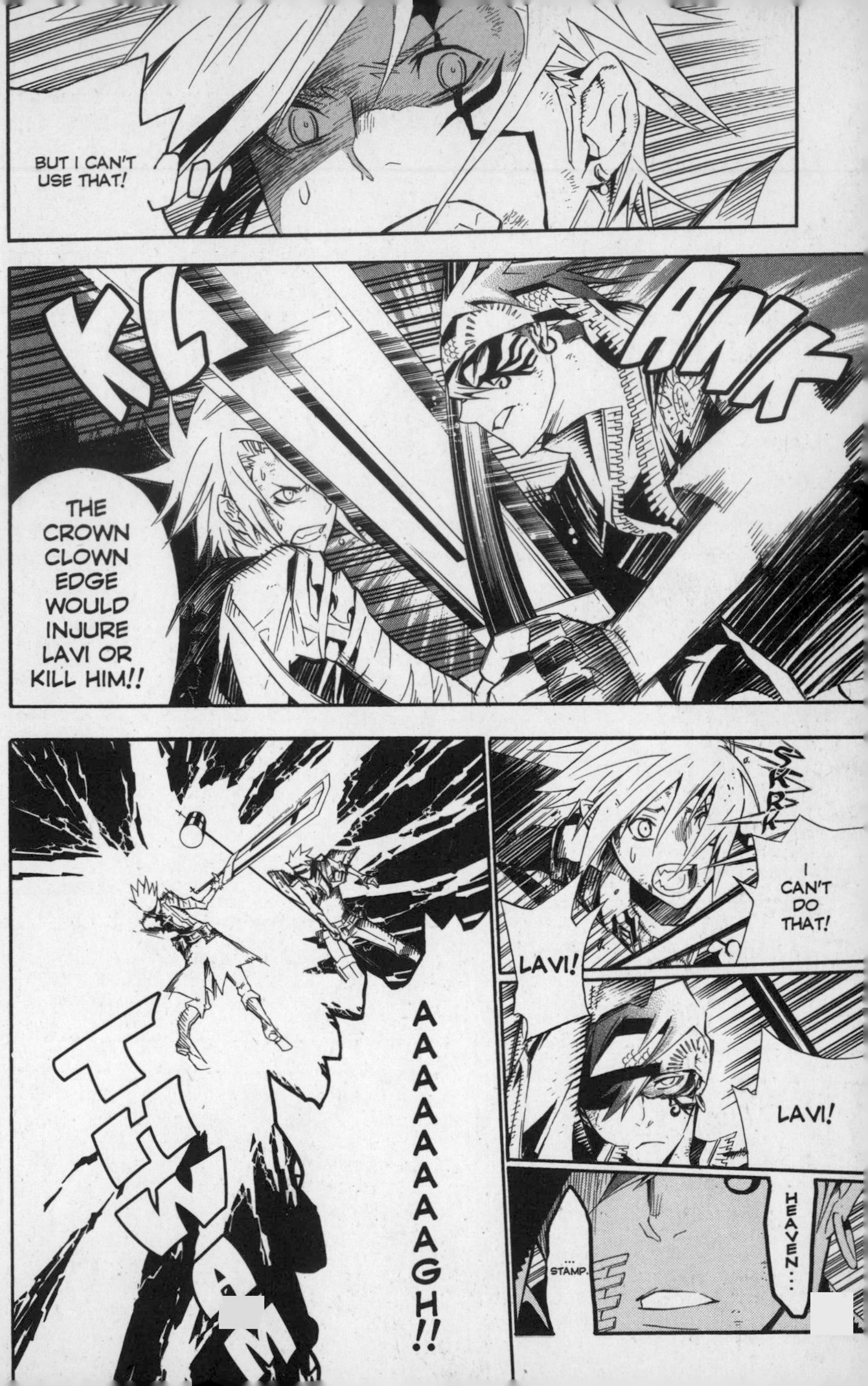
BUT I CAN'T USE THAT!
KCLANK
THE CROWN CLOWN EDGE WOULD INJURE LAVI OR KILL HIM!!
SKRK
I CAN'T DO THAT!
LAVI!
LAVI!
HEAVEN...
...STAMP.
AAAAAAAAGH!!

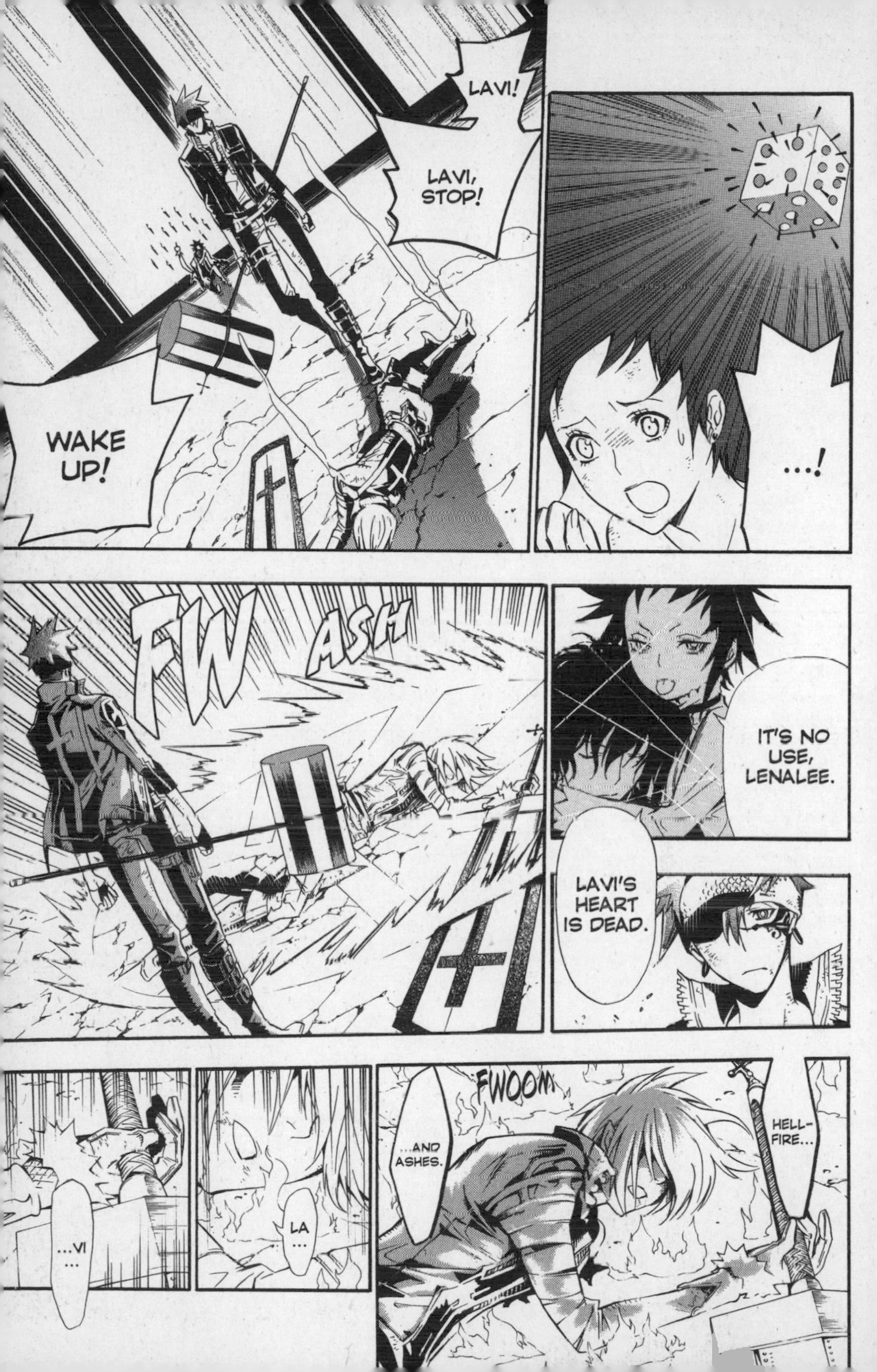
...!
LAVI!
LAVI, STOP!
WAKE UP!
IT'S NO USE, LENALEE.
LAVI'S HEART IS DEAD.
FWASH
HELL-FIRE...
FWOOM
...AND ASHES.
LA ...
...VI ...

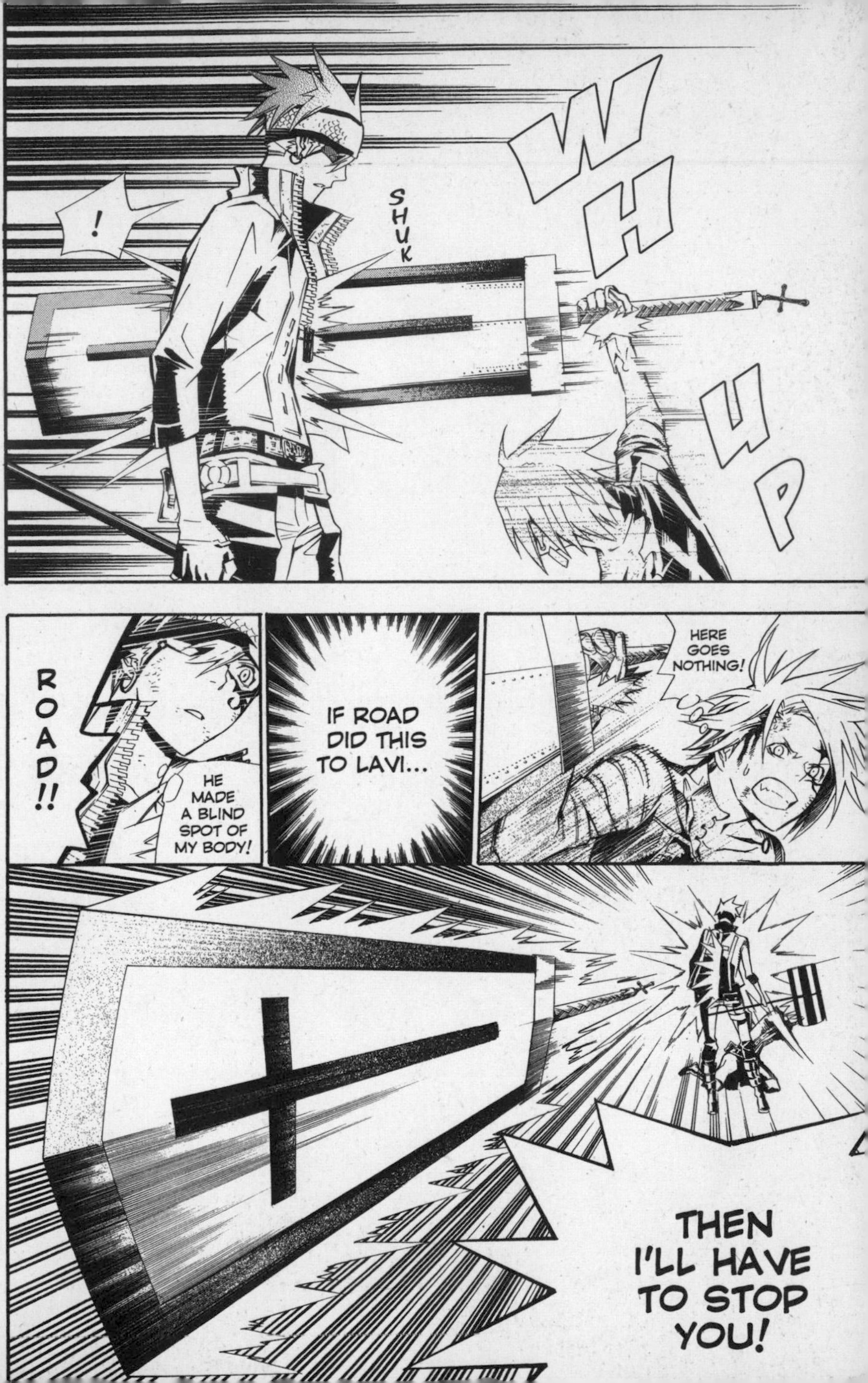
WHUP
SHUK
!
HERE GOES NOTHING!
IF ROAD DID THIS TO LAVI...
ROAD!!
HE MADE A BLIND SPOT OF MY BODY!
THEN I'LL HAVE TO STOP YOU!

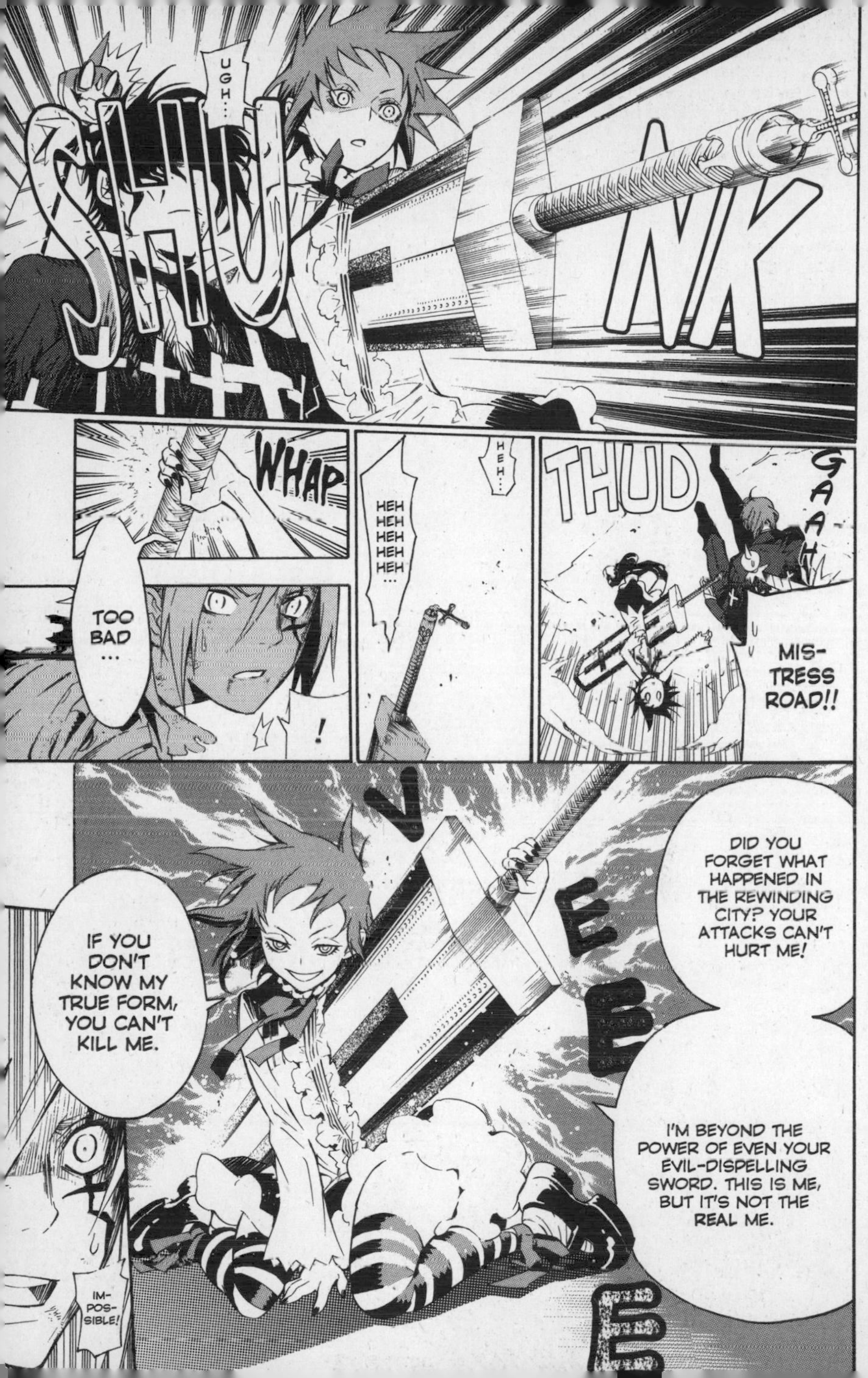
UGH...
SHU-NK
THUD
GAAAH
MISTRESS ROAD!!
HEH...
HEH HEH HEH HEH HEH...
WHAP
TOO BAD...
!
DID YOU FORGET WHAT HAPPENED IN THE REWINDING CITY? YOUR ATTACKS CAN'T HURT ME!
I'M BEYOND THE POWER OF EVEN YOUR EVIL-DISPELLING SWORD. THIS IS ME, BUT IT'S NOT THE REAL ME.
IF YOU DON'T KNOW MY TRUE FORM, YOU CAN'T KILL ME.
IMPOSSIBLE!

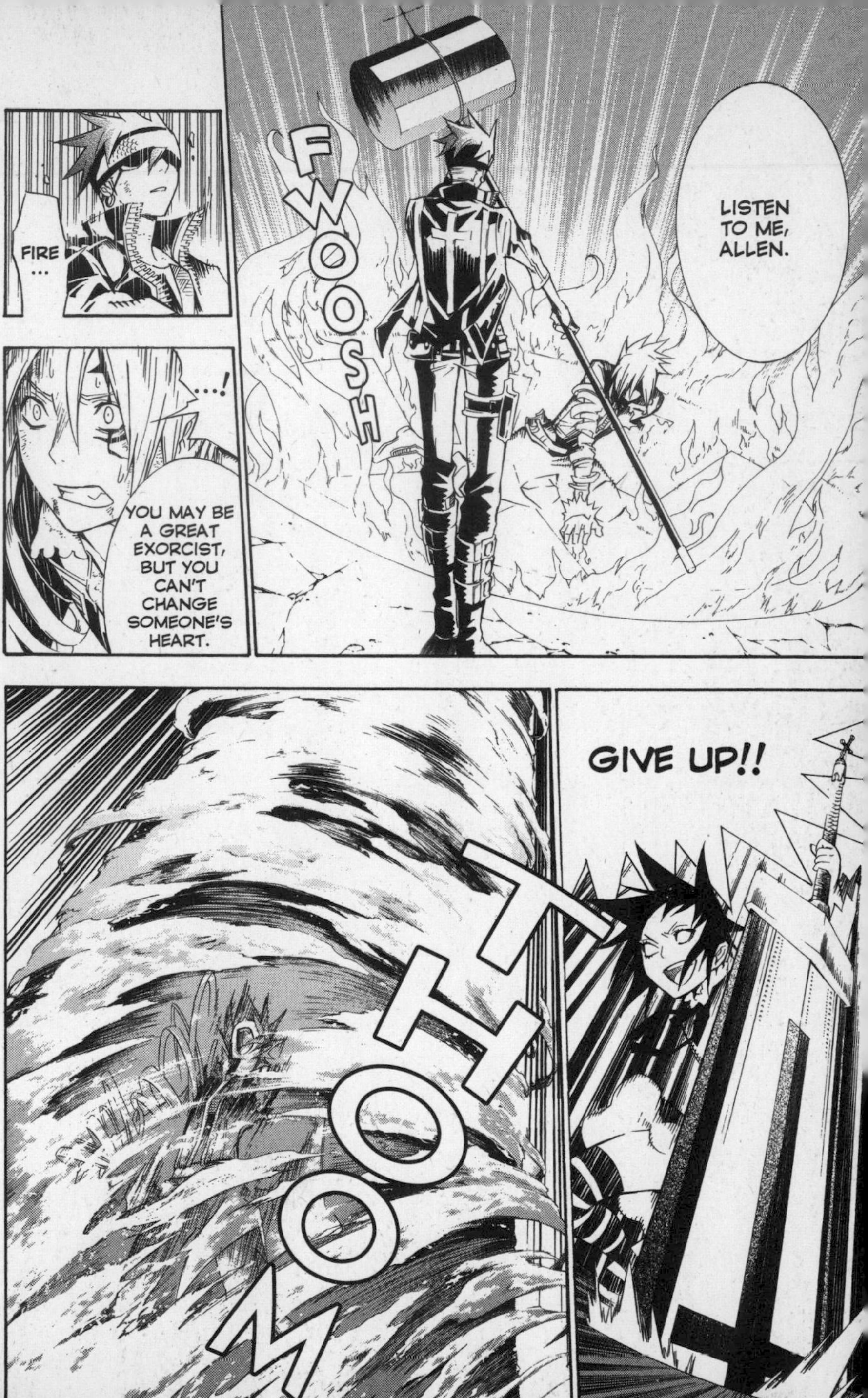
LISTEN TO ME, ALLEN.
FWOOSH
FIRE ...
...!
YOU MAY BE A GREAT EXORCIST, BUT YOU CAN'T CHANGE SOMEONE'S HEART.
GIVE UP!!
THOOOM

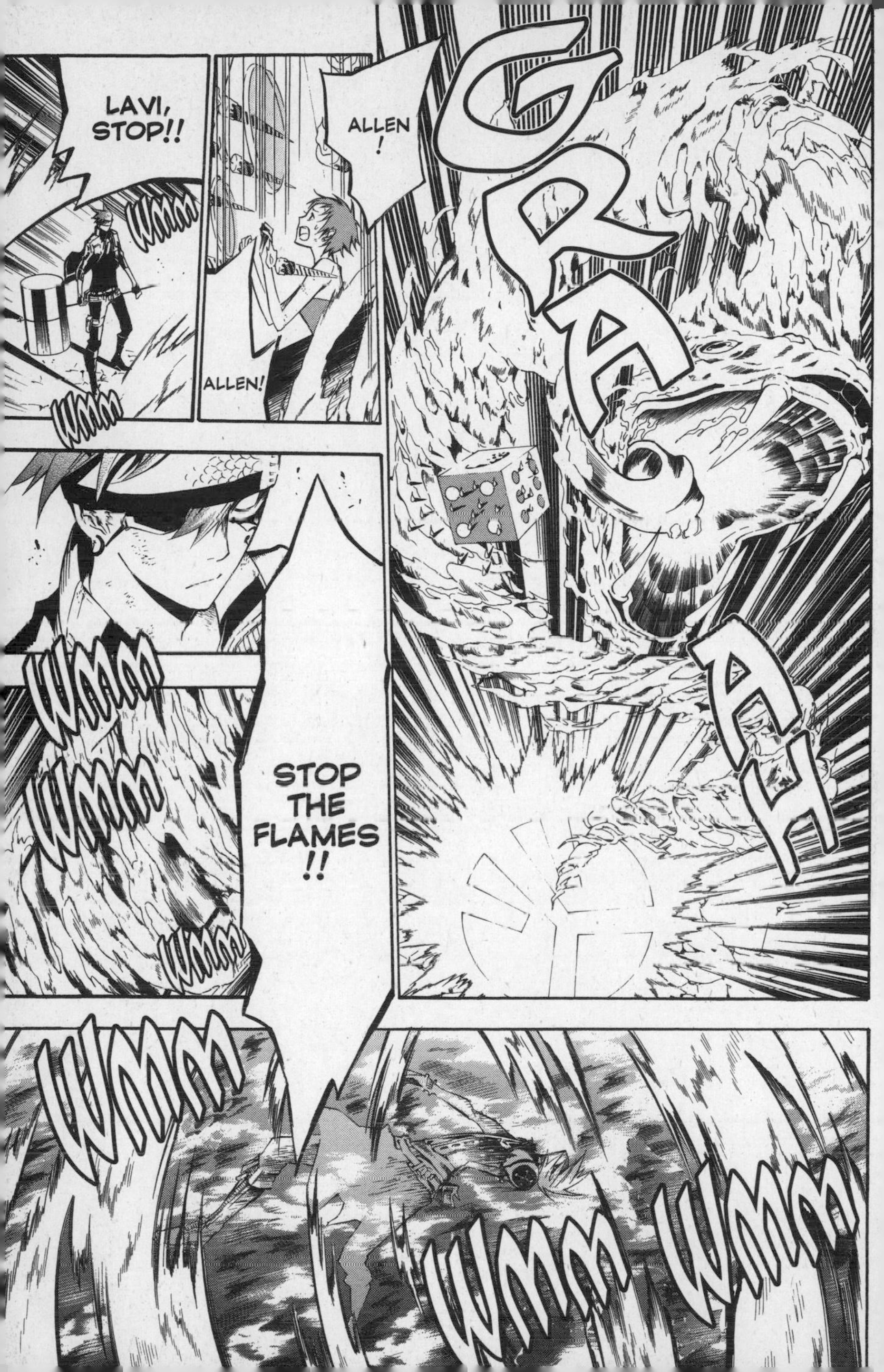
GRAAAH
ALLEN!
ALLEN!
LAVI, STOP!!
WMMM
WMMM
STOP THE FLAMES!!
WMMM
WMMM
WMMM
WMMM
WMMM WMMM

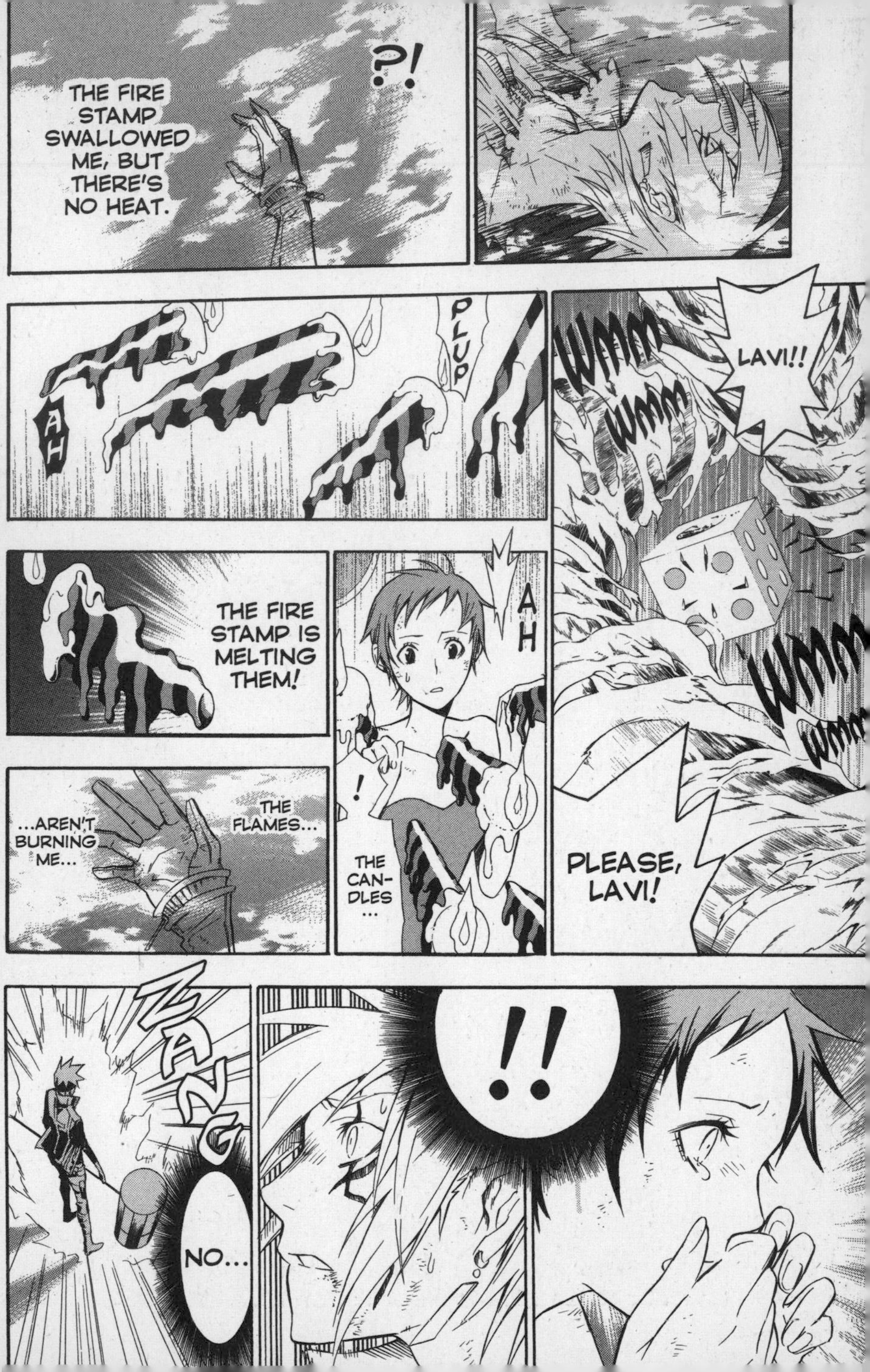
?!
THE FIRE STAMP SWALLOWED ME, BUT THERE'S NO HEAT.
LAVI!!
WMM WMM
WMM WMM
PLEASE, LAVI!
PLUP
AH
AH
!
THE CANDLES...
THE FIRE STAMP IS MELTING THEM!
THE FLAMES...
...AREN'T BURNING ME...
!!
ZANG
NO...

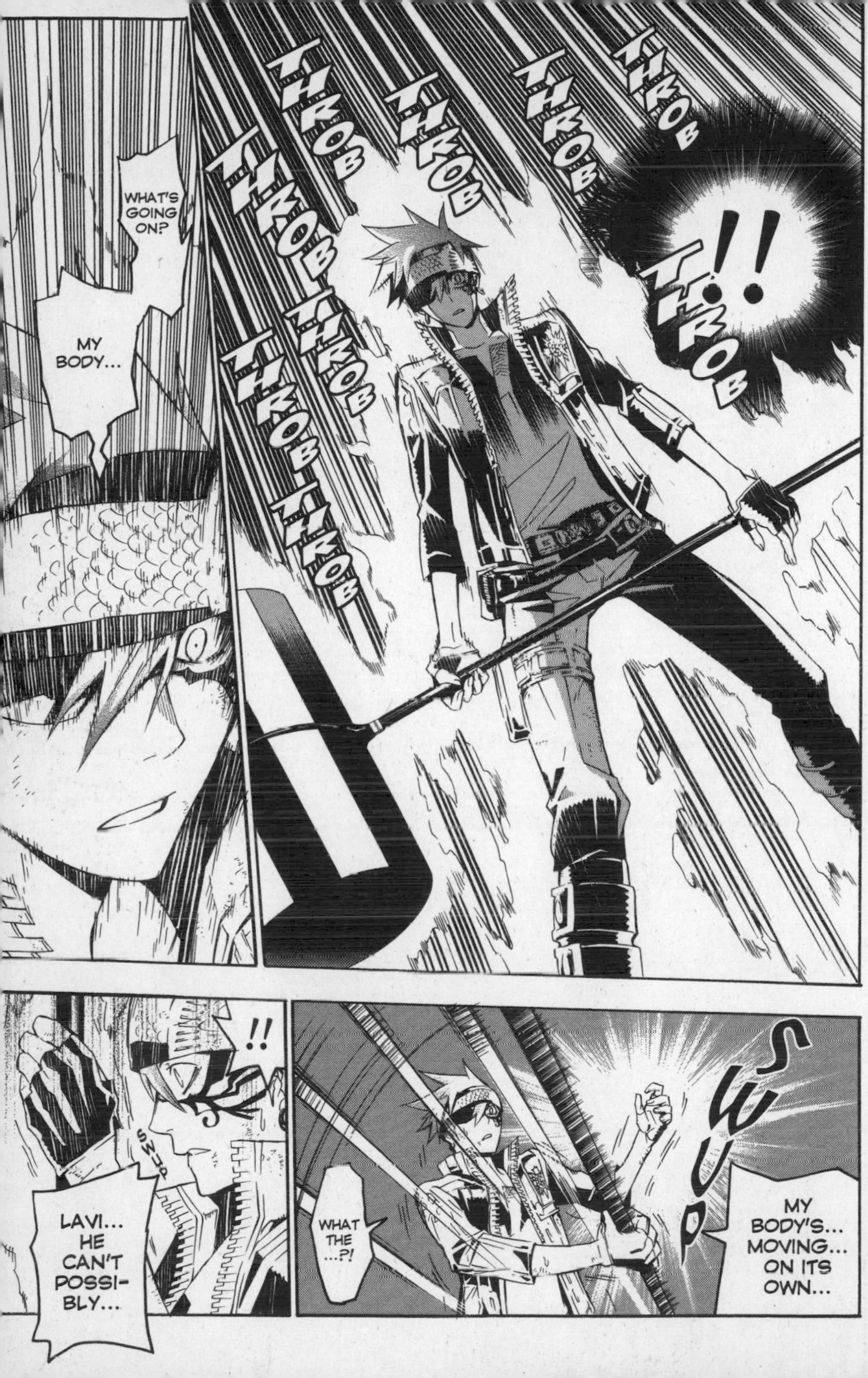
THROB
THROB
!!
THROB
THROB
THROB
THROB
THROB
THROB
THROB
THROB
WHAT'S GOING ON?
MY BODY...
SWUP
MY BODY'S... MOVING... ON ITS OWN...
WHAT THE ...?!
!!
SWUP
LAVI... HE CAN'T POSSIBLY...

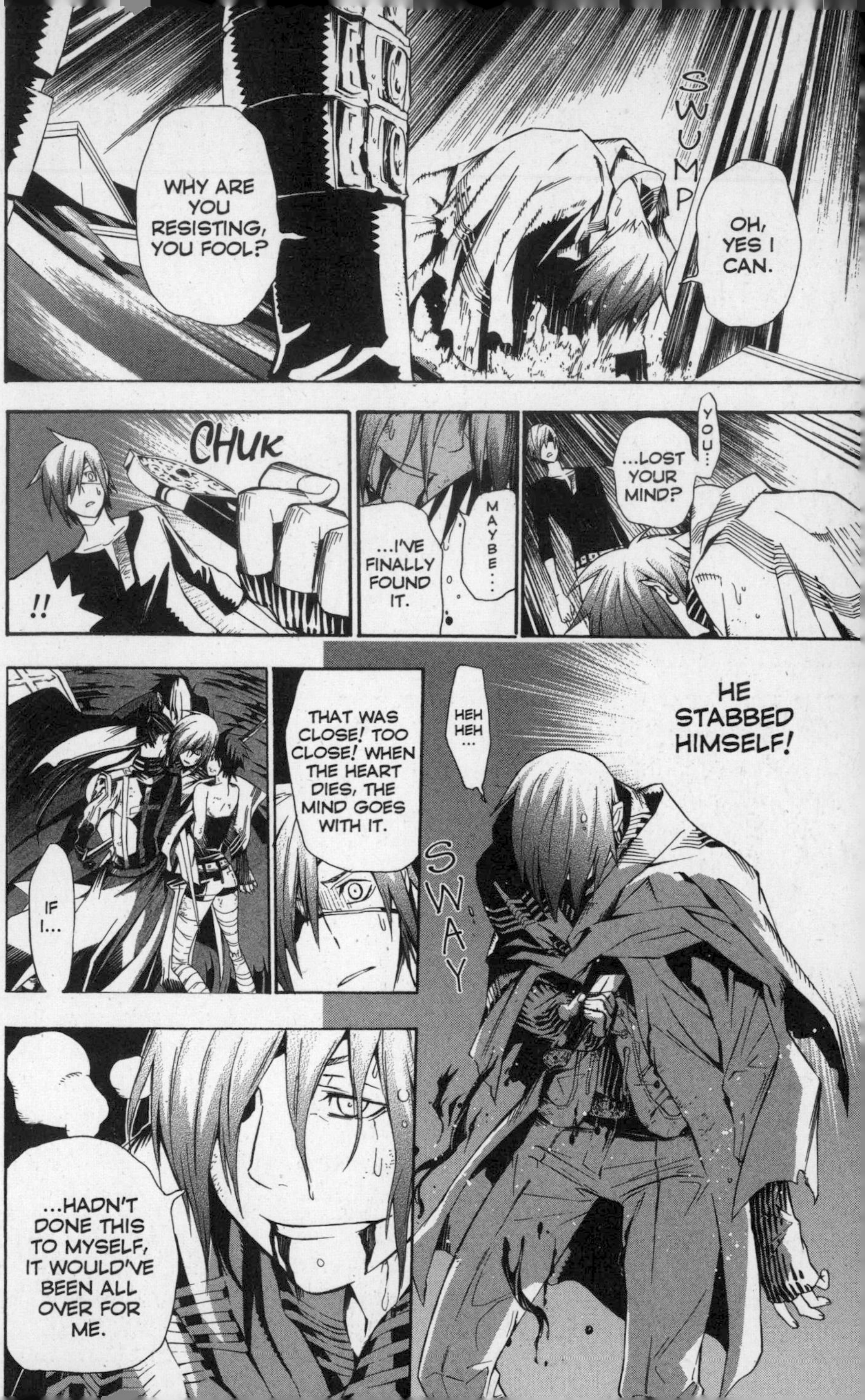
SWUMP
OH, YES I CAN.
WHY ARE YOU RESISTING, YOU FOOL?
YOU...
...LOST YOUR MIND?
MAYBE...
...I'VE FINALLY FOUND IT.
CHUK
!!
HE STABBED HIMSELF!
HEH HEH...
SWAY
THAT WAS CLOSE! TOO CLOSE! WHEN THE HEART DIES, THE MIND GOES WITH IT.
IF I...
...HADN'T DONE THIS TO MYSELF, IT WOULD'VE BEEN ALL OVER FOR ME.

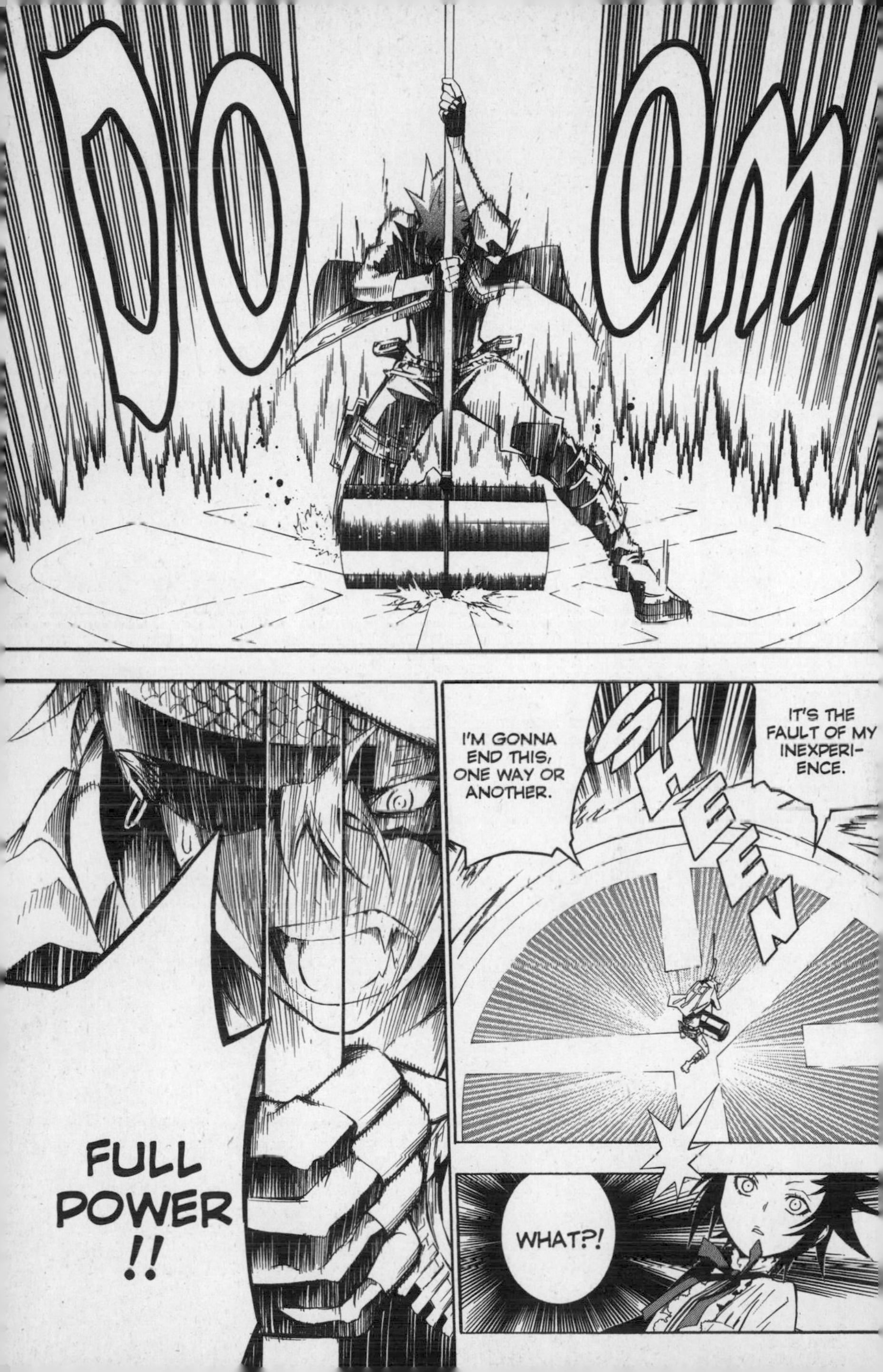
DOOM
IT'S THE FAULT OF MY INEXPERIENCE.
I'M GONNA END THIS, ONE WAY OR ANOTHER.
SHEEN
WHAT?!
FULL POWER!!

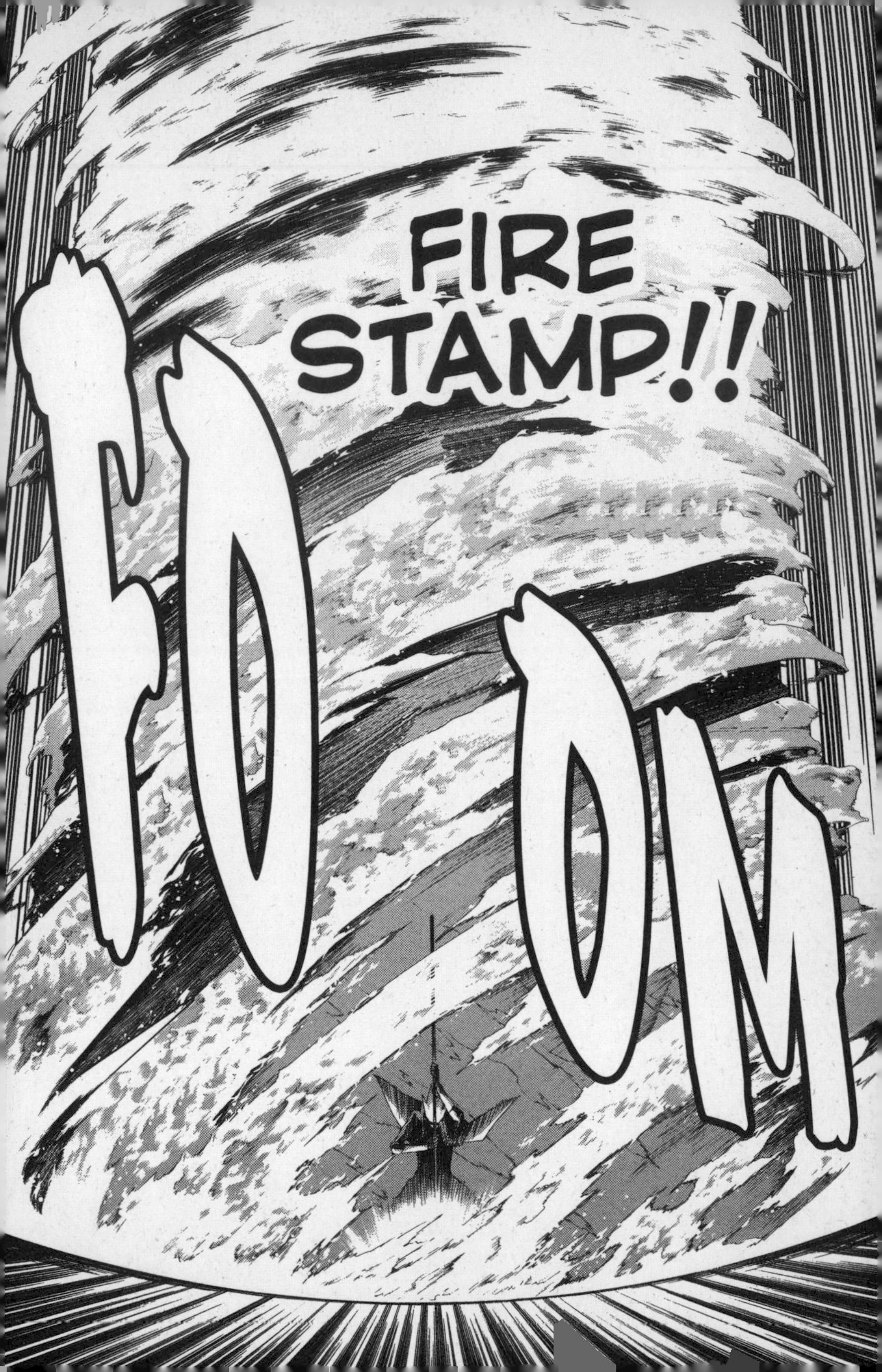
FIRE STAMP!!
FOOM

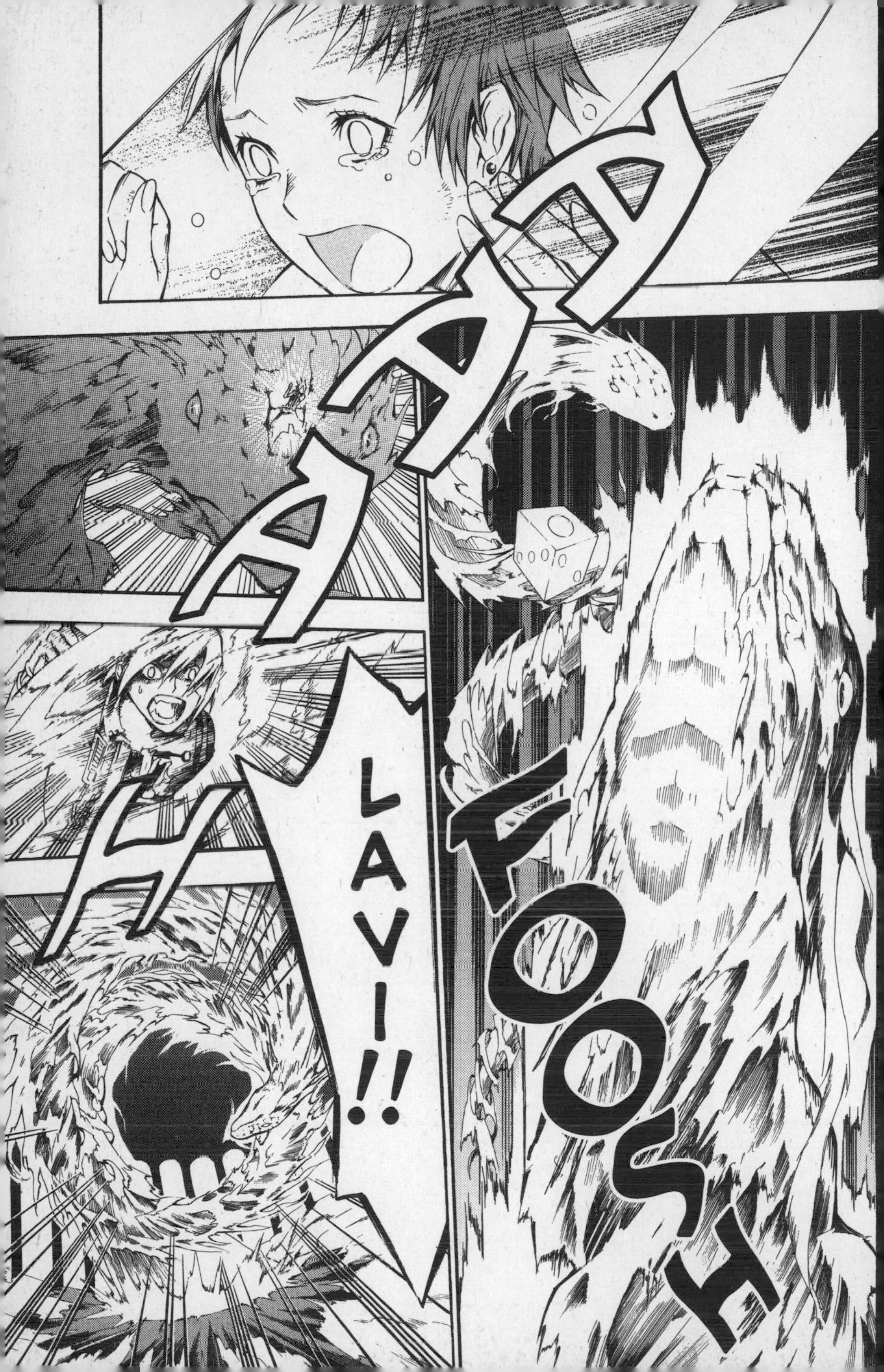

AAAAAH
LAVI!!
FOOSH

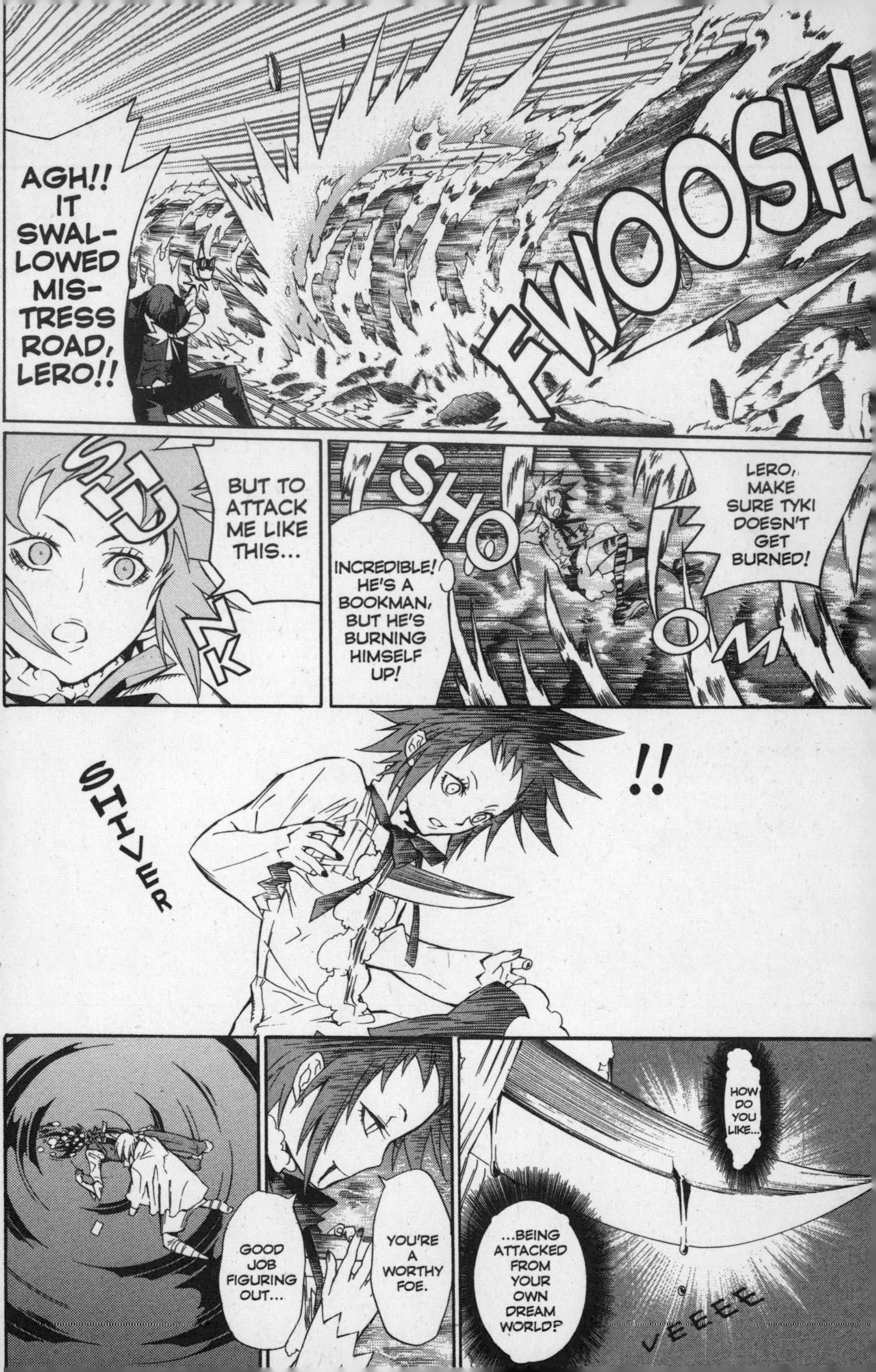
FWOOSH
AGH!! IT SWAL-LOWED MIS-TRESS ROAD, LERO!!
LERO, MAKE SURE TYKI DOESN'T GET BURNED!
SHOOOM
INCREDIBLE! HE'S A BOOKMAN, BUT HE'S BURNING HIMSELF UP!
BUT TO ATTACK ME LIKE THIS...
SHUNK
!!
SHIVER
HOW DO YOU LIKE...
...BEING ATTACKED FROM YOUR OWN DREAM WORLD?
VEEEE
YOU'RE A WORTHY FOE.
GOOD JOB FIGURING OUT...

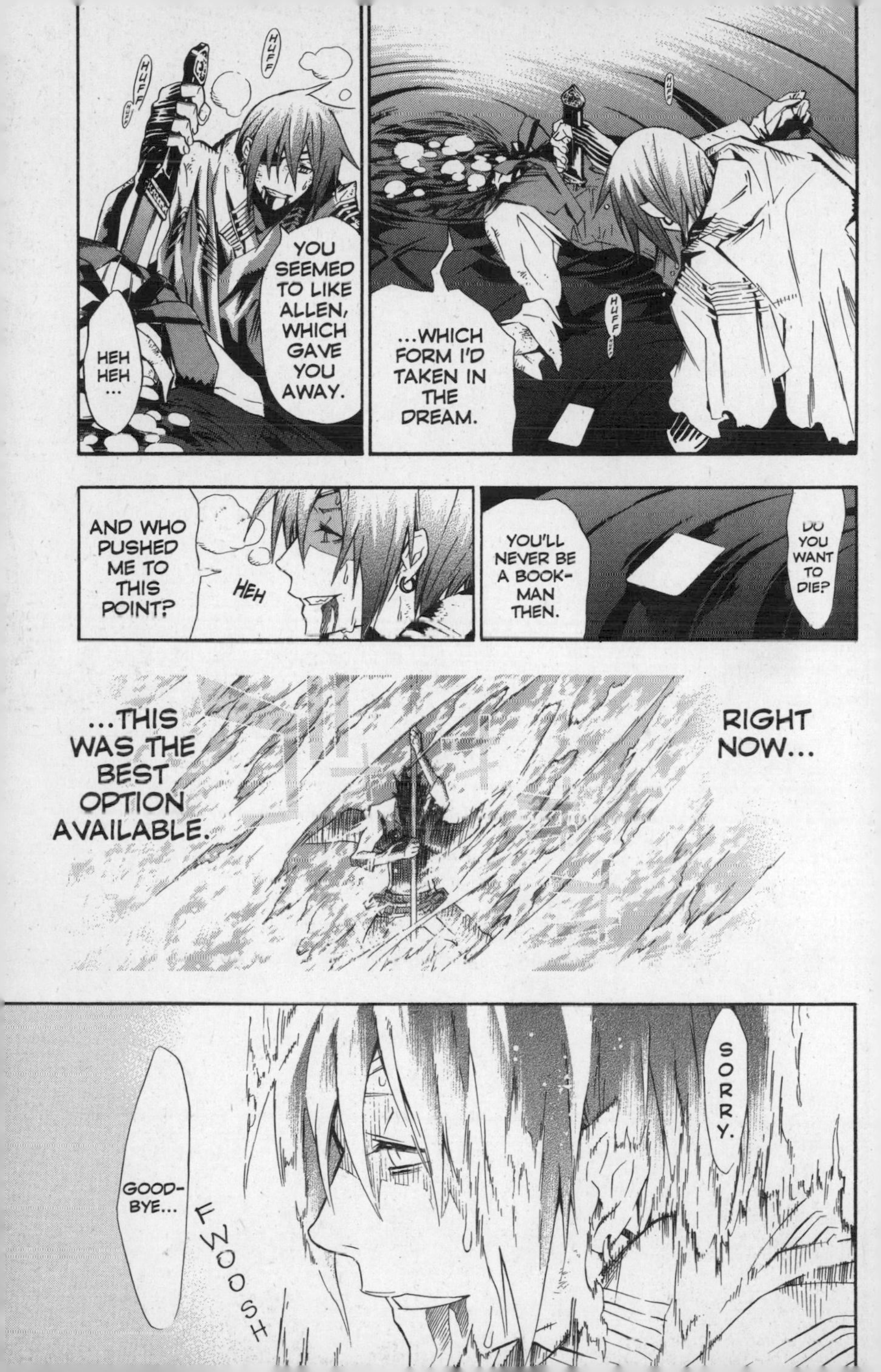
HUFF
...WHICH FORM I'D TAKEN IN THE DREAM.
HUFF
HUFF
HUFF
YOU SEEMED TO LIKE ALLEN, WHICH GAVE YOU AWAY.
HEH HEH ...
DO YOU WANT TO DIE?
YOU'LL NEVER BE A BOOK-MAN THEN.
AND WHO PUSHED ME TO THIS POINT?
HEH
RIGHT NOW...
...THIS WAS THE BEST OPTION AVAILABLE.
SORRY.
GOOD-BYE...
FWOOSH

D.GRAY-MAN INVESTIGATION SERIES (?)

FAVORITE FOODS ♥

THE NOAH EDITION

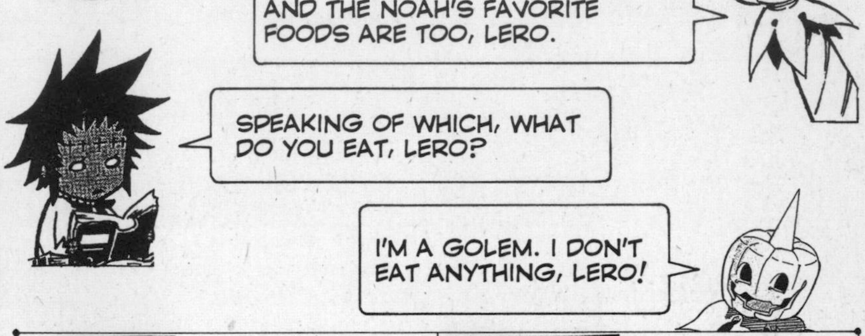

WE FOUND OUT WHAT THE EARL'S AND THE NOAH'S FAVORITE FOODS ARE TOO, LERO.
SPEAKING OF WHICH, WHAT DO YOU EAT, LERO?
I'M A GOLEM. I DON'T EAT ANYTHING, LERO!

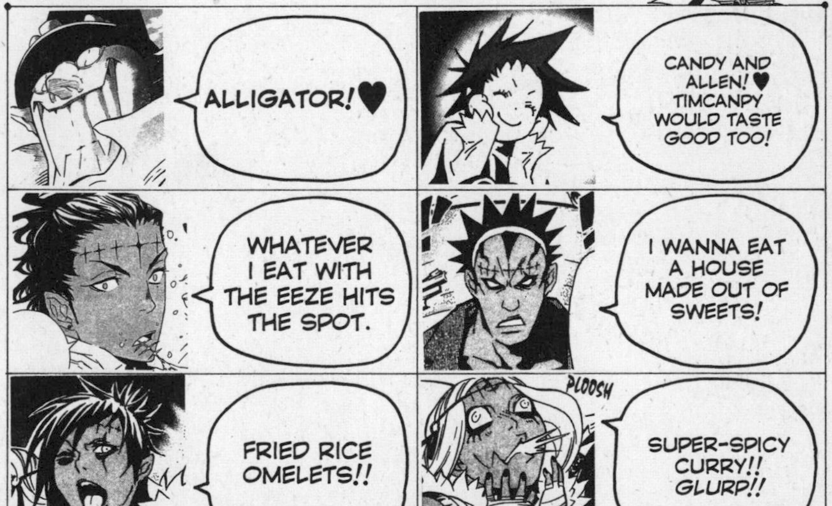

CANDY AND ALLEN! ♥ TIMCANPY WOULD TASTE GOOD TOO!
ALLIGATOR! ♥
I WANNA EAT A HOUSE MADE OUT OF SWEETS!
WHATEVER I EAT WITH THE EEZE HITS THE SPOT.
PLOOSH
SUPER-SPICY CURRY!! GLURP!!
FRIED RICE OMELETS!!

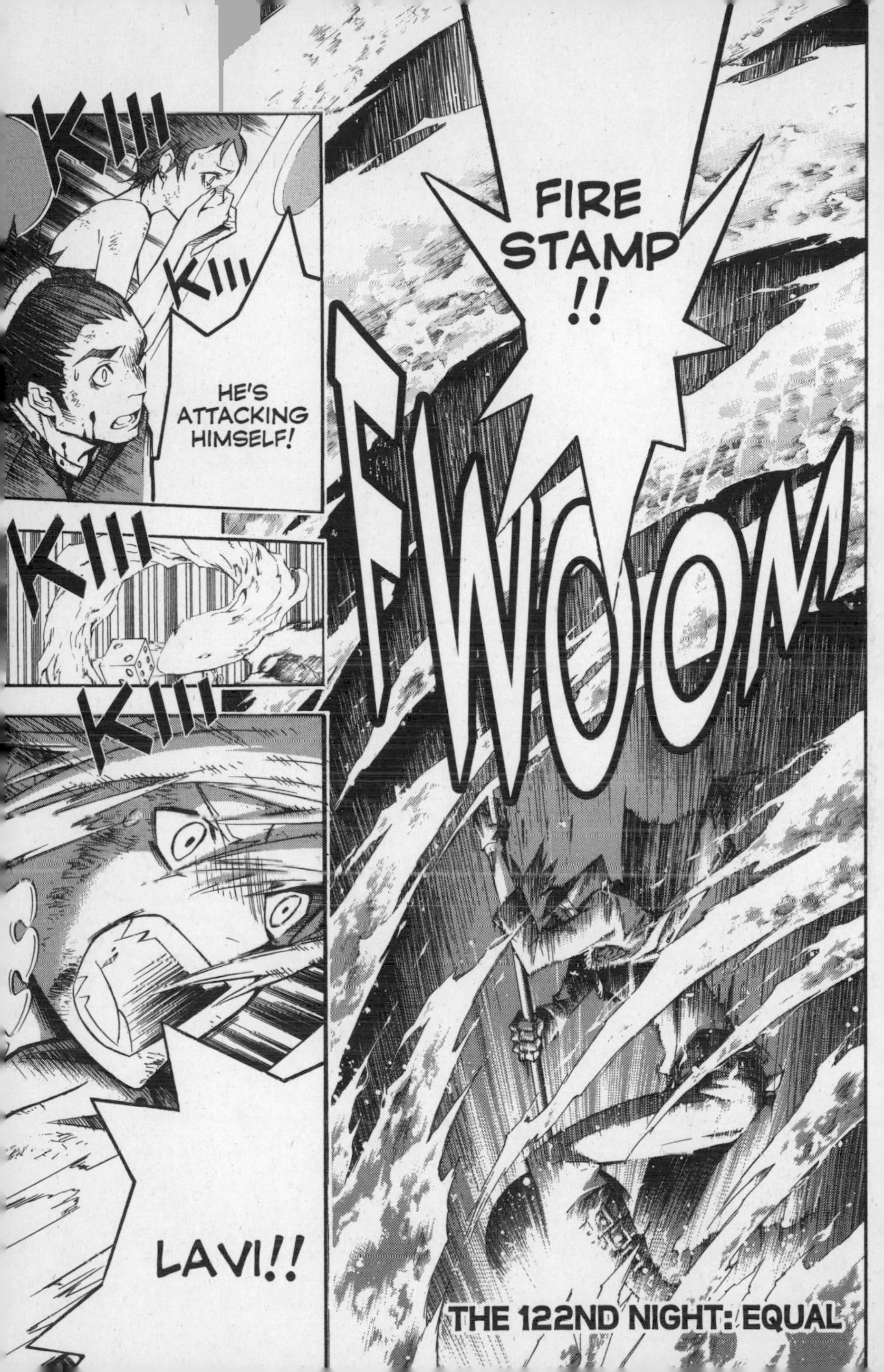
FIRE STAMP!!
FWOOM
THE 122ND NIGHT: EQUAL
KIIII
KIIII
HE'S ATTACKING HIMSELF!
KIIII
KIIII
LAVI!!

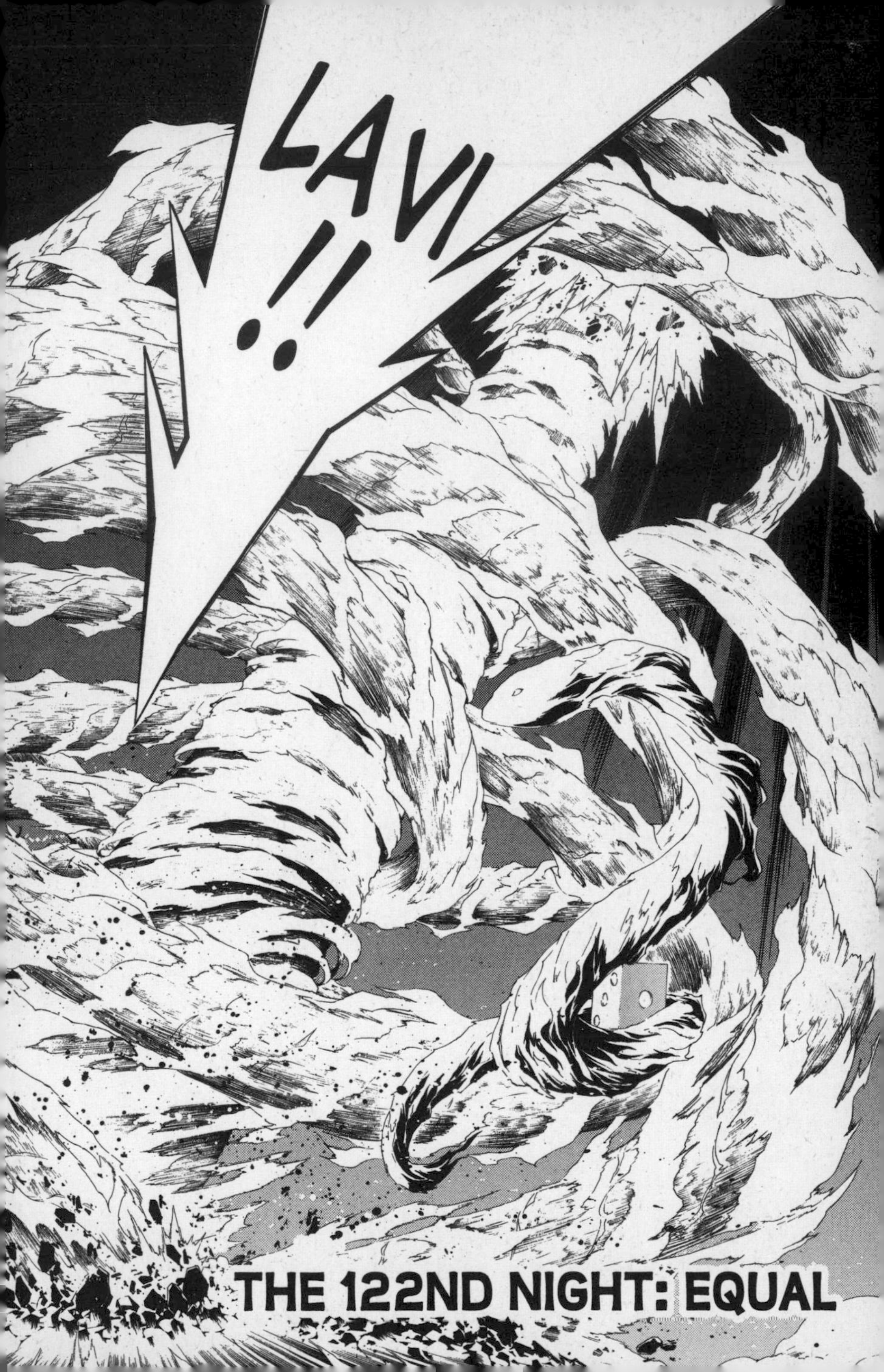
LAVI!!
THE 122ND NIGHT: EQUAL

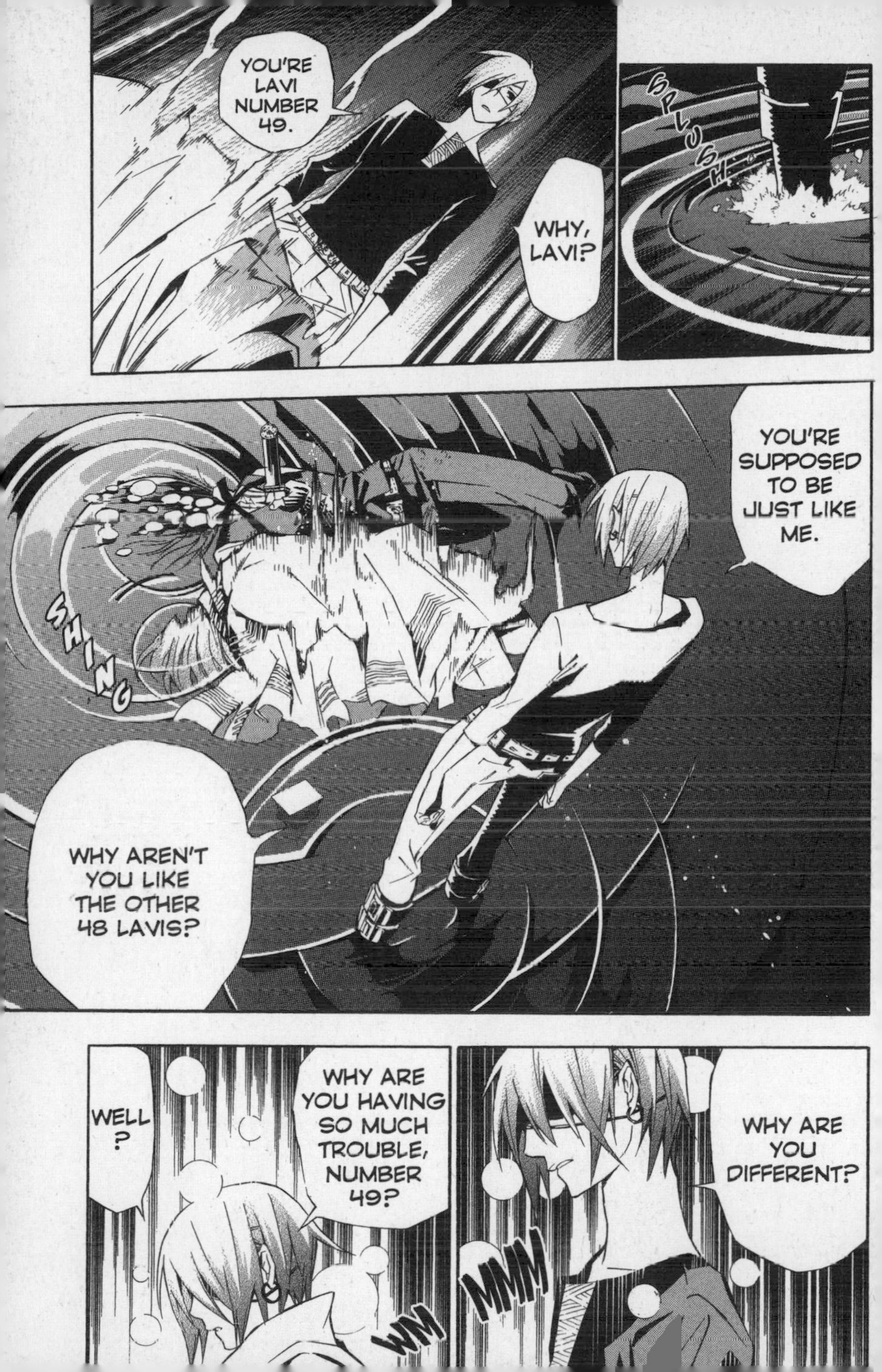
SPLUSH
YOU'RE LAVI NUMBER 49.
WHY, LAVI?
YOU'RE SUPPOSED TO BE JUST LIKE ME.
SHING
WHY AREN'T YOU LIKE THE OTHER 48 LAVIS?
WHY ARE YOU DIFFERENT?
MMM
WHY ARE YOU HAVING SO MUCH TROUBLE, NUMBER 49?
WELL?
WM

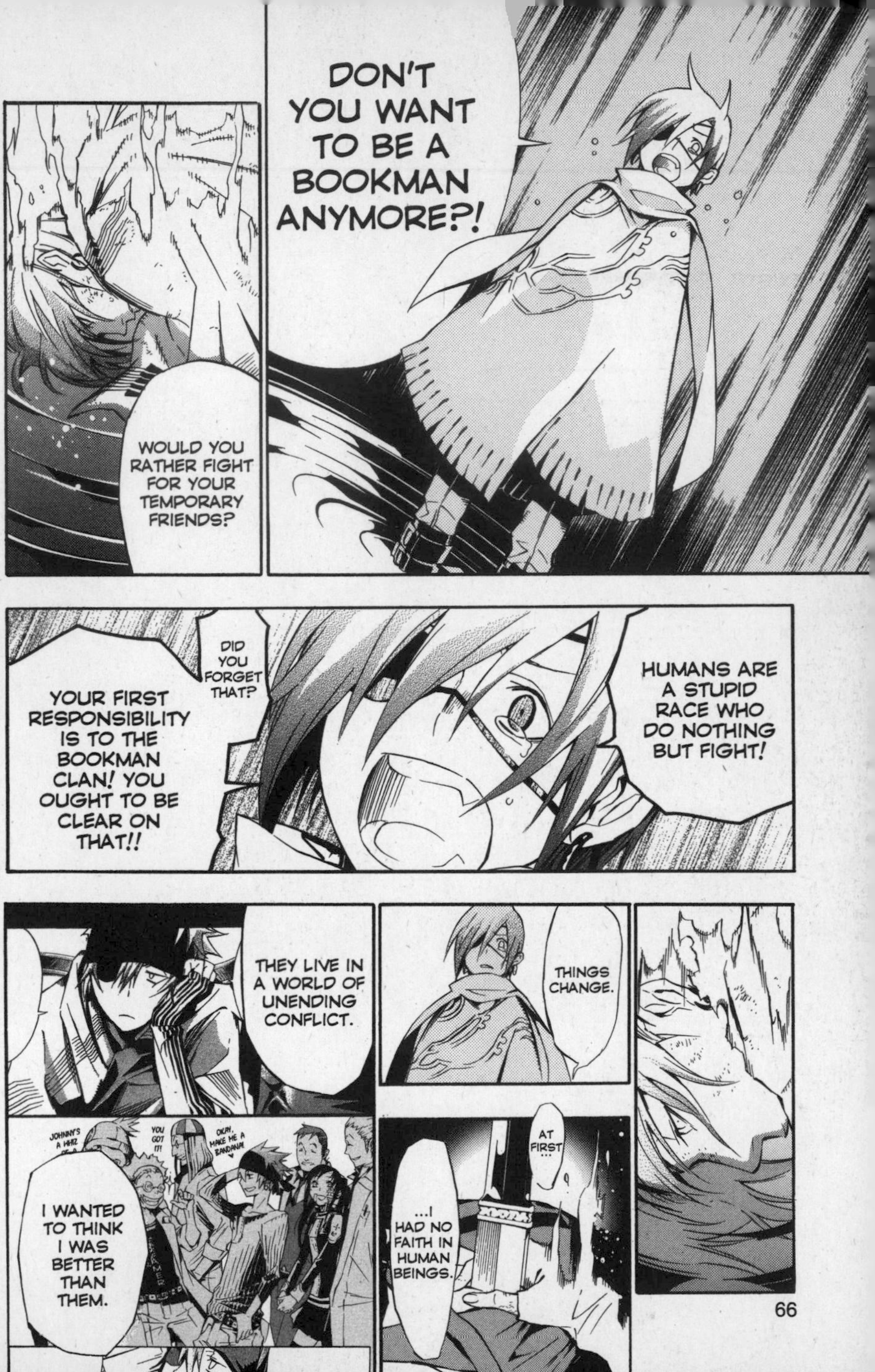
DON'T YOU WANT TO BE A BOOKMAN ANYMORE?!
WOULD YOU RATHER FIGHT FOR YOUR TEMPORARY FRIENDS?
HUMANS ARE A STUPID RACE WHO DO NOTHING BUT FIGHT!
DID YOU FORGET THAT?
YOUR FIRST RESPONSIBILITY IS TO THE BOOKMAN CLAN! YOU OUGHT TO BE CLEAR ON THAT!!
THINGS CHANGE.
THEY LIVE IN A WORLD OF UNENDING CONFLICT.
AT FIRST...
...I HAD NO FAITH IN HUMAN BEINGS.
OKAY, MAKE ME A BANDANA! ♥
YOU GOT IT!
JOHNNY'S A WHIZ
I WANTED TO THINK I WAS BETTER THAN THEM.

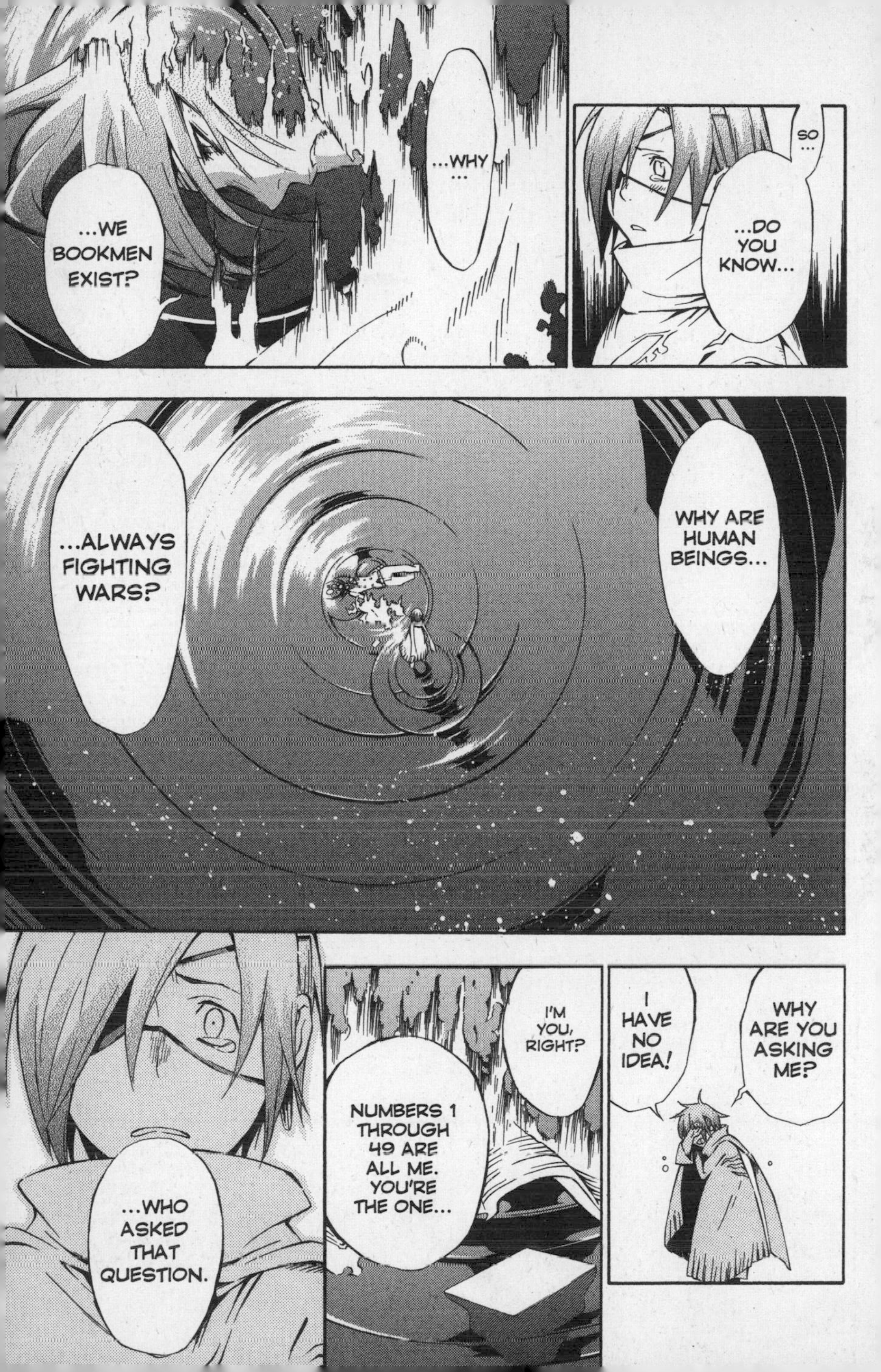
SO...
...DO YOU KNOW...
...WHY...
...WE BOOKMEN EXIST?
WHY ARE HUMAN BEINGS...
...ALWAYS FIGHTING WARS?
WHY ARE YOU ASKING ME?
I HAVE NO IDEA!
I'M YOU, RIGHT?
NUMBERS 1 THROUGH 49 ARE ALL ME. YOU'RE THE ONE...
...WHO ASKED THAT QUESTION.

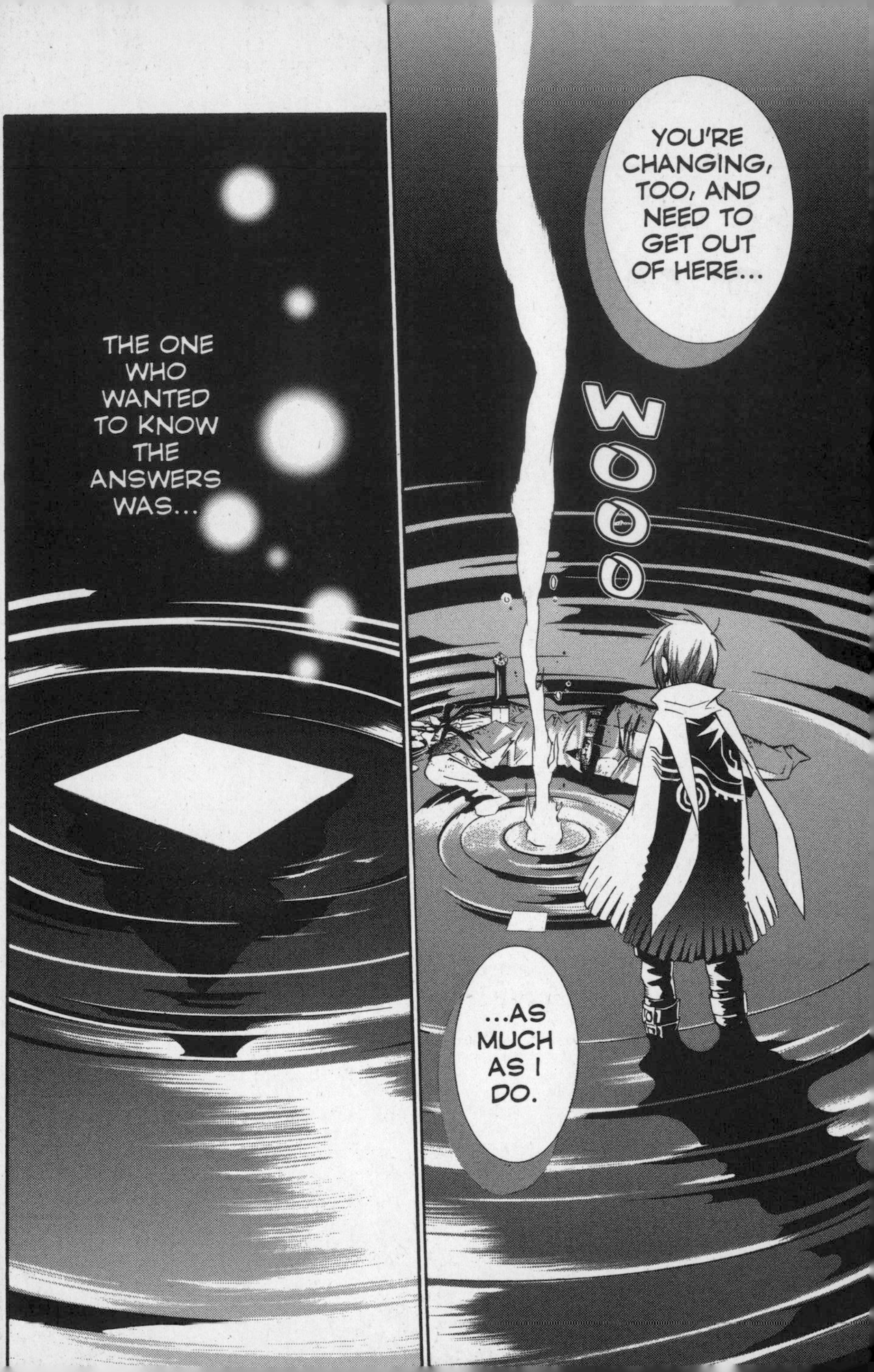
YOU'RE CHANGING, TOO, AND NEED TO GET OUT OF HERE...
WOOOO
...AS MUCH AS I DO.
THE ONE WHO WANTED TO KNOW THE ANSWERS WAS...

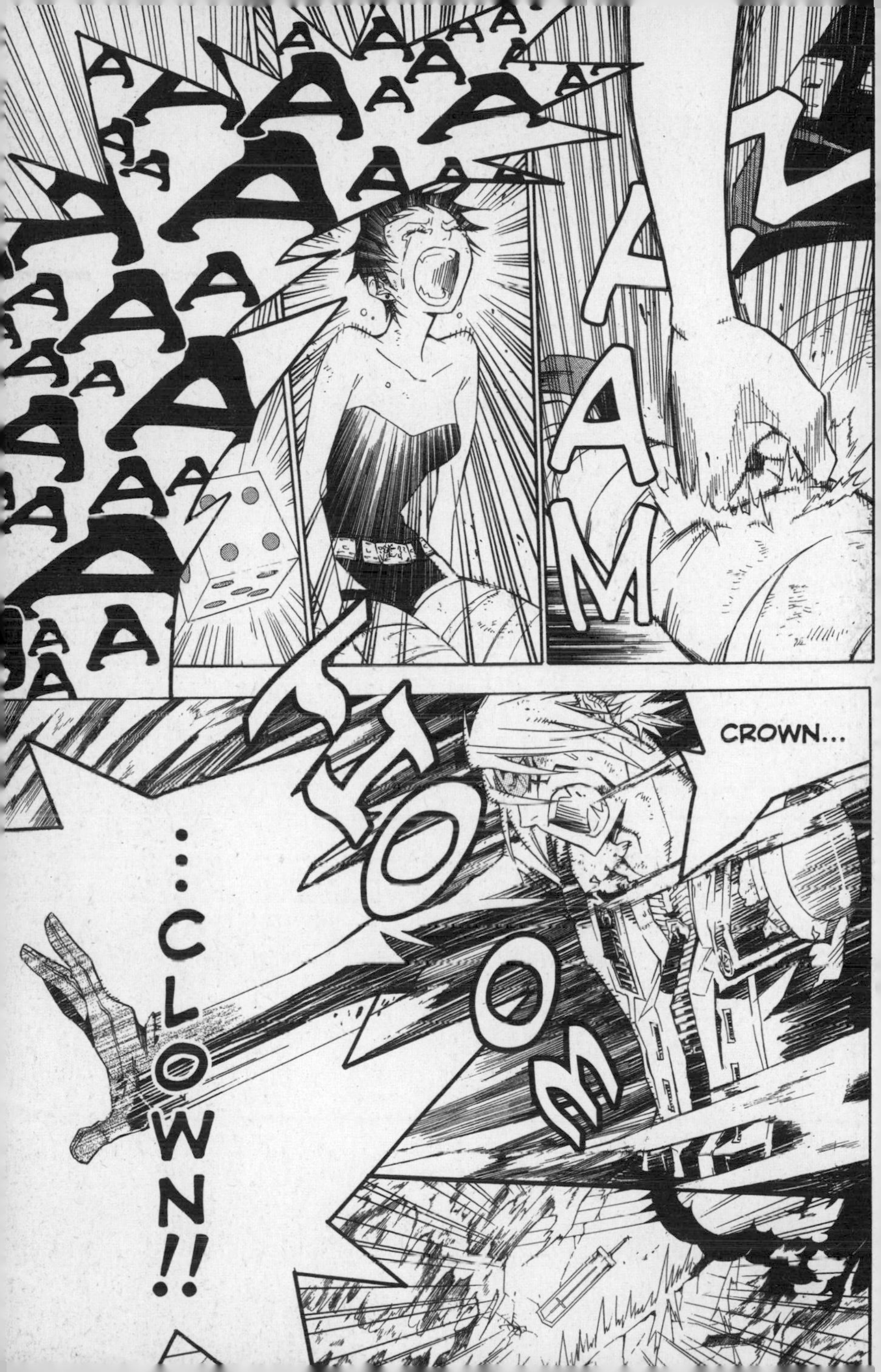
CROWN...
...CLOWN!!

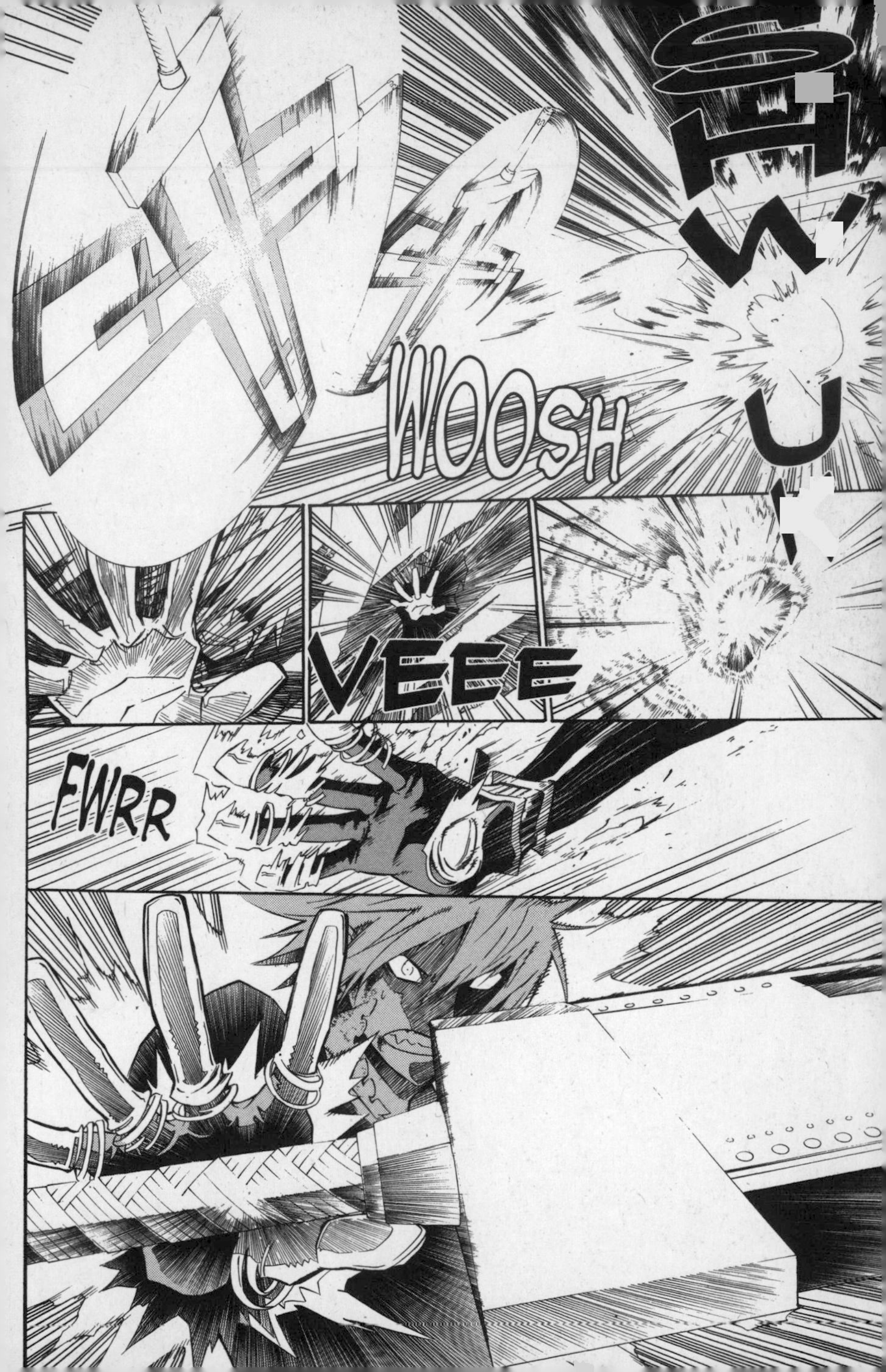
WOOSH
VEEE
FWRR

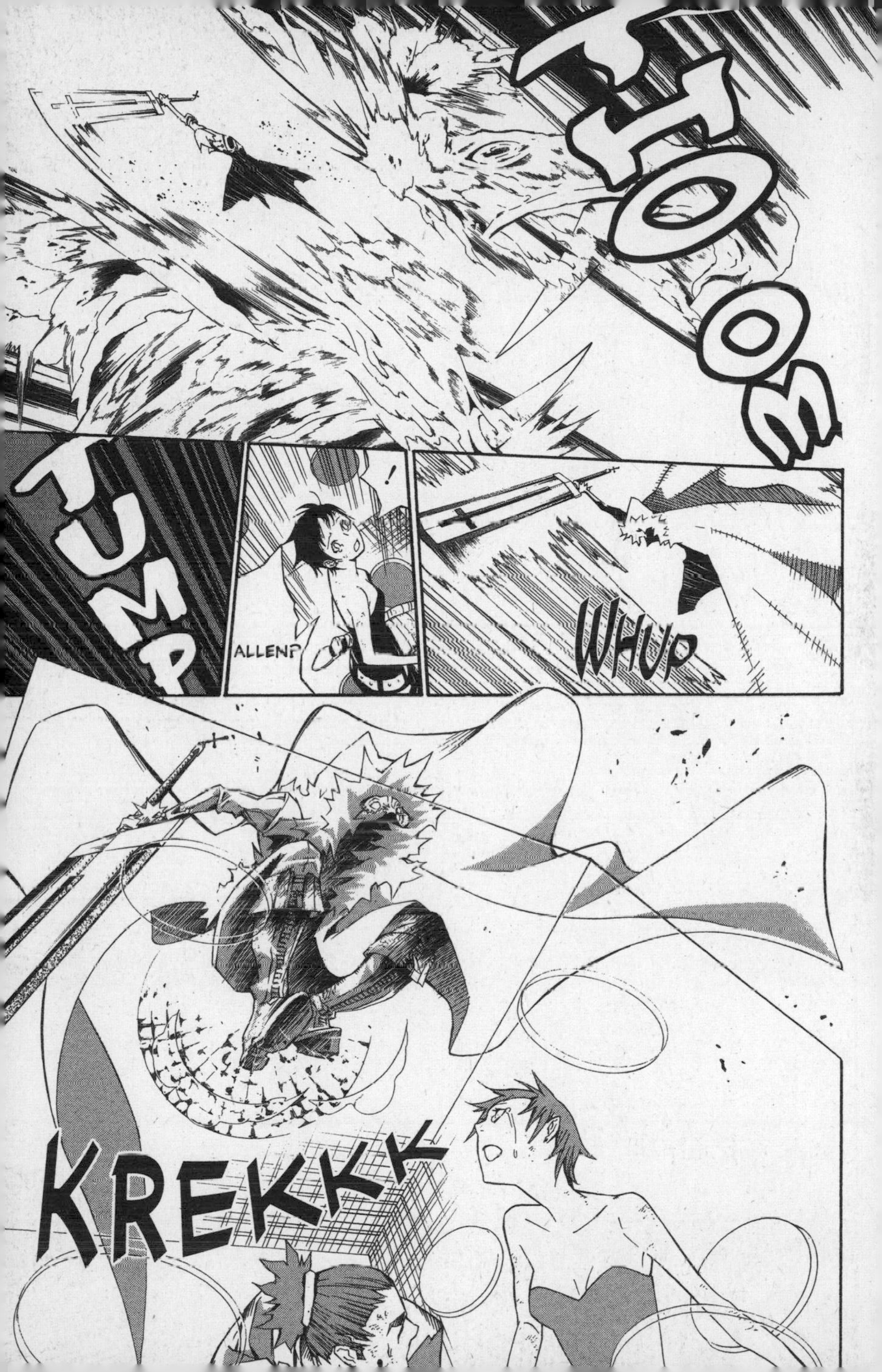
WHUP
!
ALLEN?
FUMP
KREKKK

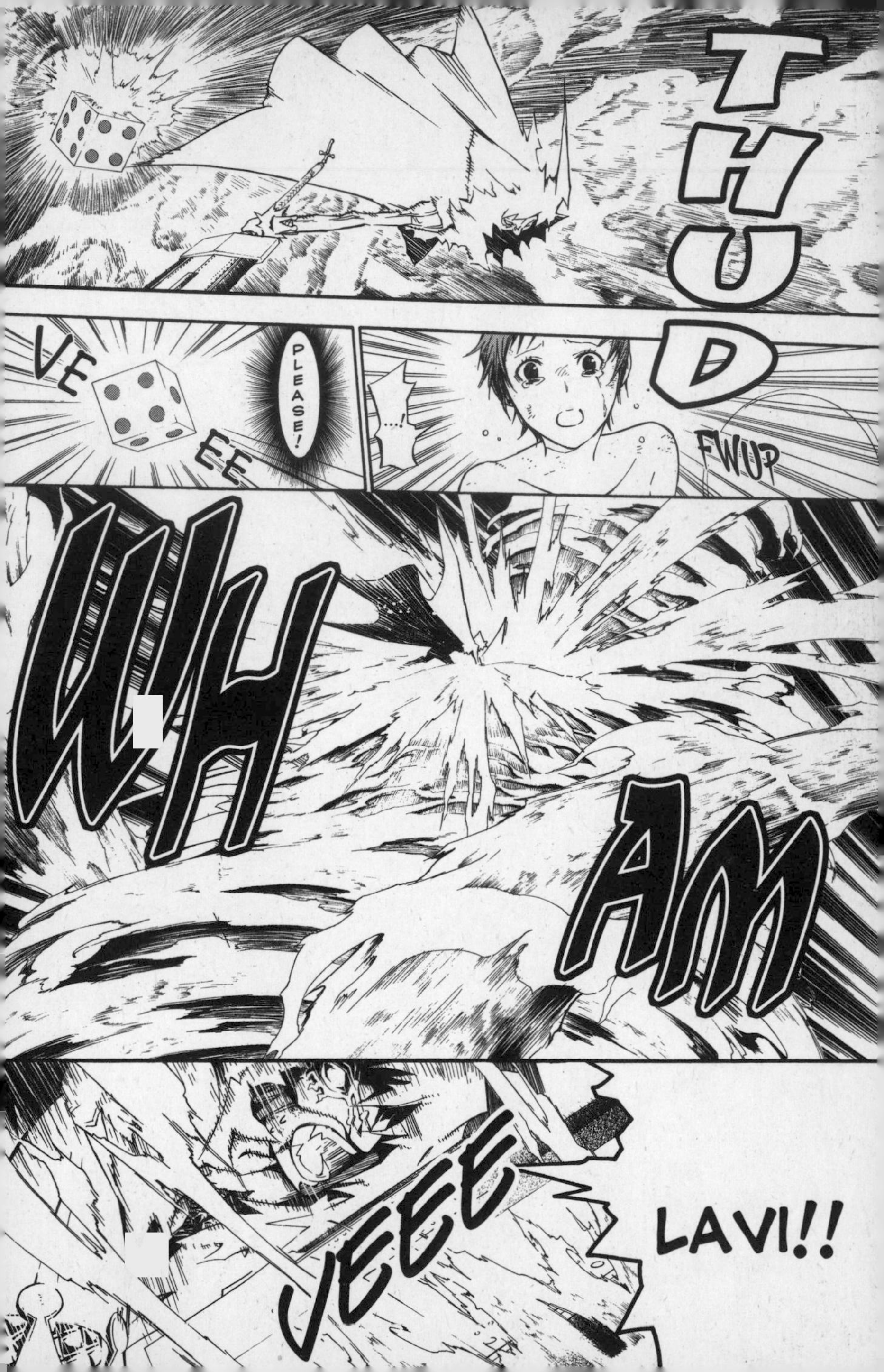
THUD
FWUP
...!
PLEASE!
VE
EE
WH
AM
LAVI!!
JEEE

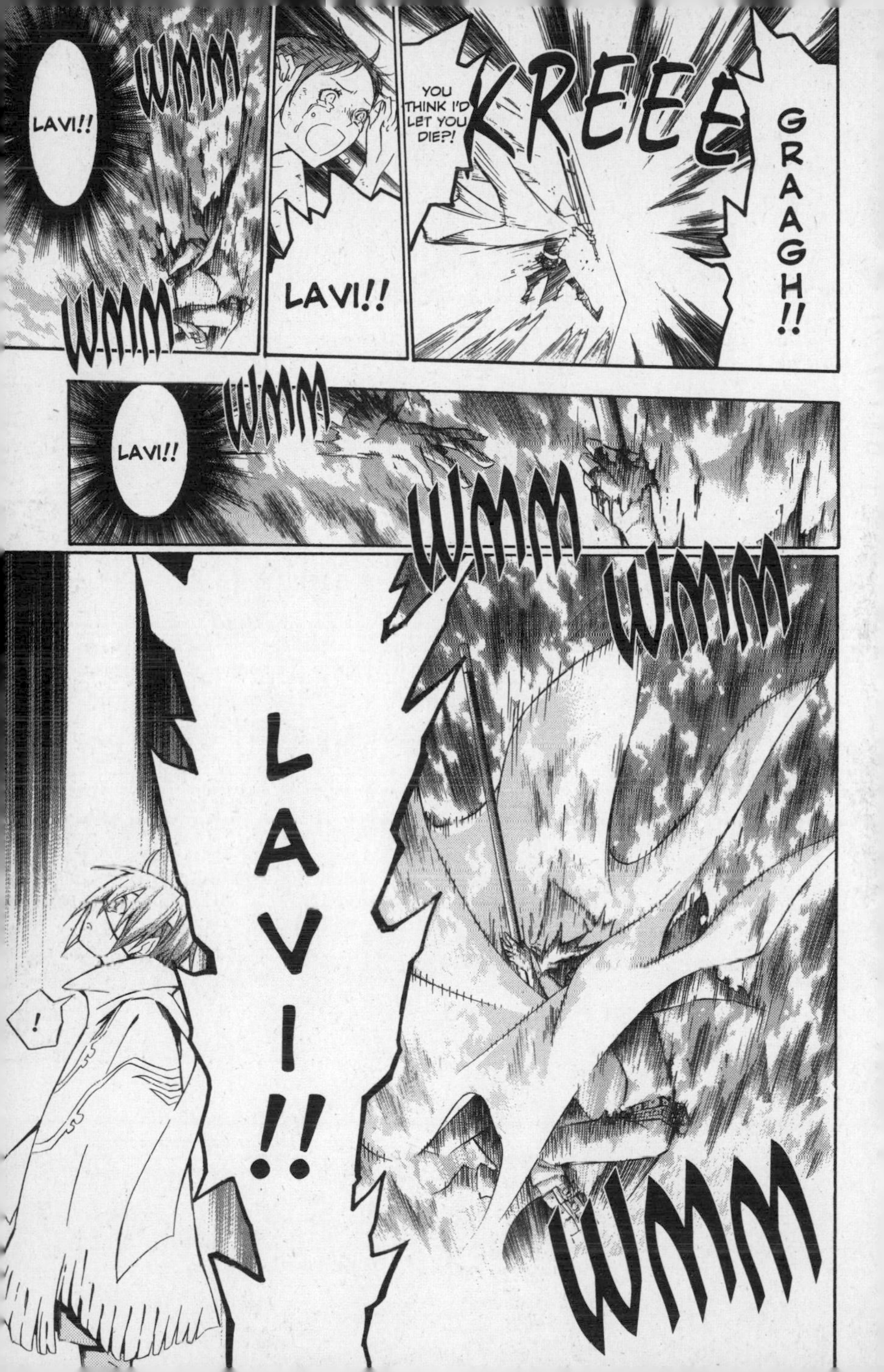
GRAAGH!!
KREEE
YOU THINK I'D LET YOU DIE?!
LAVI!!
WMM
LAVI!!
WMM
WMM
WMM
LAVI!!
WMMM
LAVI!!
WMMM
!

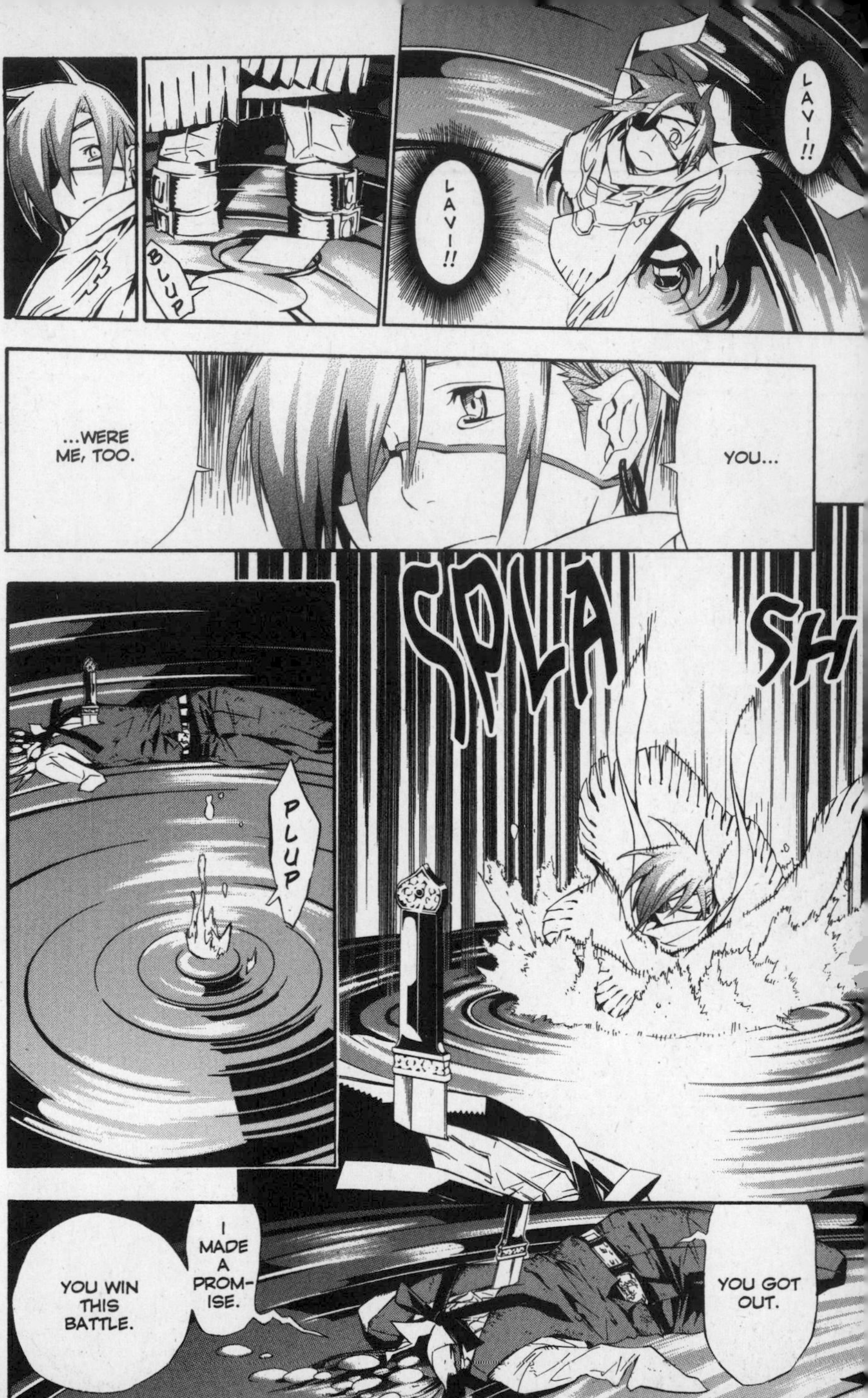
LAVI!!
LAVI!!
BLUP
YOU...
...WERE ME, TOO.
SPLASH
PLUP
YOU GOT OUT.
I MADE A PROMISE.
YOU WIN THIS BATTLE.

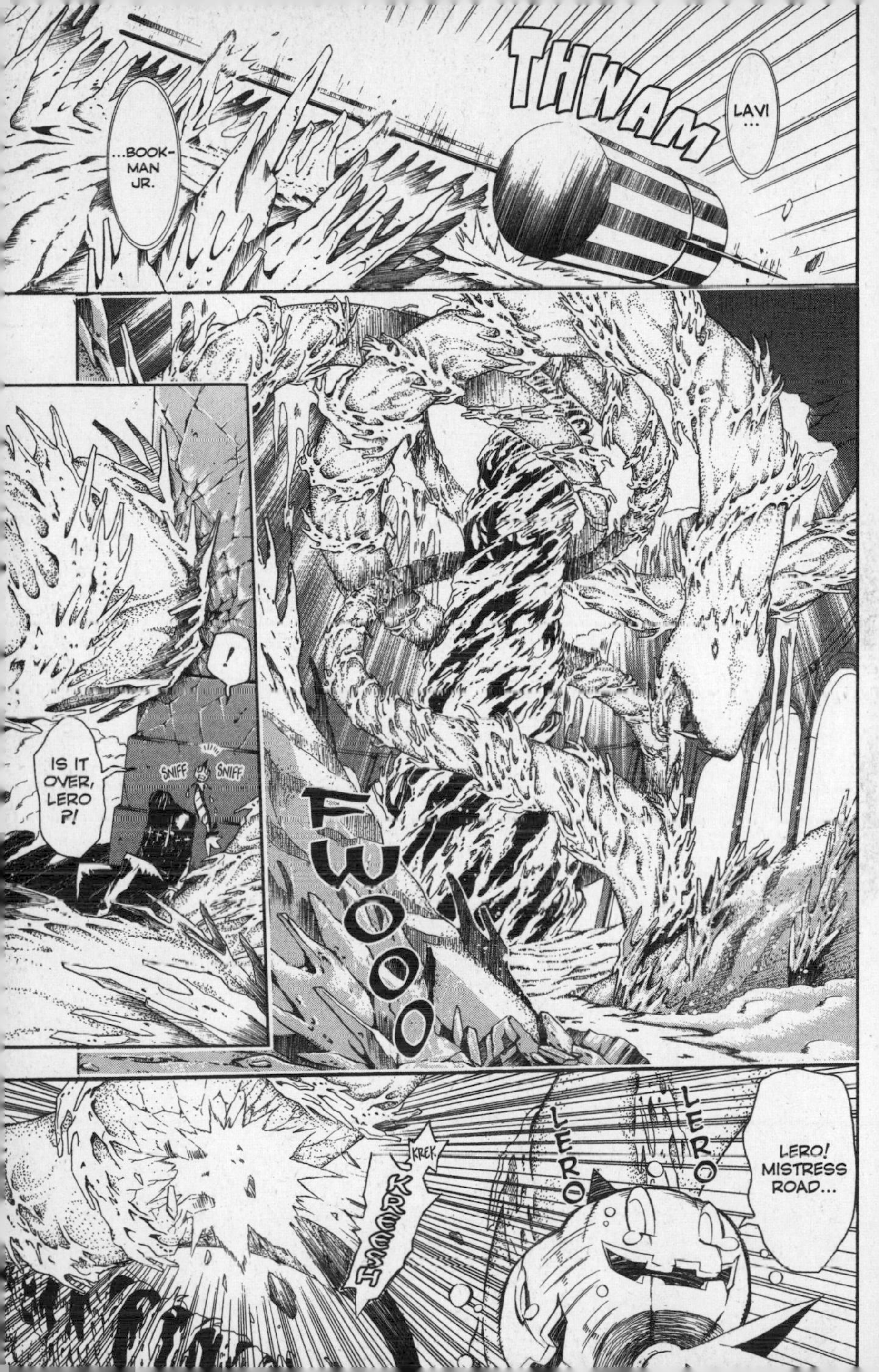
THWAM
LAVI...
...BOOKMAN JR.
FWOOO
!
SNIFF
SNIFF
IS IT OVER, LERO?!
LERO! MISTRESS ROAD...
LERO
LERO
KREK.

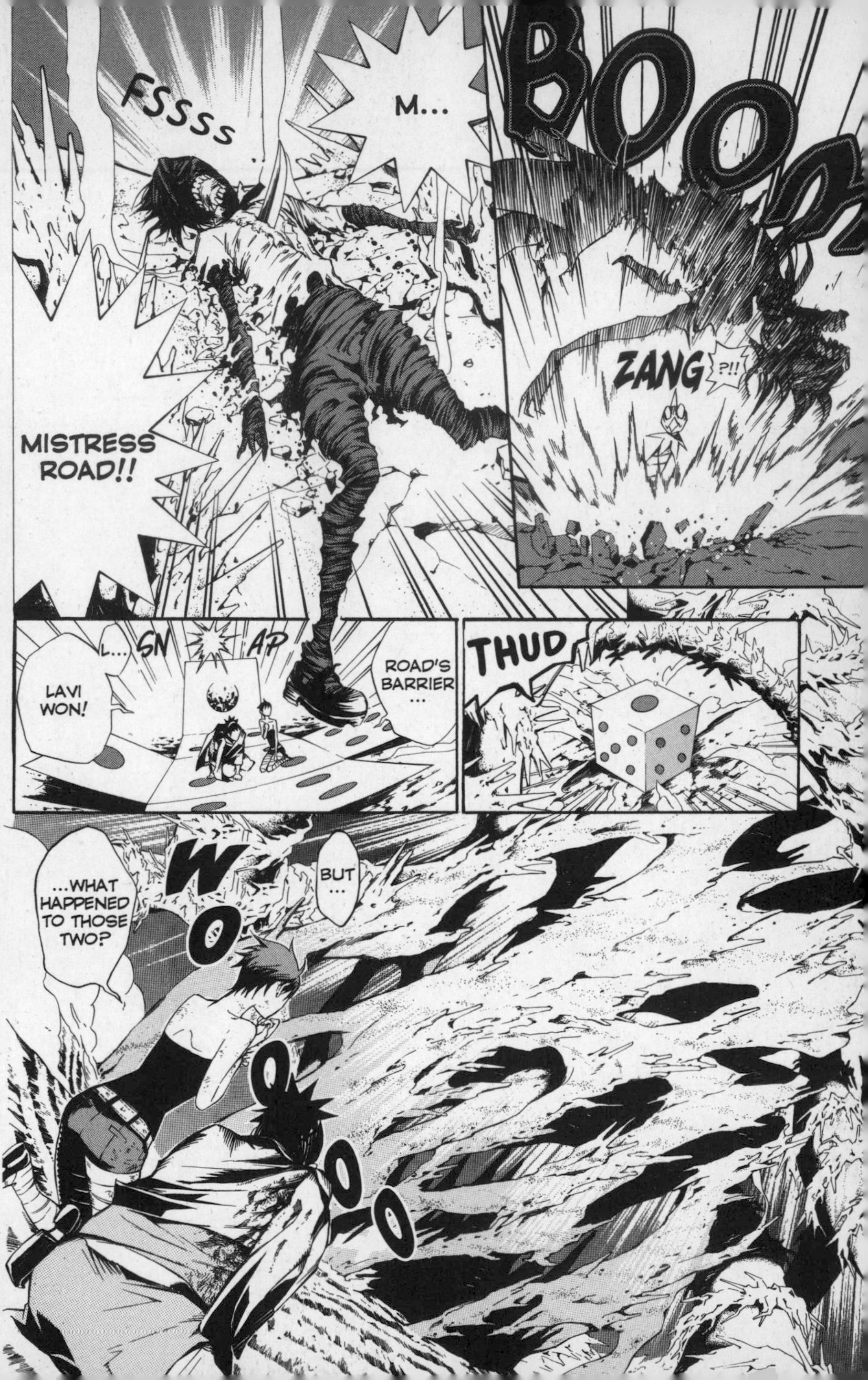

BOOM
ZANG ?!!
M...
FSSSS
MISTRESS ROAD!!
THUD
ROAD'S BARRIER ...
SNAP
L...
LAVI WON!
BUT ...
WOOOOO
...WHAT HAPPENED TO THOSE TWO?

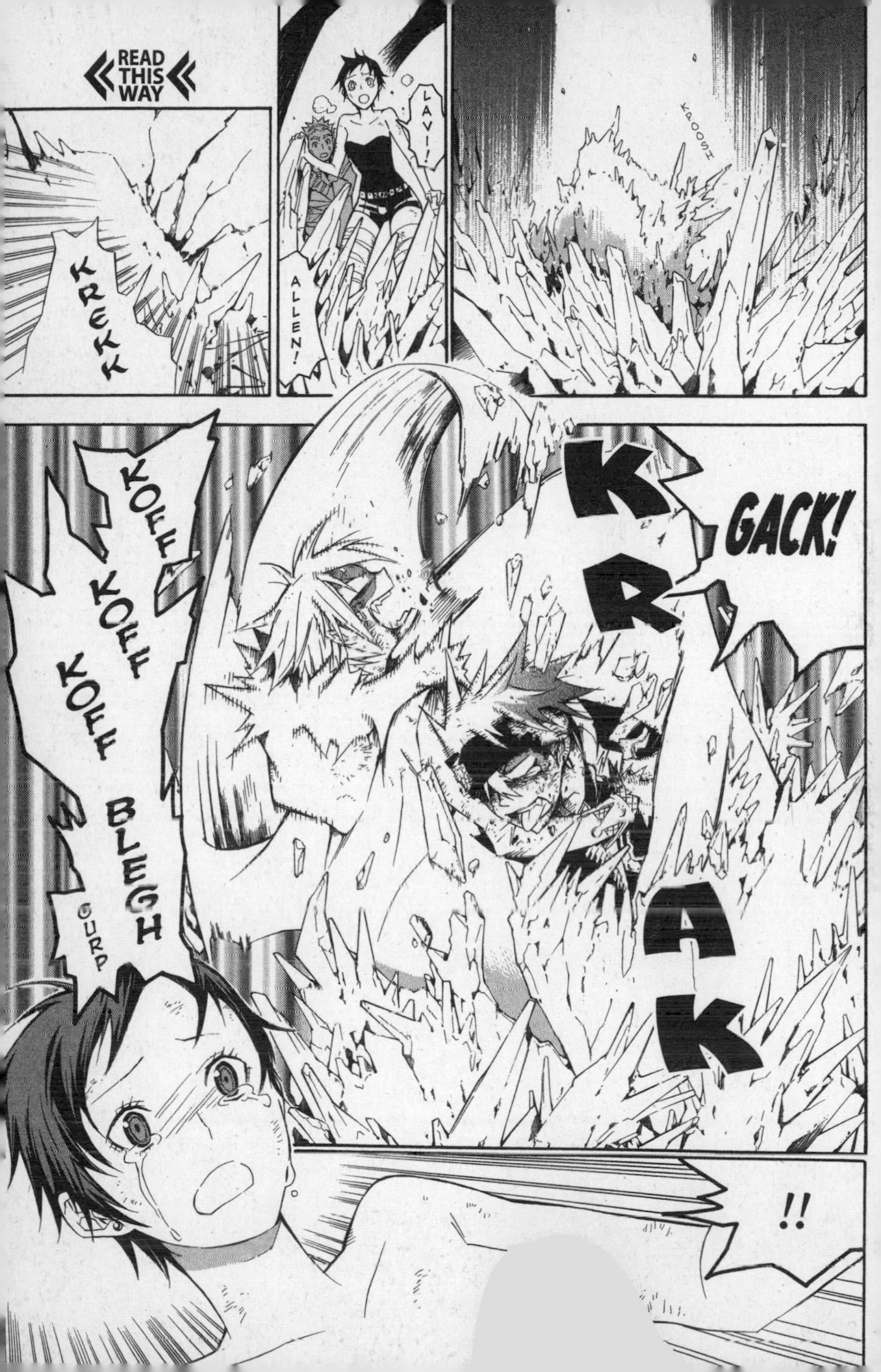
READ THIS WAY
KROOSH
LAVI!
ALLEN!
KREKK
KRAAK
GACK!
KOFF KOFF KOFF KOFF
BLEGH
GURP
!!

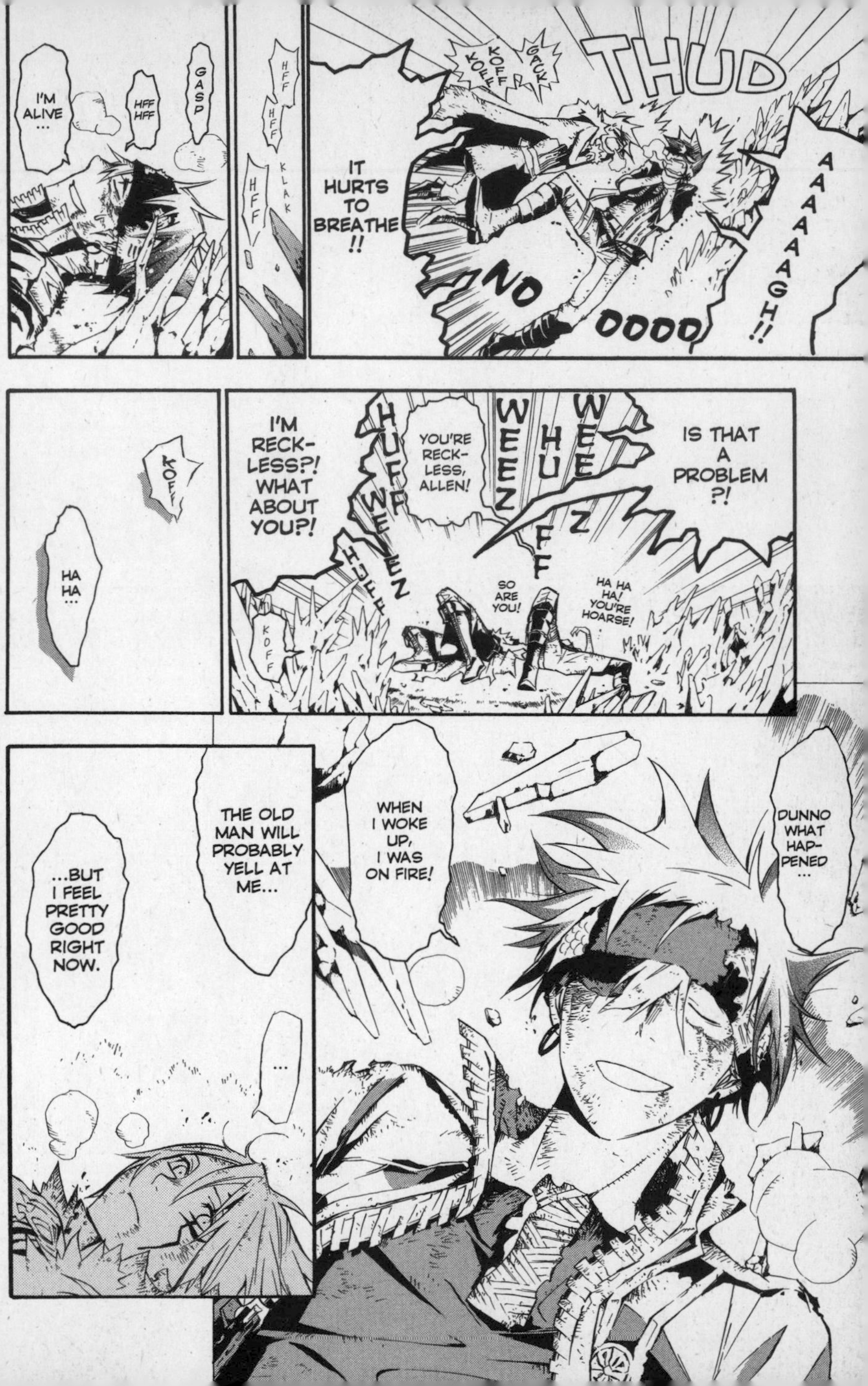
THUD
GACK
KOFF KOFF
AAAAAAAGH!!
NOOOOO
IT HURTS TO BREATHE!!
HFF HFF
HFF HFF!
KLAK
GASP
HFF HFF
I'M ALIVE...
IS THAT A PROBLEM?!
WEEZ
HEUFF
WEEZ
YOU'RE RECKLESS, ALLEN!
HUFF WEEZ
HUFF
I'M RECKLESS?! WHAT ABOUT YOU?!
HA HA HA! YOU'RE HOARSE!
SO ARE YOU!
KOFF
KOFF
HA HA...
DUNNO WHAT HAPPENED...
WHEN I WOKE UP, I WAS ON FIRE!
THE OLD MAN WILL PROBABLY YELL AT ME...
...BUT I FEEL PRETTY GOOD RIGHT NOW.
...

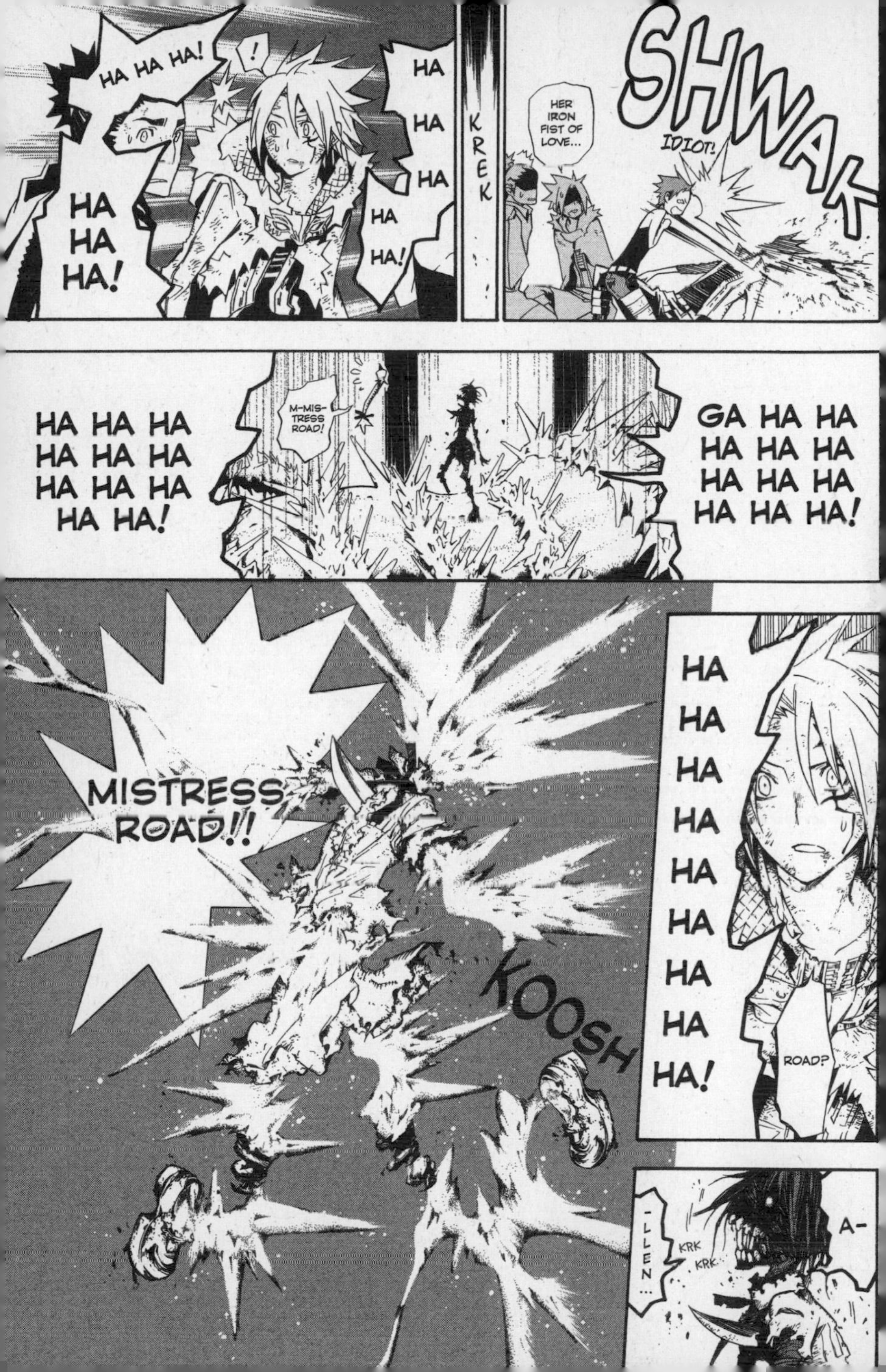
SHWAK
IDIOT!
HER IRON FIST OF LOVE...
KREK
HA HA HA!
!
HA HA HA HA HA!
HA HA HA!
GA HA HA HA HA HA HA HA HA HA HA HA!
M-MISTRESS ROAD!
HA HA HA HA HA HA HA HA HA HA HA!
HA HA HA HA HA HA HA HA HA HA!
ROAD?
A-
KRK KRK
-LLEN...
MISTRESS ROAD!!
KOOSH

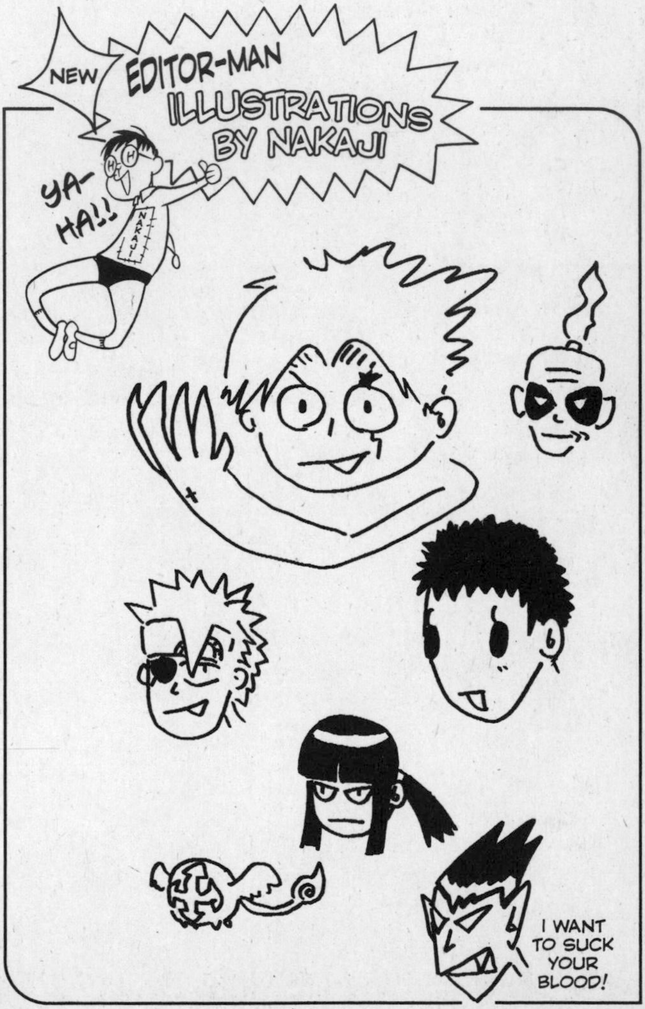
NEW
EDITOR-MAN
ILLUSTRATIONS
BY NAKAJI
YA-HA!!
NAKAJI
I WANT TO SUCK YOUR BLOOD!

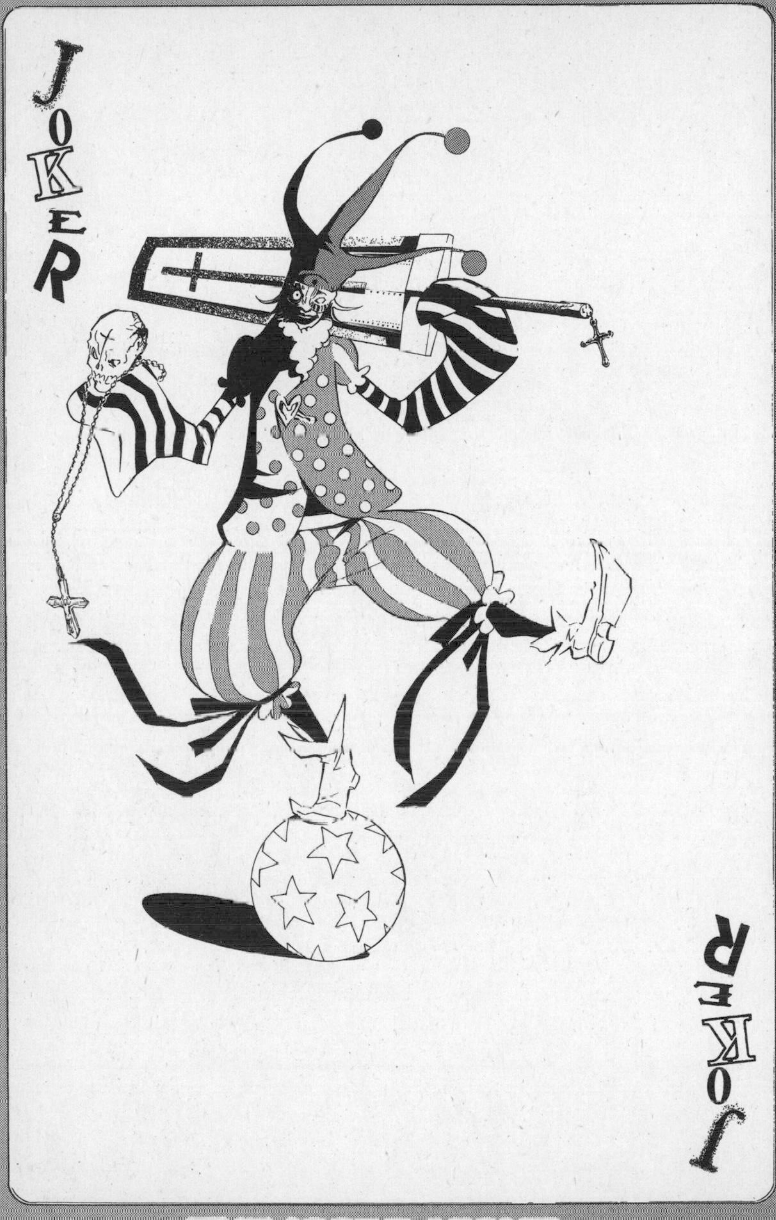
JOKER
JOKER

THE 123RD NIGHT:
THE VOICE OF DARKNESS

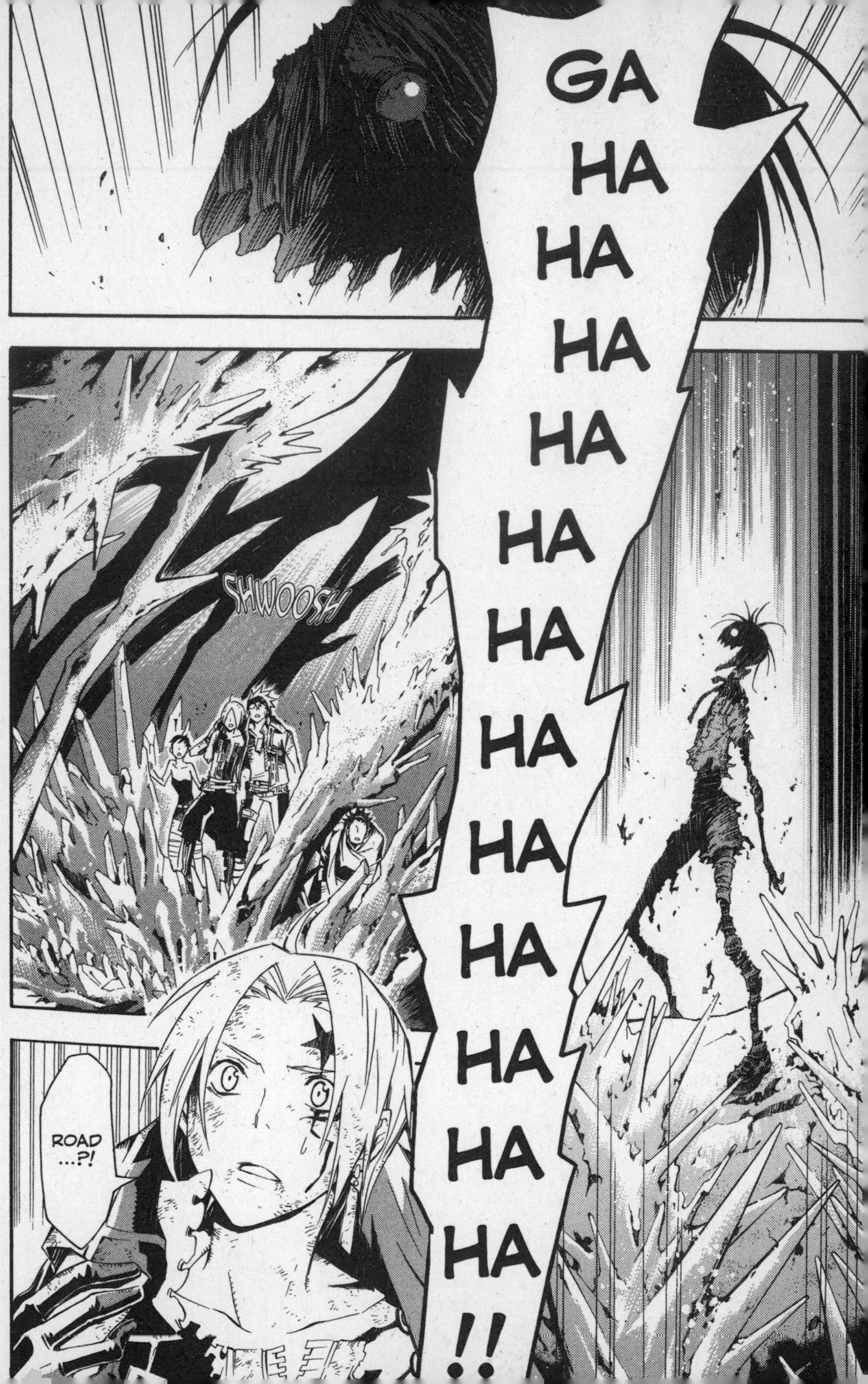
GA HA HA HA HA HA HA HA HA HA HA HA HA!!
SHWOOSH
ROAD ...?!

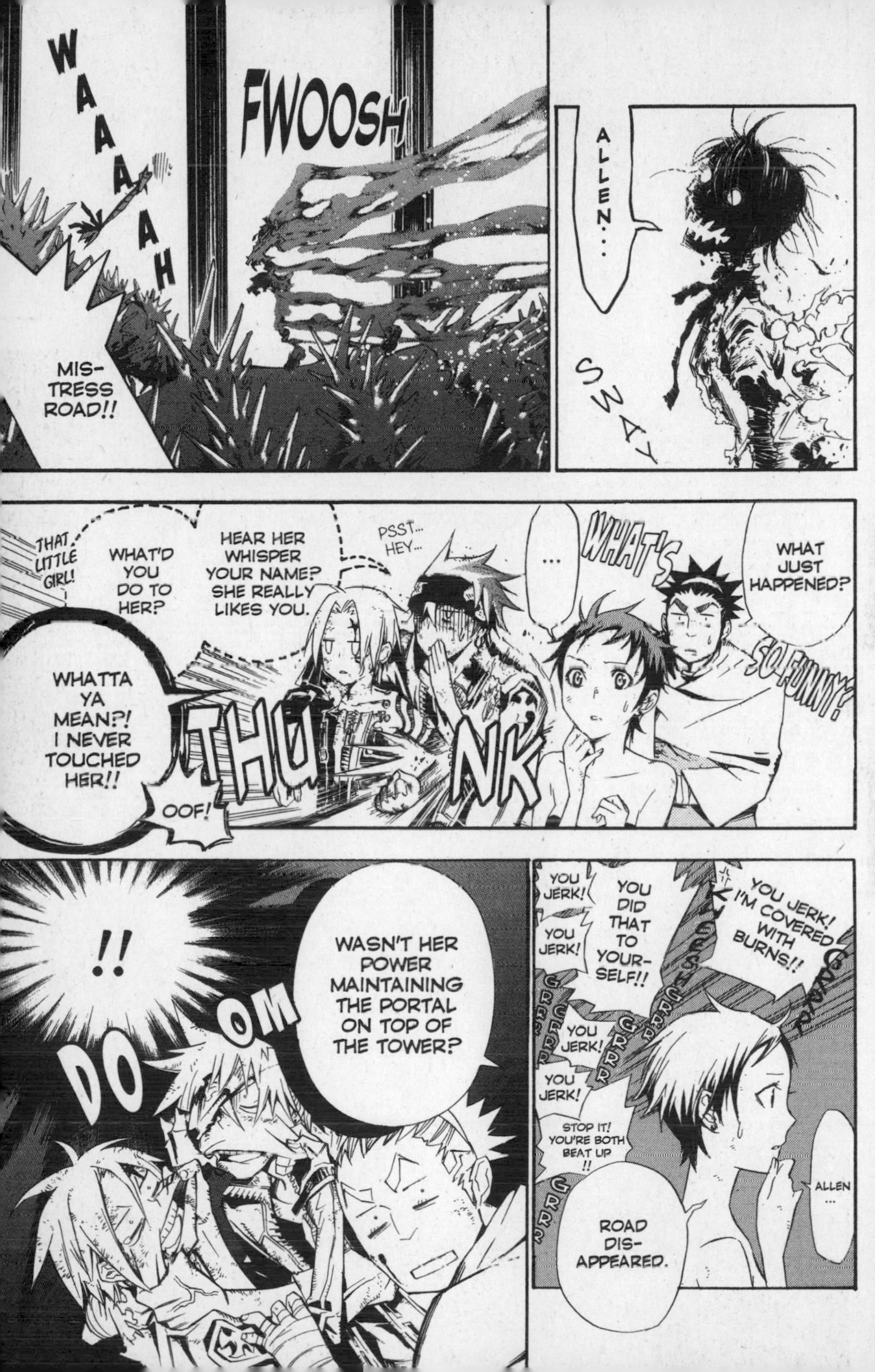
ALLEN...
SWAY
FWOOSH
WAAAAH
MIS-
TRESS
ROAD!!
WHAT JUST HAPPENED?
WHAT'S SO FUNNY?
...
PSST... HEY...
HEAR HER WHISPER YOUR NAME? SHE REALLY LIKES YOU.
WHAT'D YOU DO TO HER?
THAT LITTLE GIRL!
THUNK
WHATTA YA MEAN?! I NEVER TOUCHED HER!!
OOF!
YOU JERK! I'M COVERED WITH BURNS!!
YOU DID THAT TO YOUR-SELF!!
YOU JERK!
YOU JERK!
YOU JERK!
YOU JERK!
GRRR
STOP IT! YOU'RE BOTH BEAT UP!!
ALLEN...
ROAD DIS-APPEARED.
!!
DOOM
WASN'T HER POWER MAINTAINING THE PORTAL ON TOP OF THE TOWER?

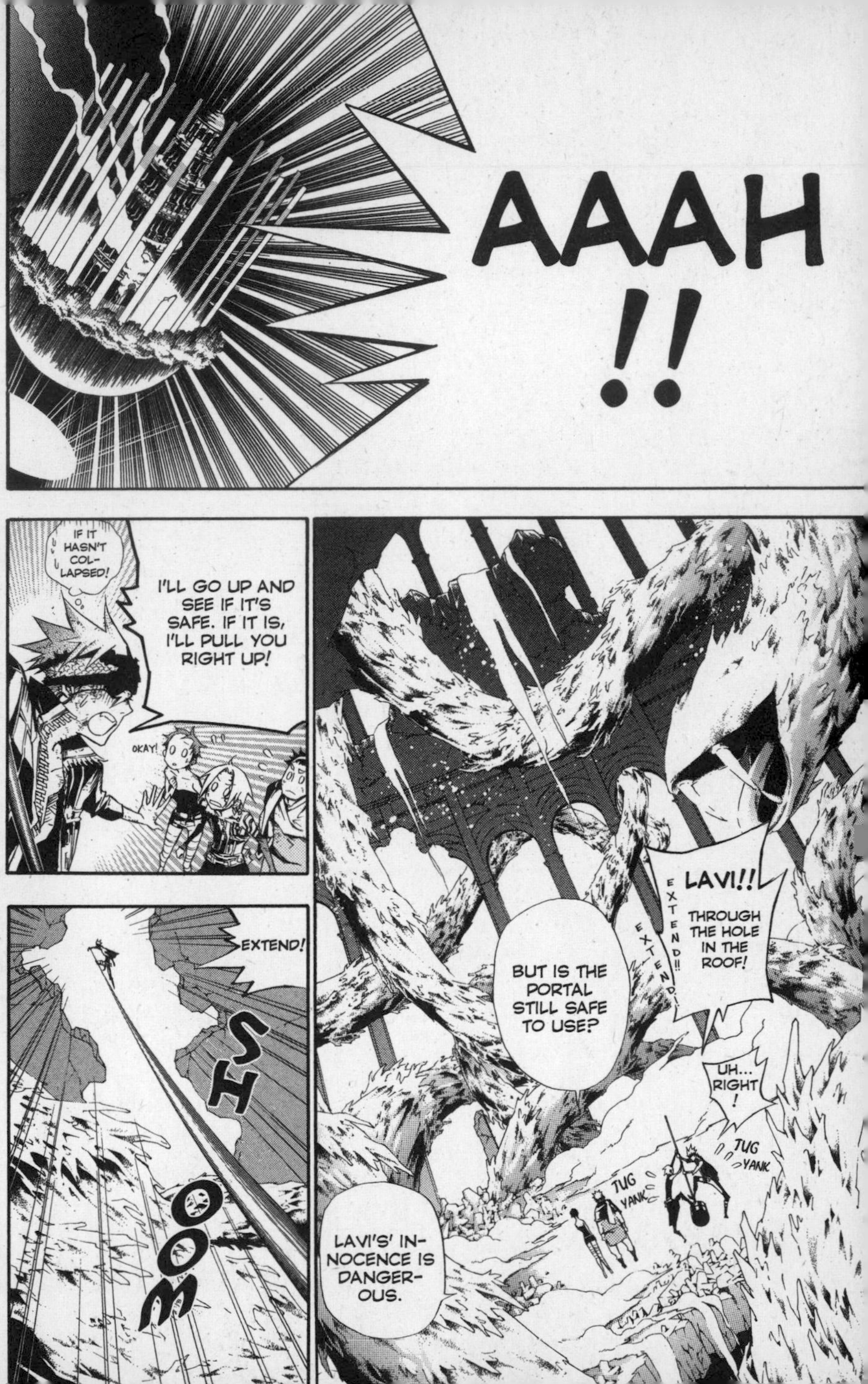
AAAH!!
LAVI!!
THROUGH THE HOLE IN THE ROOF!
EXTEND!!
EXTEND!!
BUT IS THE PORTAL STILL SAFE TO USE?
UH... RIGHT!
TUG
YANK
TUG
YANK
LAVI'S IN-NOCENCE IS DANGER-OUS.
I'LL GO UP AND SEE IF IT'S SAFE. IF IT IS, I'LL PULL YOU RIGHT UP!
IF IT HASN'T COL-LAPSED!
OKAY!
EXTEND!
SHOOM

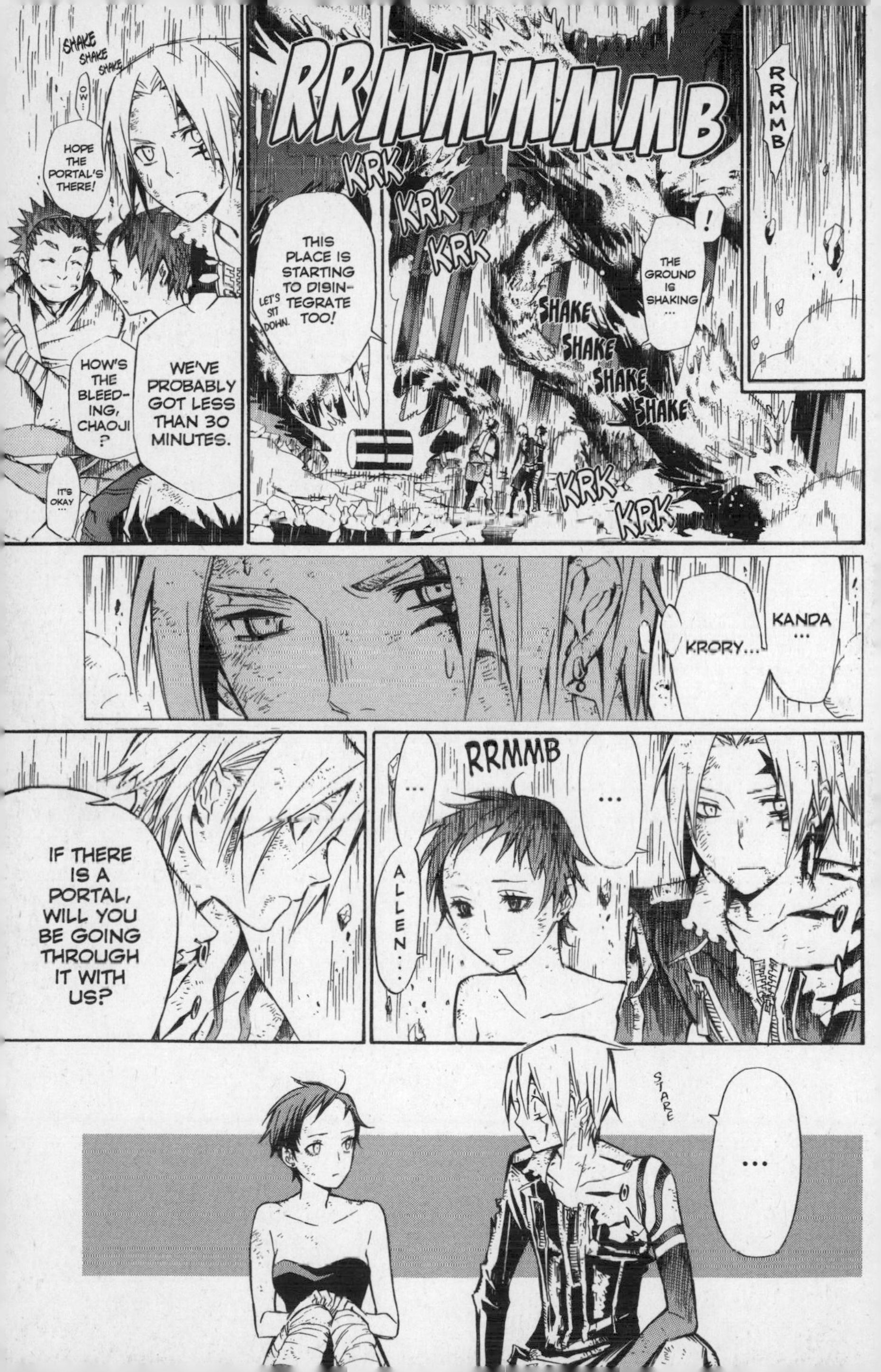
RRMMMMMMMB
RRMMB
!
THE GROUND IS SHAKING...
SHAKE SHAKE SHAKE SHAKE
KRK KRK KRK
THIS PLACE IS STARTING TO DISINTEGRATE TOO!
LET'S SIT DOWN.
KRK KRK
SHAKE SHAKE SHAKE
OW...
HOPE THE PORTAL'S THERE!
WE'VE PROBABLY GOT LESS THAN 30 MINUTES.
HOW'S THE BLEEDING, CHAOJI?
IT'S OKAY...
KANDA...
KRORY...
...
RRMMB
...
ALLEN...
IF THERE IS A PORTAL, WILL YOU BE GOING THROUGH IT WITH US?
STARE
...

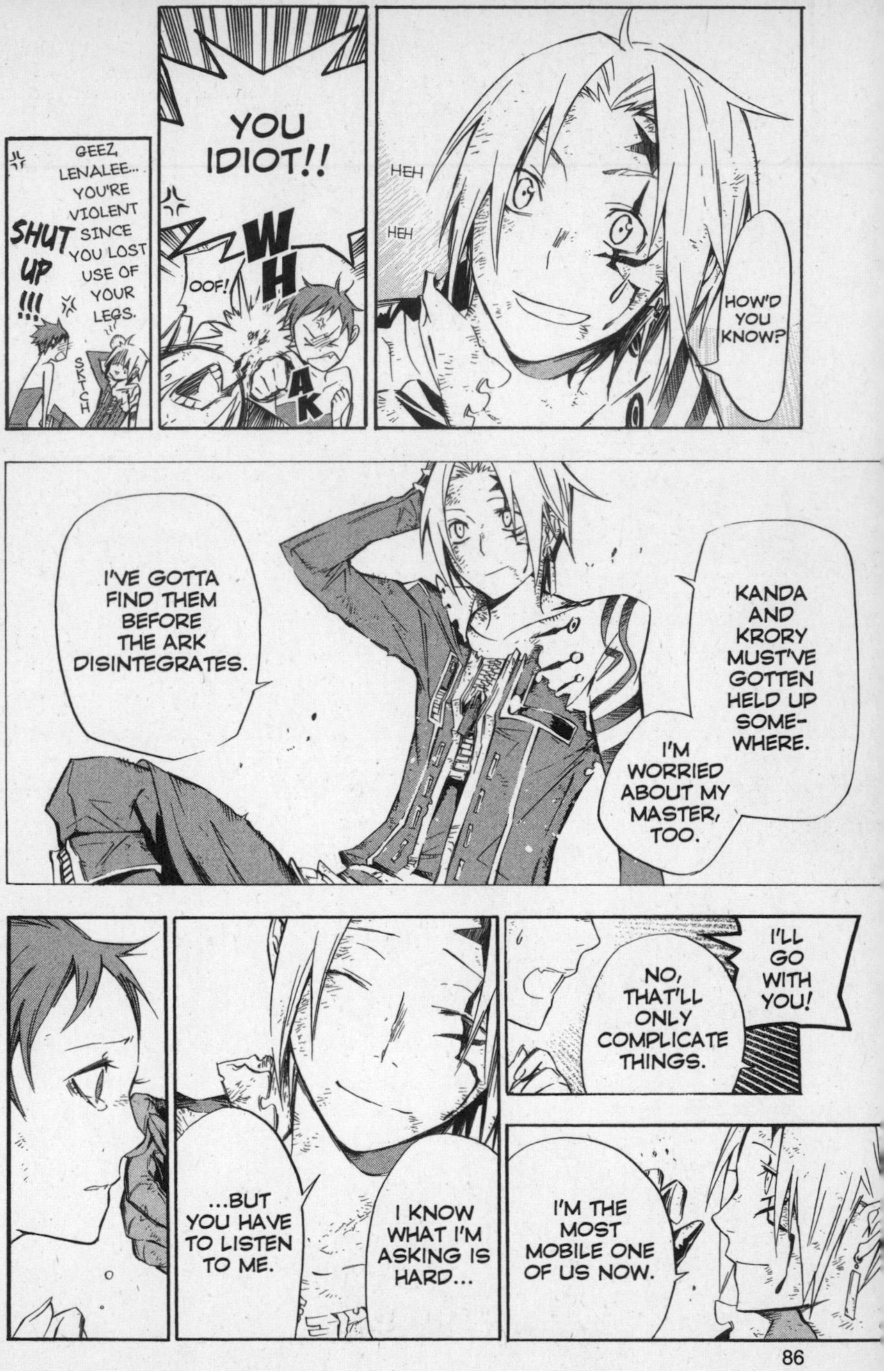
HEH
HEH
HOW'D YOU KNOW?
YOU IDIOT!!
WHAK
OOF!
GEEZ, LENALEE... YOU'RE VIOLENT SINCE YOU LOST USE OF YOUR LEGS.
SHUT UP!!!
SKTCH
KANDA AND KRORY MUST'VE GOTTEN HELD UP SOME-WHERE.
I'M WORRIED ABOUT MY MASTER, TOO.
I'VE GOTTA FIND THEM BEFORE THE ARK DISINTEGRATES.
I'LL GO WITH YOU!
NO, THAT'LL ONLY COMPLICATE THINGS.
I'M THE MOST MOBILE ONE OF US NOW.
I KNOW WHAT I'M ASKING IS HARD...
...BUT YOU HAVE TO LISTEN TO ME.

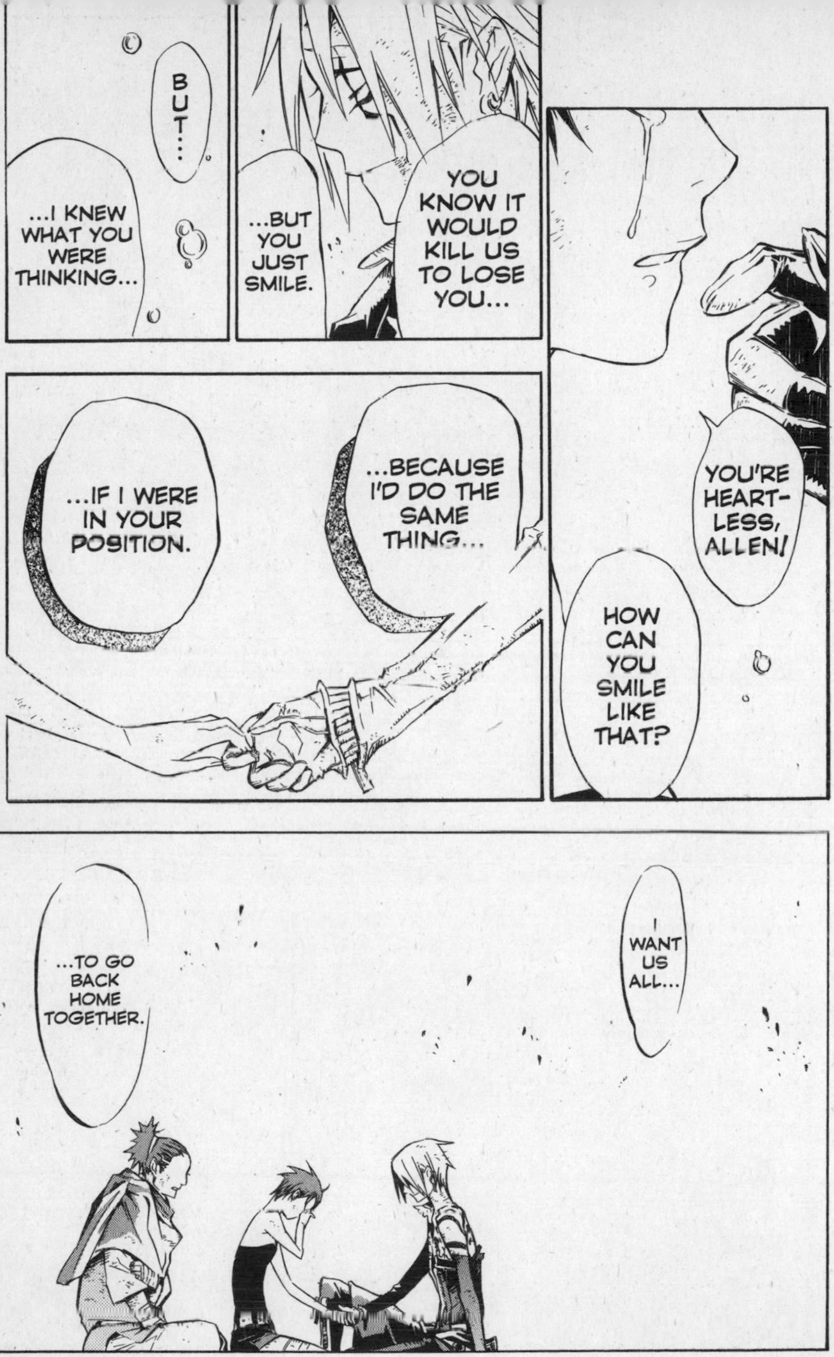
YOU'RE HEART-LESS, ALLEN!
HOW CAN YOU SMILE LIKE THAT?
YOU KNOW IT WOULD KILL US TO LOSE YOU...
...BUT YOU JUST SMILE.
BUT...
...I KNEW WHAT YOU WERE THINKING...
...BECAUSE I'D DO THE SAME THING...
...IF I WERE IN YOUR POSITION.
I WANT US ALL...
...TO GO BACK HOME TOGETHER.

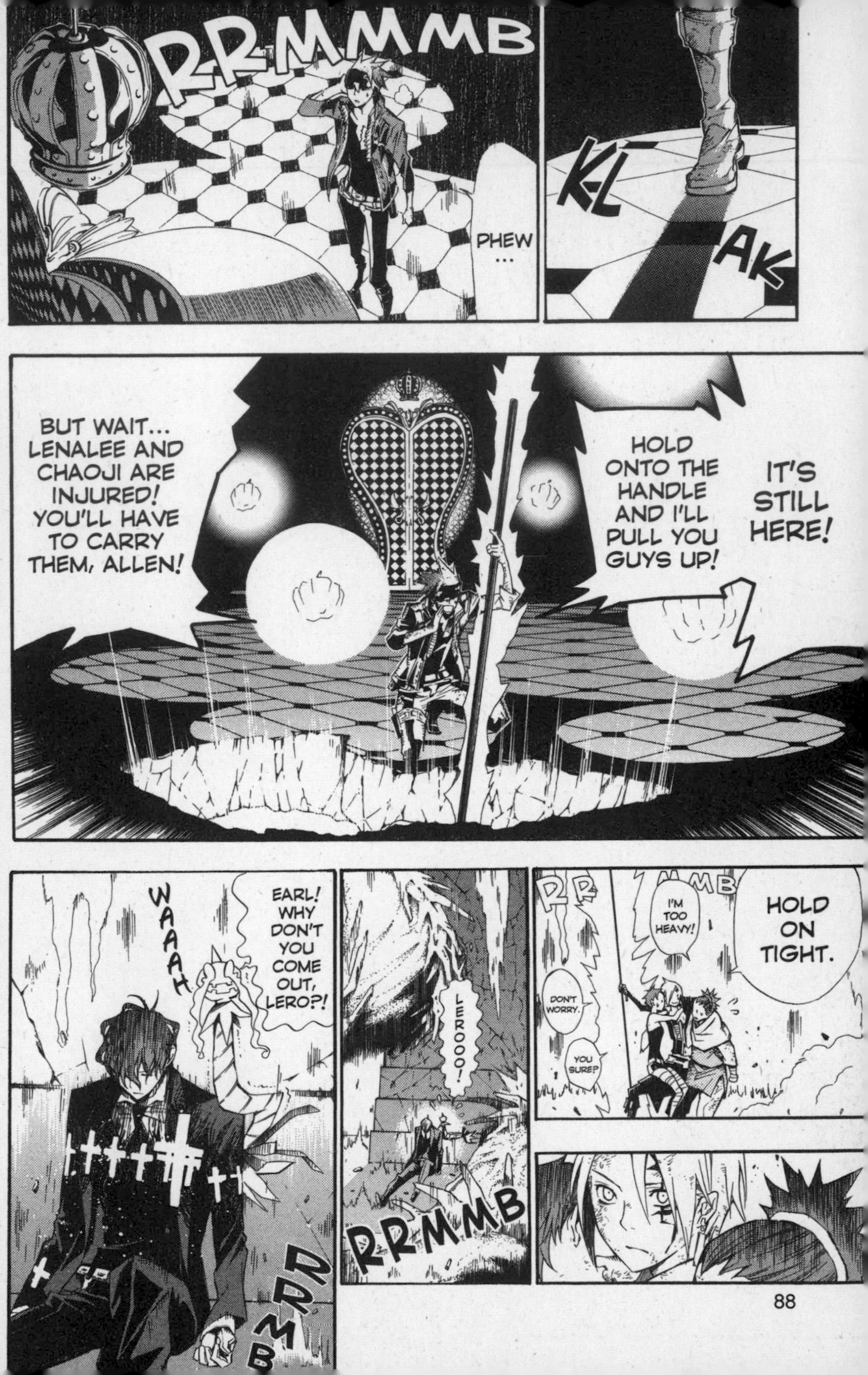
K-L
AK
RRMMMB
PHEW ...
IT'S STILL HERE!
HOLD ONTO THE HANDLE AND I'LL PULL YOU GUYS UP!
BUT WAIT... LENALEE AND CHAOJI ARE INJURED! YOU'LL HAVE TO CARRY THEM, ALLEN!
HOLD ON TIGHT.
RR
MB
I'M TOO HEAVY!
DON'T WORRY.
YOU SURE?
LEROOO!
RRMMB
EARL! WHY DON'T YOU COME OUT, LERO?!
WAAAAH
RRMMB

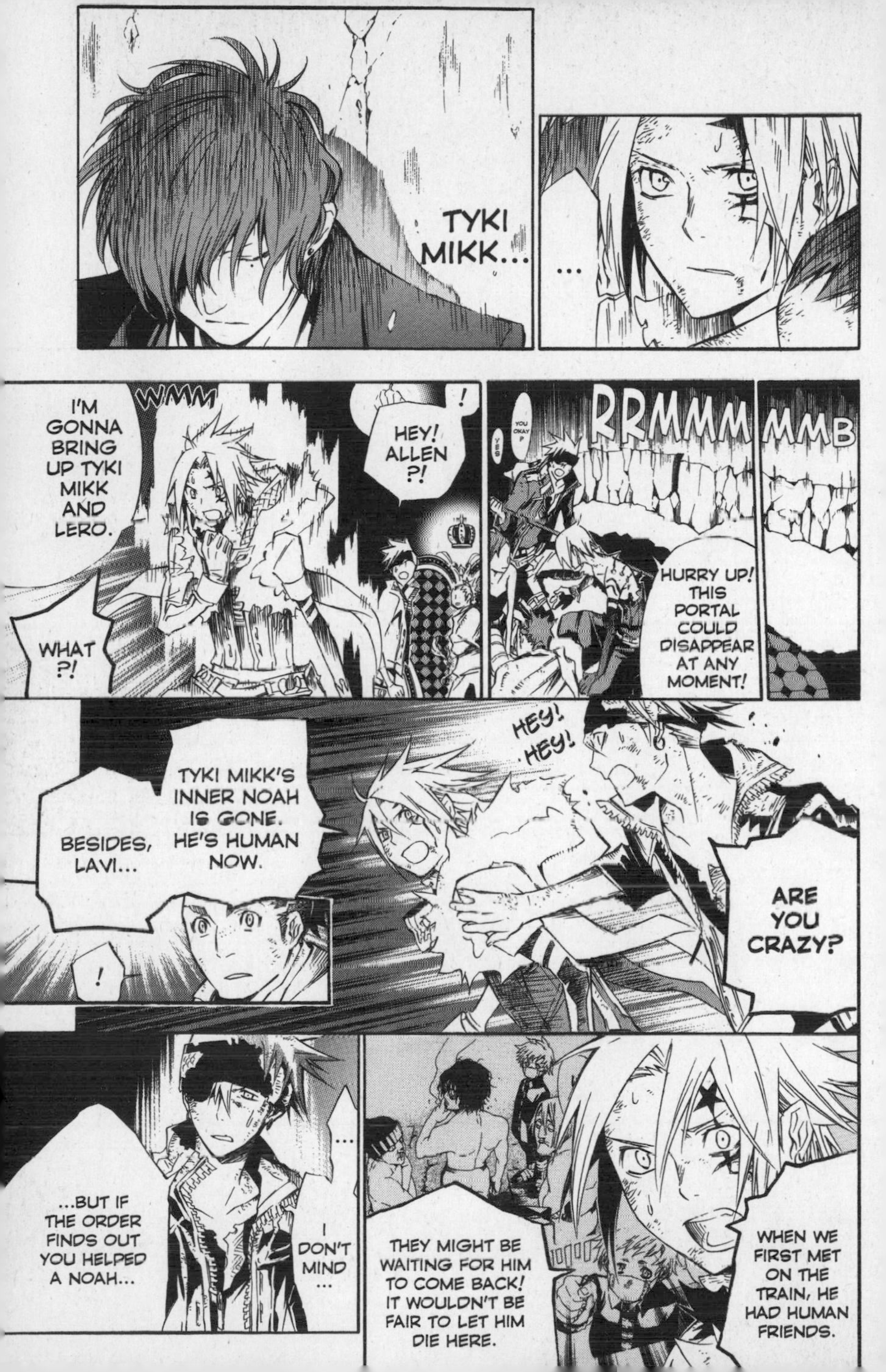
...
TYKI MIKK...
RRMMMM
MMB
YOU OKAY?
YES
HURRY UP! THIS PORTAL COULD DISAPPEAR AT ANY MOMENT!
!
HEY! ALLEN?!
WMM
I'M GONNA BRING UP TYKI MIKK AND LERO.
WHAT?!
HEY! HEY!
ARE YOU CRAZY?
TYKI MIKK'S INNER NOAH IS GONE. HE'S HUMAN NOW.
BESIDES, LAVI...
!
WHEN WE FIRST MET ON THE TRAIN, HE HAD HUMAN FRIENDS.
THEY MIGHT BE WAITING FOR HIM TO COME BACK! IT WOULDN'T BE FAIR TO LET HIM DIE HERE.
...
...BUT IF THE ORDER FINDS OUT YOU HELPED A NOAH...
I DON'T MIND...

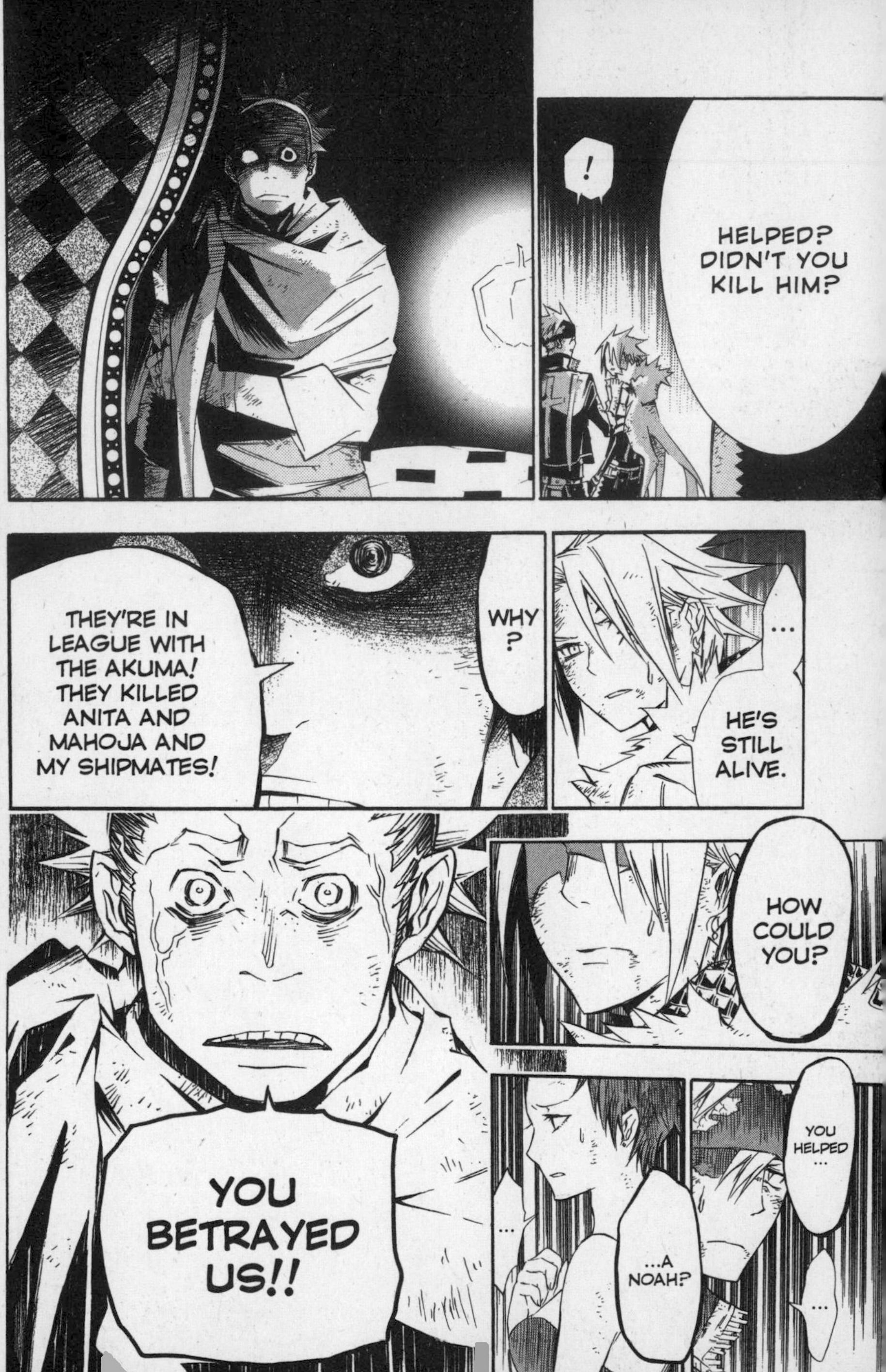
!
HELPED? DIDN'T YOU KILL HIM?
...
HE'S STILL ALIVE.
WHY?
THEY'RE IN LEAGUE WITH THE AKUMA! THEY KILLED ANITA AND MAHOJA AND MY SHIPMATES!
HOW COULD YOU?
YOU HELPED ...
...
...A NOAH?
...
YOU BETRAYED US!!

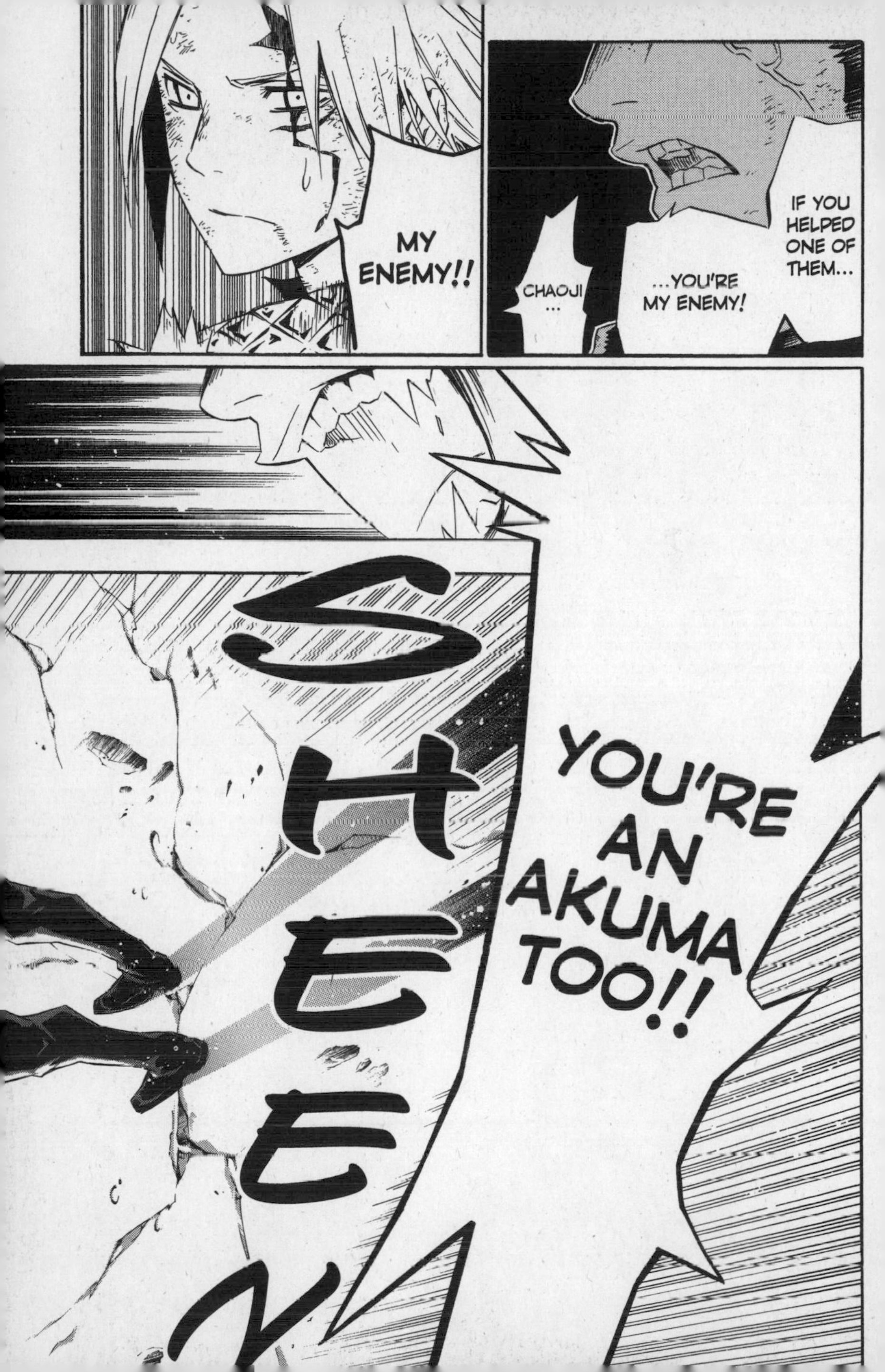
IF YOU HELPED ONE OF THEM...
...YOU'RE MY ENEMY!
CHAOJI...
MY ENEMY!!
YOU'RE AN AKUMA TOO!!
SHEEN

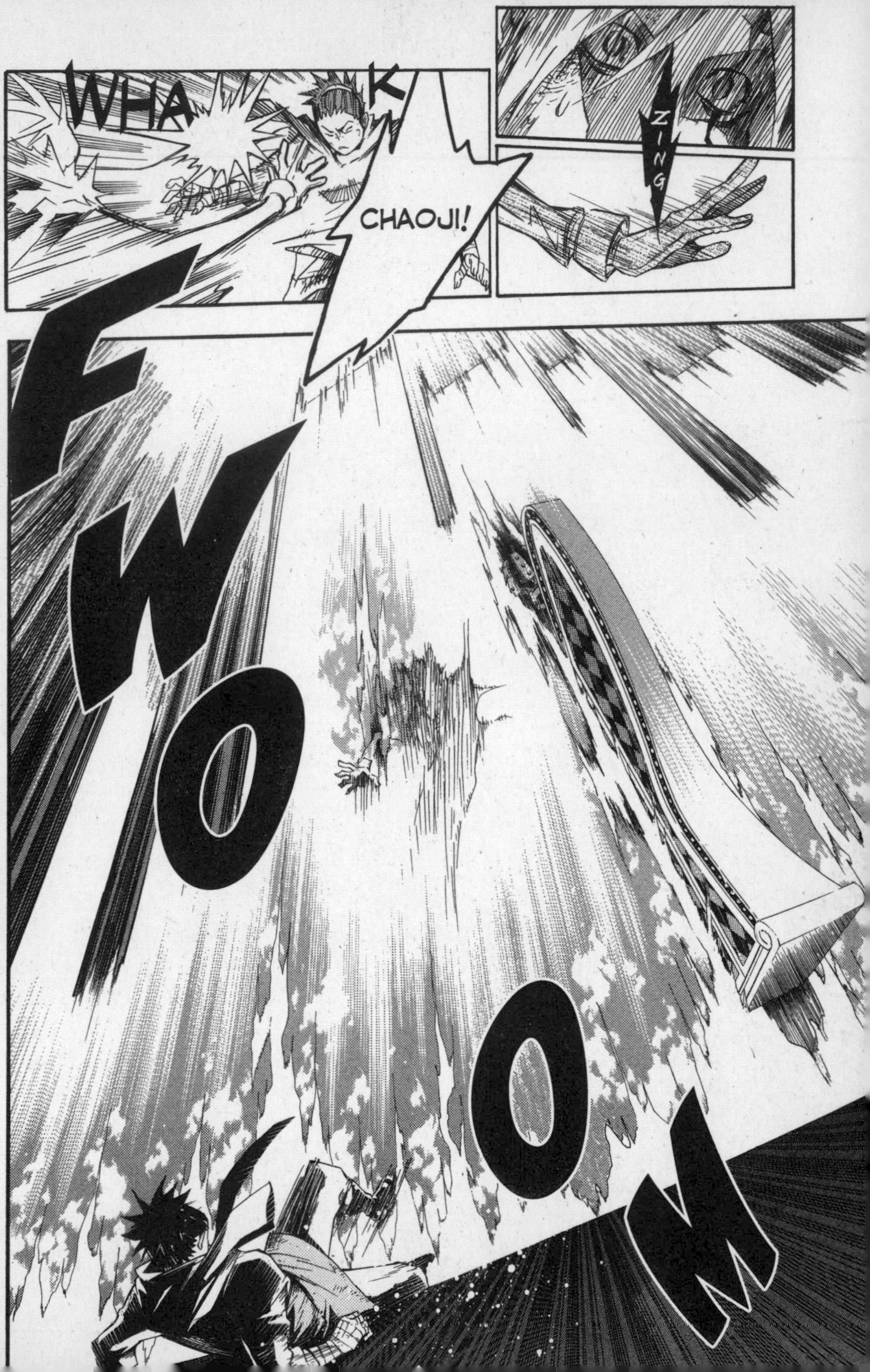
ZING
WHA K
CHAOJI!
FWOOOM

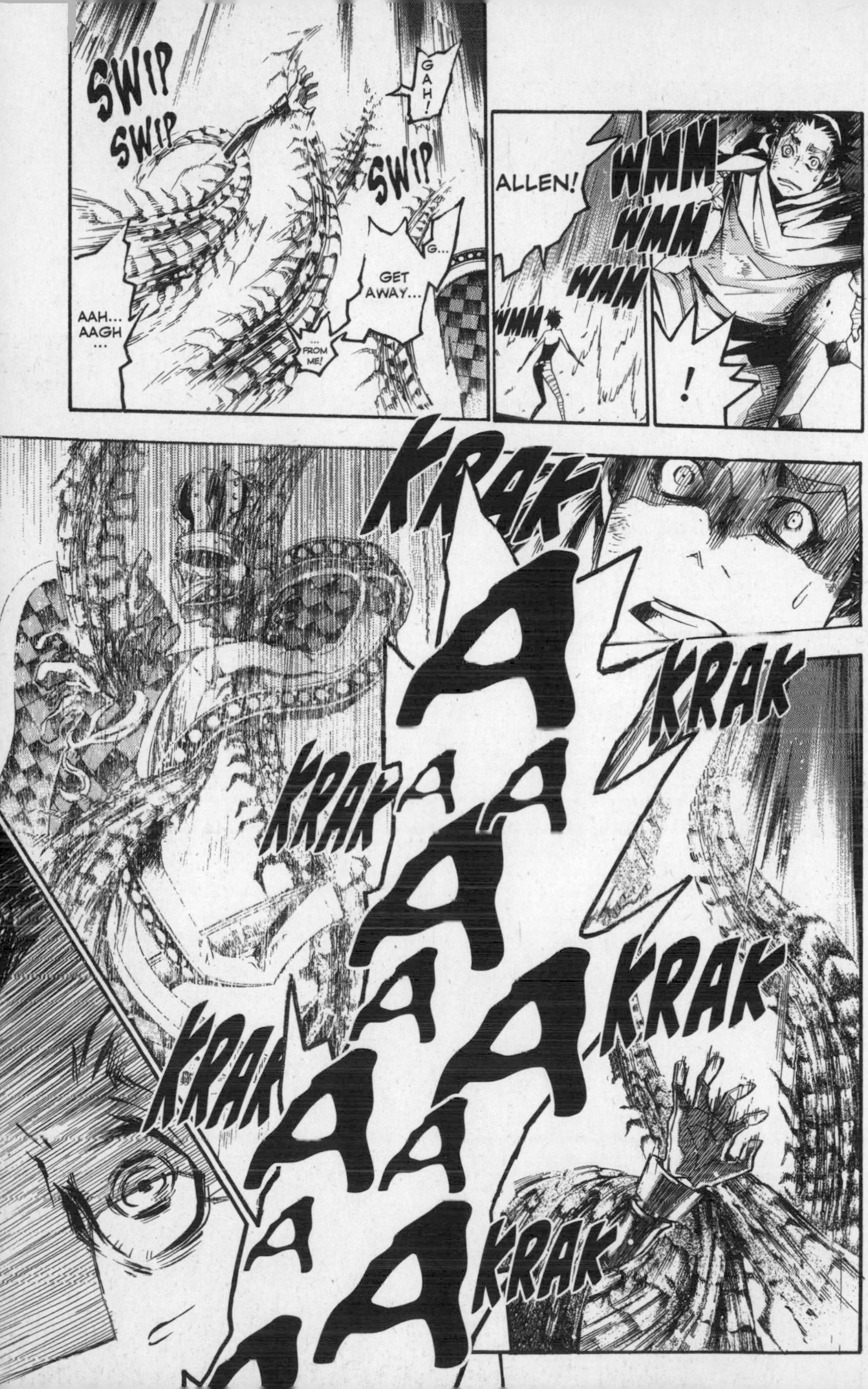
!
WMM WMM WMM WMM
ALLEN!
GAH!
SWIP
G...
GET AWAY...
...FROM ME!
SWIP SWIP
AAH... AAGH...
KRAK
KRAK
AAAAAAAAAAAA
KRAK
KRAK
KRAK
KRAK

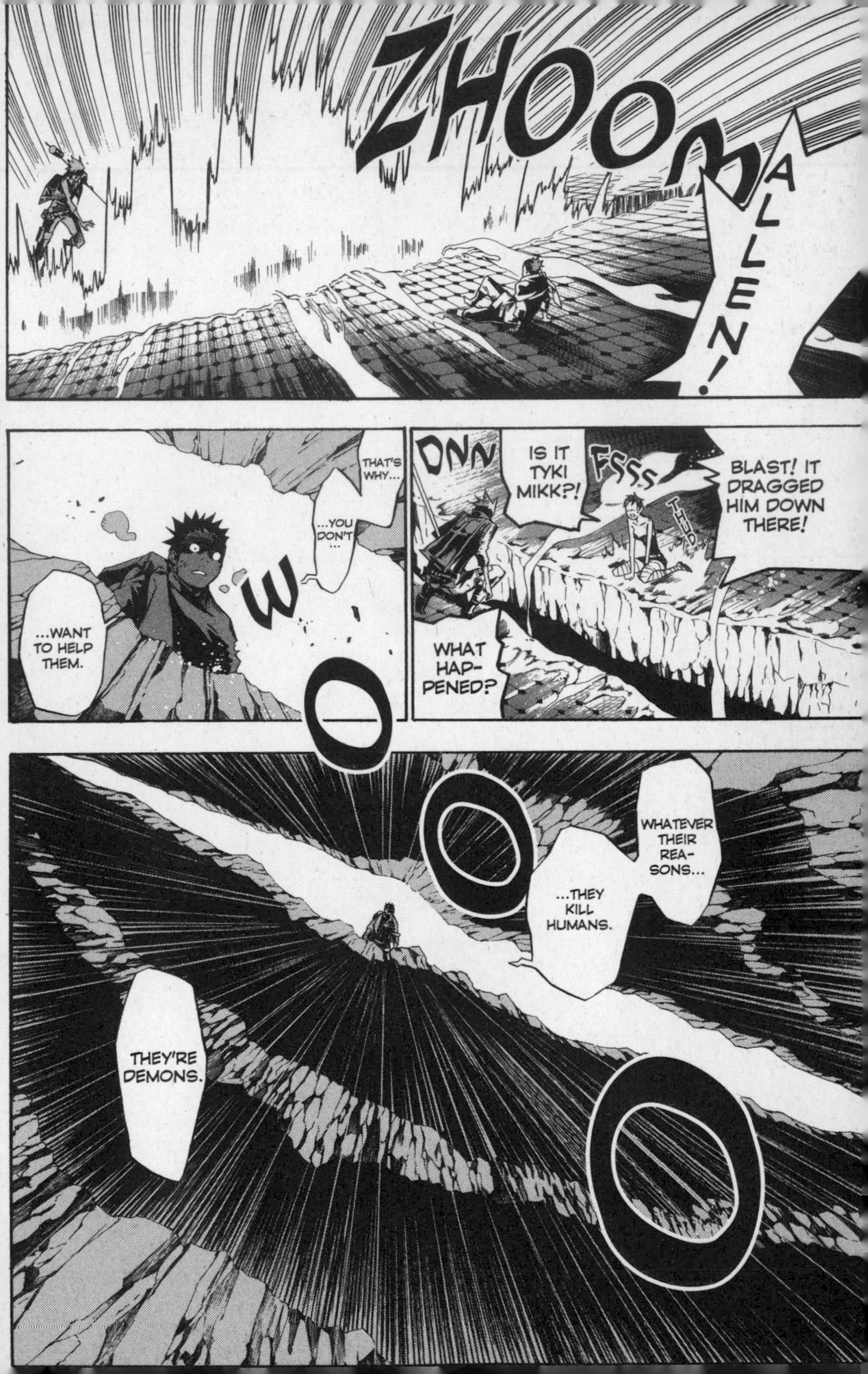
ZHOOM
ALLEN!
BLAST! IT DRAGGED HIM DOWN THERE!
THUD
FSSS
IS IT TYKI MIKK?!
DNN
WHAT HAP-PENED?
THAT'S WHY...
...YOU DON'T...
...WANT TO HELP THEM.
WOOOO
WHATEVER THEIR REA-SONS...
...THEY KILL HUMANS.
THEY'RE DEMONS.

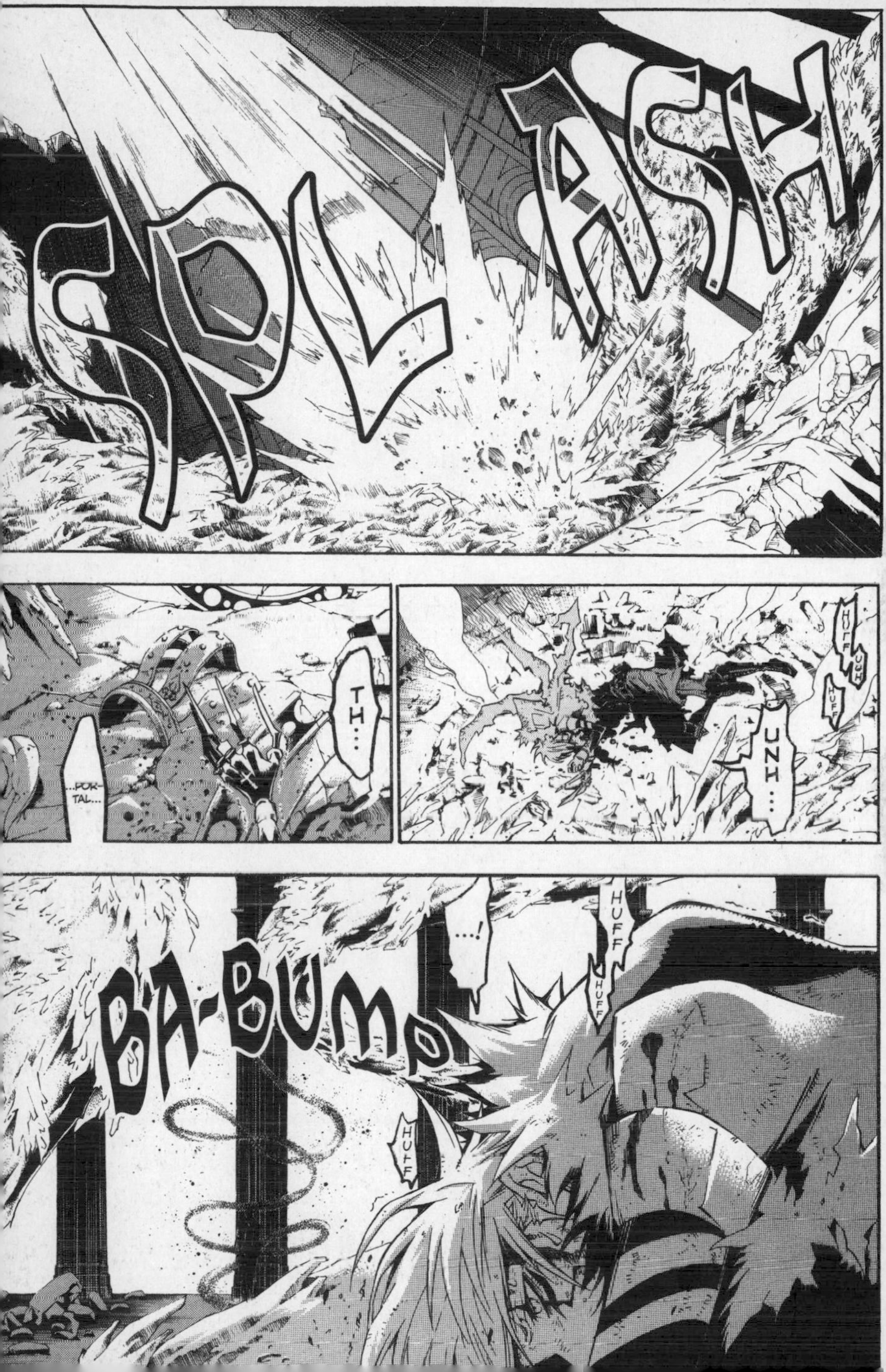
SPLASH
HUFF
UGH
HUFF
UNH...
TH...
...POR-
TAL...
HUFF
HUFF
...!
BA-BUMP
HUFF

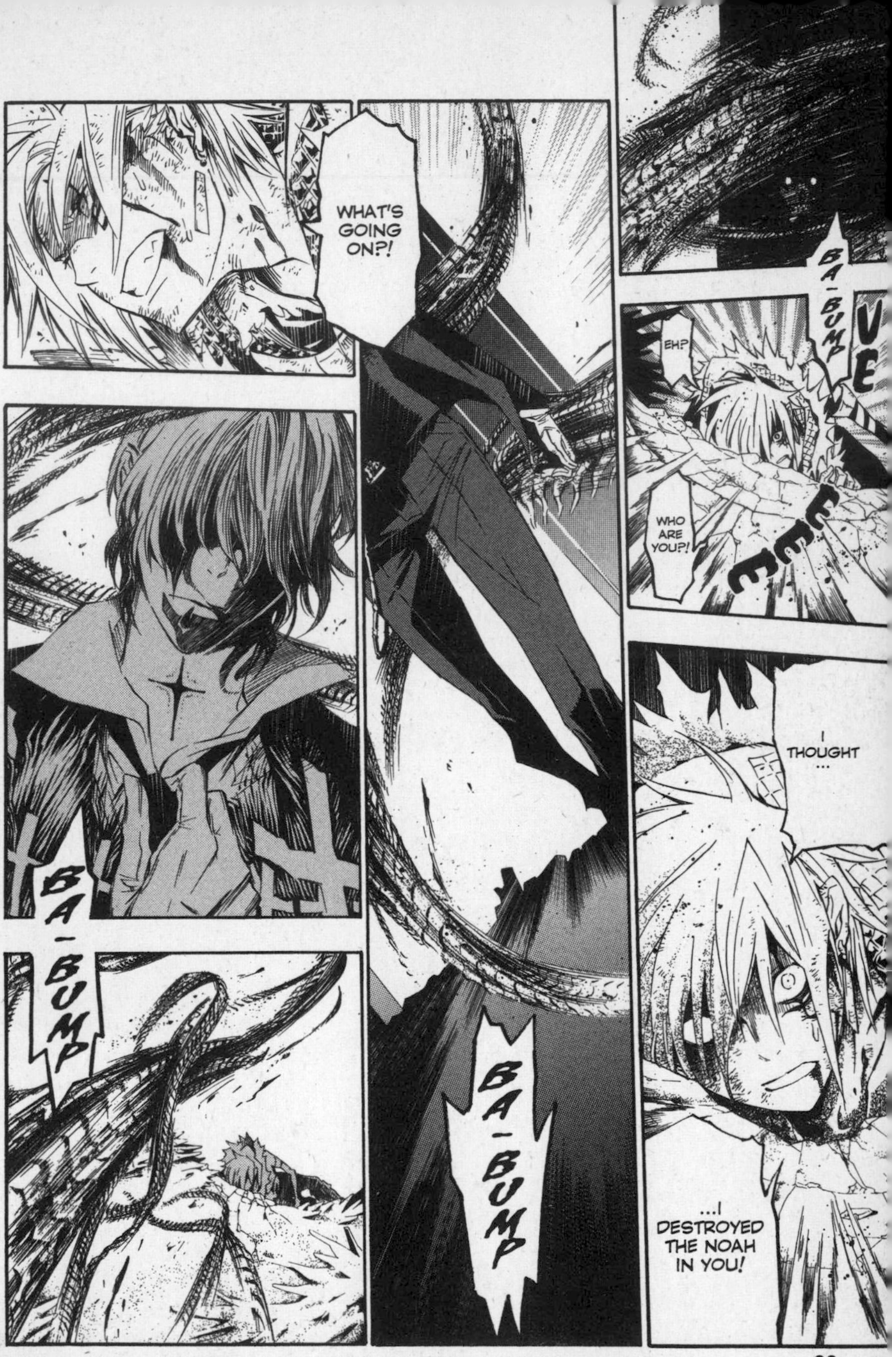
BA-BUMP
EH?
VEEEE
WHO ARE YOU?!
I THOUGHT...
...I DESTROYED THE NOAH IN YOU!
BA-BUMP
WHAT'S GOING ON?!
BA-BUMP
BA-BUMP

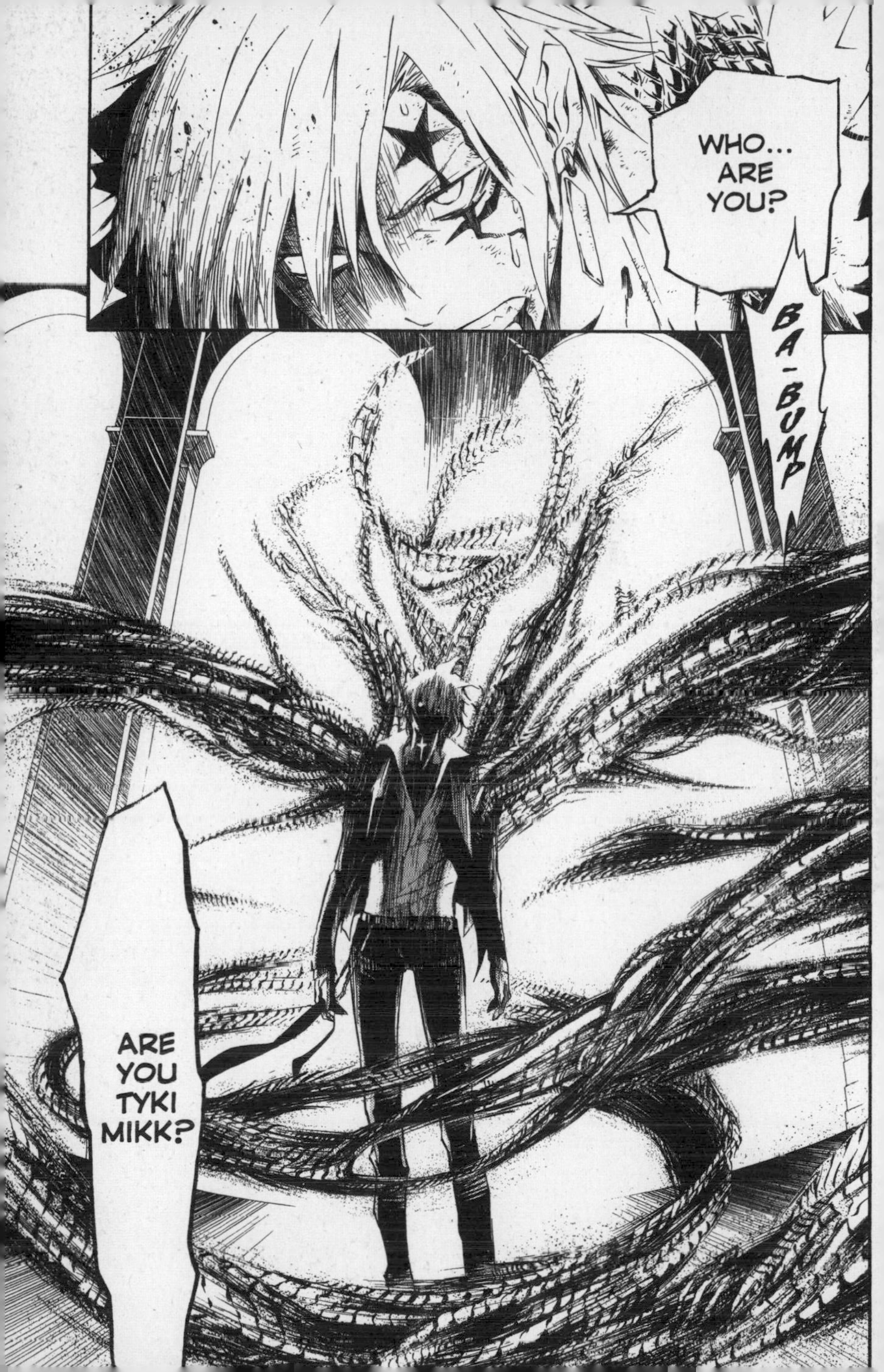
WHO... ARE YOU?
BA-BUMP
ARE YOU TYKI MIKK?

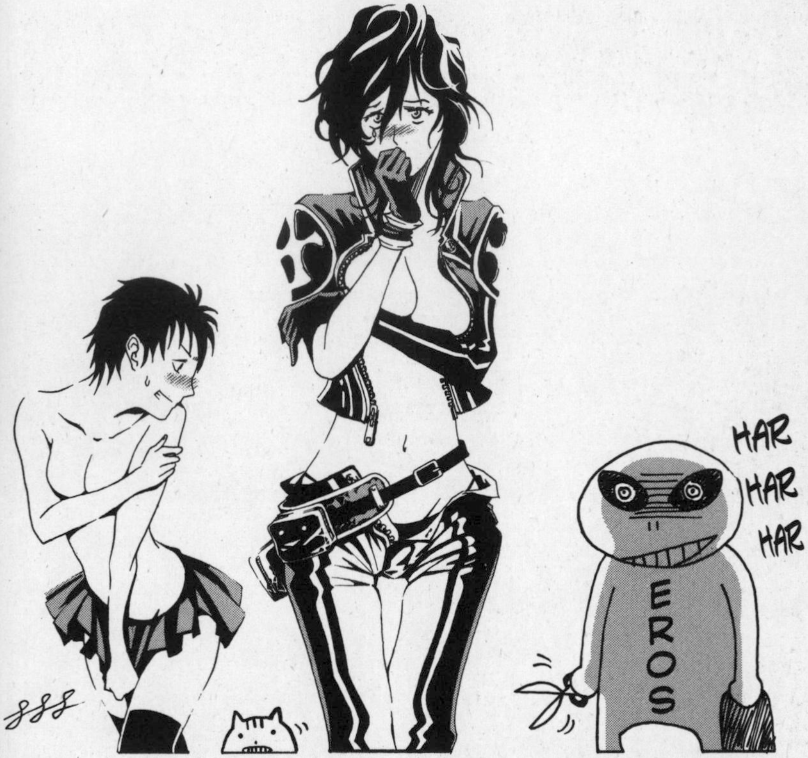
HAR
HAR
HAR
EROS

THE D.GRAY-MAN ELITE CORPS

ILLUSTRATION BY MURAKAMI-KUN

MURAKAMI IS A MAN WHO USES HIS UNIQUE CONVERSATIONAL SKILLS TO GIVE EVERYONE A HARD TIME. HE LIKES TO BRING SWEETS TO THE WORKPLACE, BUT WHEN THEY AREN'T VERY GOOD, PEOPLE COMPLAIN. THEY SAY HE SPENDS A LOT OF TIME HANGING AROUND THE SHOPS UNDER THE BUILDING.

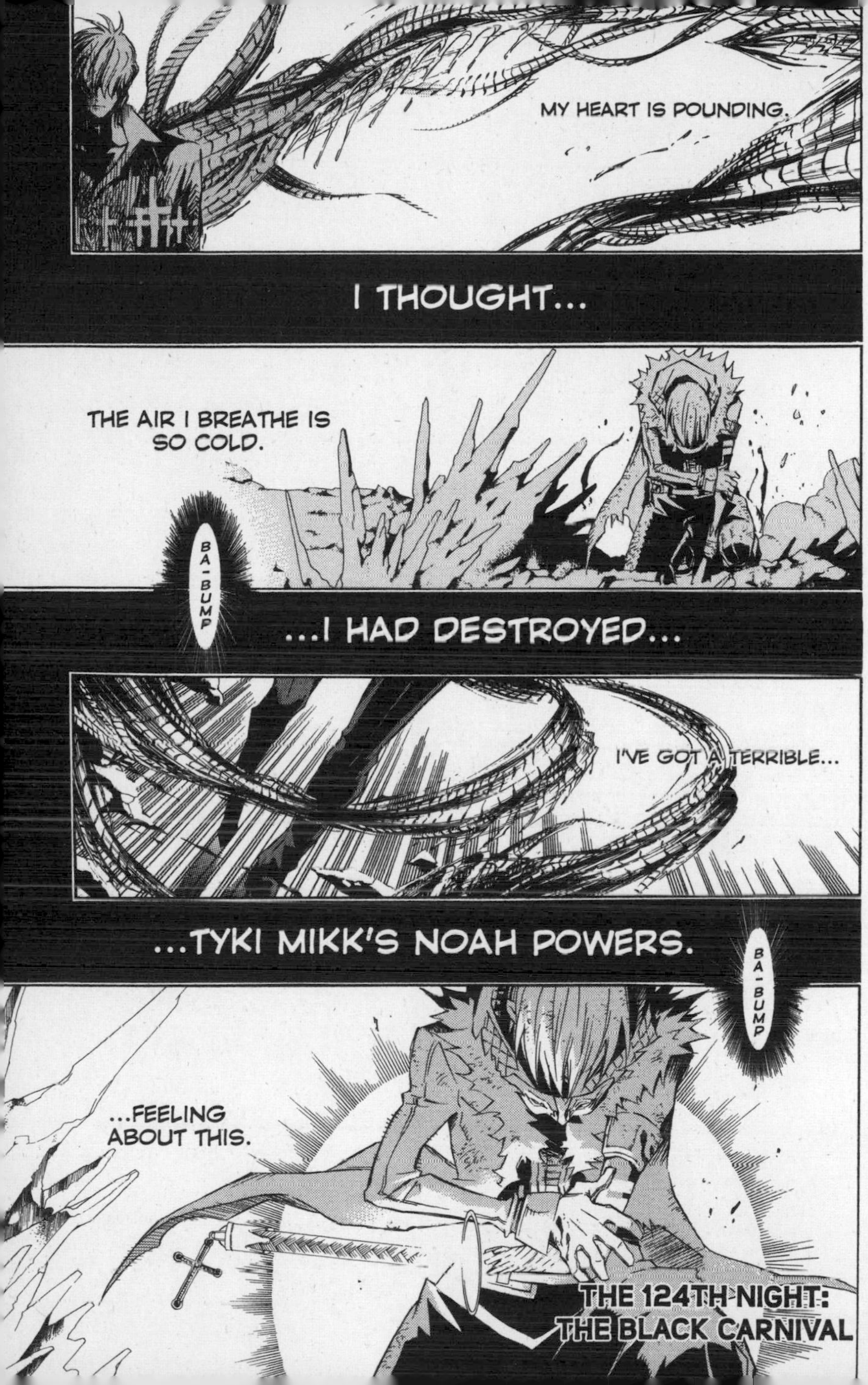
MY HEART IS POUNDING.
I THOUGHT...
THE AIR I BREATHE IS SO COLD.
BA-BUMP
...I HAD DESTROYED...
I'VE GOT A TERRIBLE...
...TYKI MIKK'S NOAH POWERS.
BA-BUMP
...FEELING ABOUT THIS.
THE 124TH NIGHT: THE BLACK CARNIVAL

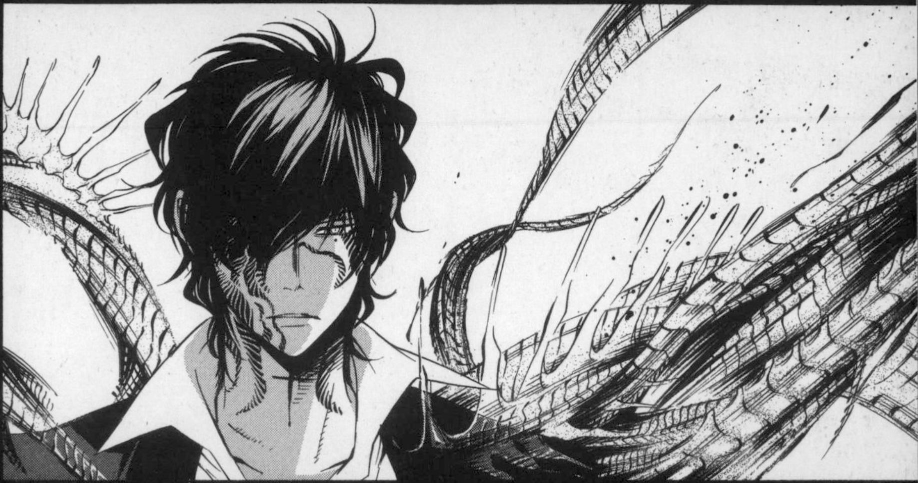

THE 124TH NIGHT: THE BLACK CARNIVAL

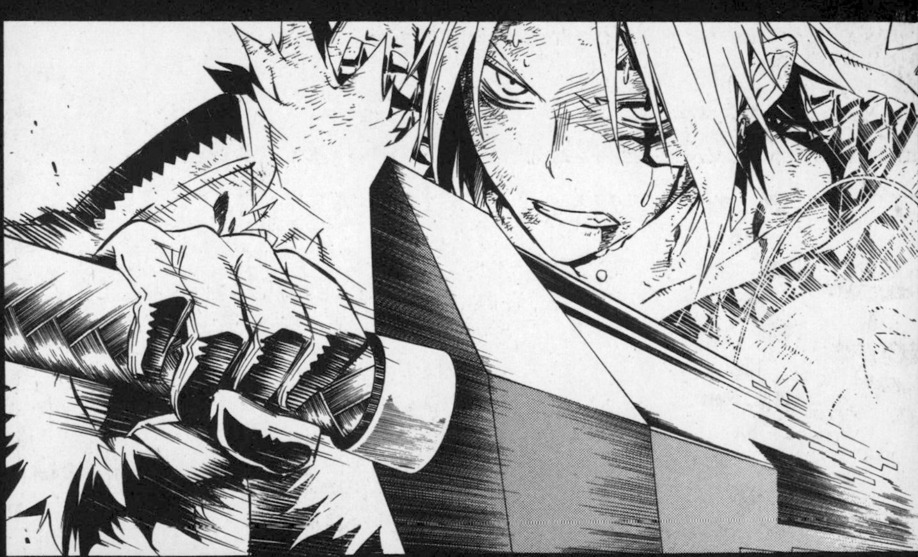

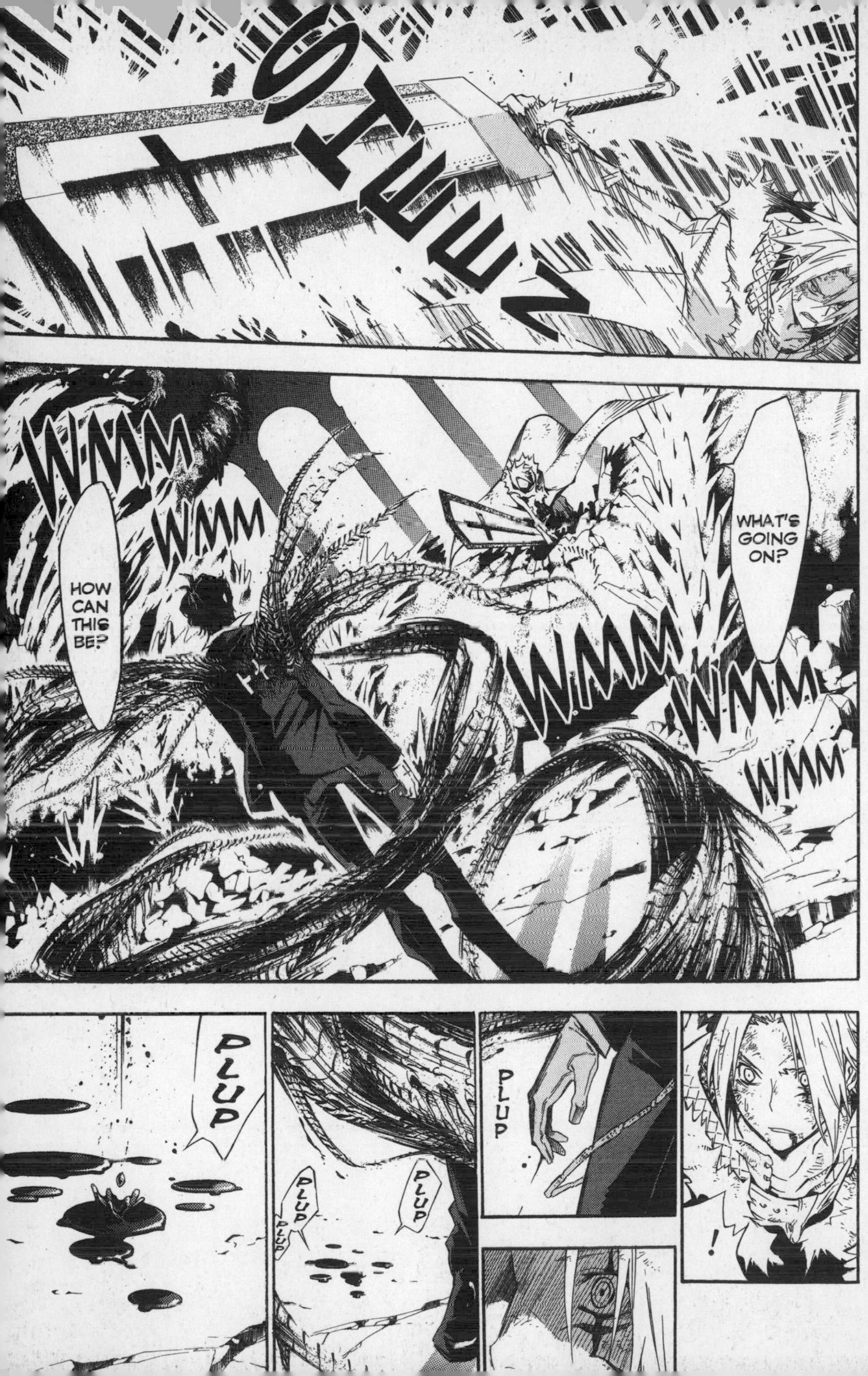
WHAT'S GOING ON?
WMM WMM WMM
WMM WMM
HOW CAN THIS BE?
!
PLUP
PLUP
PLUP
PLUP
PLUP

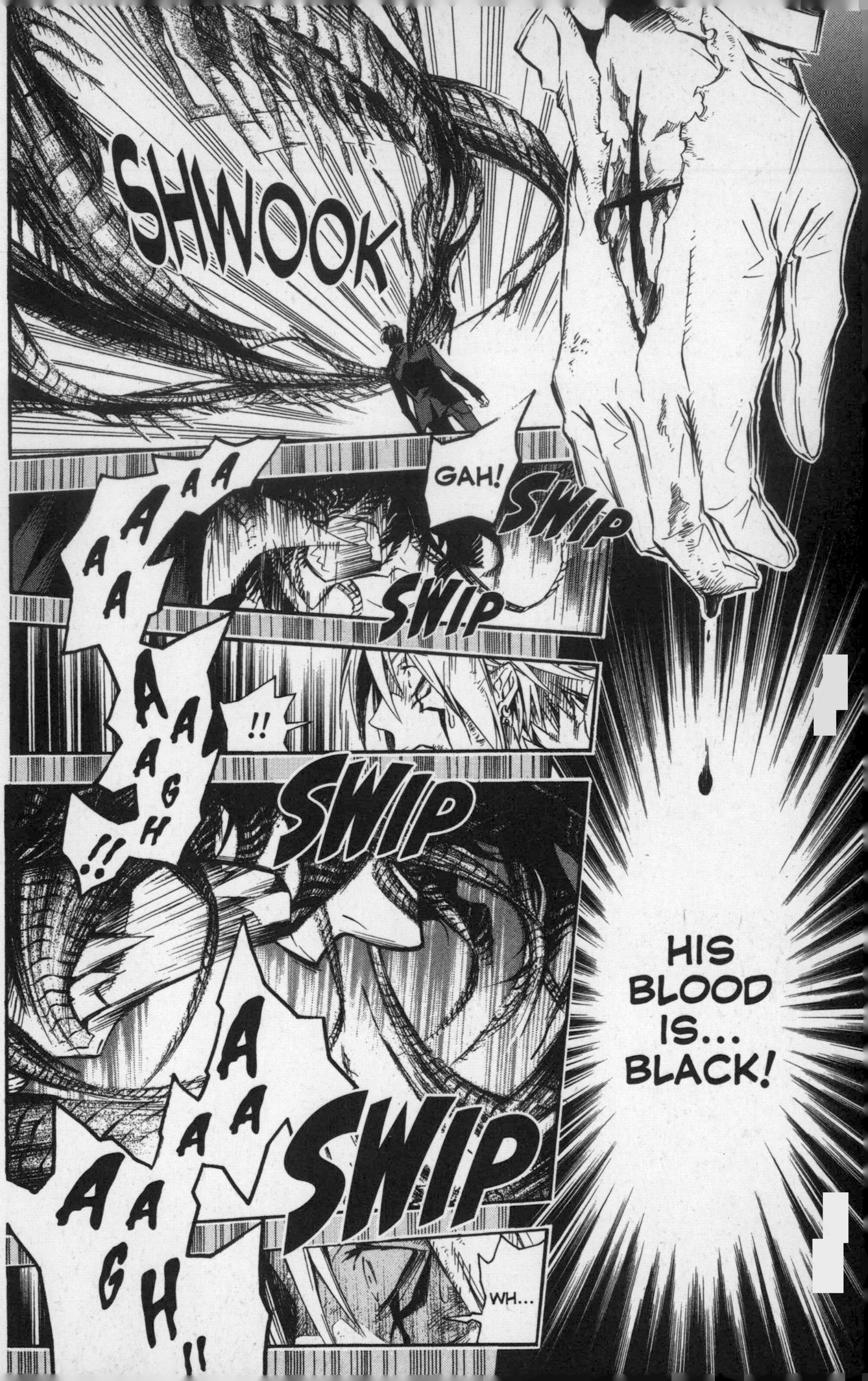
HIS BLOOD IS... BLACK!
SHWOOK
GAH!
AAAAAAAAAAAAGH!!
SWIP
SWIP
!!
SWIP
AAAAAAGH!!
SWIP
WH...

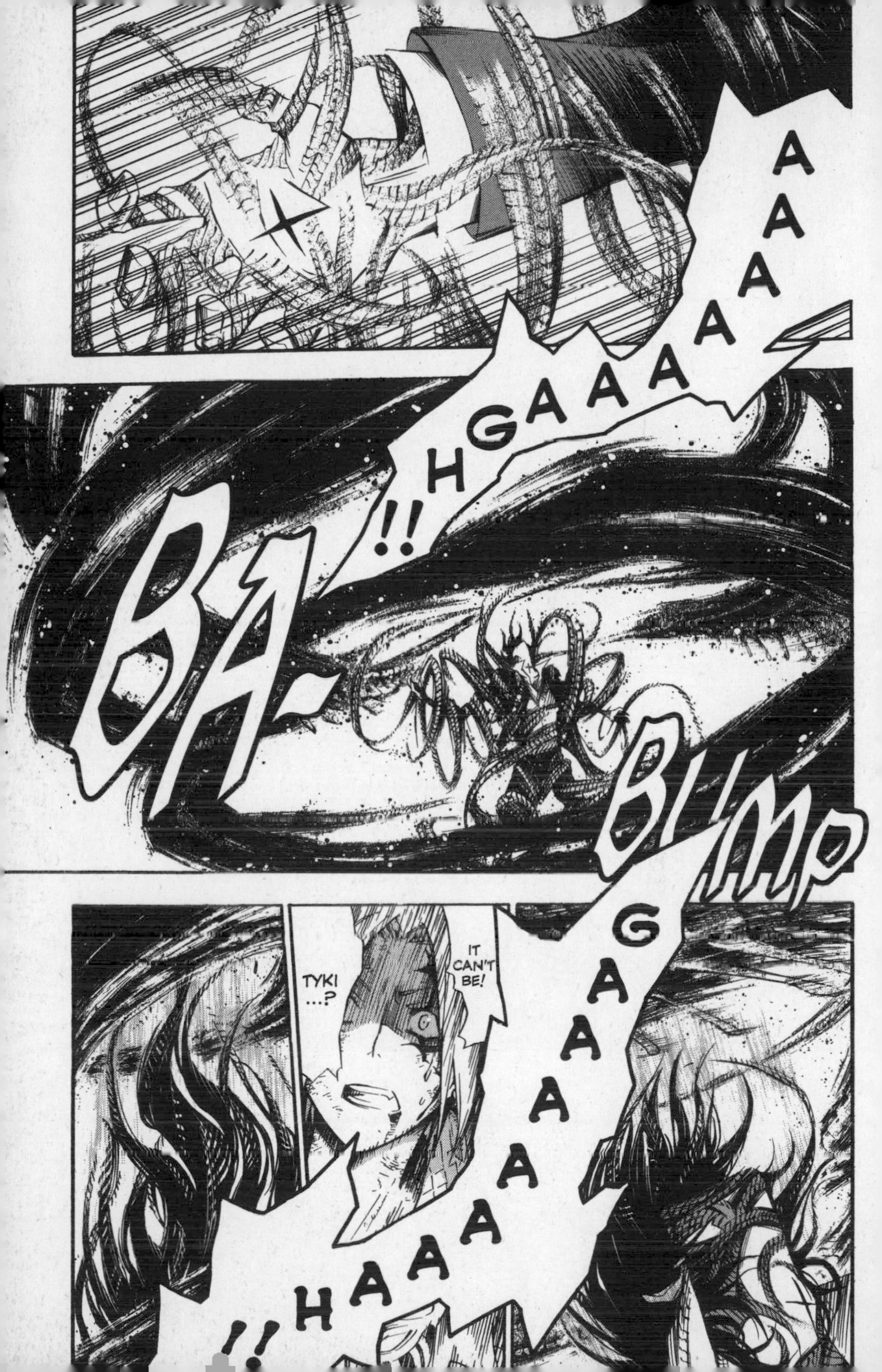
AAAAAAAGH!!
BA-BUMP
GAAAAAAAAH!!
IT CAN'T BE!
TYKI ...?

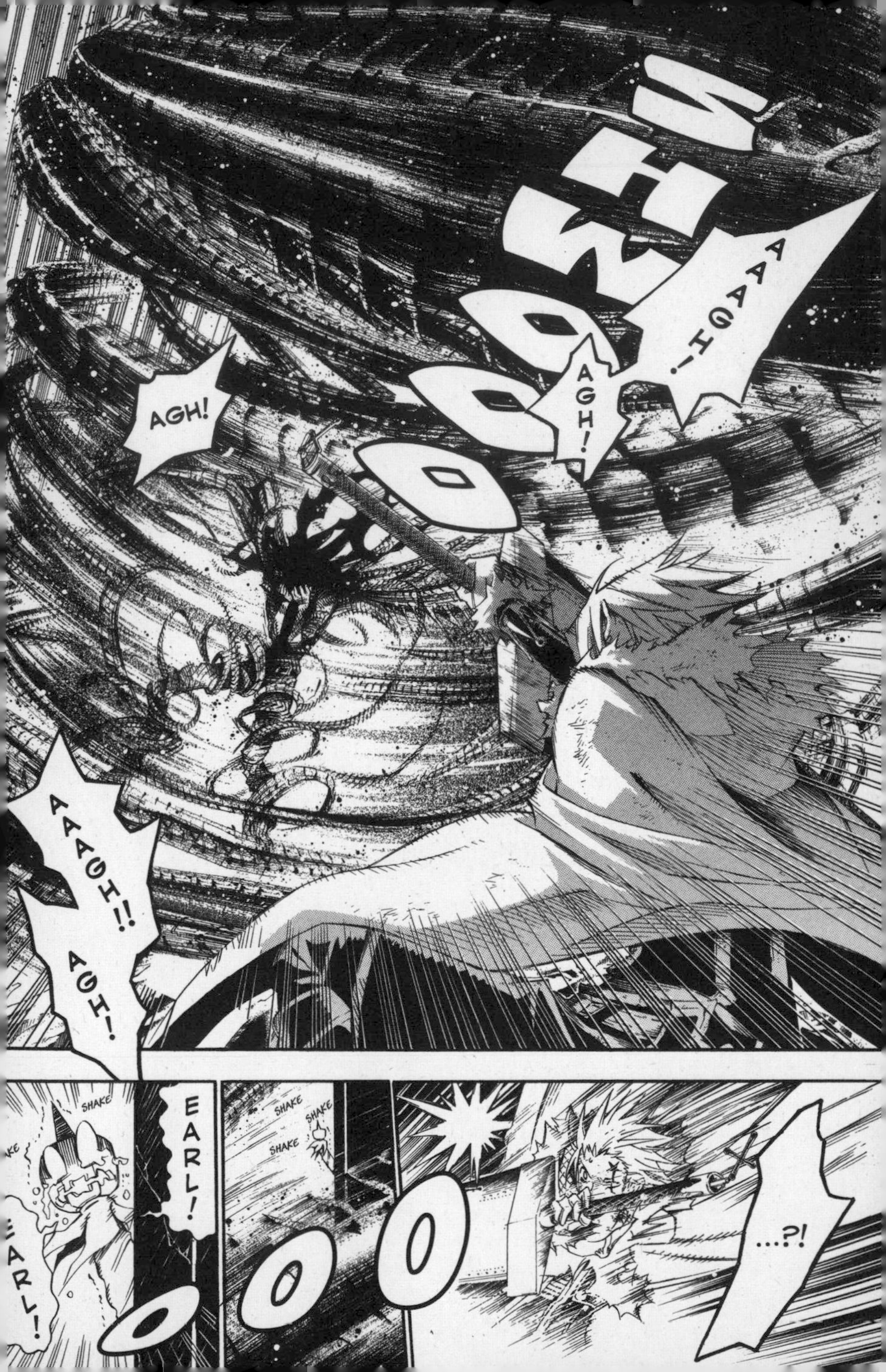
SWOOO
AAAGH!
AGH!
AGH!
AAAGH!! AGH!
...?!
OOOO
SHAKE
SHAKE
SHAKE
EARL!
SHAKE
SHAKE
EARL!

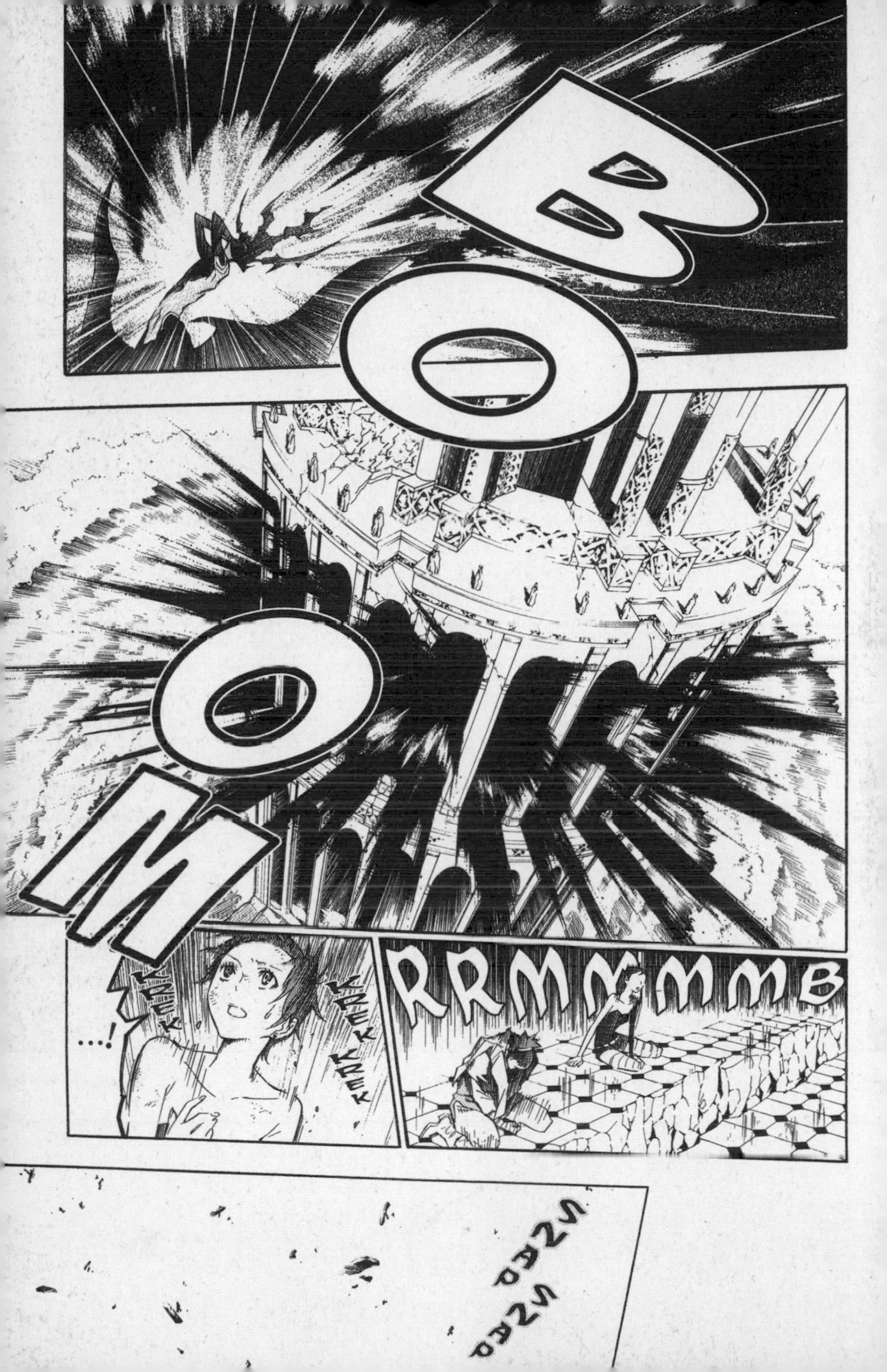
BOOM
KREK
KREK KREK
...!
RRMMMMMB

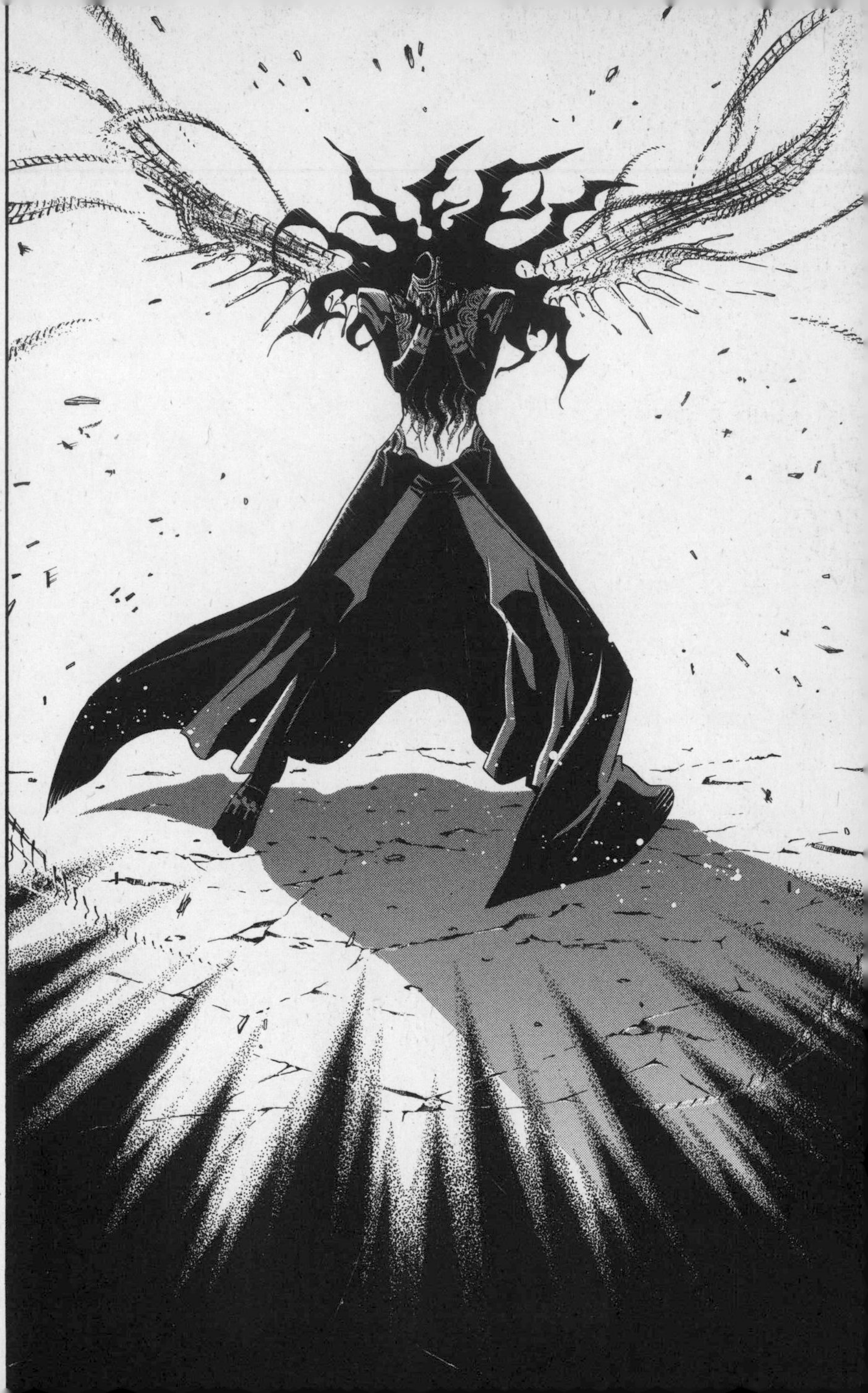

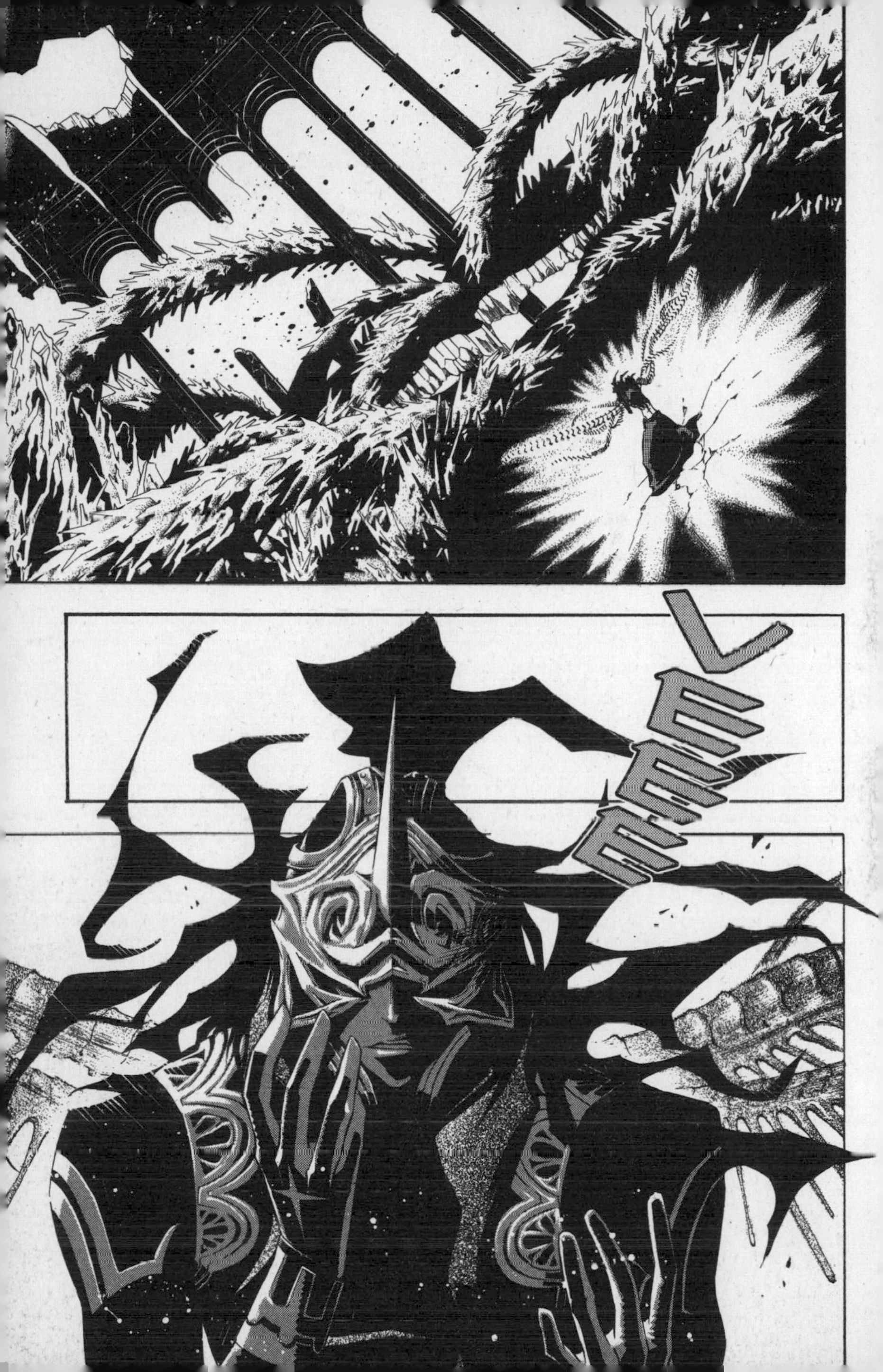
VÈEEE

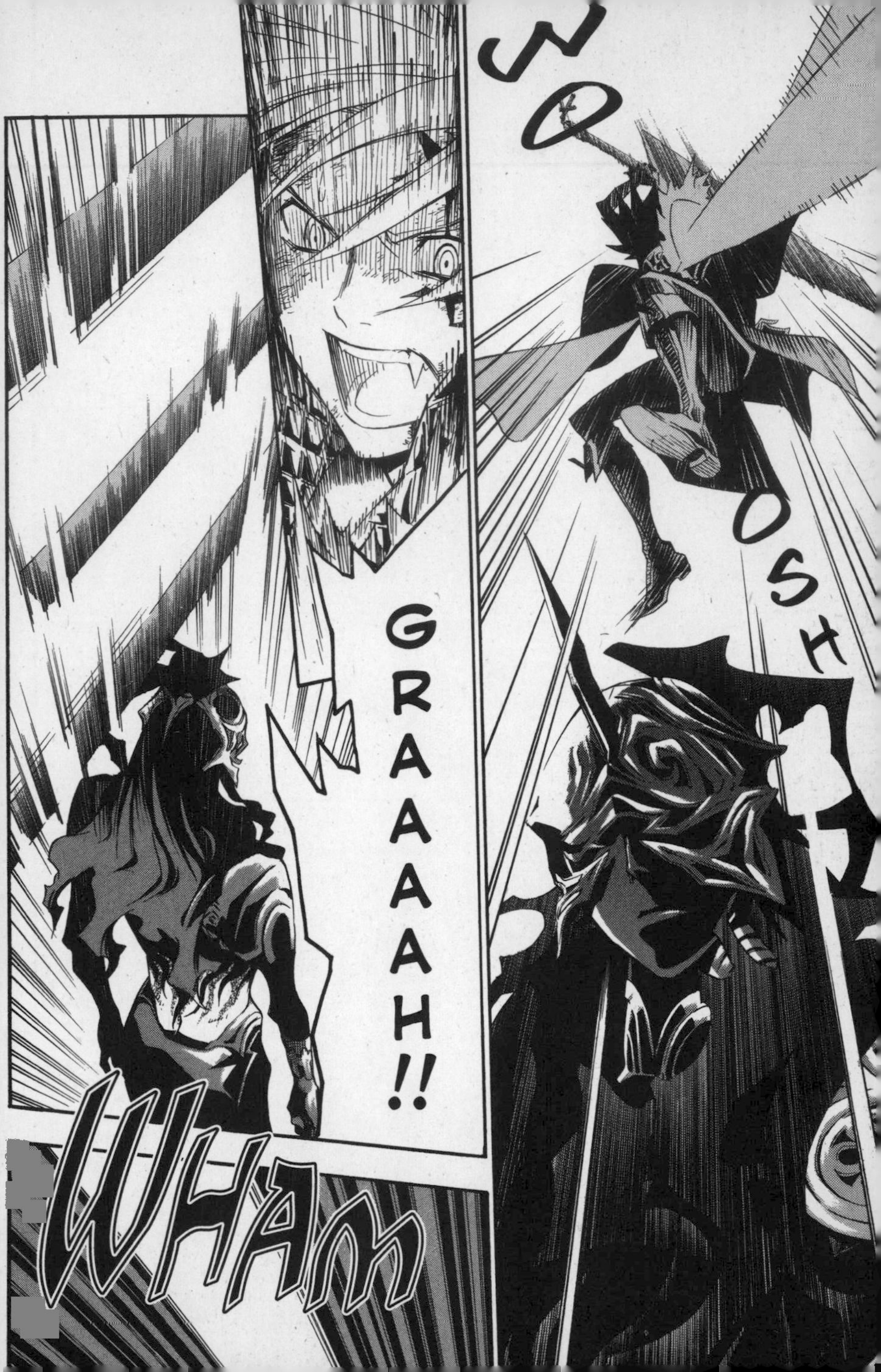
WOOSH
GRAAAAH!!
WHAM

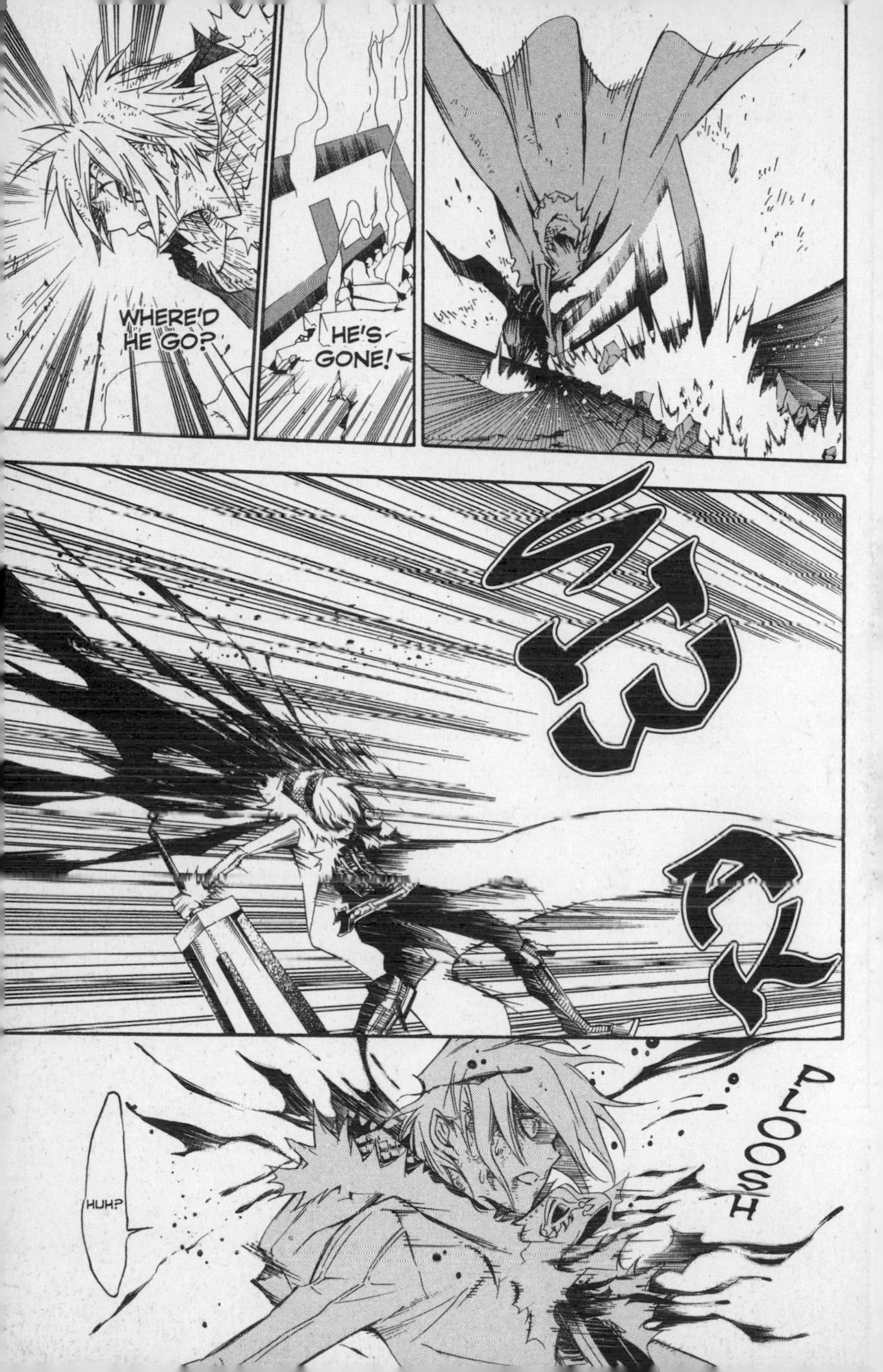
HE'S GONE!
WHERE'D HE GO?
PLOOSH
HUH?

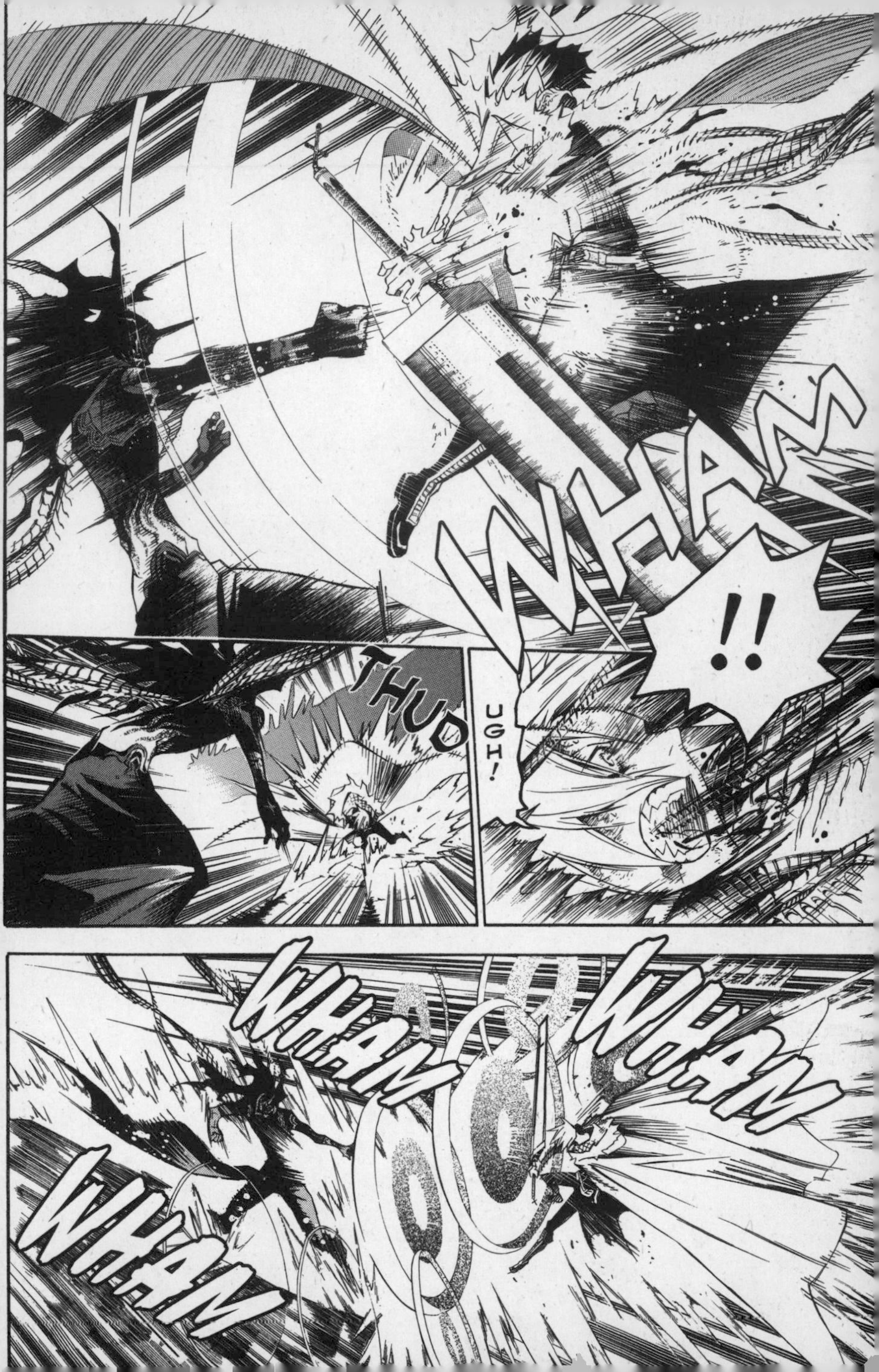
WHAM!!
UGH!
THUD
WHAM
WHAM
WHAM

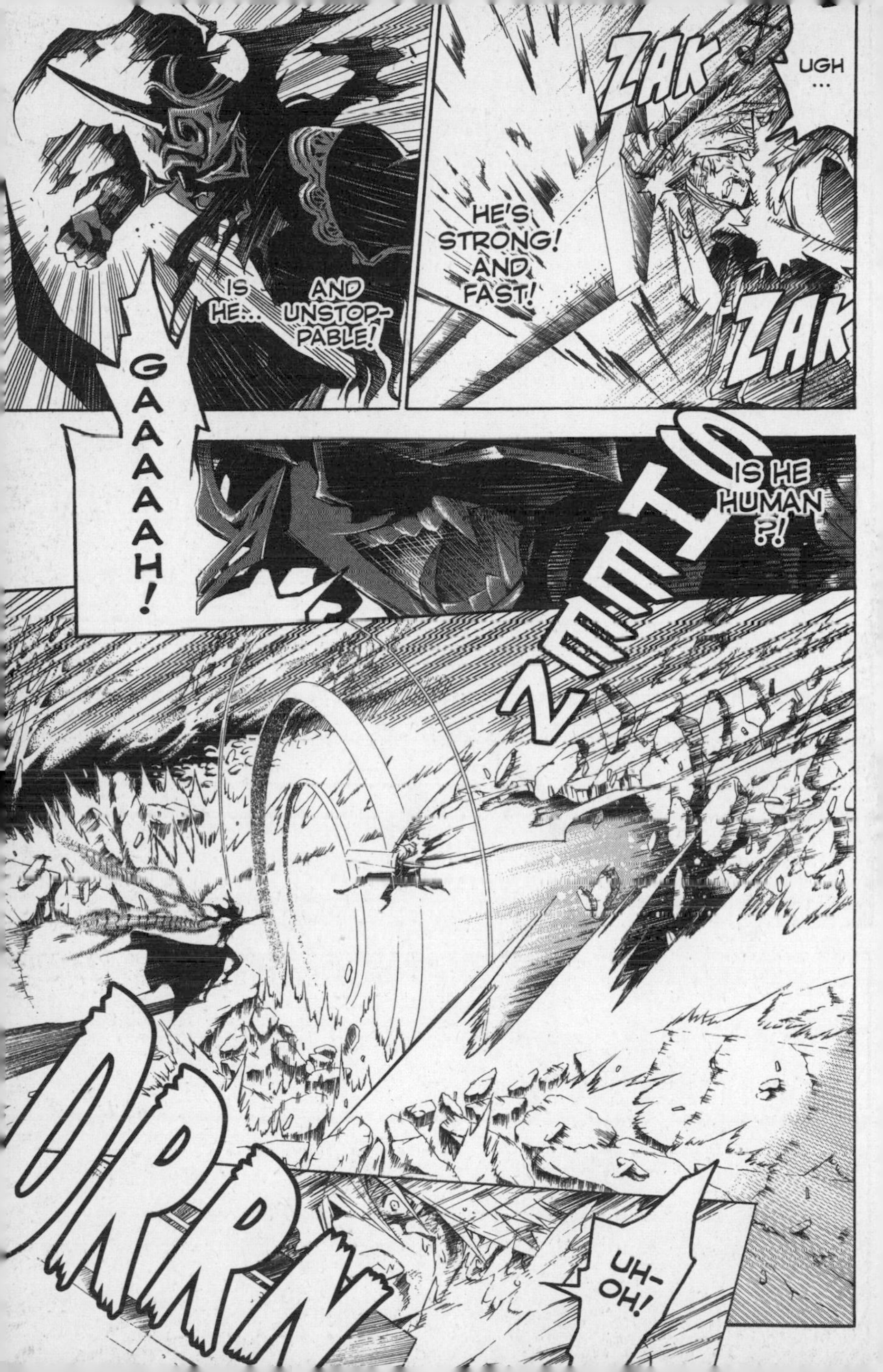
ZAK
UGH ...
HE'S STRONG! AND FAST!
ZAK
IS HE...
AND UNSTOP-PABLE!
GAAAAAAH!
IS HE HUMAN ?!
UH-OH!

...TO TYKI MIKK?

SHWAK

WHAT HAPPENED...

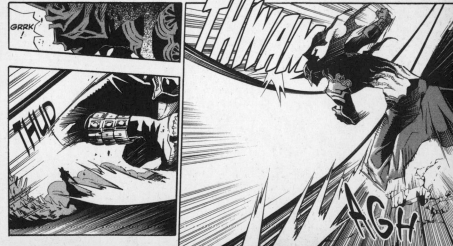

GRRK!

THUD

THWAM

AGH

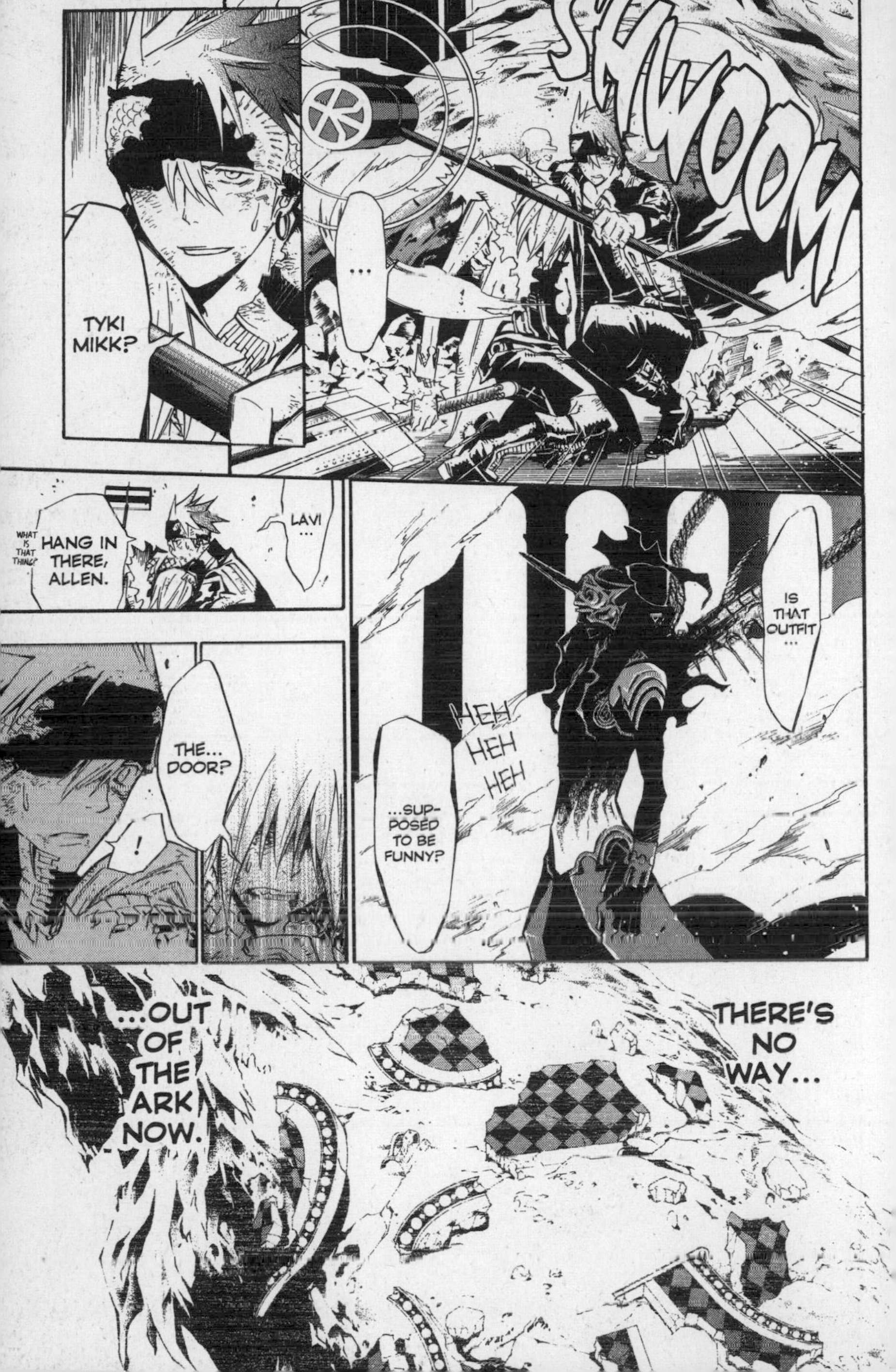
SHWOOM
...
TYKI MIKK?
IS THAT OUTFIT...
HEH HEH HEH
...SUP-POSED TO BE FUNNY?
LAVI...
HANG IN THERE, ALLEN.
WHAT IS THAT THING?
THE... DOOR?
!
THERE'S NO WAY...
...OUT OF THE ARK NOW.

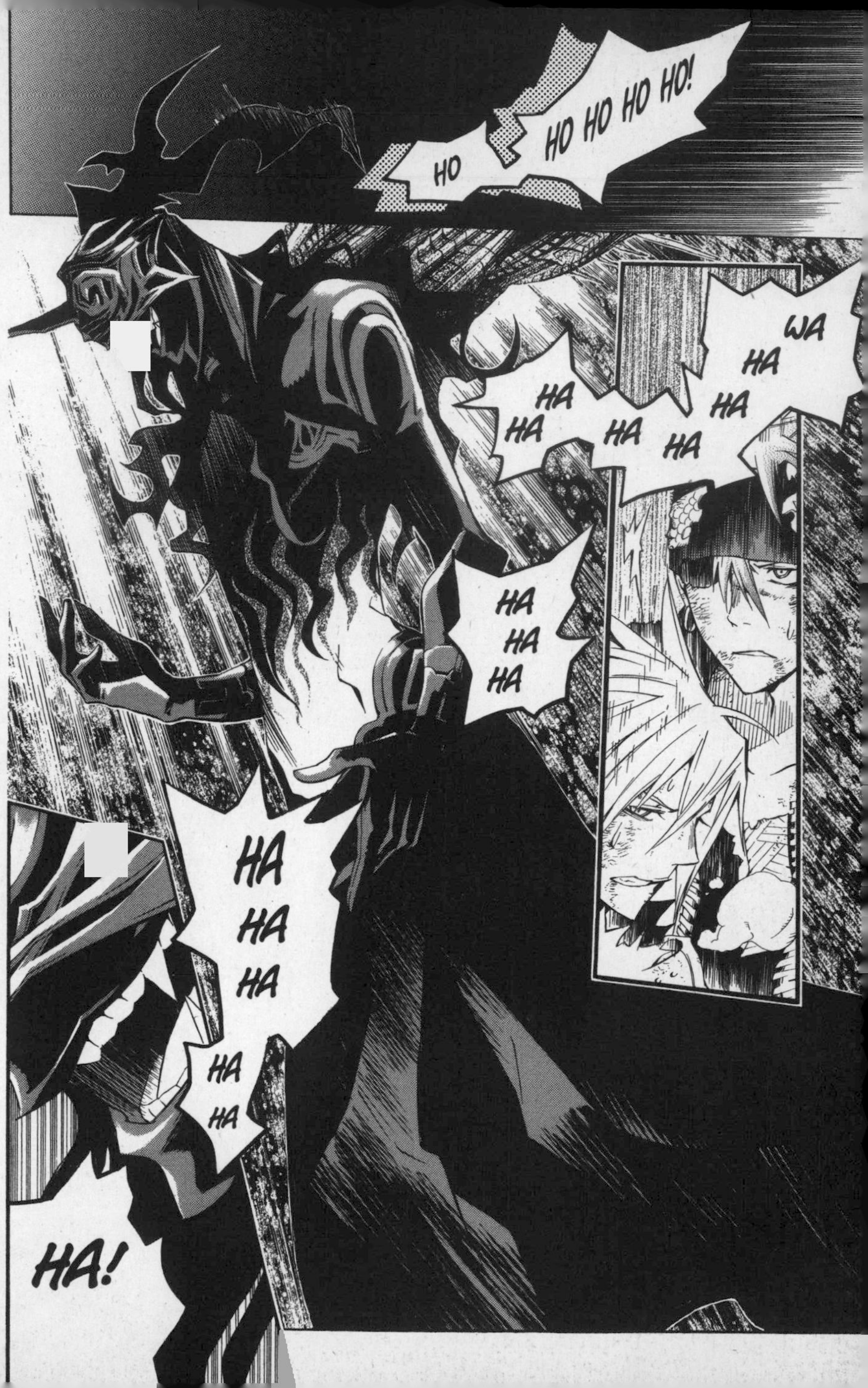
HO HO HO HO HO!
WA HA HA HA HA HA HA HA
HA HA HA
HA HA HA HA HA
HA!

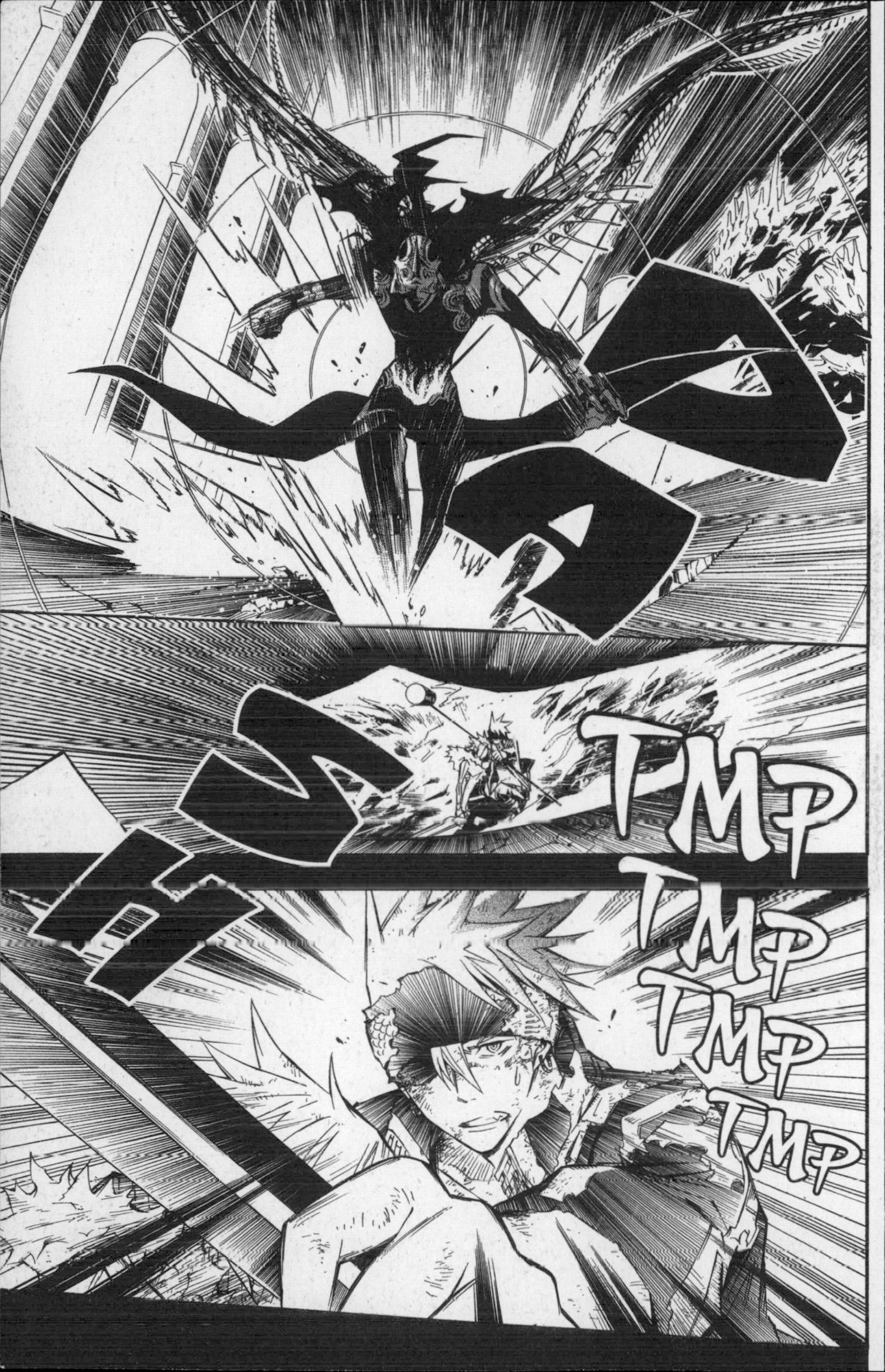
TMP
TMP
TMP
TMP

NOAH

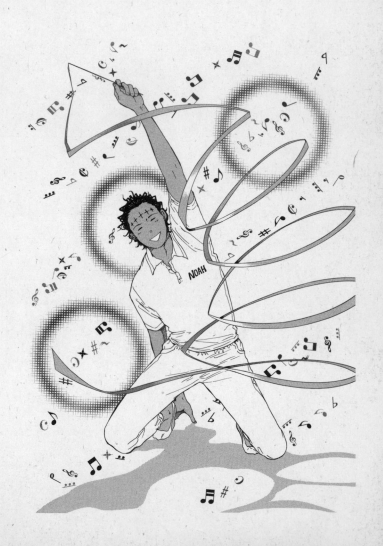

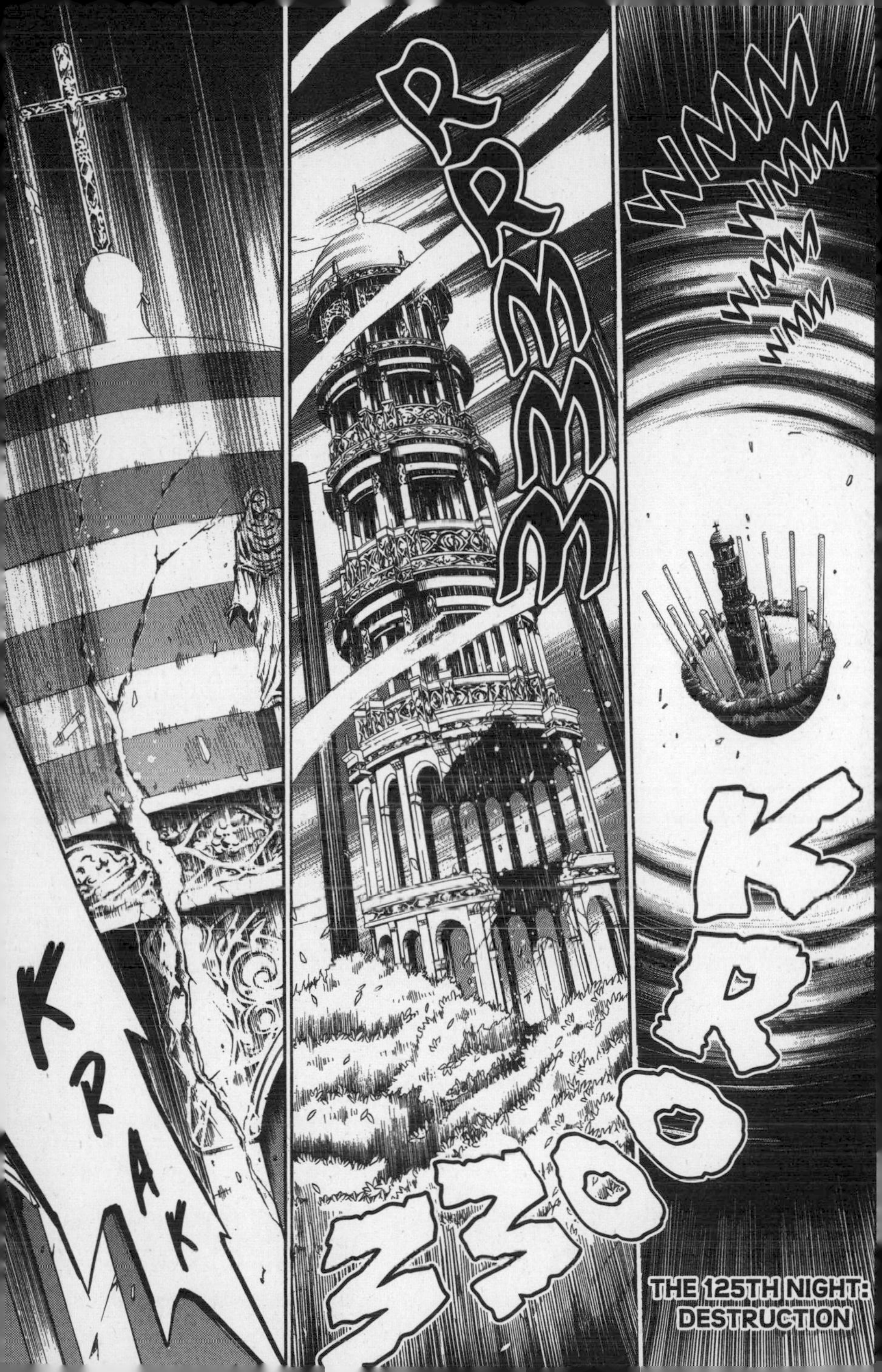
WMMM
WMMM
WMMM
WMMM
KRAK

THE 125TH NIGHT:
DESTRUCTION

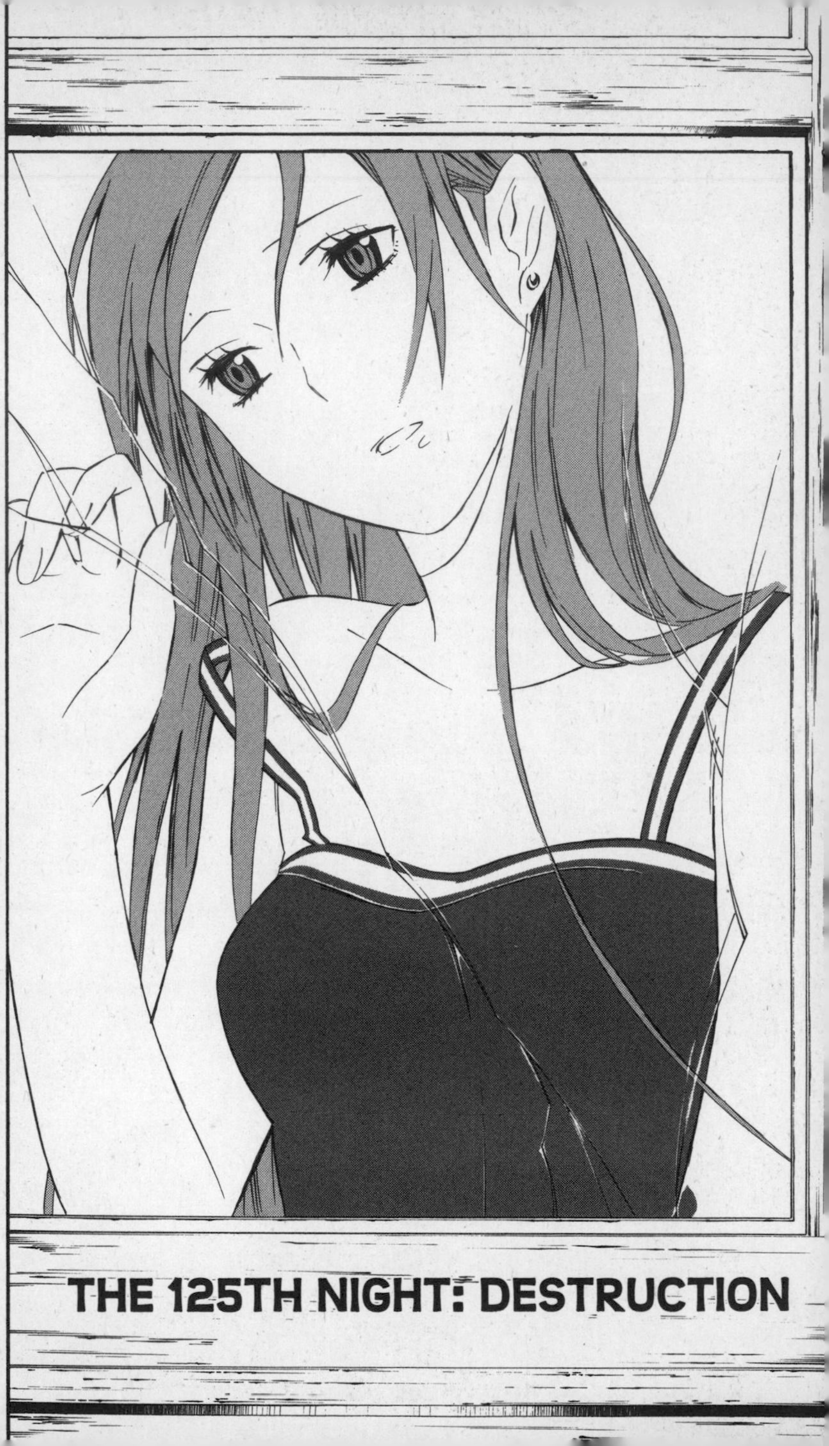
THE 125TH NIGHT: DESTRUCTION

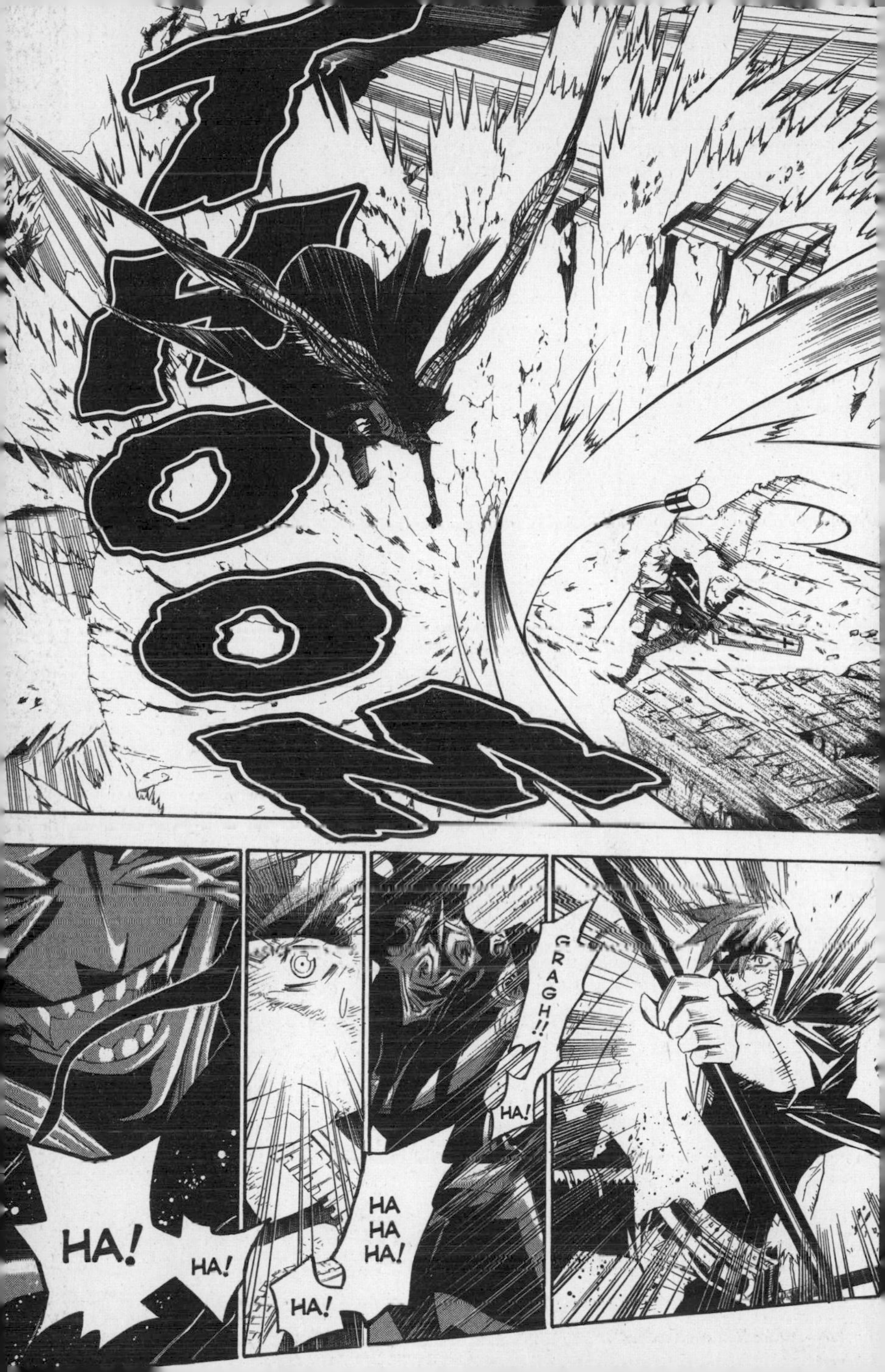
GRAGH!!
HA!
HA
HA
HA!
HA!
HA!
HA!

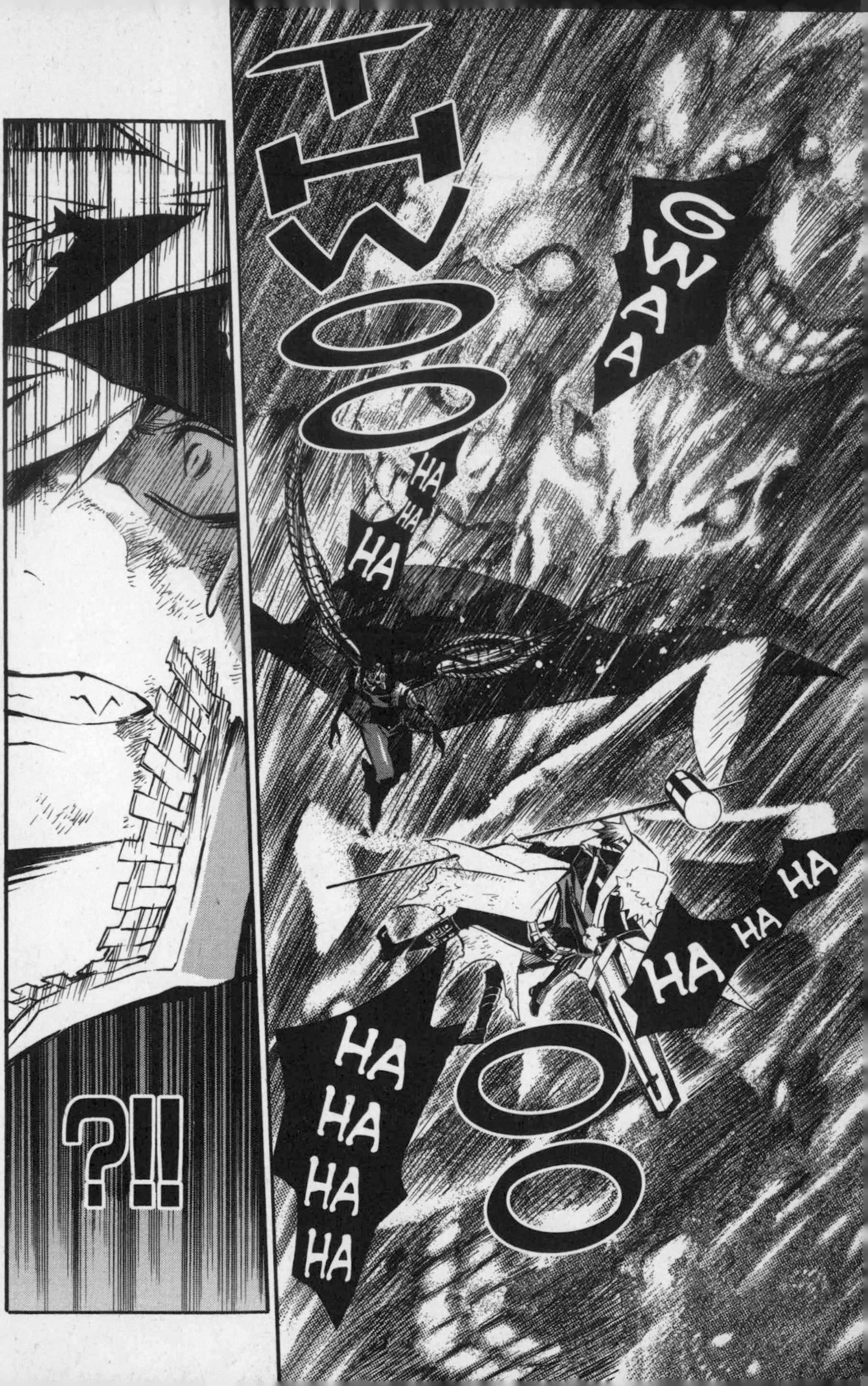
THWOOOO
GWAAA
HA HA HA
HA HA HA HA
HA HA HA HA HA
?!!

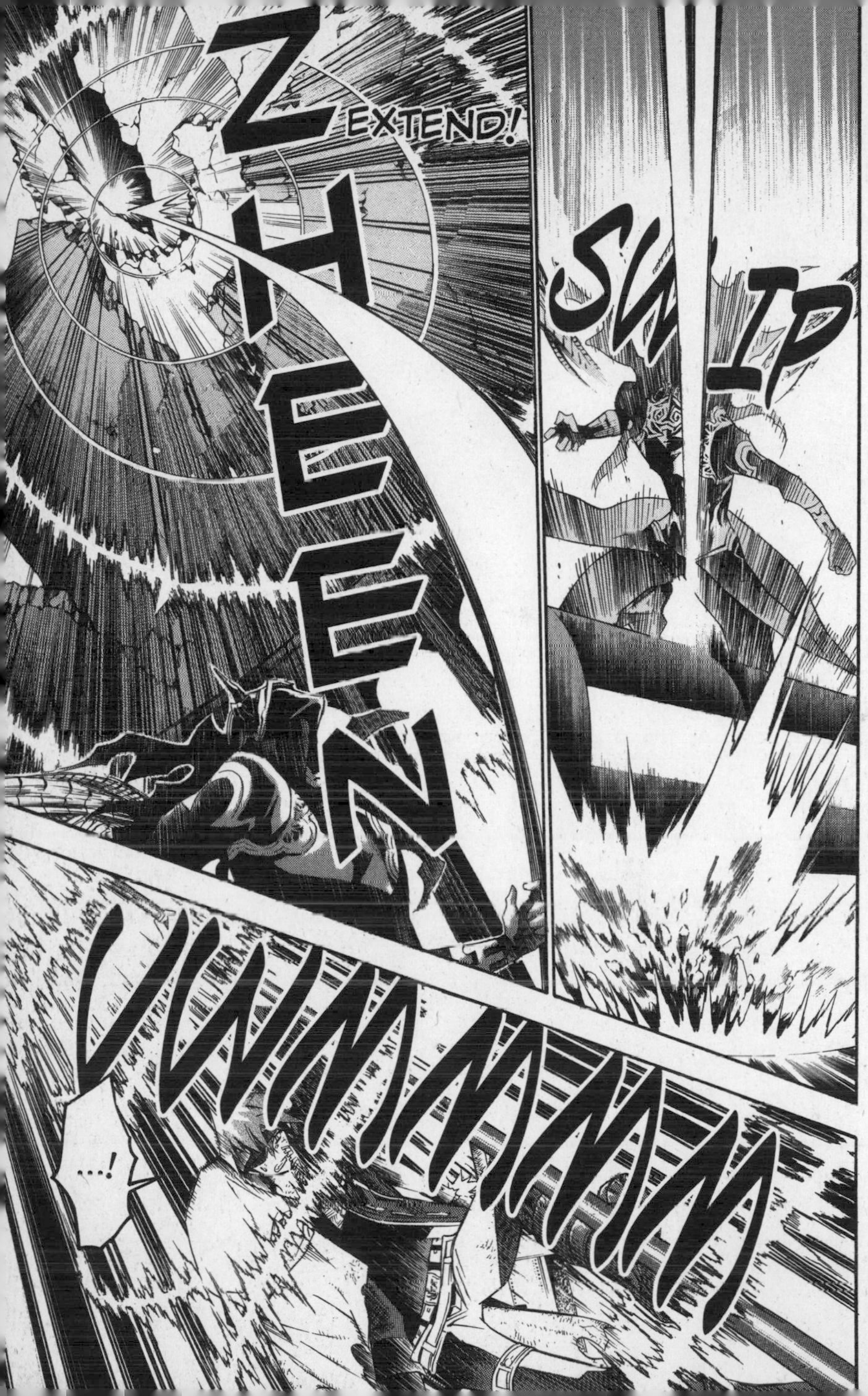
EXTEND!
ZHEEEN
....!

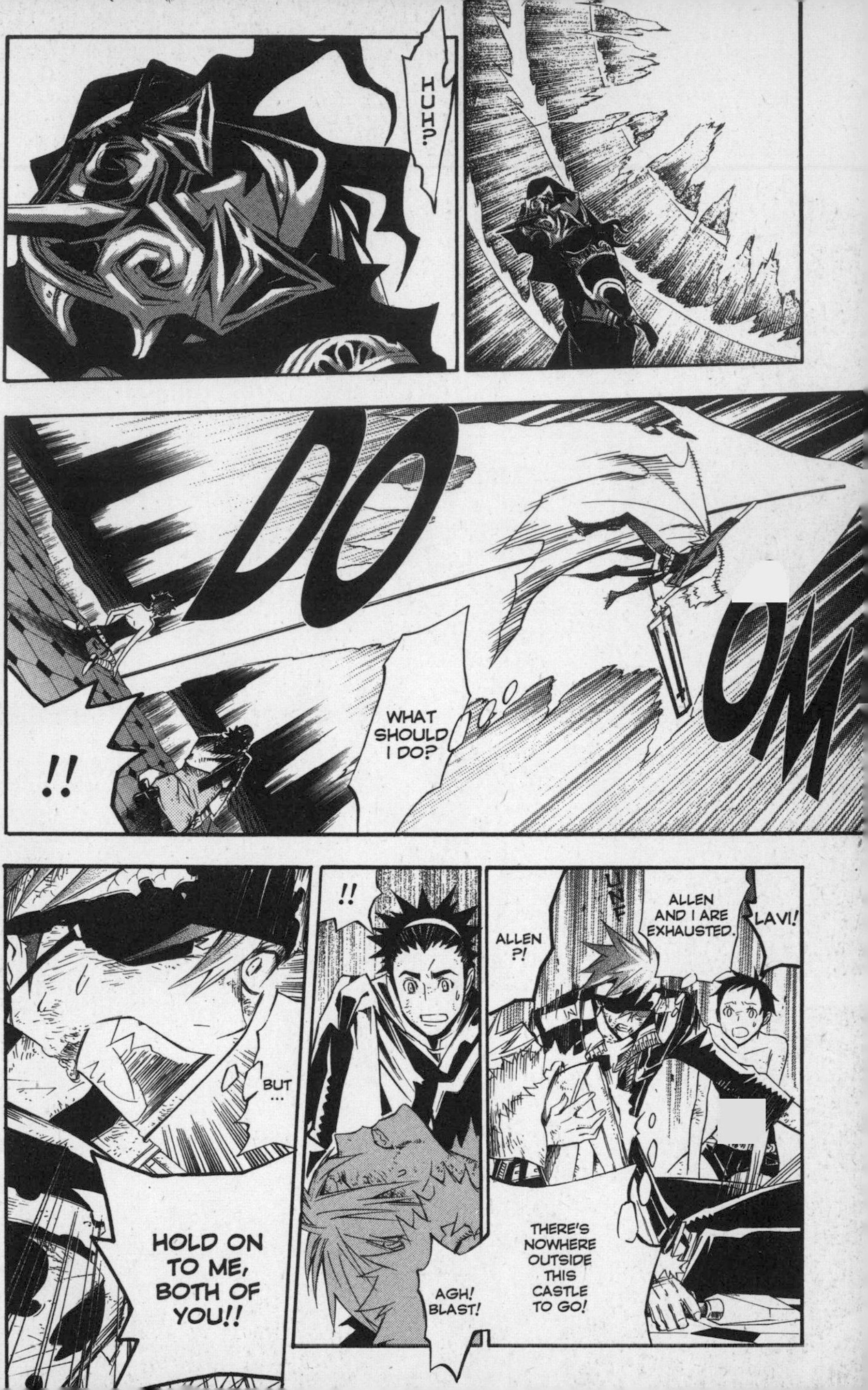
HUH?
DO
OM
WHAT SHOULD I DO?
!!
LAVI!
ALLEN AND I ARE EXHAUSTED.
ALLEN ?!
THERE'S NOWHERE OUTSIDE THIS CASTLE TO GO!
!!
AGH! BLAST!
BUT ...
HOLD ON TO ME, BOTH OF YOU!!

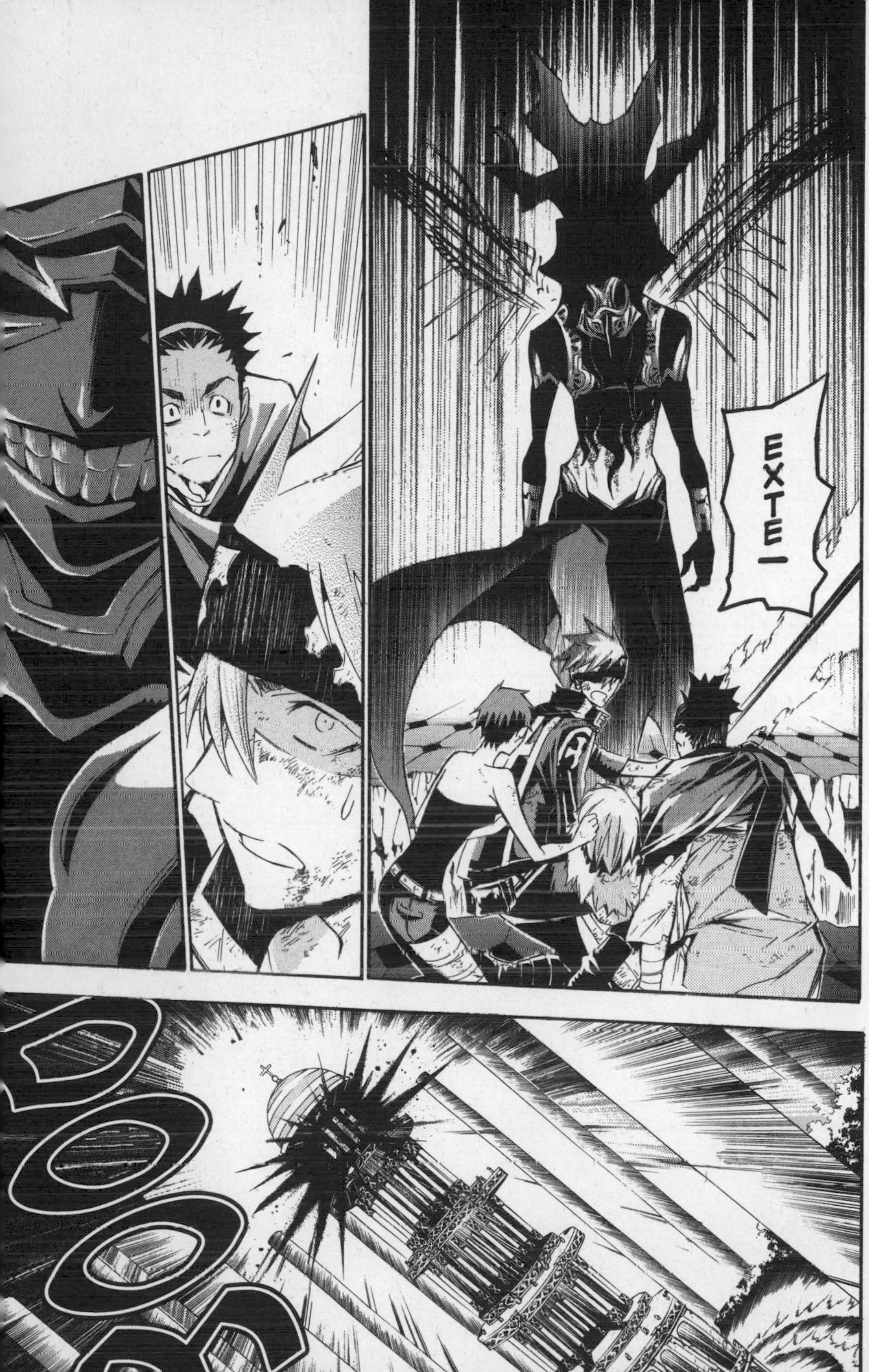
EXTE—

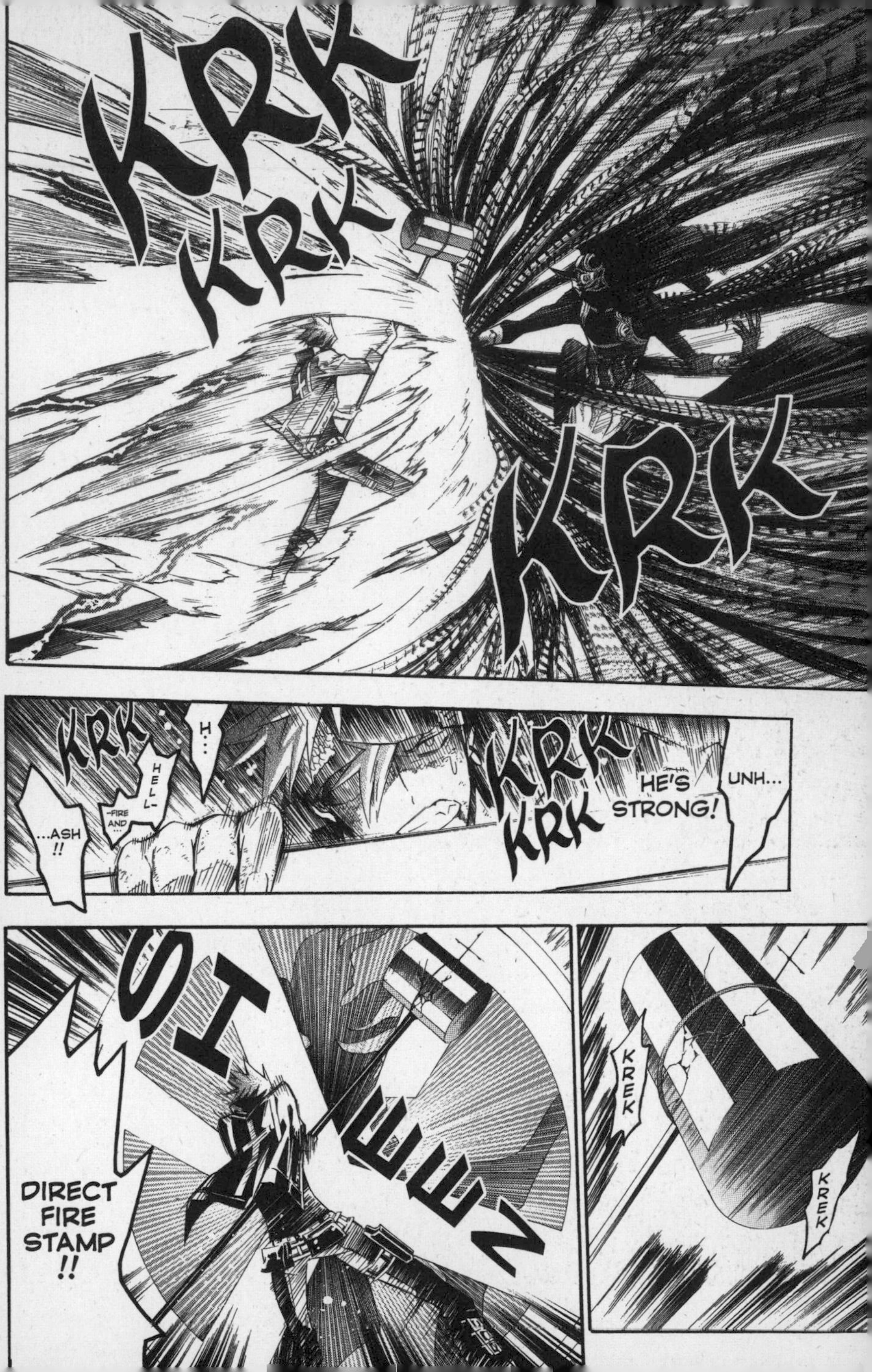
KRK
KRK
KRK
UNH...
HE'S STRONG!
KRK
KRK
H...
HELL-FIRE AND...
...ASH!!
KRK
KREK
KREK
SHWEN
DIRECT FIRE STAMP!!

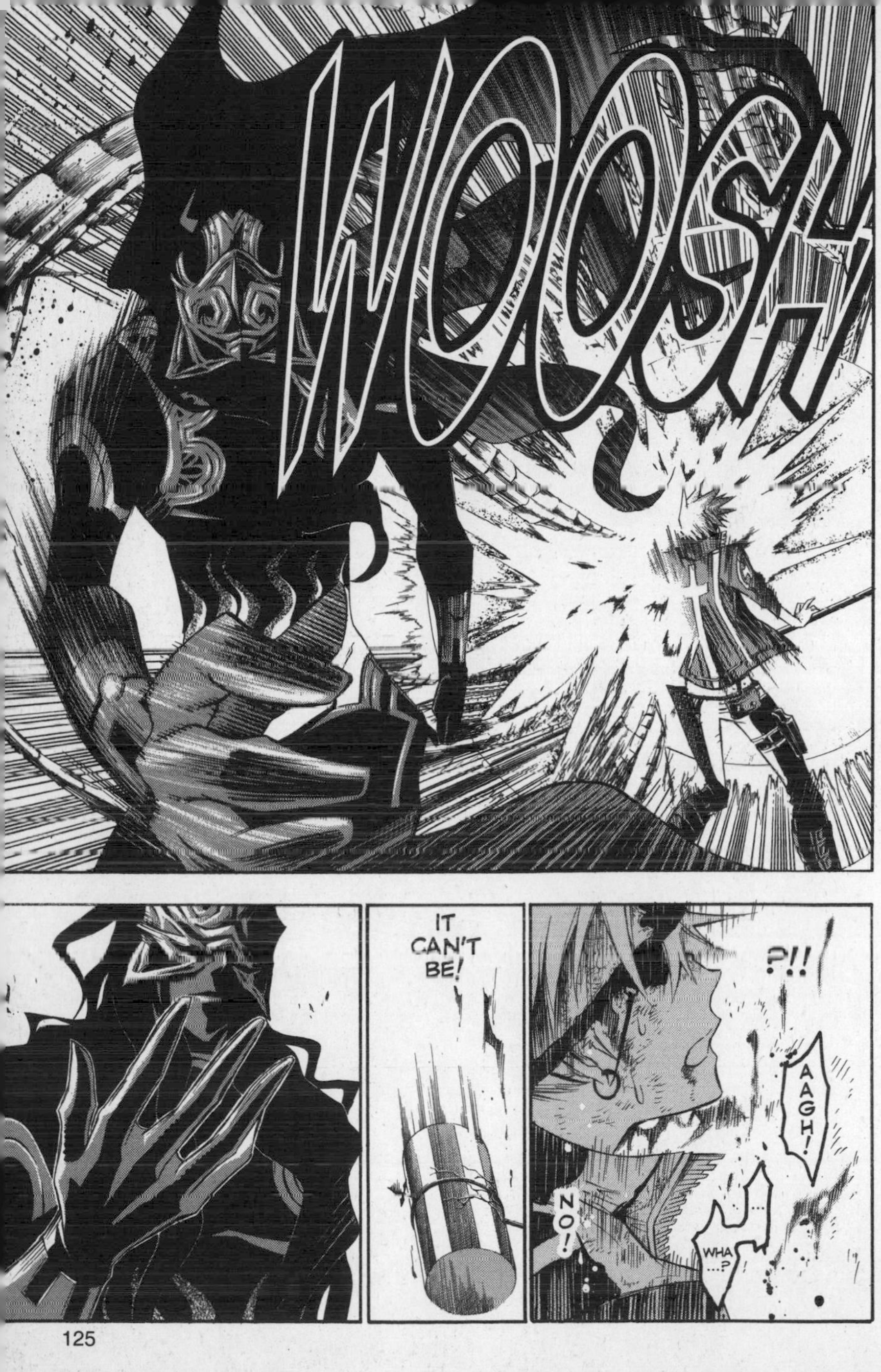
WOOSH
?!!
AAGH!
... WHA ...?
NO!
IT CAN'T BE!

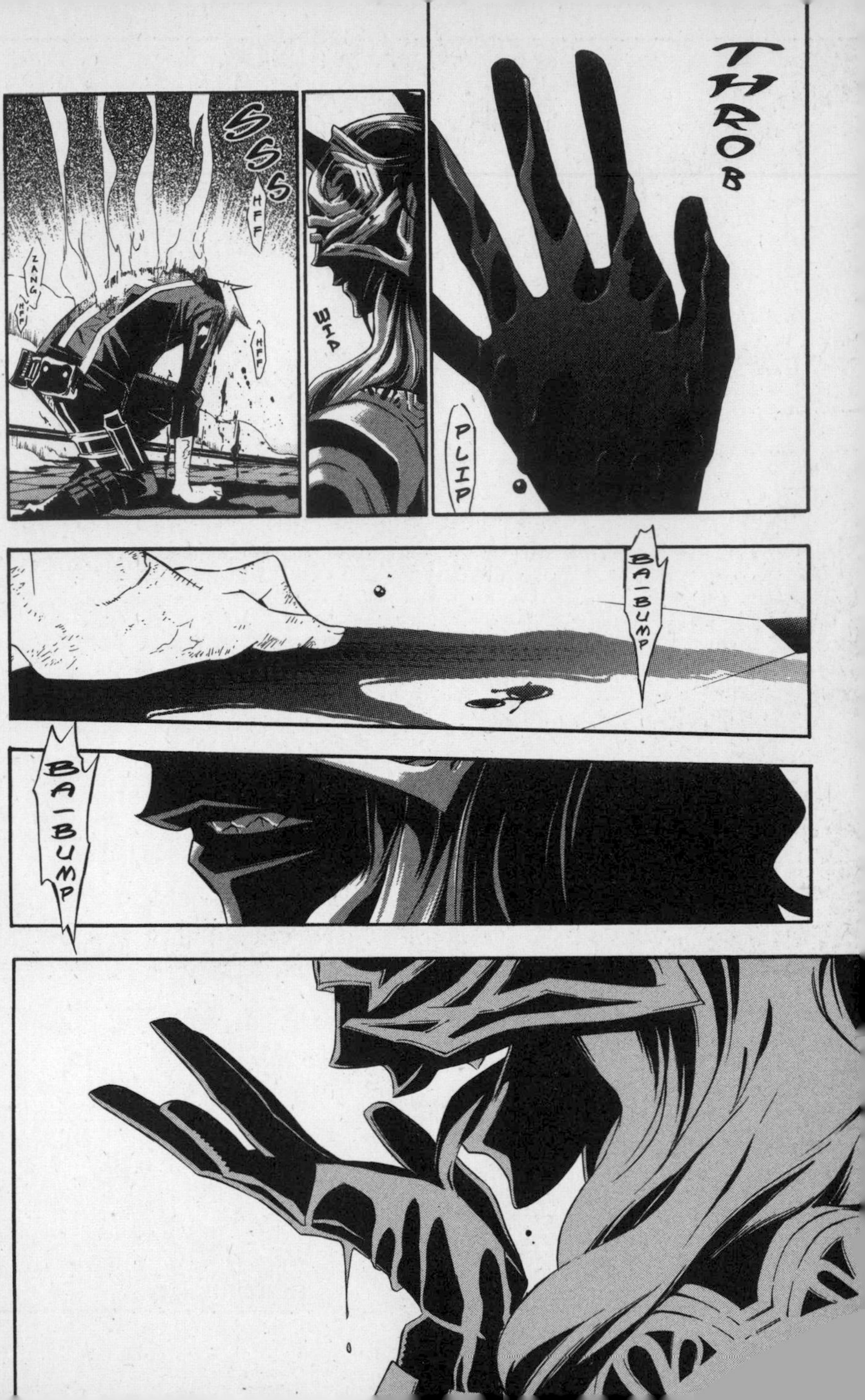
THROB
PLIP
WIP
SSSS
HFF
ZANG
HFF
HFF
BA-BUMP
BA-BUMP

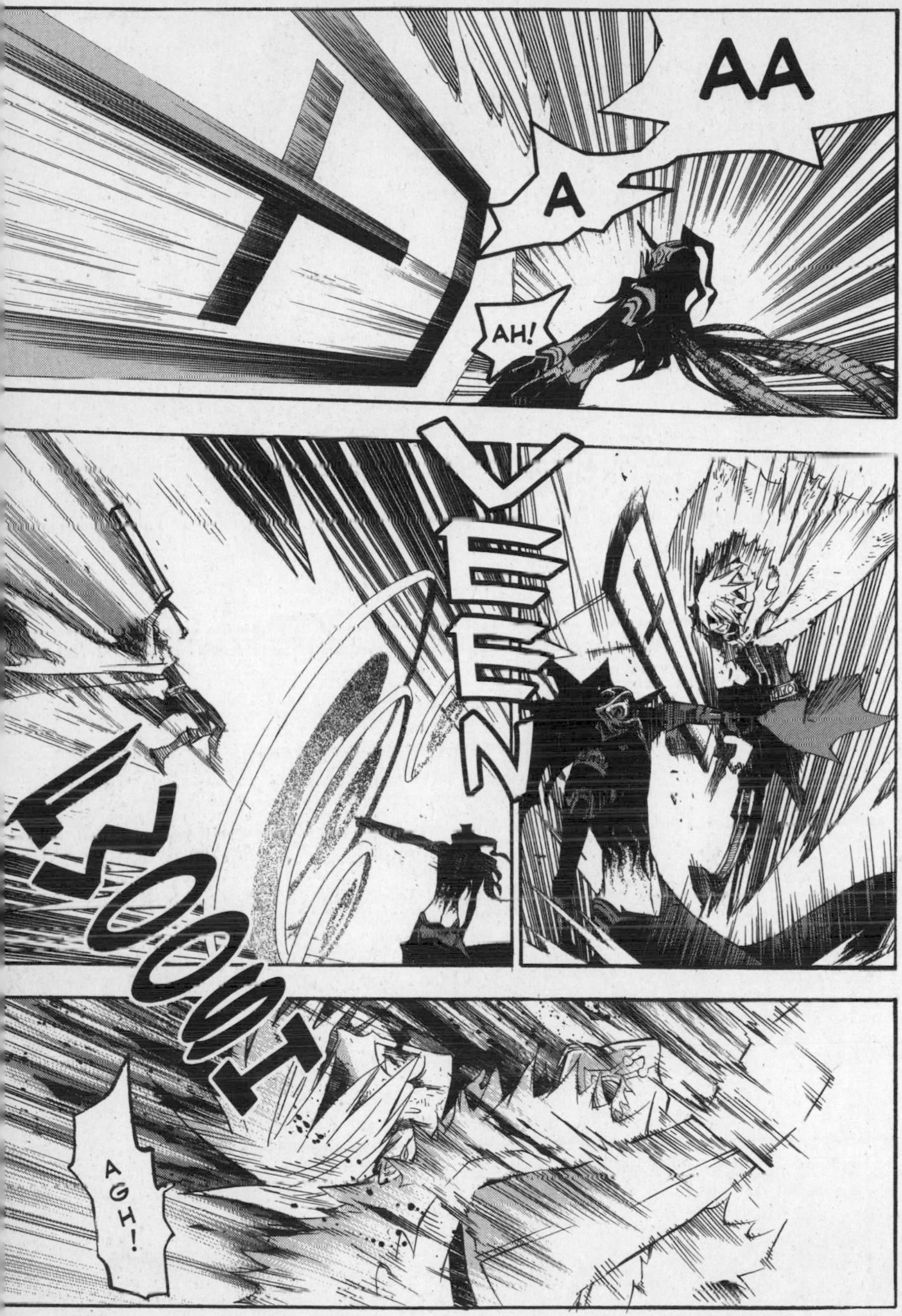
AA
A
AH!
VEEEEN
WOOOT
AGH!

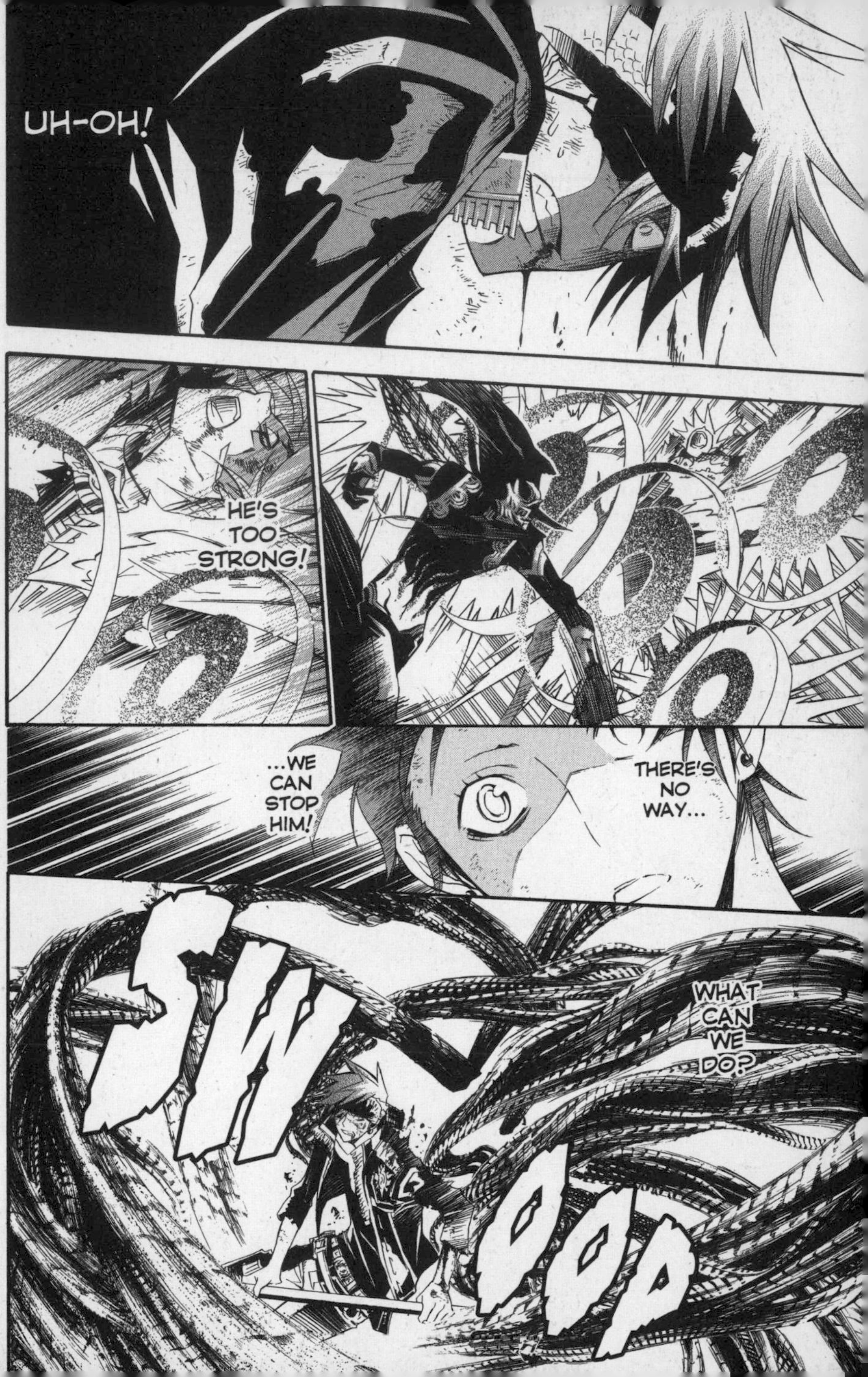
UH-OH!
HE'S TOO STRONG!
THERE'S NO WAY...
...WE CAN STOP HIM!
WHAT CAN WE DO?
SWOOP

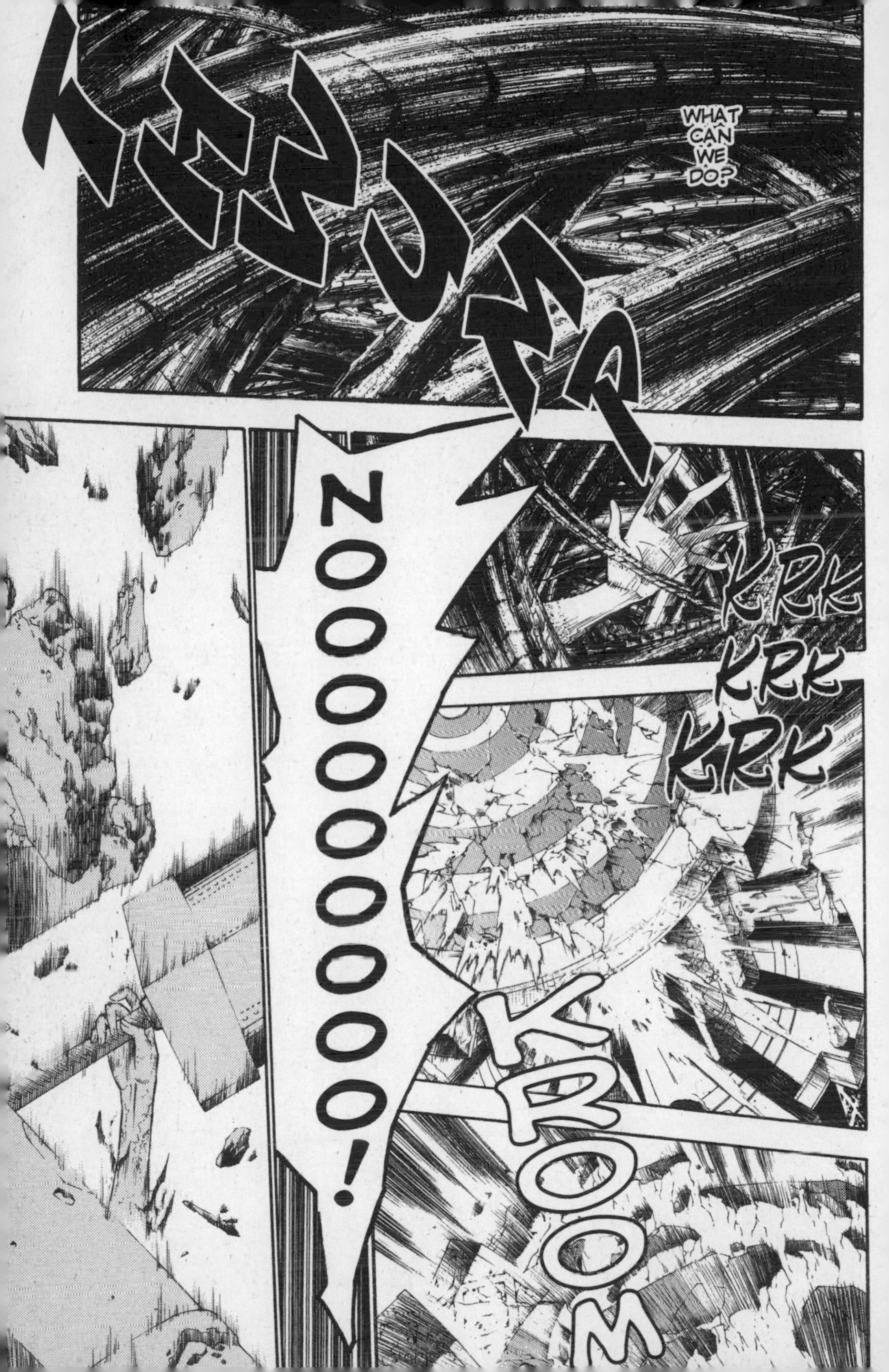
WHAT CAN WE DO?
KRK KRK KRK
NOOOOOOOOO!
KROOM

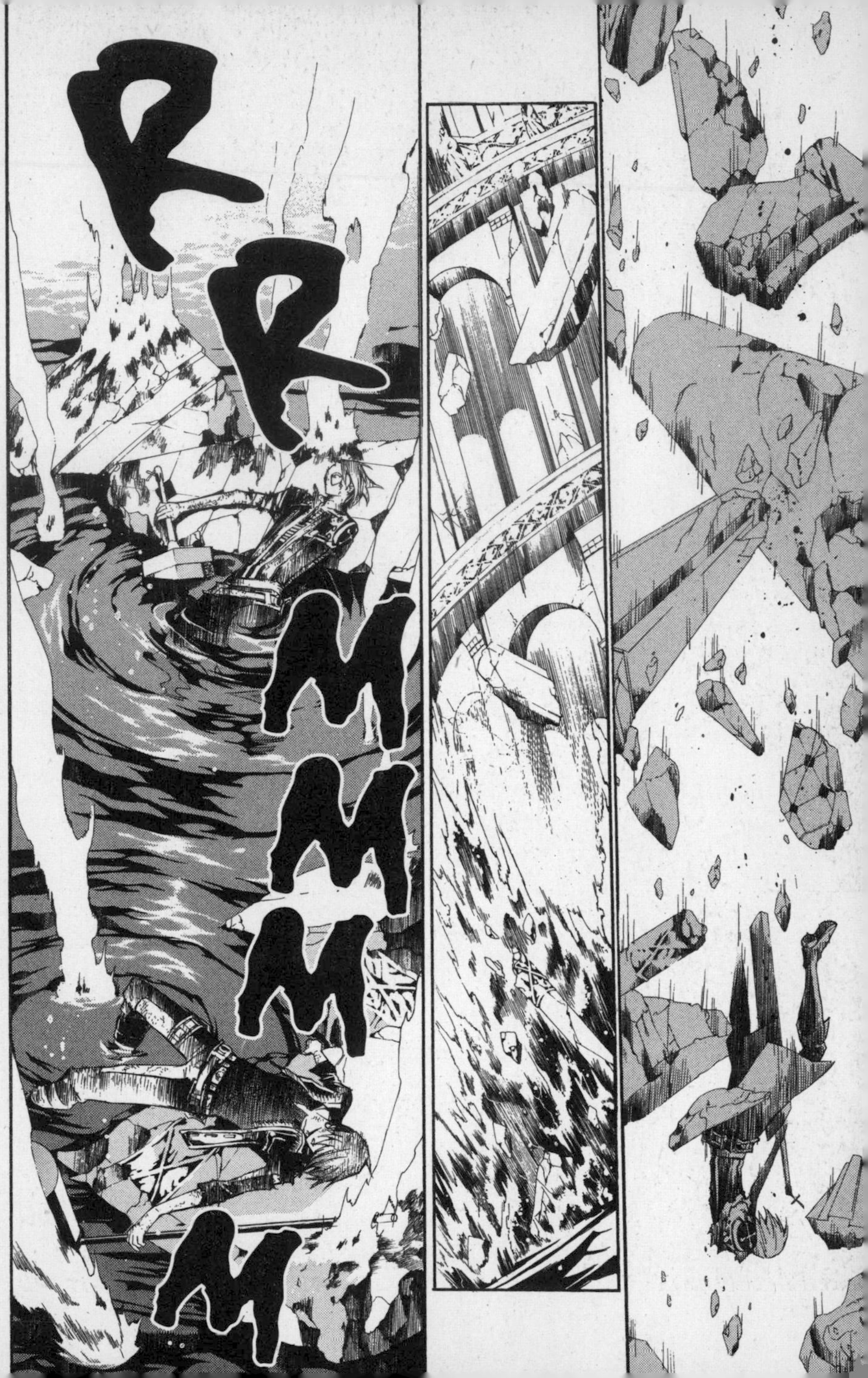
RRMMMM

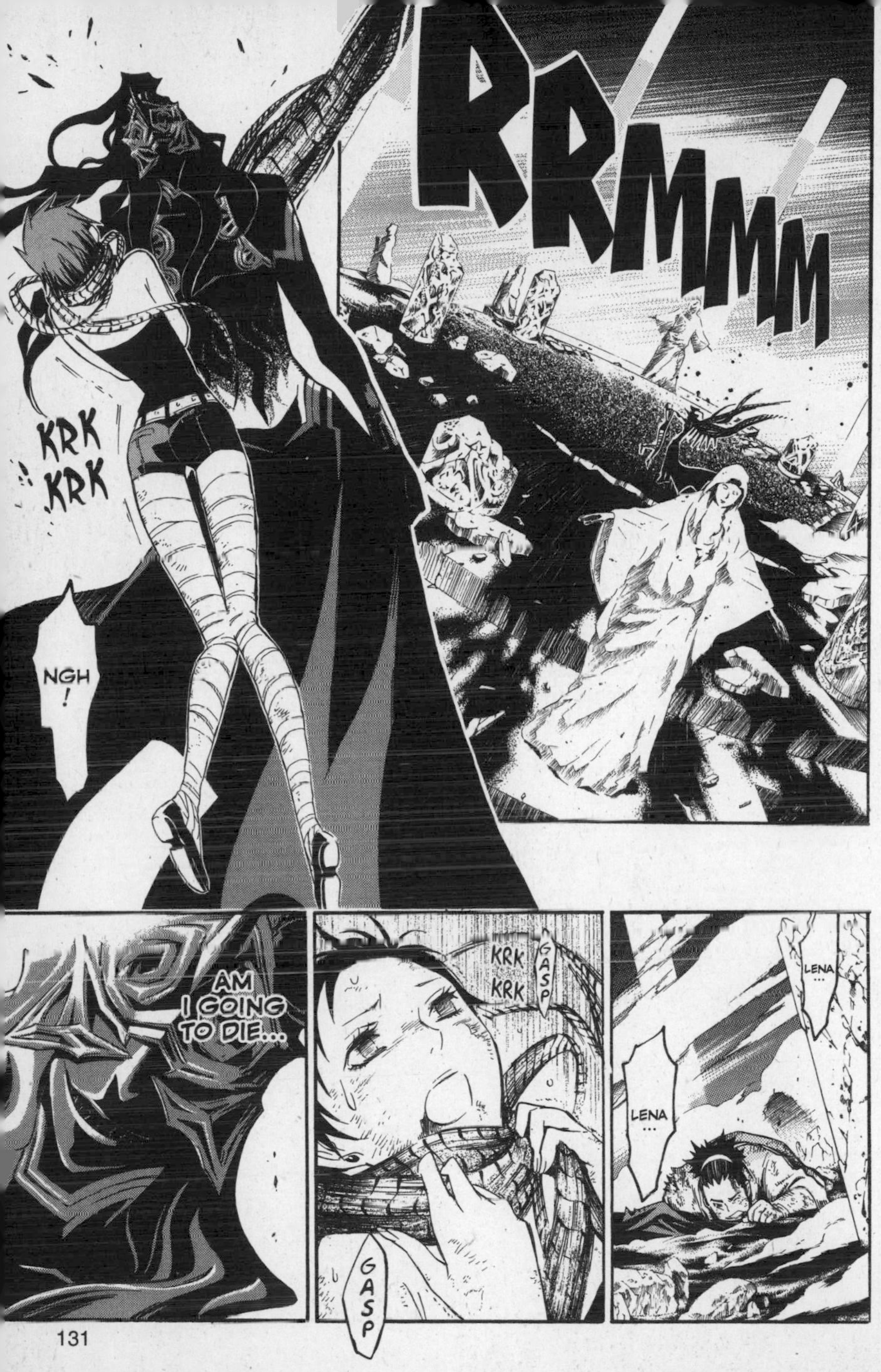
RRMMMM
KRK KRK
NGH!
LENA...
LENA...
KRK KRK
GASP
GASP
AM I GOING TO DIE...

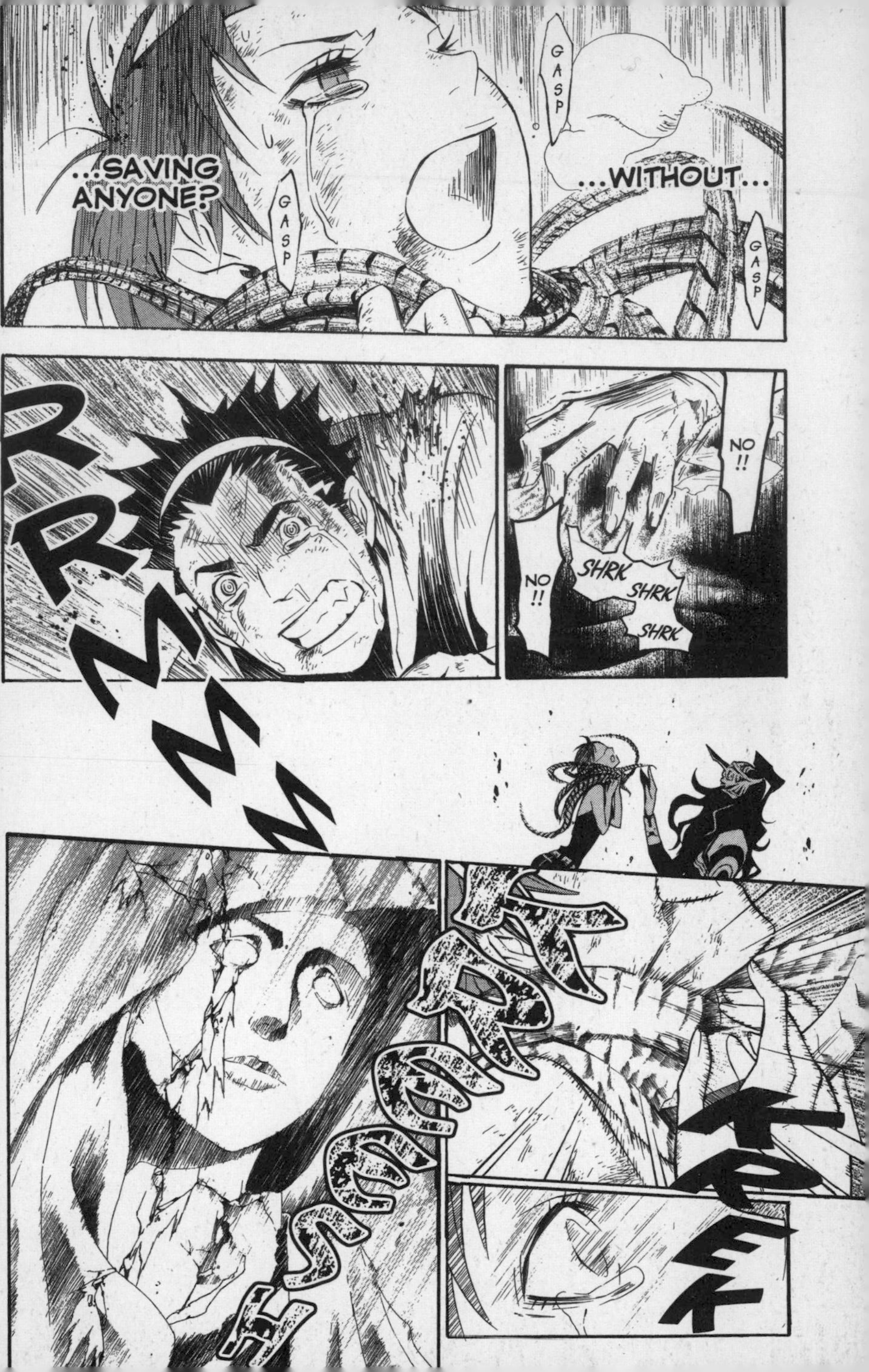
GASP
...WITHOUT...
GASP
...SAVING ANYONE?
GASP
NO!!
SHRK
SHRK
SHRK
NO!!

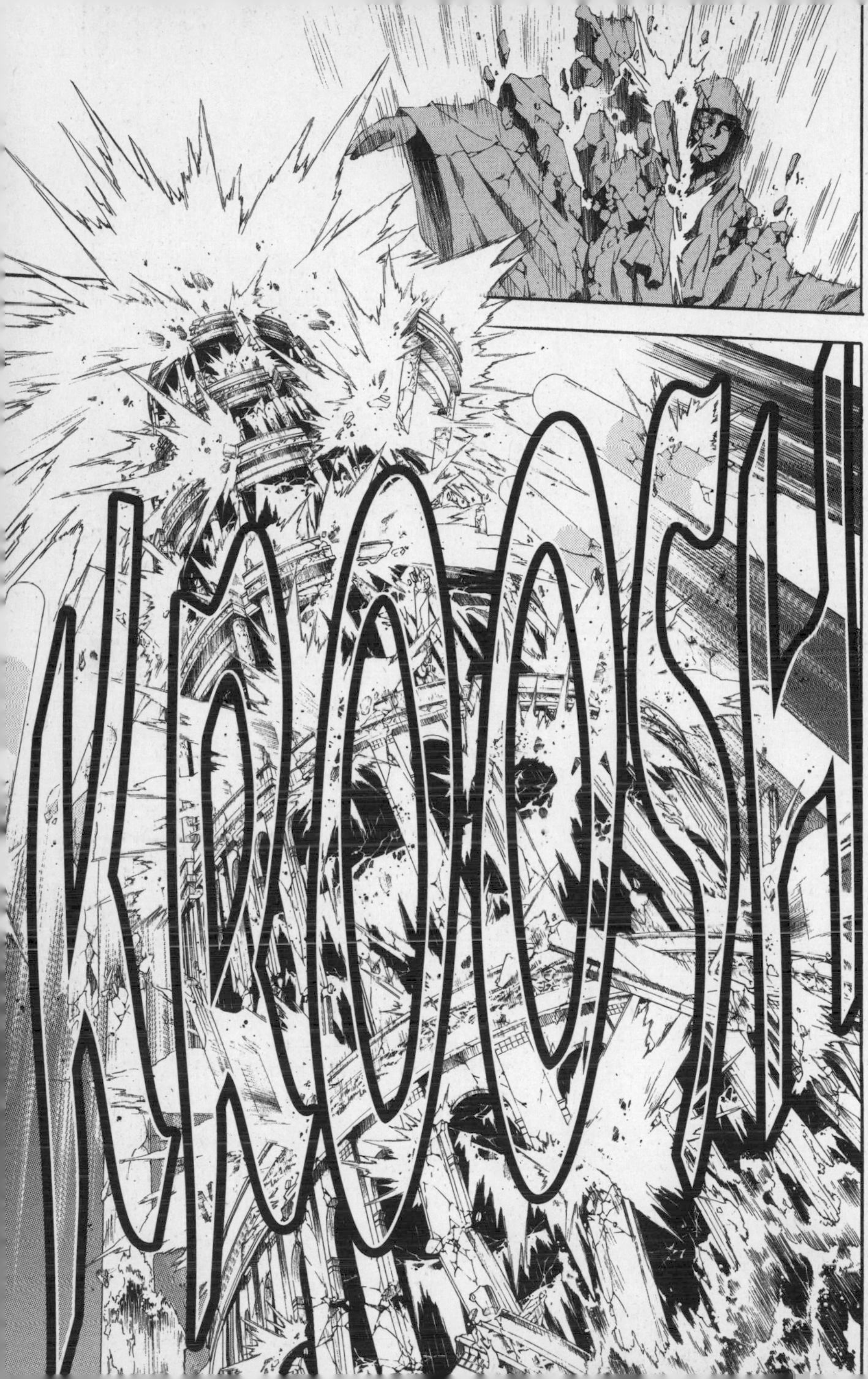
KROOSH

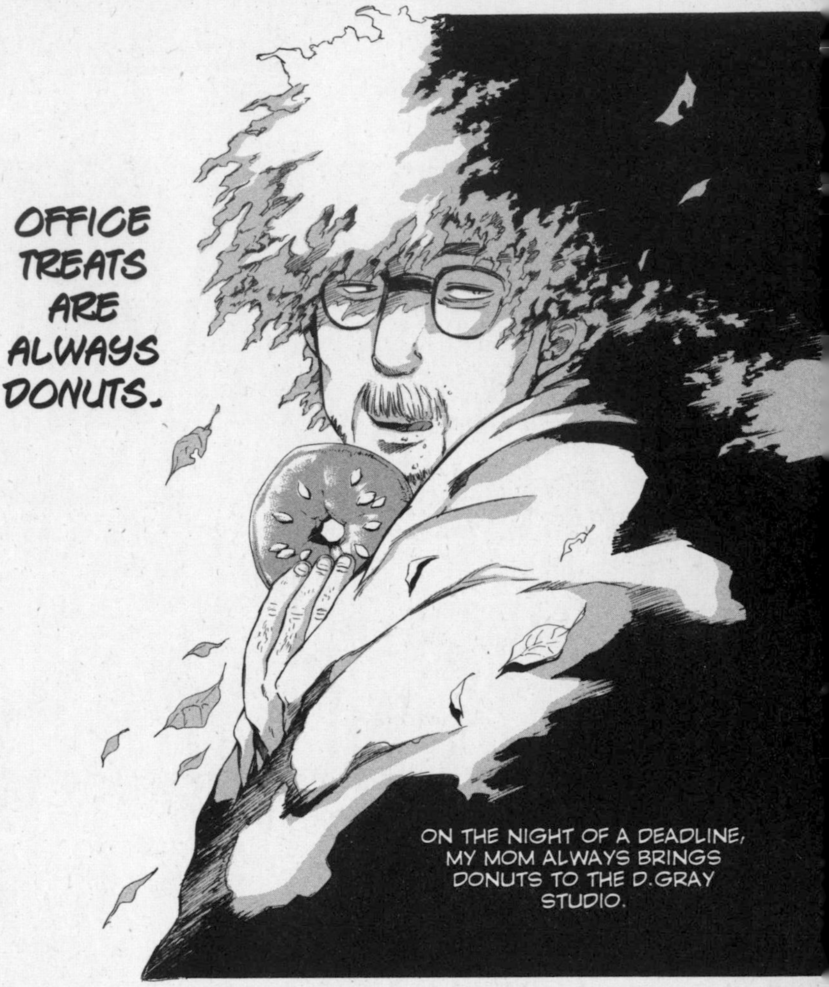
OFFICE TREATS ARE ALWAYS DONUTS.
ON THE NIGHT OF A DEADLINE, MY MOM ALWAYS BRINGS DONUTS TO THE D.GRAY STUDIO.

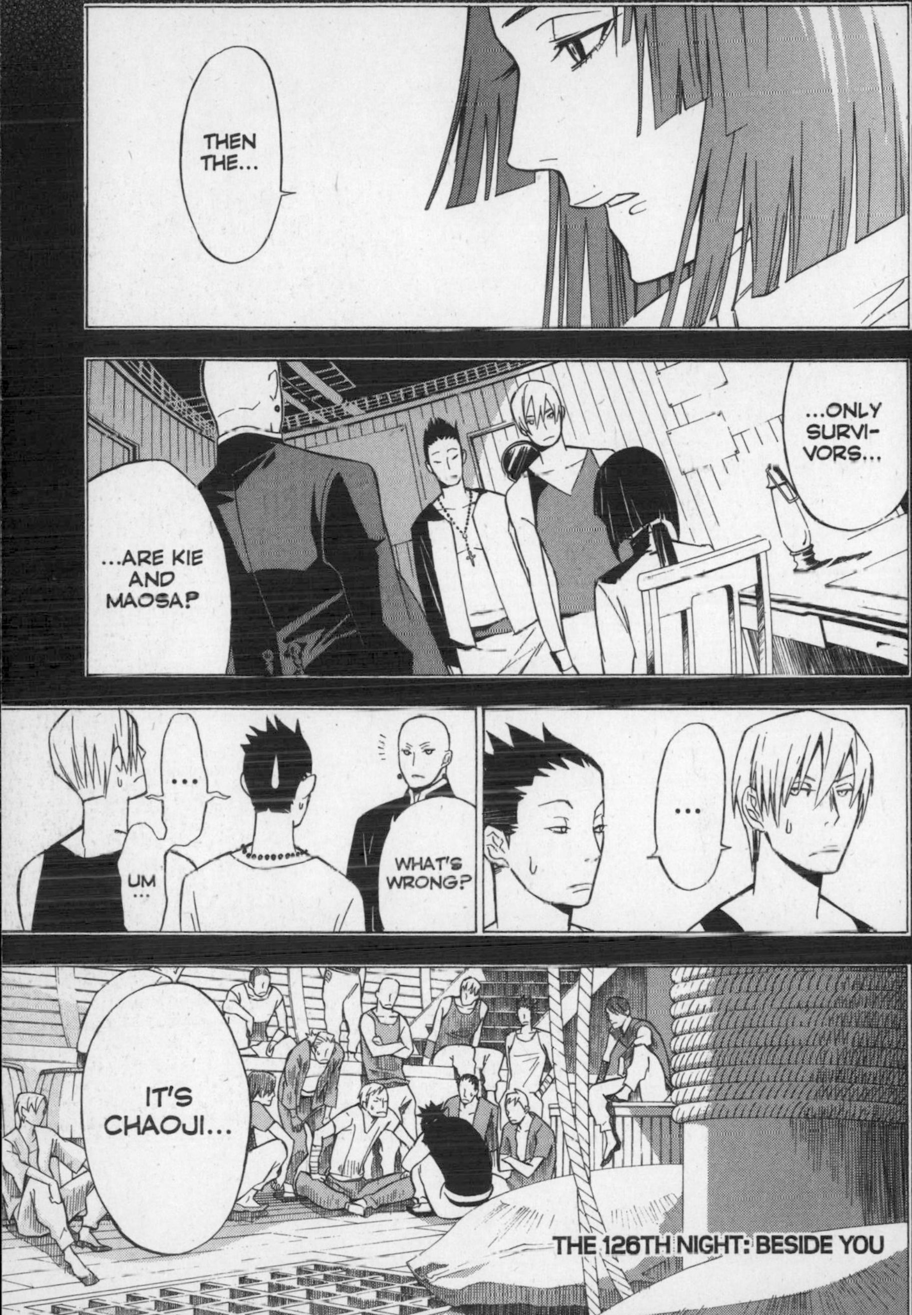
THEN THE...
...ONLY SURVIVORS...
...ARE KIE AND MAOSA?
...
WHAT'S WRONG?
...
UM ...
IT'S CHAOJI...
THE 126TH NIGHT: BESIDE YOU

THE 126TH NIGHT: BESIDE YOU

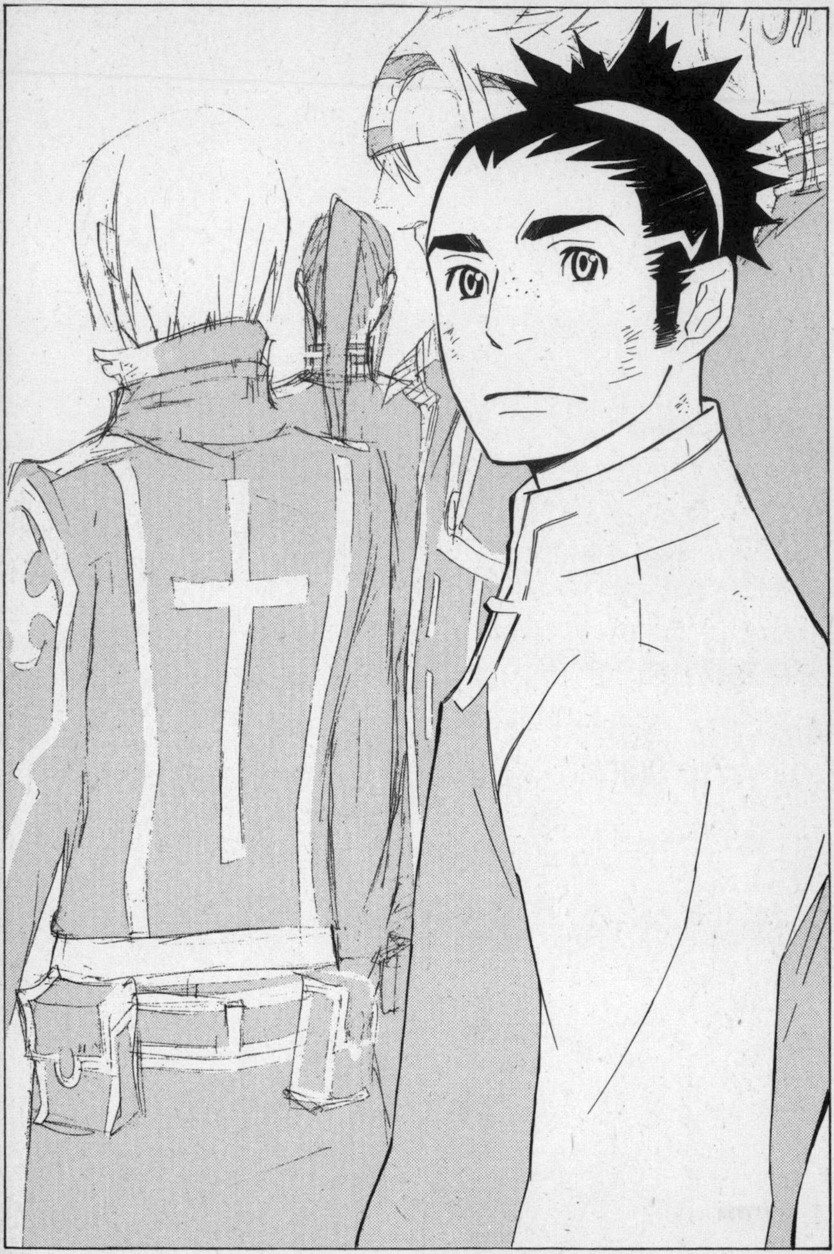

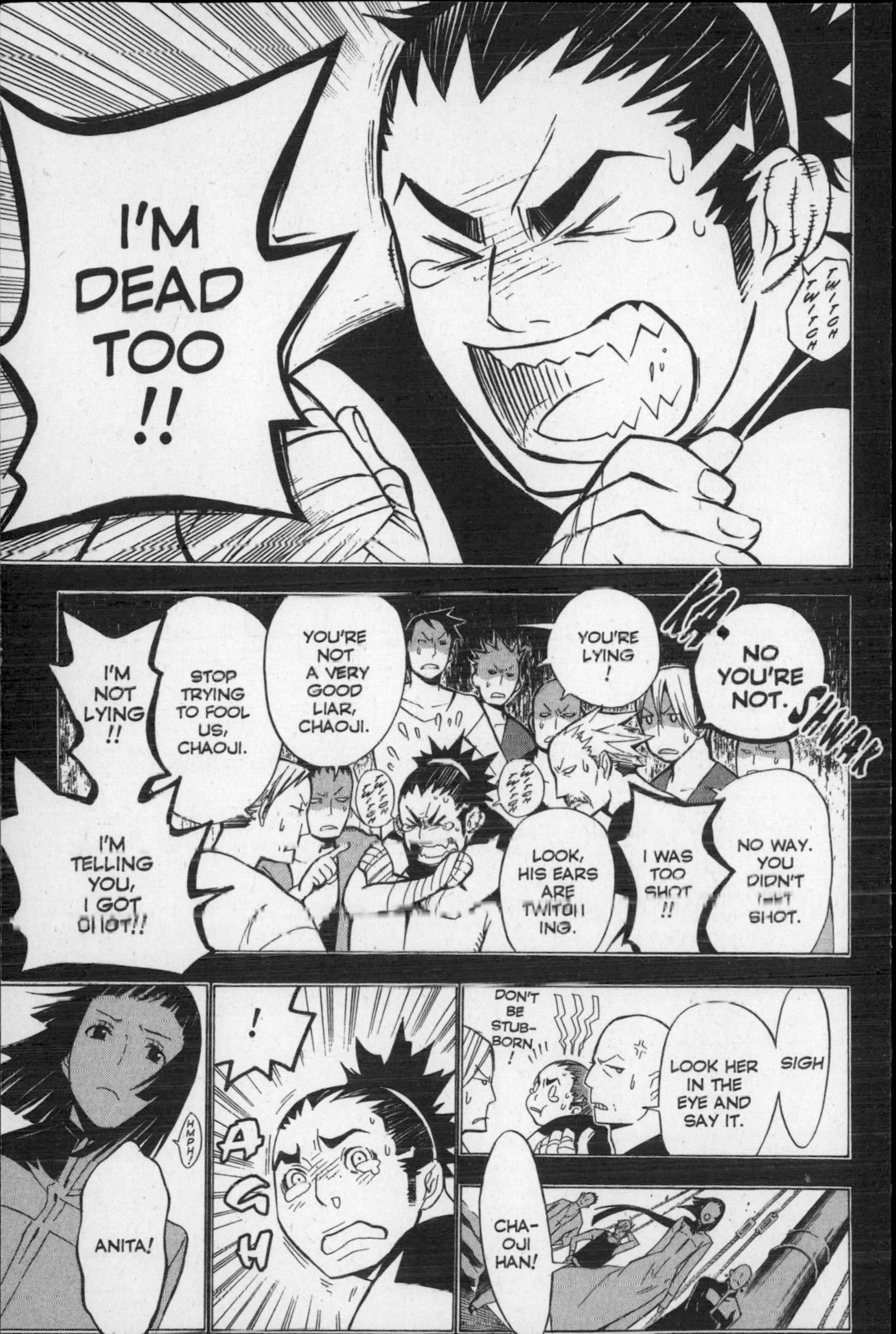
I'M DEAD TOO !!
TWITCH TWITCH
KA-
SHWAK
NO YOU'RE NOT.
YOU'RE LYING !
YOU'RE NOT A VERY GOOD LIAR, CHAOJI.
STOP TRYING TO FOOL US, CHAOJI.
I'M NOT LYING !!
NO WAY. YOU DIDN'T GET SHOT.
I WAS TOO SHOT !!
LOOK, HIS EARS ARE TWITCHING.
I'M TELLING YOU, I GOT SHOT!!
SIGH
LOOK HER IN THE EYE AND SAY IT.
DON'T BE STUBBORN !
CHA-OJI HAN!
!
AGH
HMPH!
ANITA!

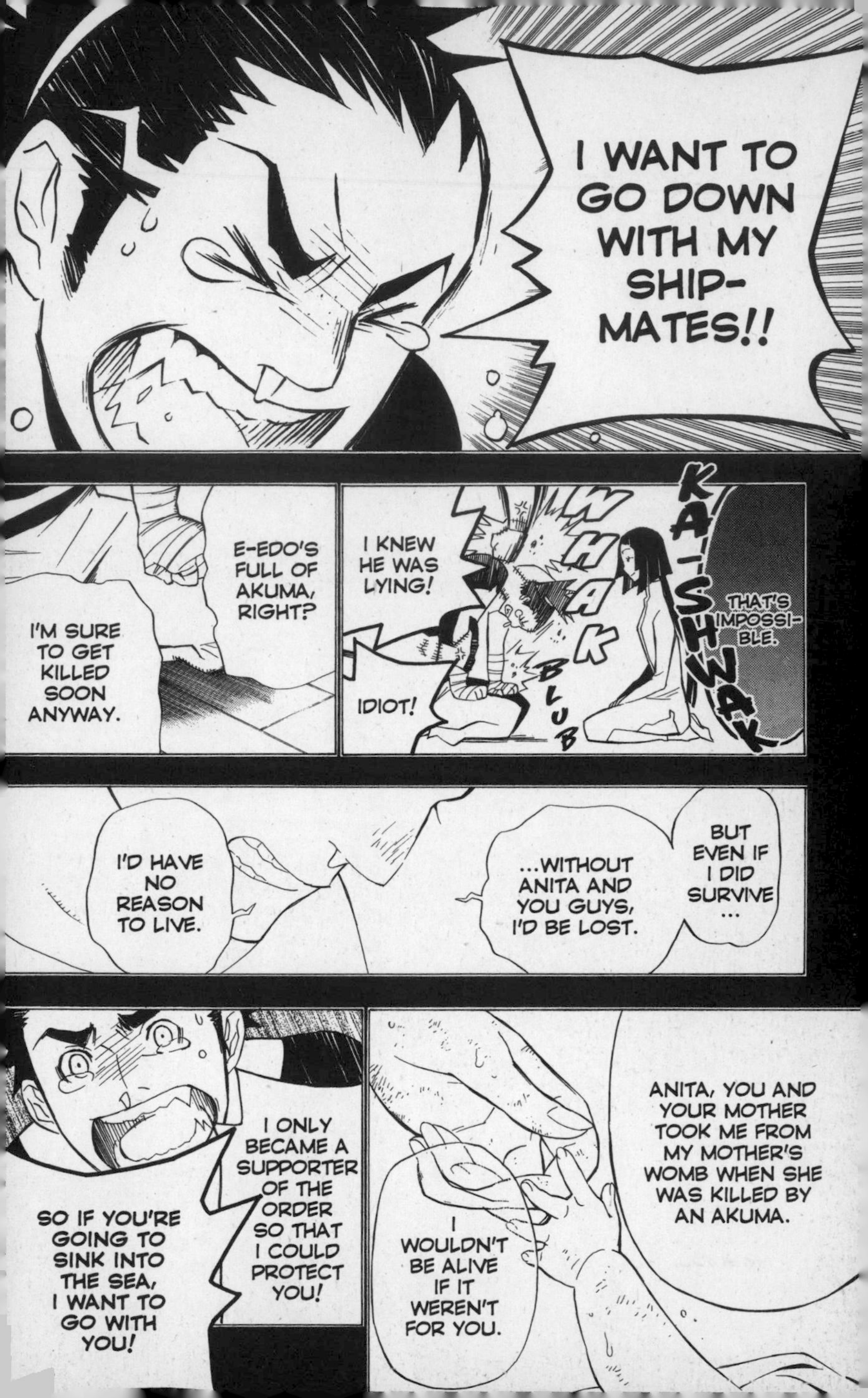
I WANT TO GO DOWN WITH MY SHIP-MATES!!
KA-SHWAK
THAT'S IMPOSSIBLE.
WHAK
I KNEW HE WAS LYING!
BLUB
IDIOT!
E-EDO'S FULL OF AKUMA, RIGHT?
I'M SURE TO GET KILLED SOON ANYWAY.
BUT EVEN IF I DID SURVIVE...
...WITHOUT ANITA AND YOU GUYS, I'D BE LOST.
I'D HAVE NO REASON TO LIVE.
ANITA, YOU AND YOUR MOTHER TOOK ME FROM MY MOTHER'S WOMB WHEN SHE WAS KILLED BY AN AKUMA.
I WOULDN'T BE ALIVE IF IT WEREN'T FOR YOU.
I ONLY BECAME A SUPPORTER OF THE ORDER SO THAT I COULD PROTECT YOU!
SO IF YOU'RE GOING TO SINK INTO THE SEA, I WANT TO GO WITH YOU!

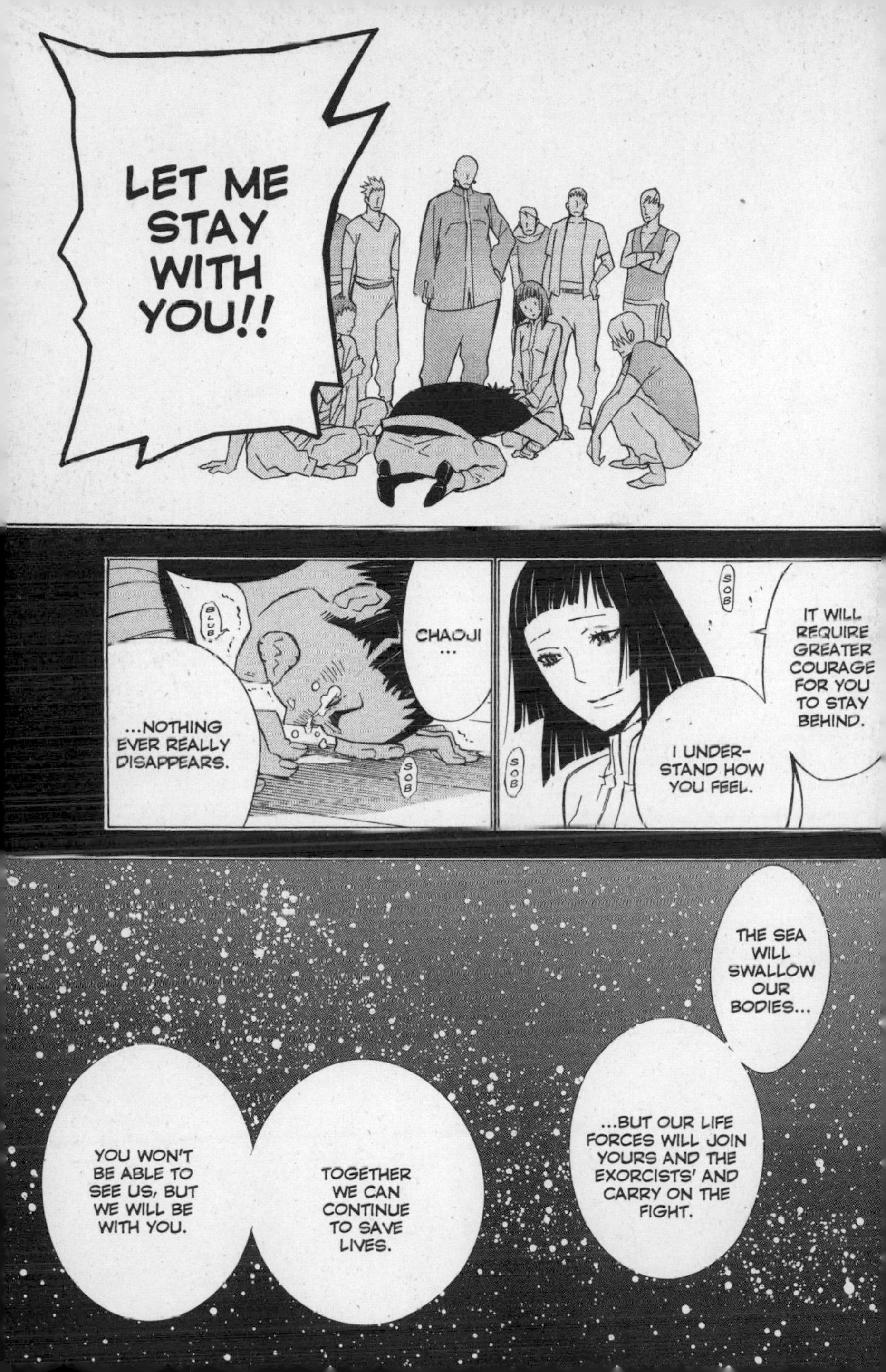
LET ME STAY WITH YOU!!
SOB
IT WILL REQUIRE GREATER COURAGE FOR YOU TO STAY BEHIND.
I UNDER-STAND HOW YOU FEEL.
SOB
BLUB
CHAOJI ...
...NOTHING EVER REALLY DISAPPEARS.
SOB
THE SEA WILL SWALLOW OUR BODIES...
...BUT OUR LIFE FORCES WILL JOIN YOURS AND THE EXORCISTS' AND CARRY ON THE FIGHT.
TOGETHER WE CAN CONTINUE TO SAVE LIVES.
YOU WON'T BE ABLE TO SEE US, BUT WE WILL BE WITH YOU.

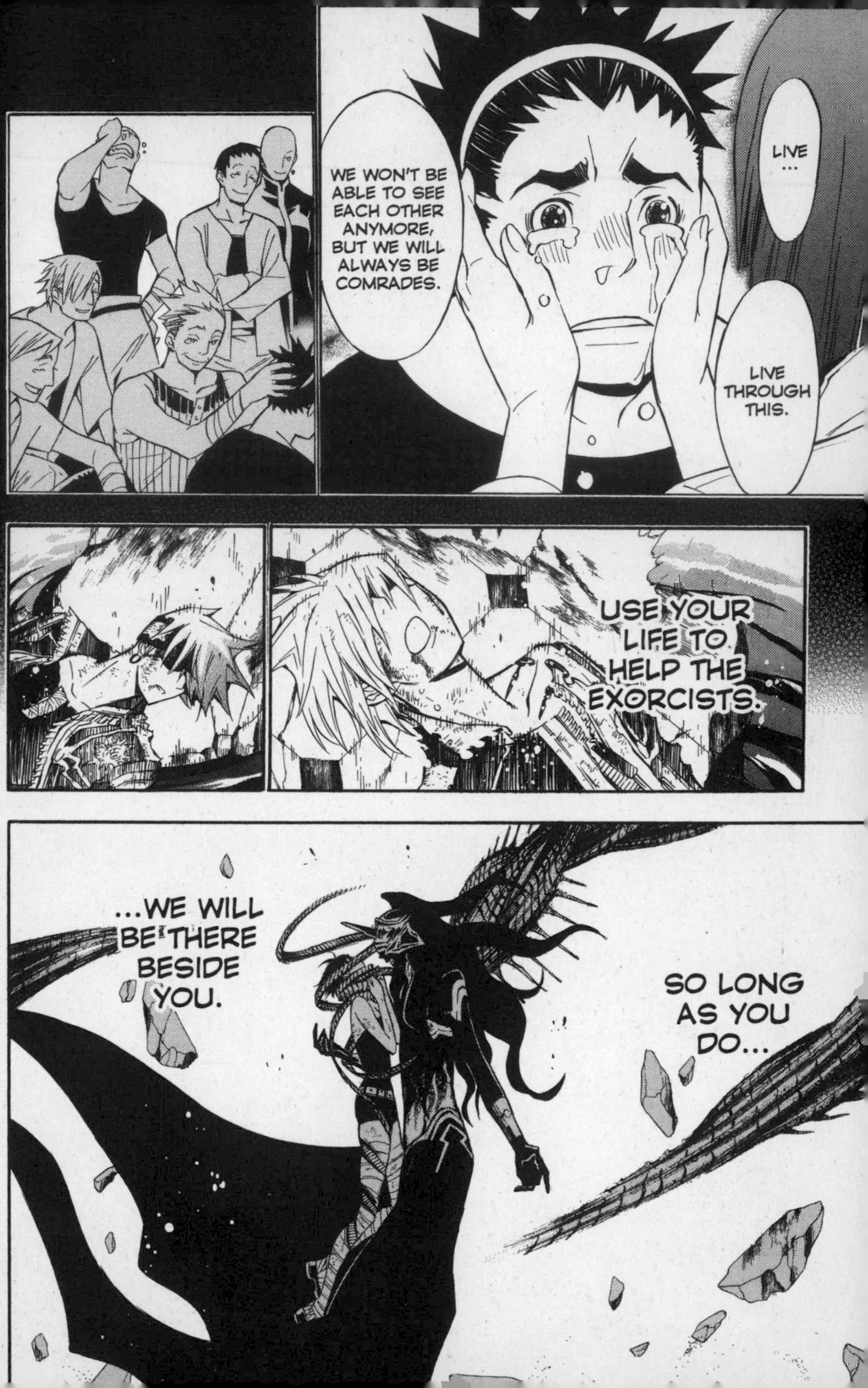
LIVE ...
LIVE THROUGH THIS.
WE WON'T BE ABLE TO SEE EACH OTHER ANYMORE, BUT WE WILL ALWAYS BE COMRADES.
USE YOUR LIFE TO HELP THE EXORCISTS.
SO LONG AS YOU DO...
...WE WILL BE THERE BESIDE YOU.

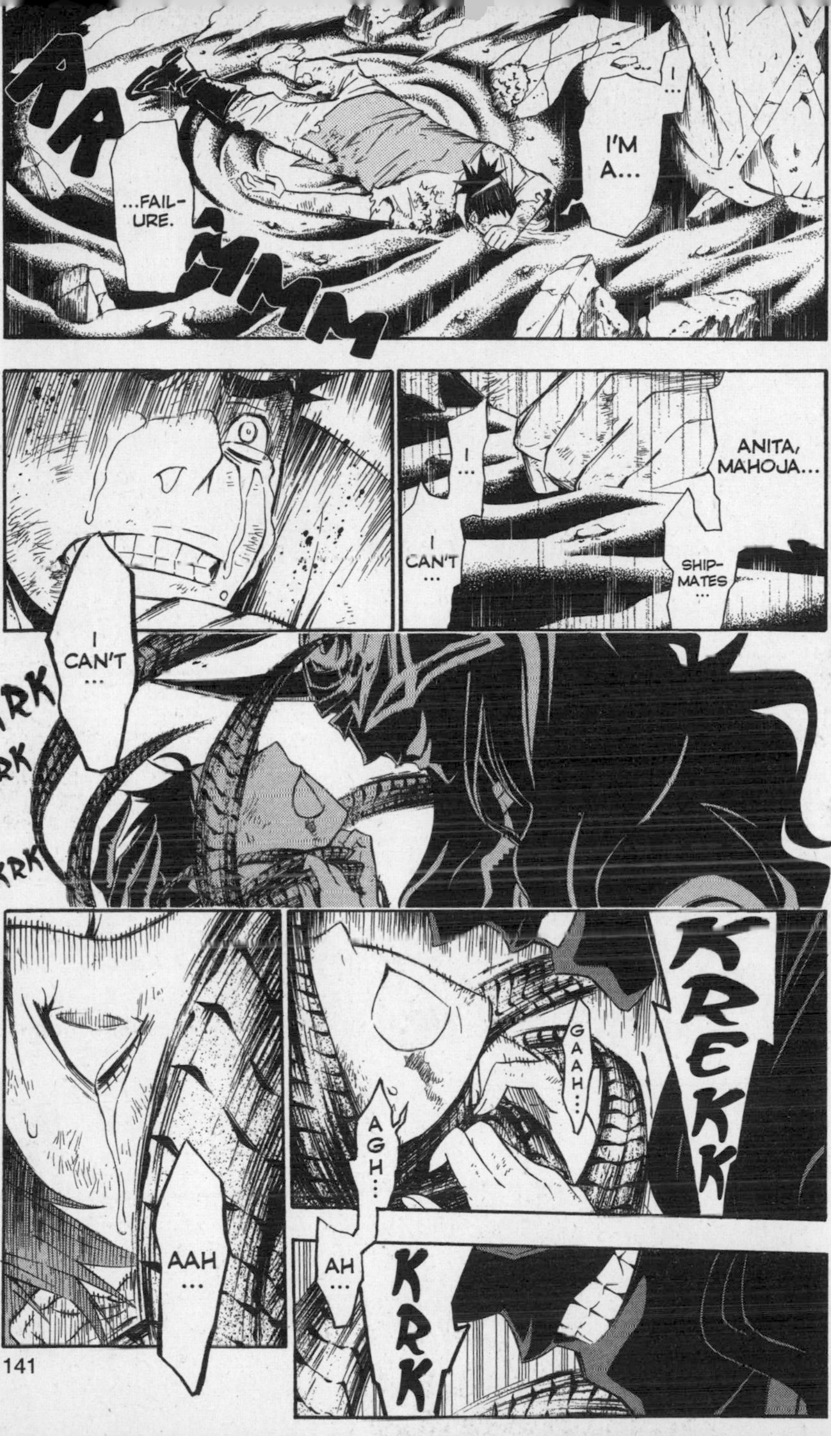
I...
I'M A...
...FAIL-URE.
RRUMMM
ANITA, MAHOJA...
SHIP-MATES...
I...
I CAN'T...
I CAN'T...
KRK KRK KRK
KREKK
GAAH...
AGH...
AAH...
AH...
KRK

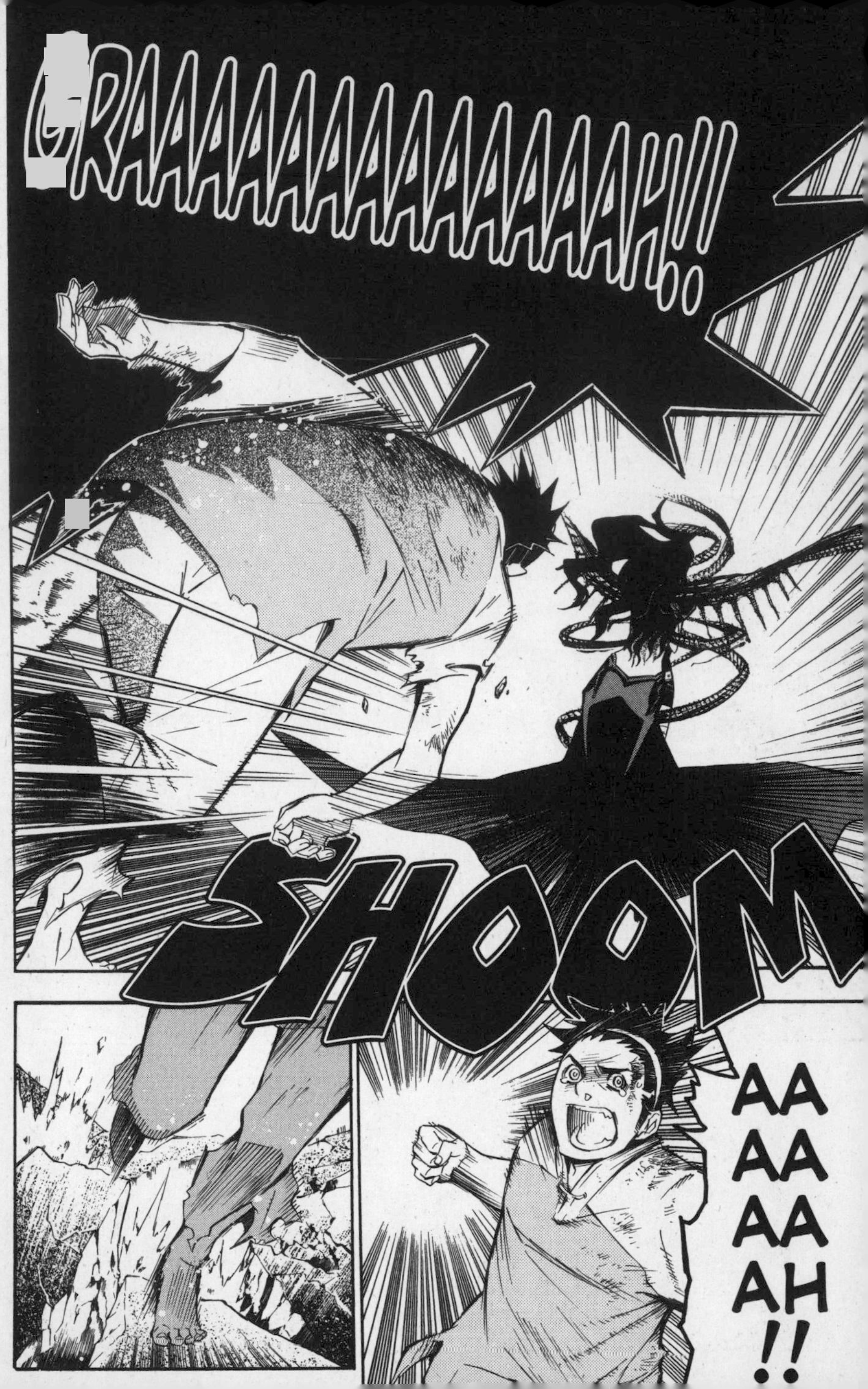
GRAAAAAAAAAAAAAH!!
SHOOM
AAAAAAAH!!

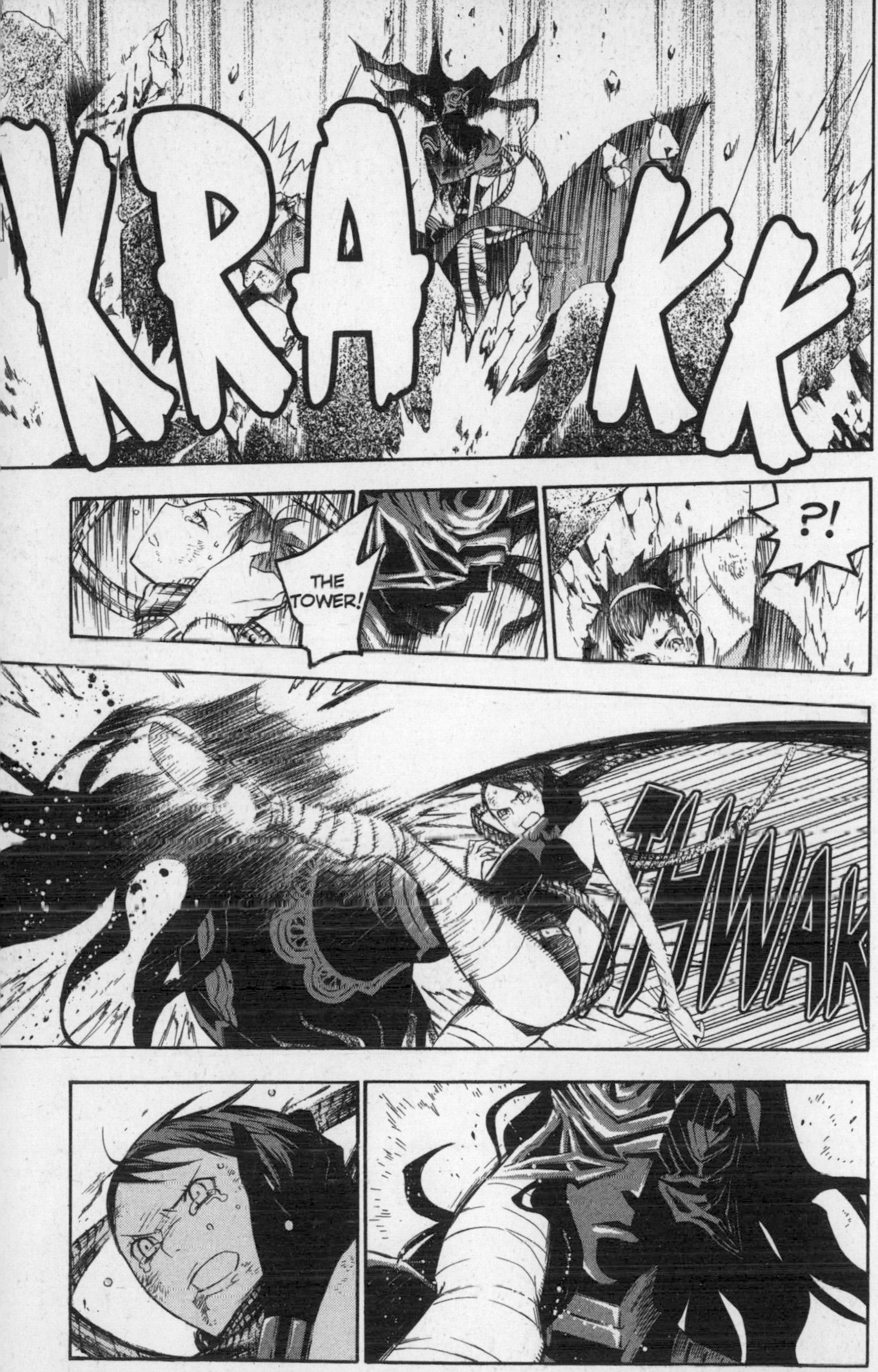
KRAKK
?!
THE TOWER!
THWAK

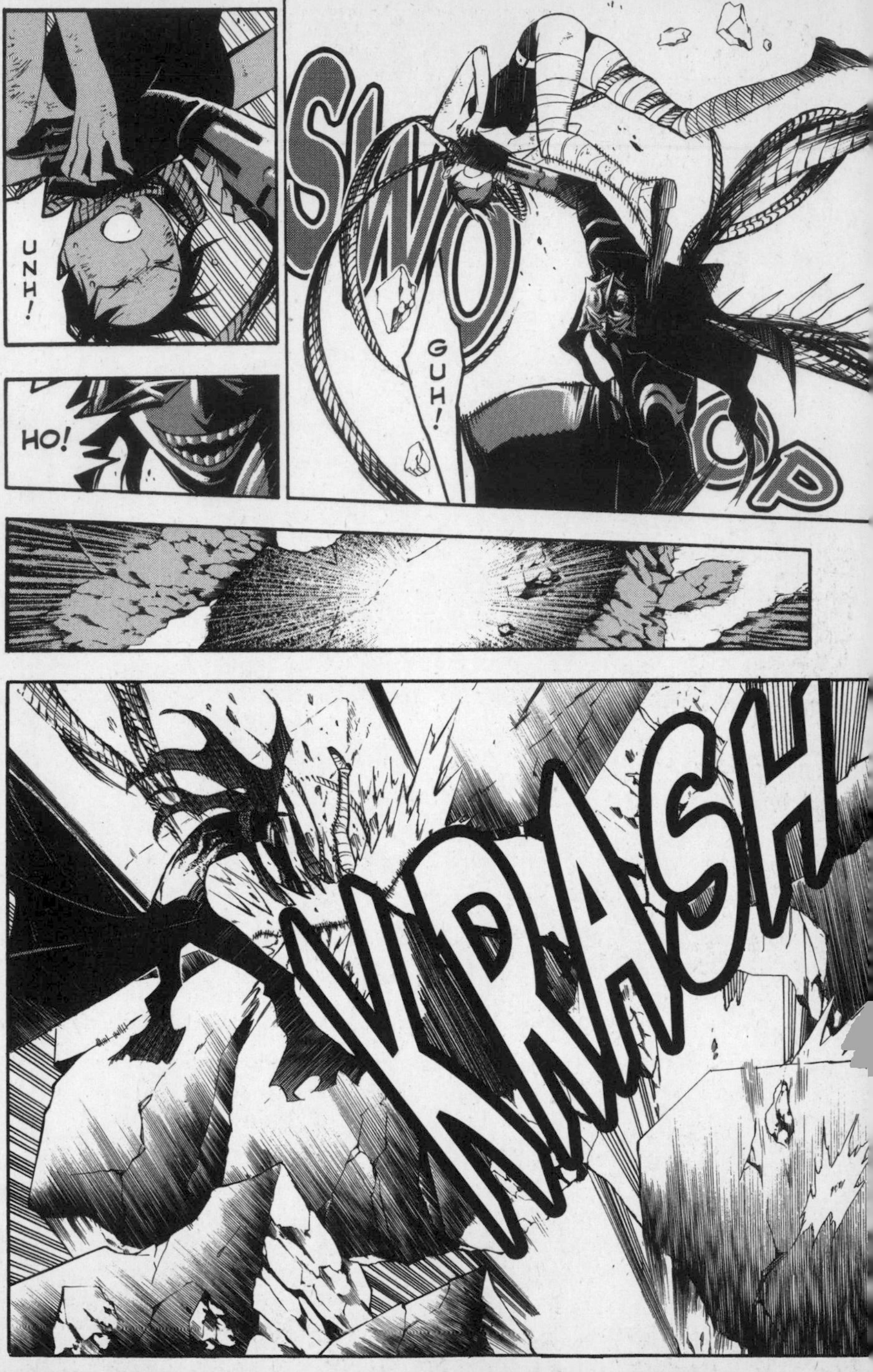
SWOOP
GUH!
UNH!
HO!
KRASH

READ THIS WAY

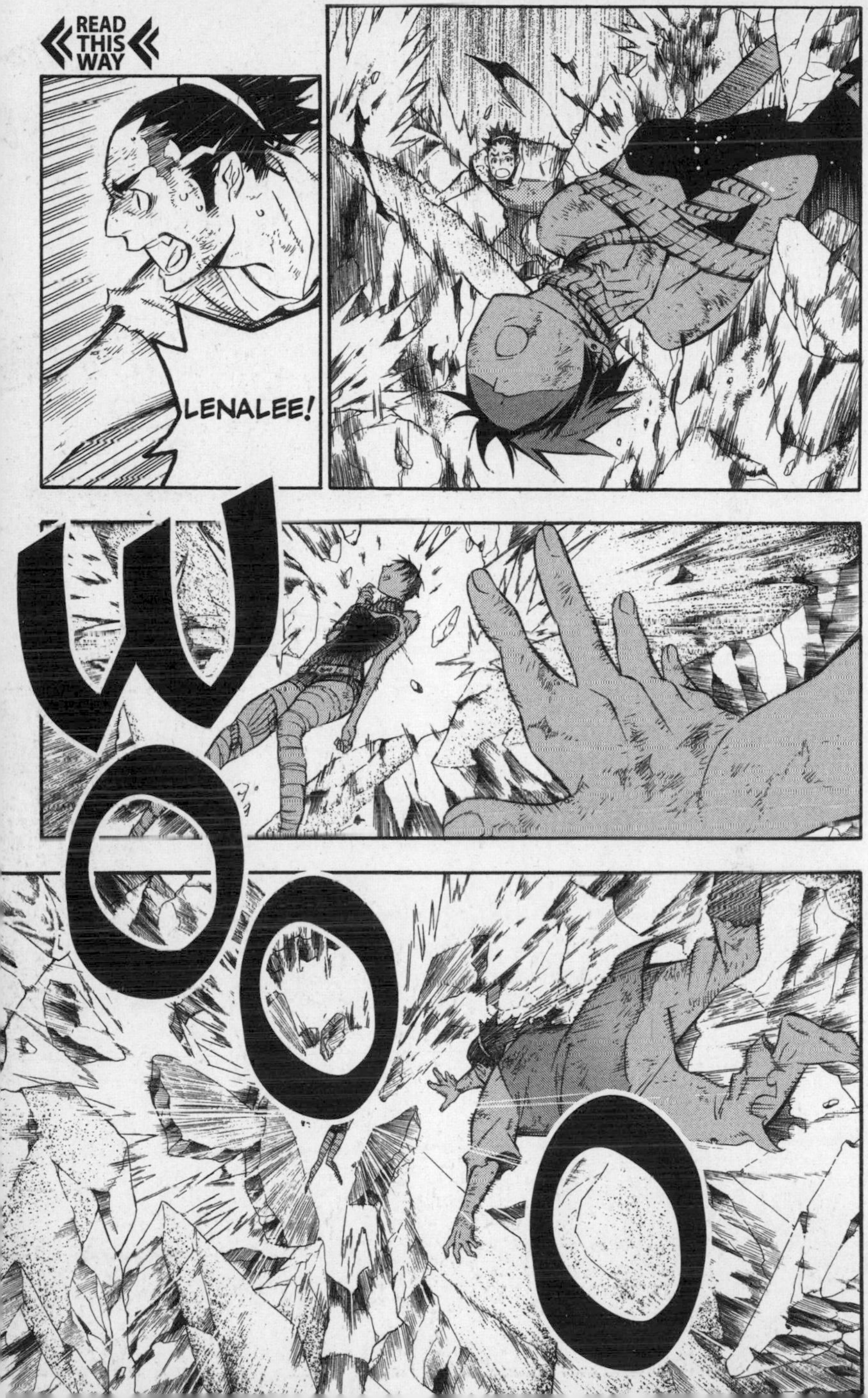
LENALEE!
WOOO

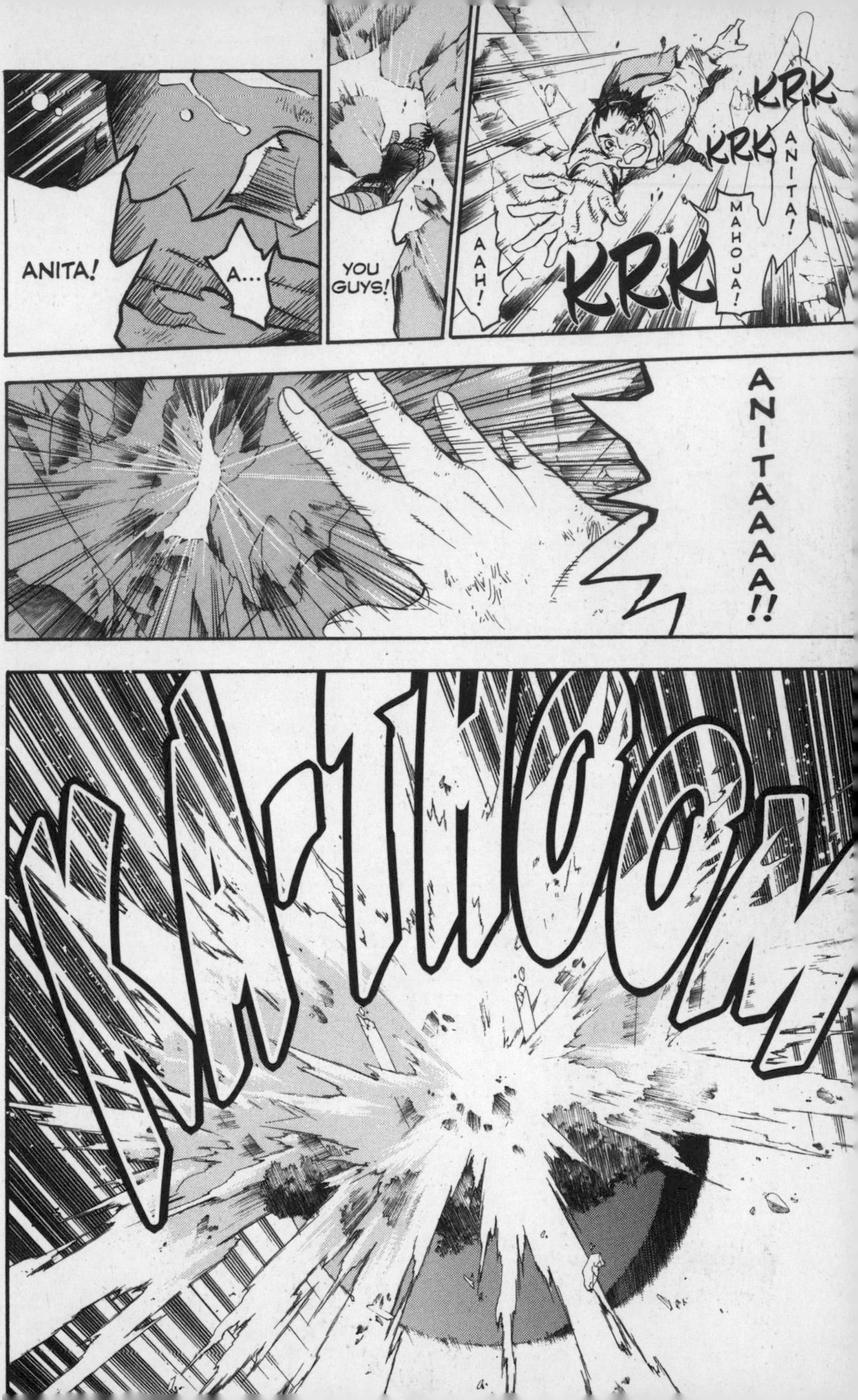
KRK
KRK
ANITA!
MAHOJA!
KRK
AAH!
YOU GUYS!
A...
ANITA!
ANITAAAAA!!

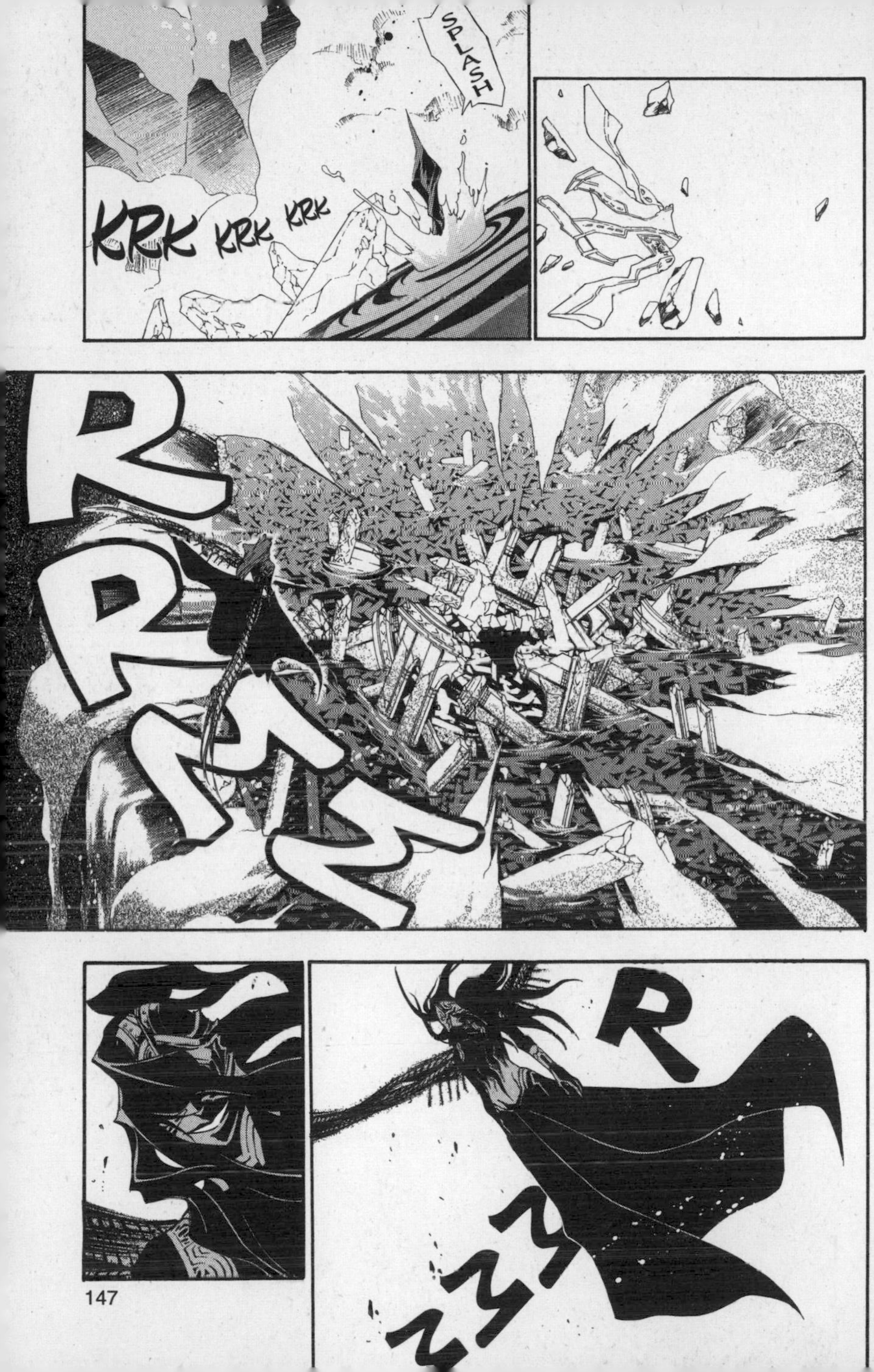
SPLASH
KRK KRK KRK
RRMM
RMMM

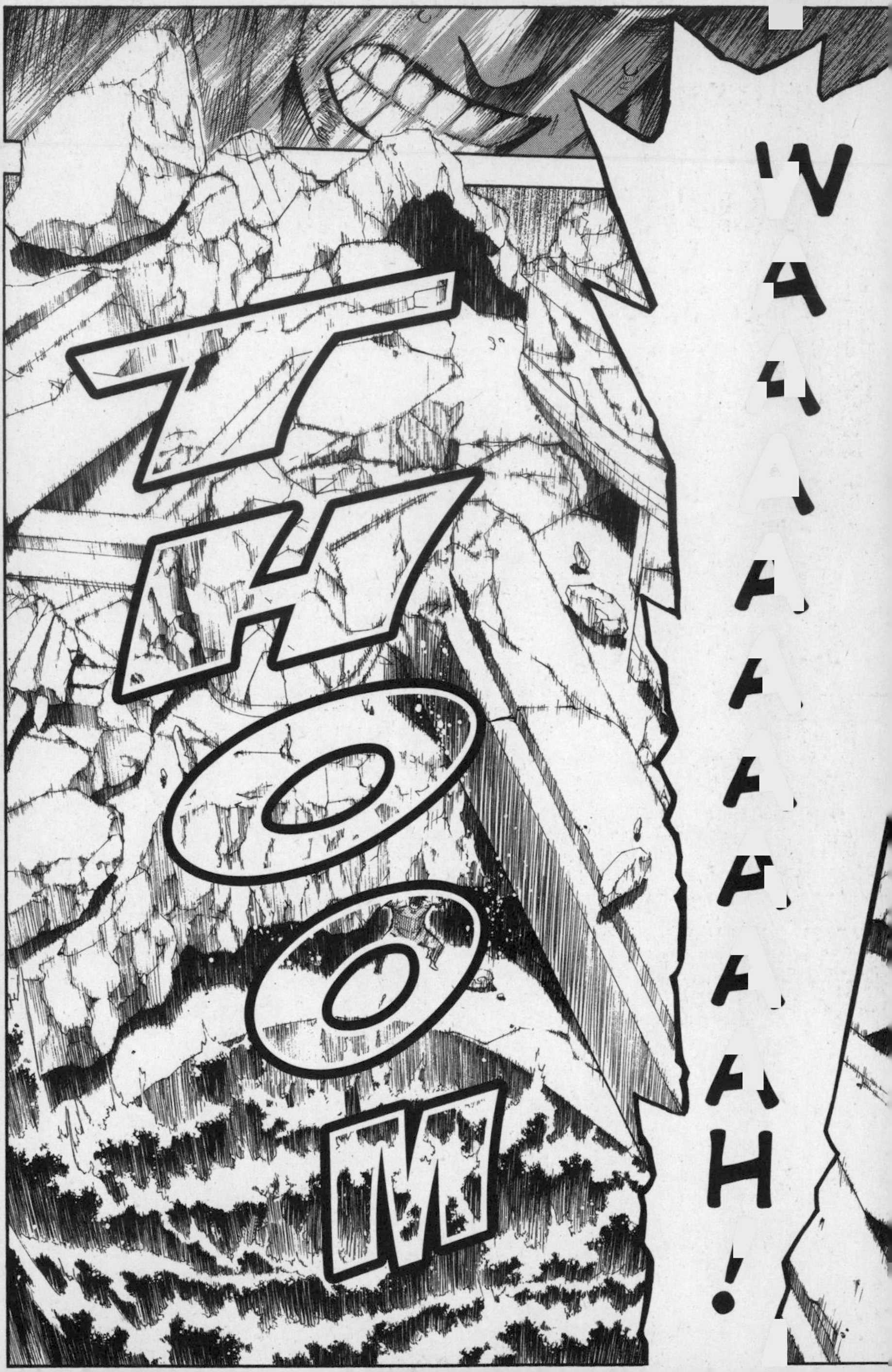
WAAAAAAAAAH!
THOOM

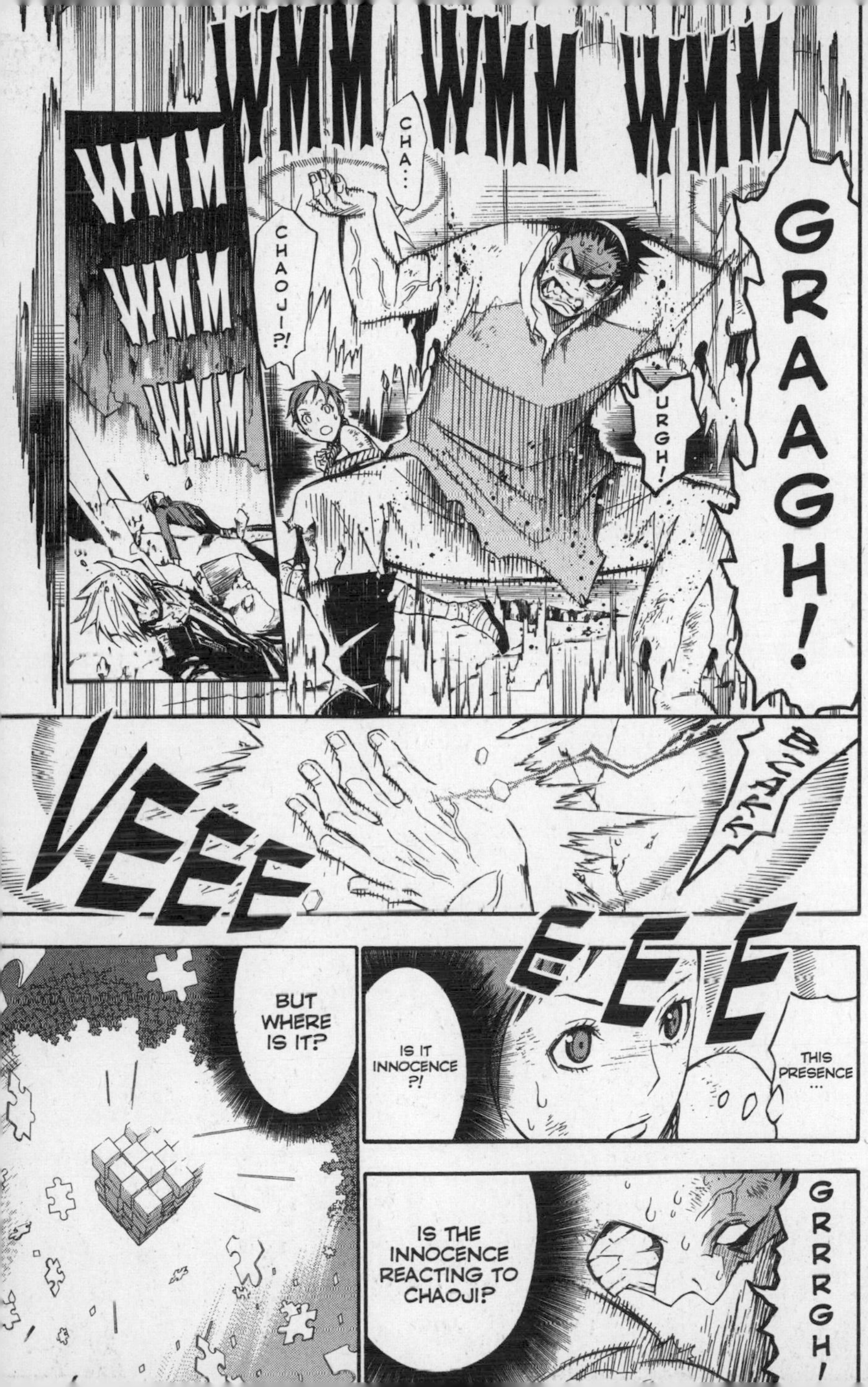
WMM WMM WMM
GRAAGH!
CHA...
URGH!
CHAOJI?!
WMM
WMM
WMM
VEEE
EEE
THIS PRESENCE...
IS IT INNOCENCE?!
GRRRGH!
IS THE INNOCENCE REACTING TO CHAOJI?
BUT WHERE IS IT?

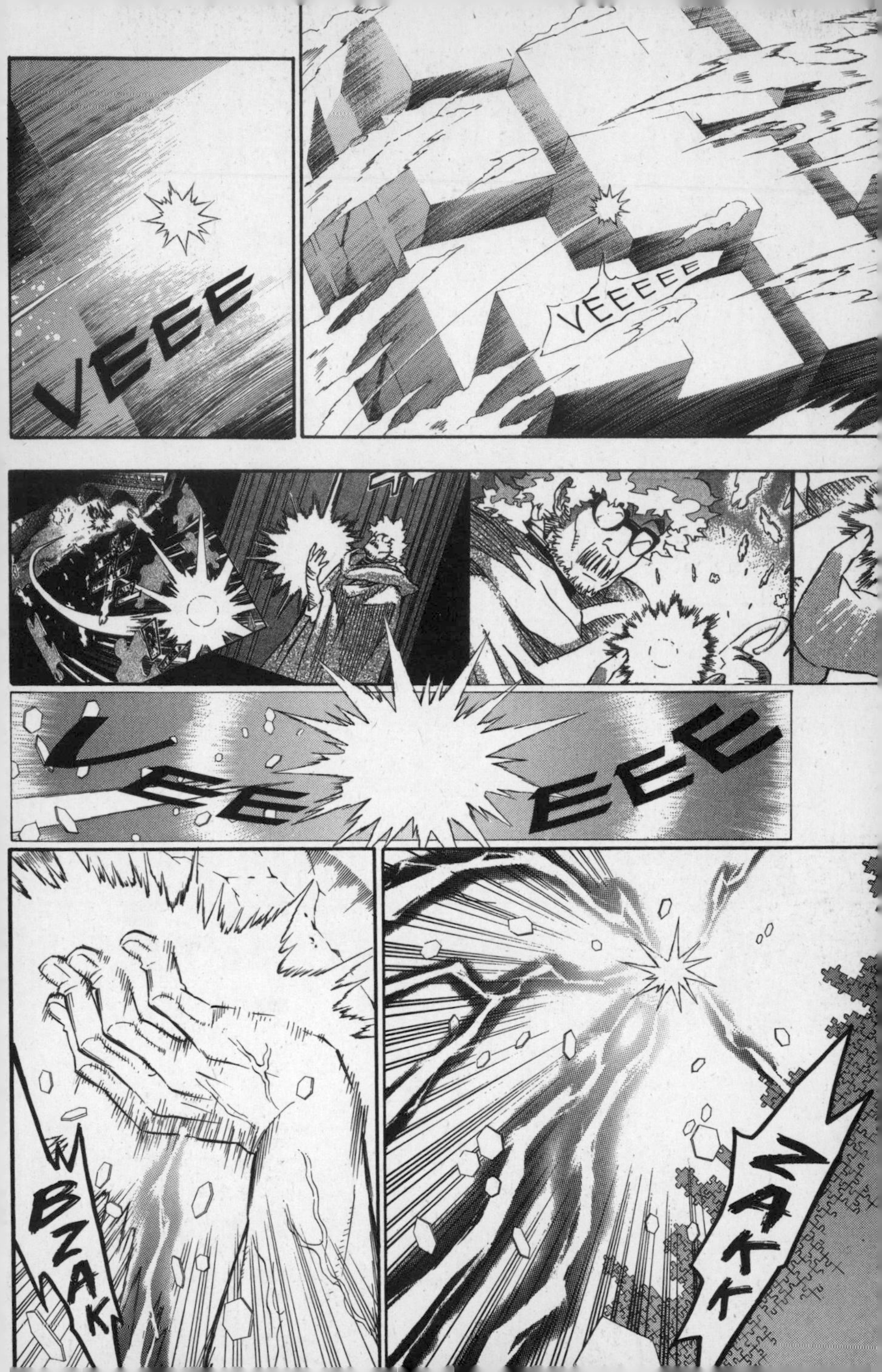
VEEE
VEEEEE
VEE
EEE
ZAKK
BZAK

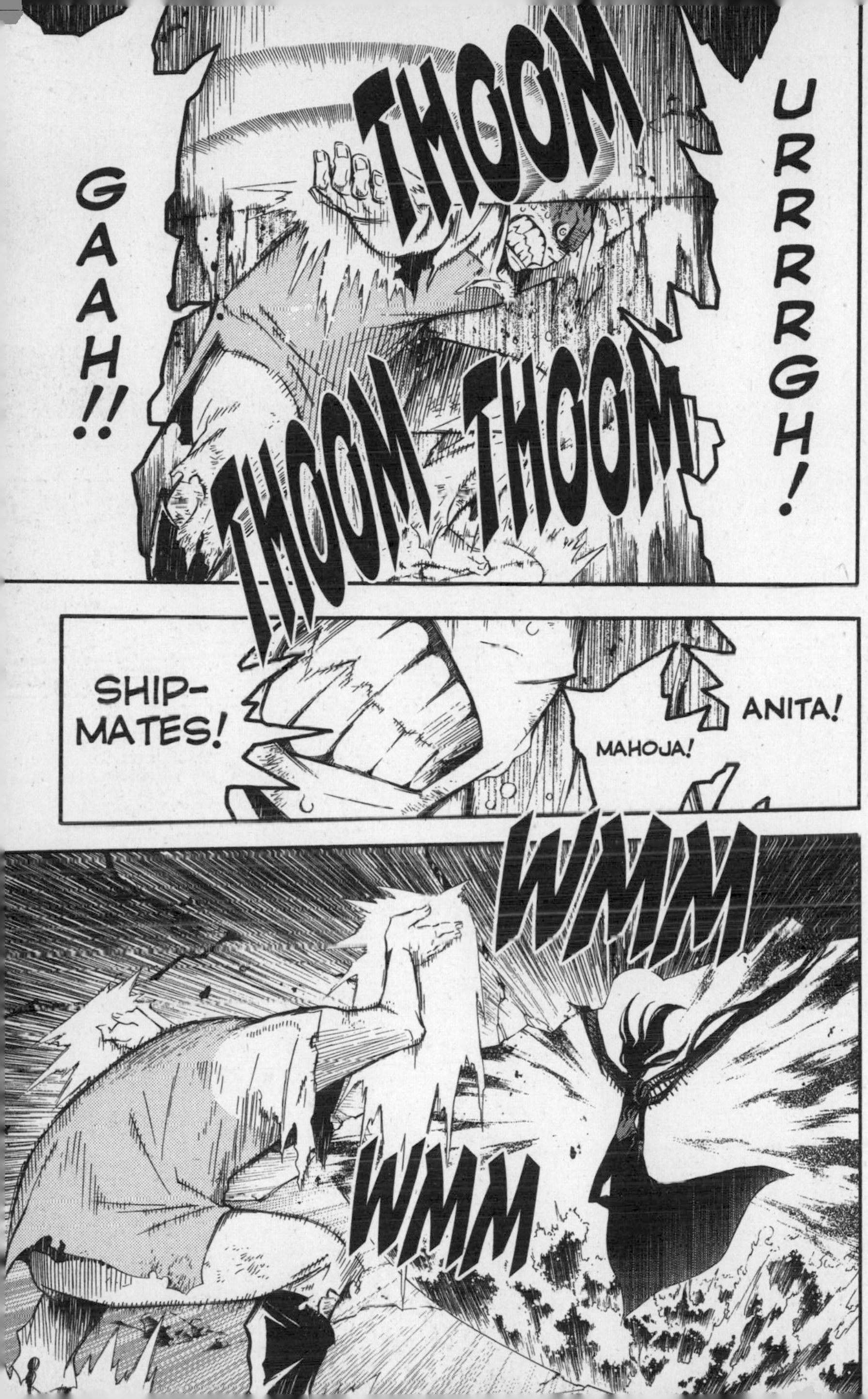
URRRRGH!
THOOM
GAAH!!
THOOM THOOM
ANITA!
MAHOJA!
SHIP-
MATES!
WMM
WMM

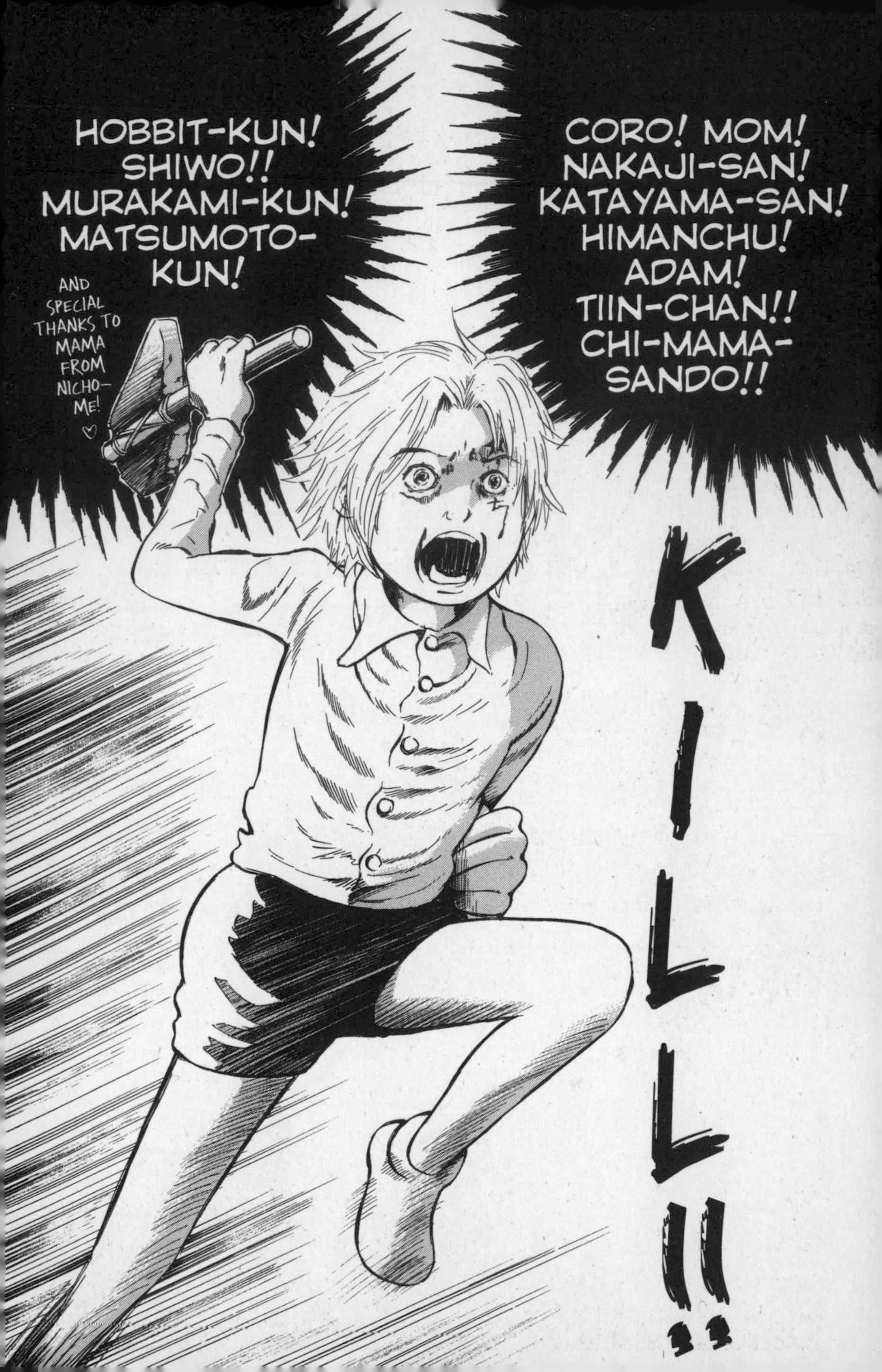
CORO! MOM! NAKAJI-SAN! KATAYAMA-SAN! HIMANCHU! ADAM! TIIN-CHAN!! CHI-MAMA-SANDO!!
HOBBIT-KUN! SHIWO!! MURAKAMI-KUN! MATSUMOTO-KUN!
AND SPECIAL THANKS TO MAMA FROM NICHO-ME! ♡
KILL!!

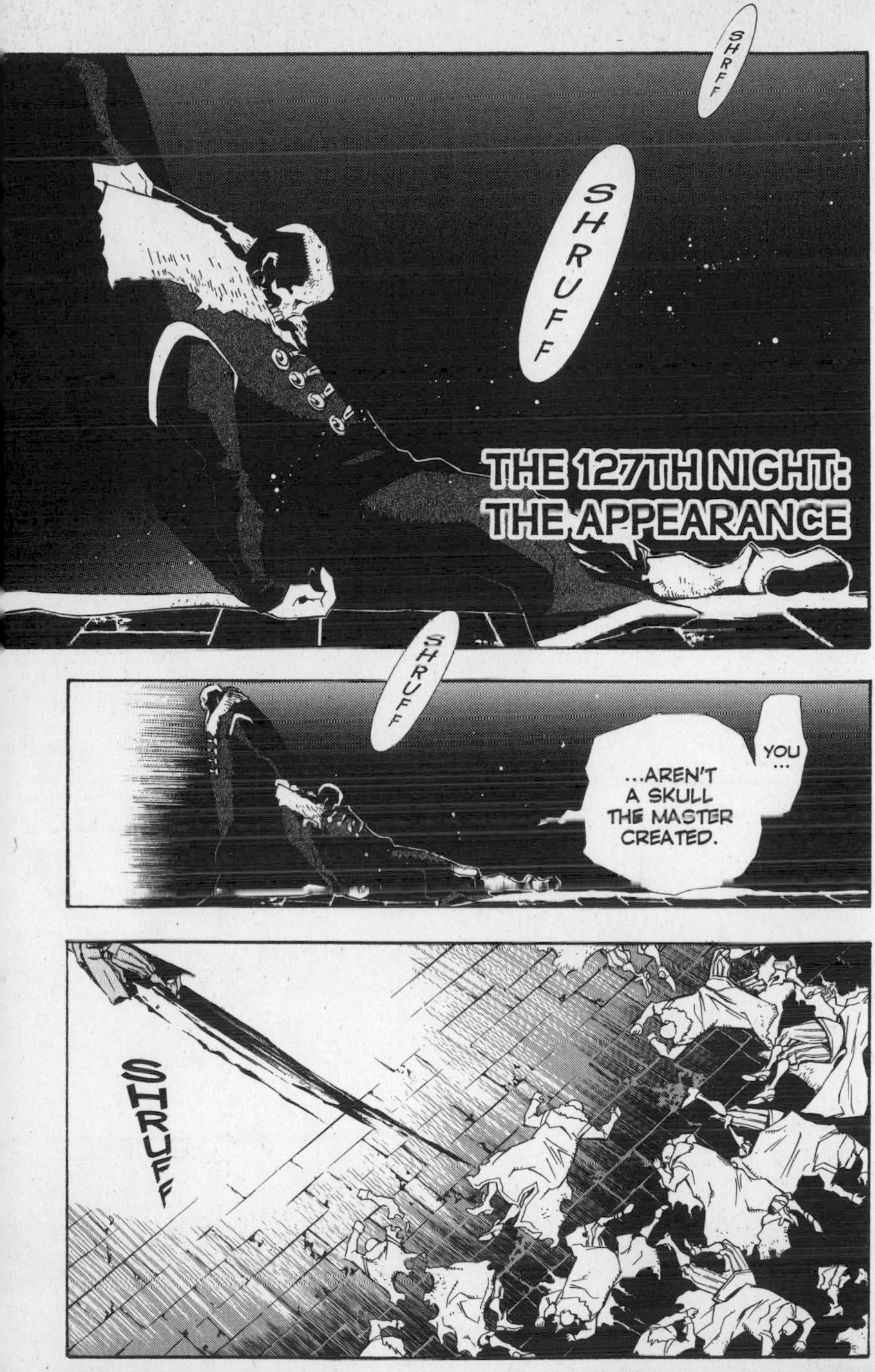
SHRFF
SHRUFF
THE 127TH NIGHT: THE APPEARANCE
SHRUFF
YOU ...
...AREN'T A SKULL THE MASTER CREATED.
SHRUFF

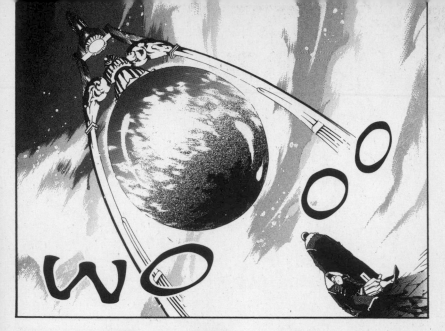

WO

SO THIS IS
THE EGG
YOU WERE
WATCHING.

WAH!

WHOO

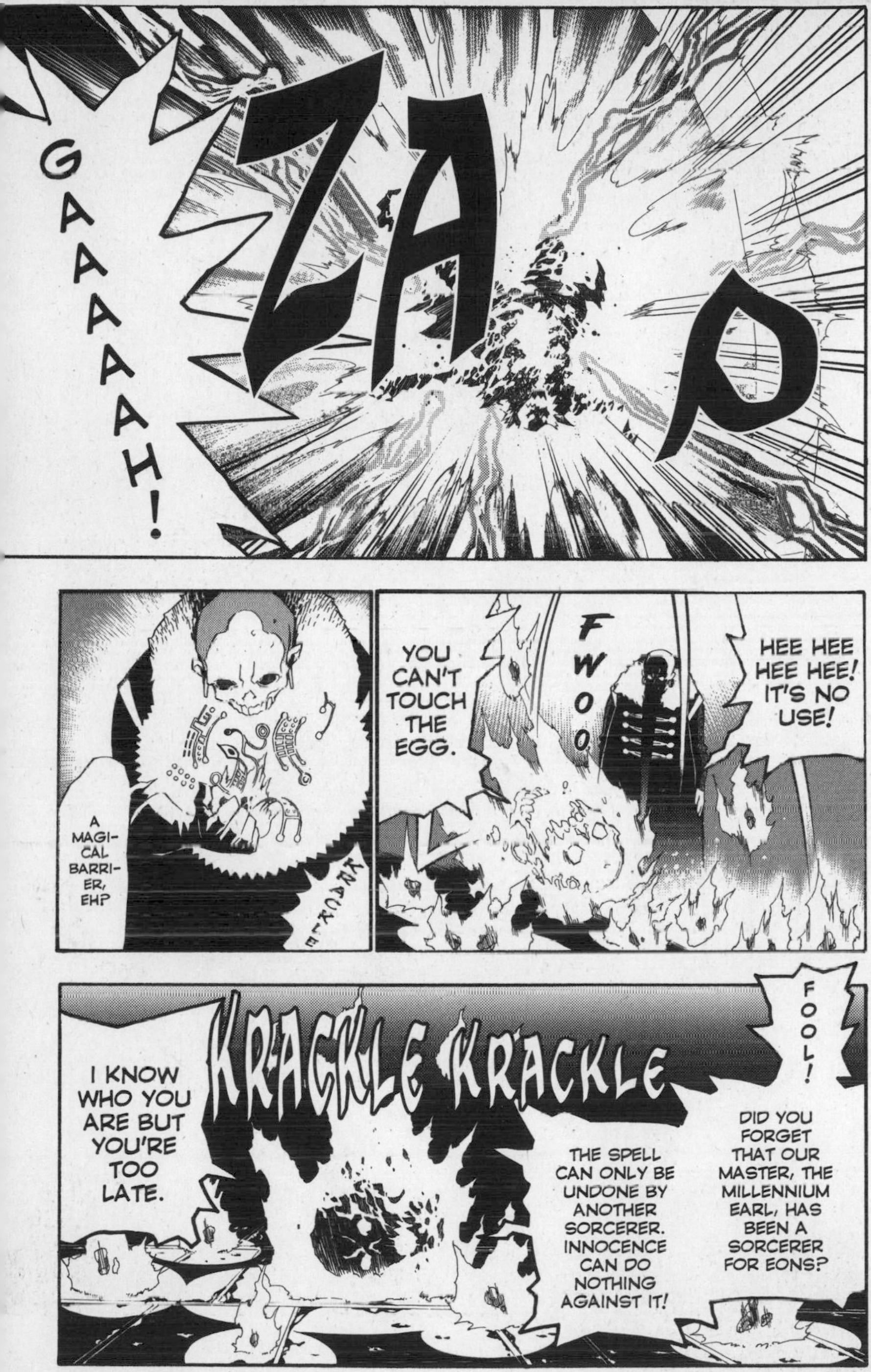
ZAP
GAAAAAH!
HEE HEE HEE HEE! IT'S NO USE!
FWOO
YOU CAN'T TOUCH THE EGG.
KRACKLE
A MAGI-CAL BARRI-ER, EH?
FOOL!
DID YOU FORGET THAT OUR MASTER, THE MILLENNIUM EARL, HAS BEEN A SORCERER FOR EONS?
THE SPELL CAN ONLY BE UNDONE BY ANOTHER SORCERER. INNOCENCE CAN DO NOTHING AGAINST IT!
KRACKLE KRACKLE
I KNOW WHO YOU ARE BUT YOU'RE TOO LATE.

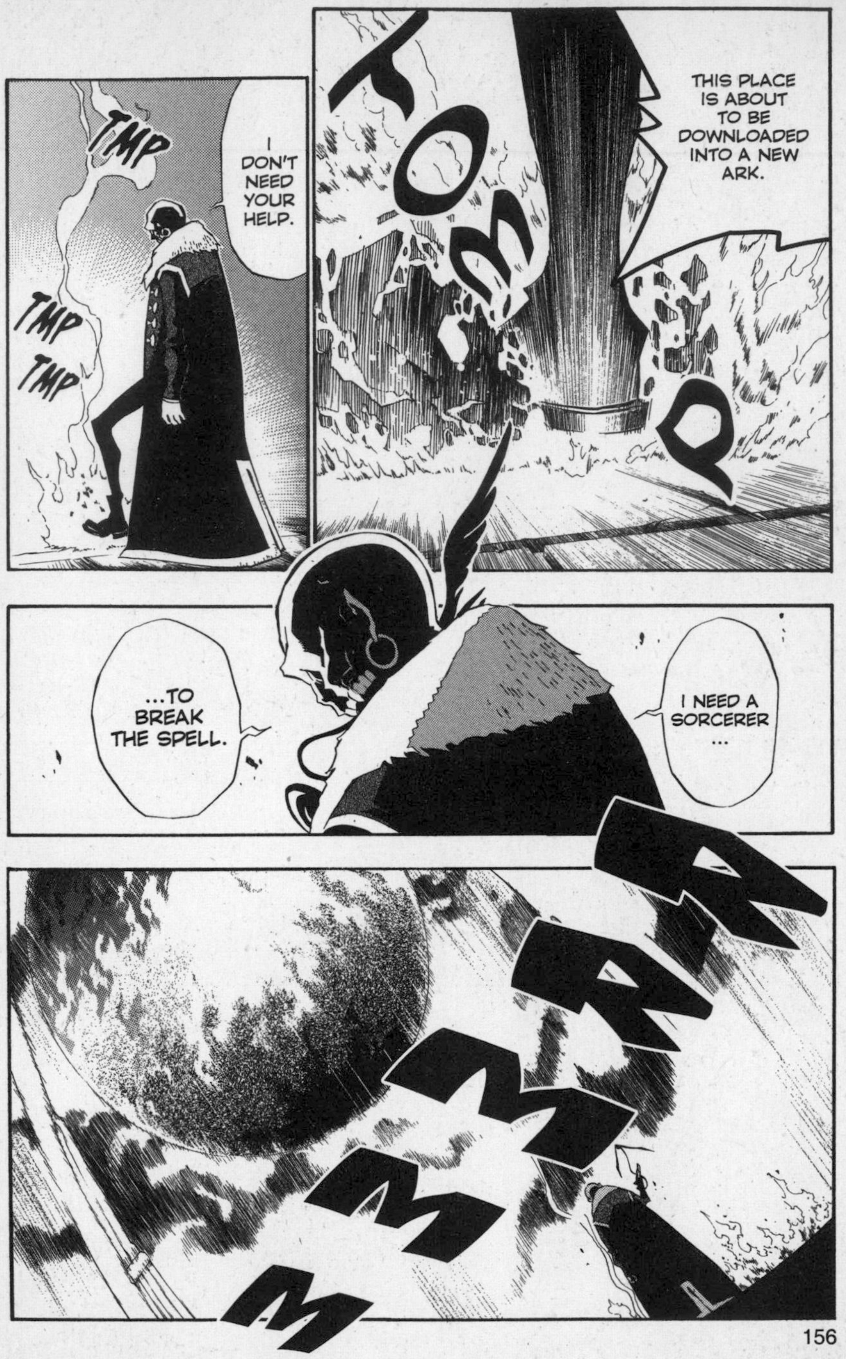
THIS PLACE IS ABOUT TO BE DOWNLOADED INTO A NEW ARK.
TMP
I DON'T NEED YOUR HELP.
TMP
TMP
I NEED A SORCERER ...
...TO BREAK THE SPELL.

READ THIS WAY

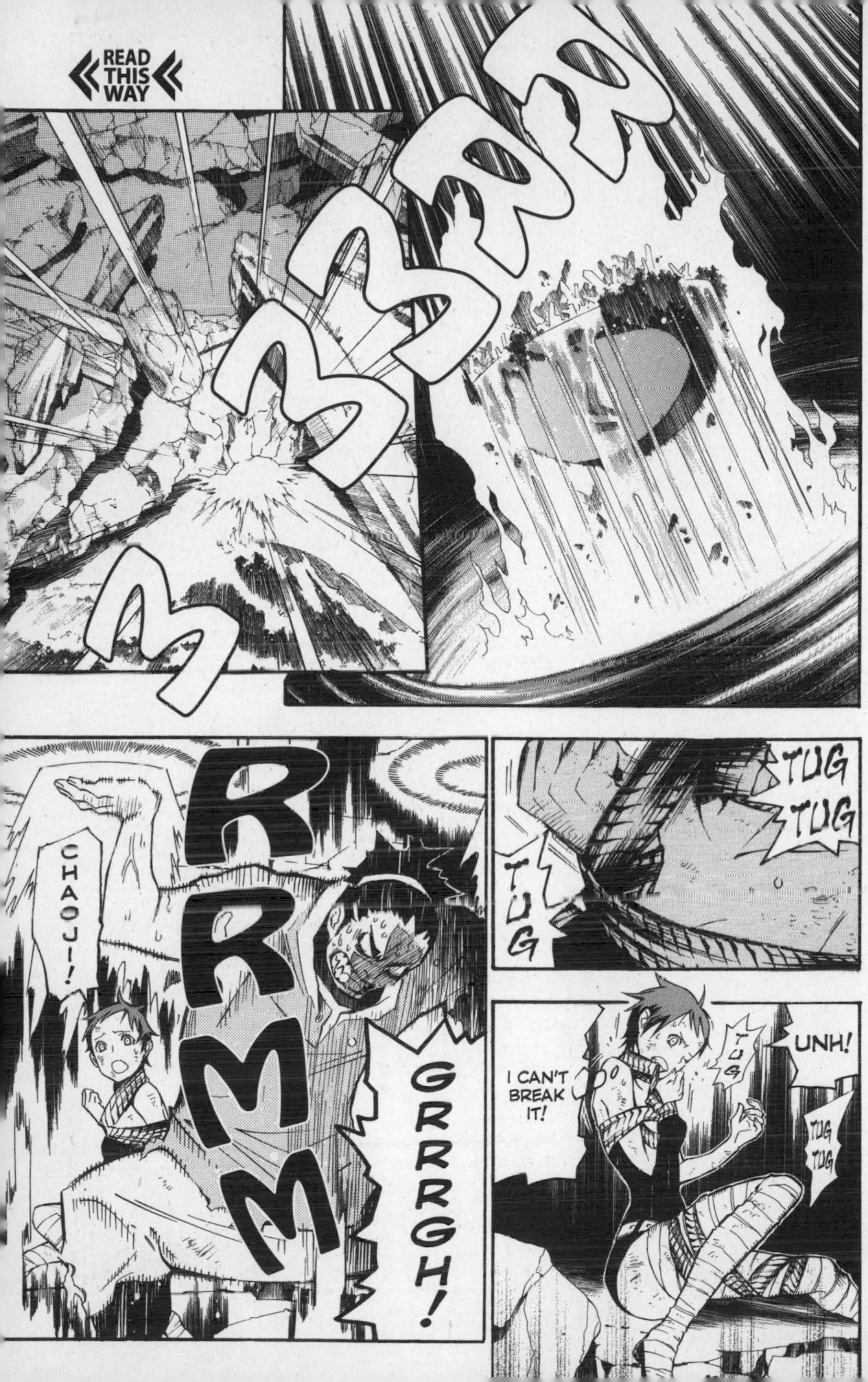
TUG TUG
TUG
UNH!
TUG
I CAN'T BREAK IT!
TUG TUG
RRMMM
GRRRGH!
CHAOJI!

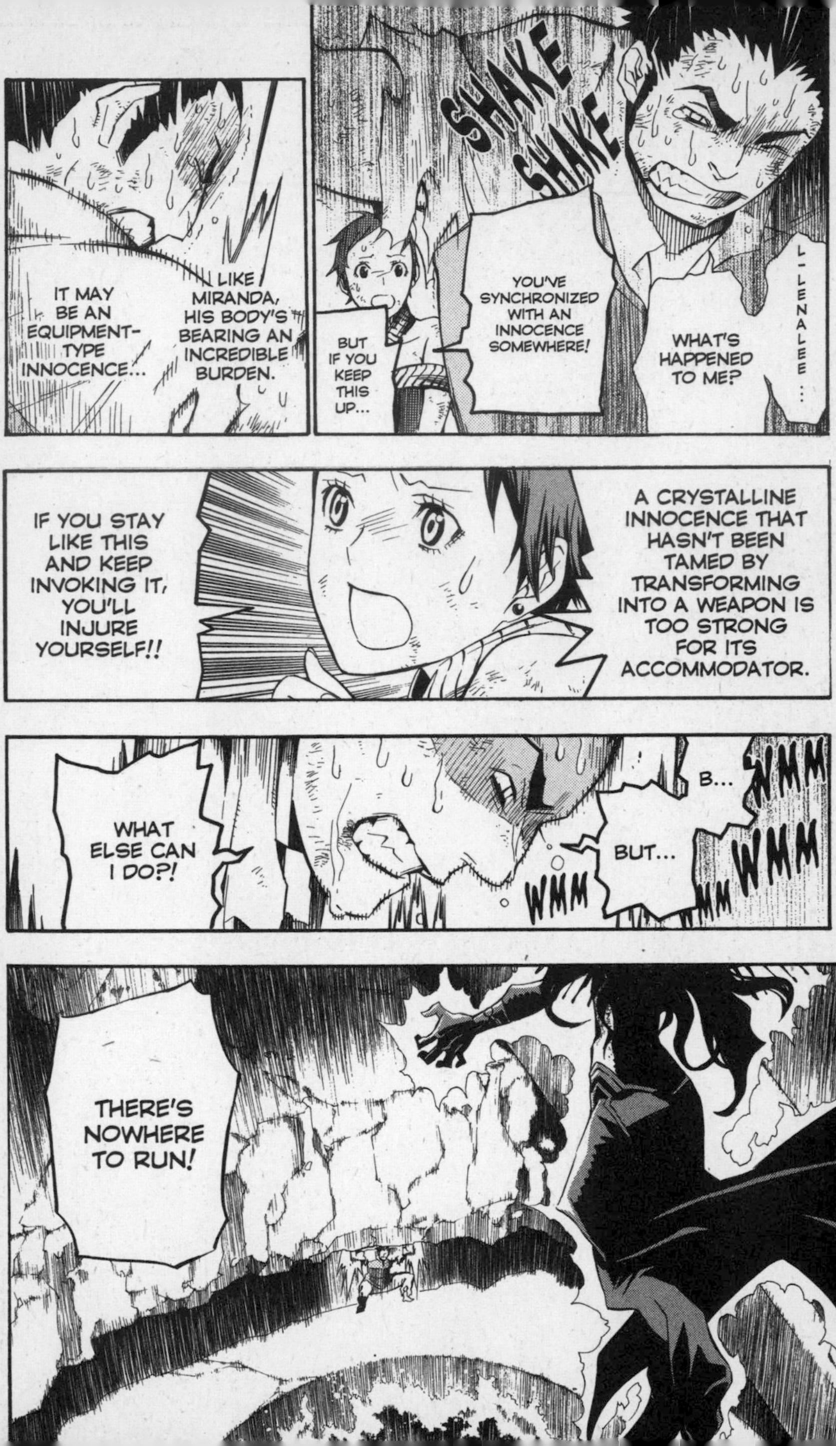
SHAKE SHAKE
L-LENALEE...
WHAT'S HAPPENED TO ME?
YOU'VE SYNCHRONIZED WITH AN INNOCENCE SOMEWHERE!
BUT IF YOU KEEP THIS UP...
LIKE MIRANDA, HIS BODY'S BEARING AN INCREDIBLE BURDEN.
IT MAY BE AN EQUIPMENT-TYPE INNOCENCE...
A CRYSTALLINE INNOCENCE THAT HASN'T BEEN TAMED BY TRANSFORMING INTO A WEAPON IS TOO STRONG FOR ITS ACCOMMODATOR.
IF YOU STAY LIKE THIS AND KEEP INVOKING IT, YOU'LL INJURE YOURSELF!!
WMM WMM WMM
B...
BUT...
WMM
WHAT ELSE CAN I DO?!
THERE'S NOWHERE TO RUN!

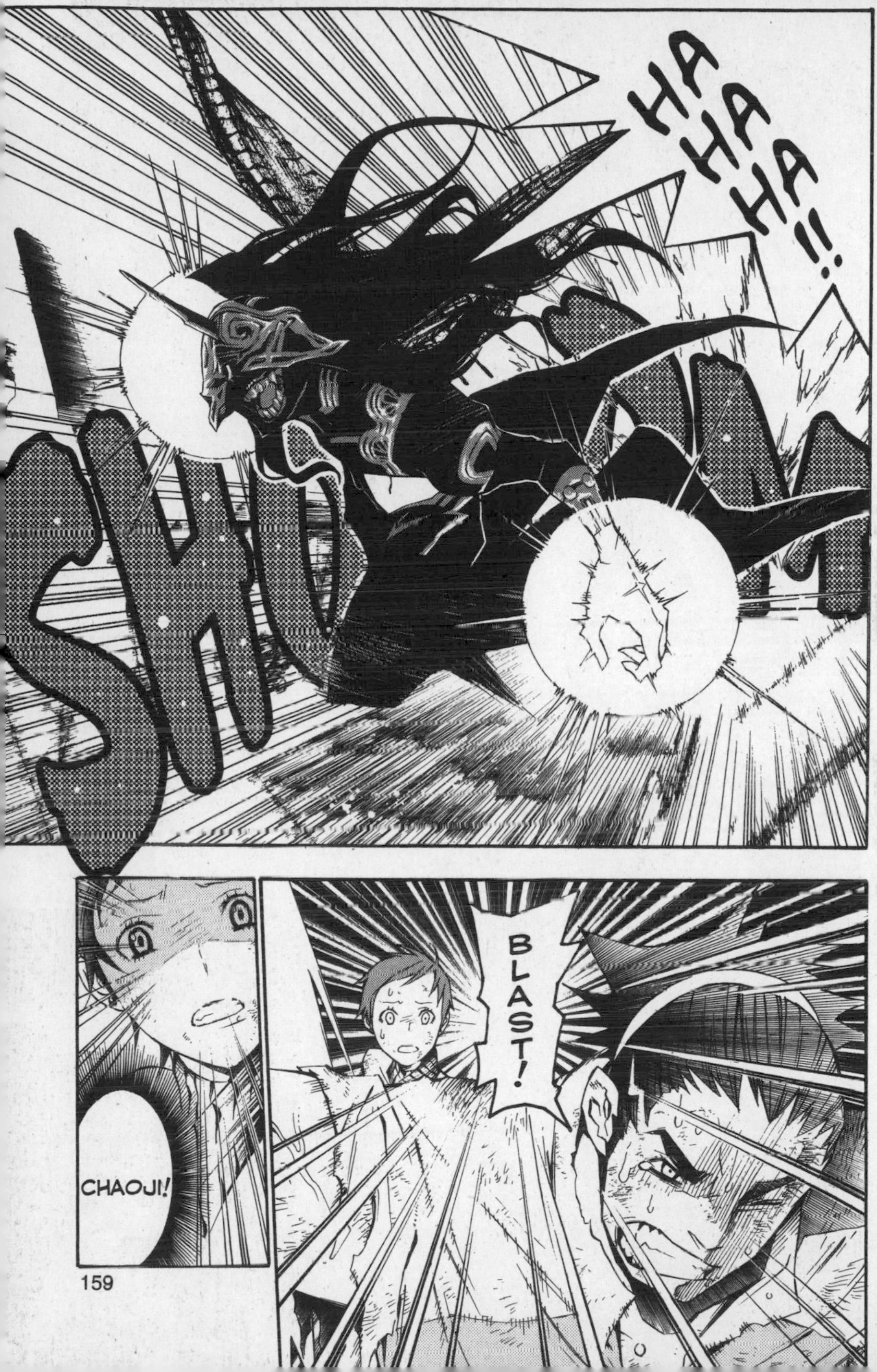
HA HA HA!!
BLAST!
CHAOJI!

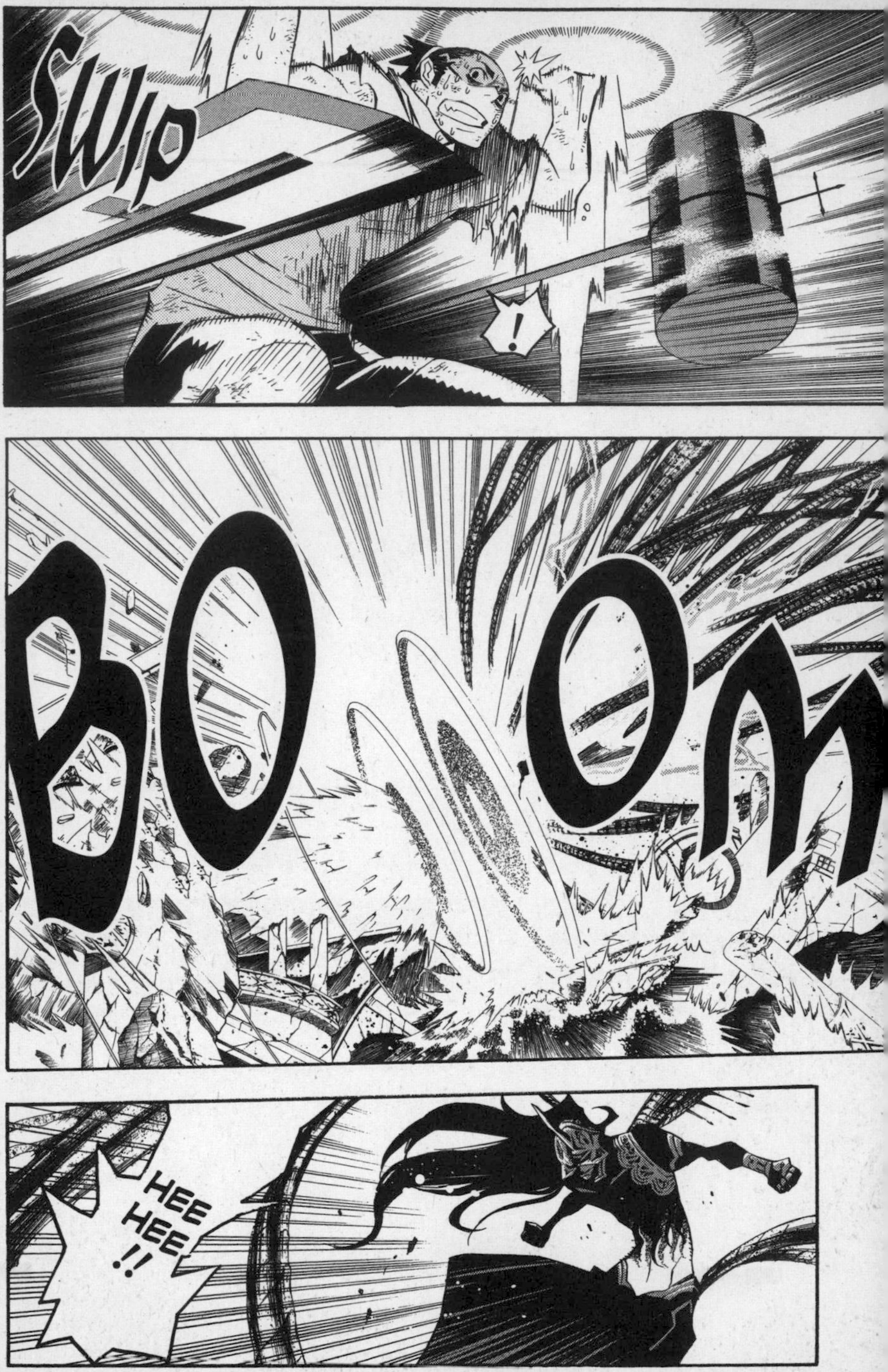
SWIP
!
BOOM
HEE HEE!!

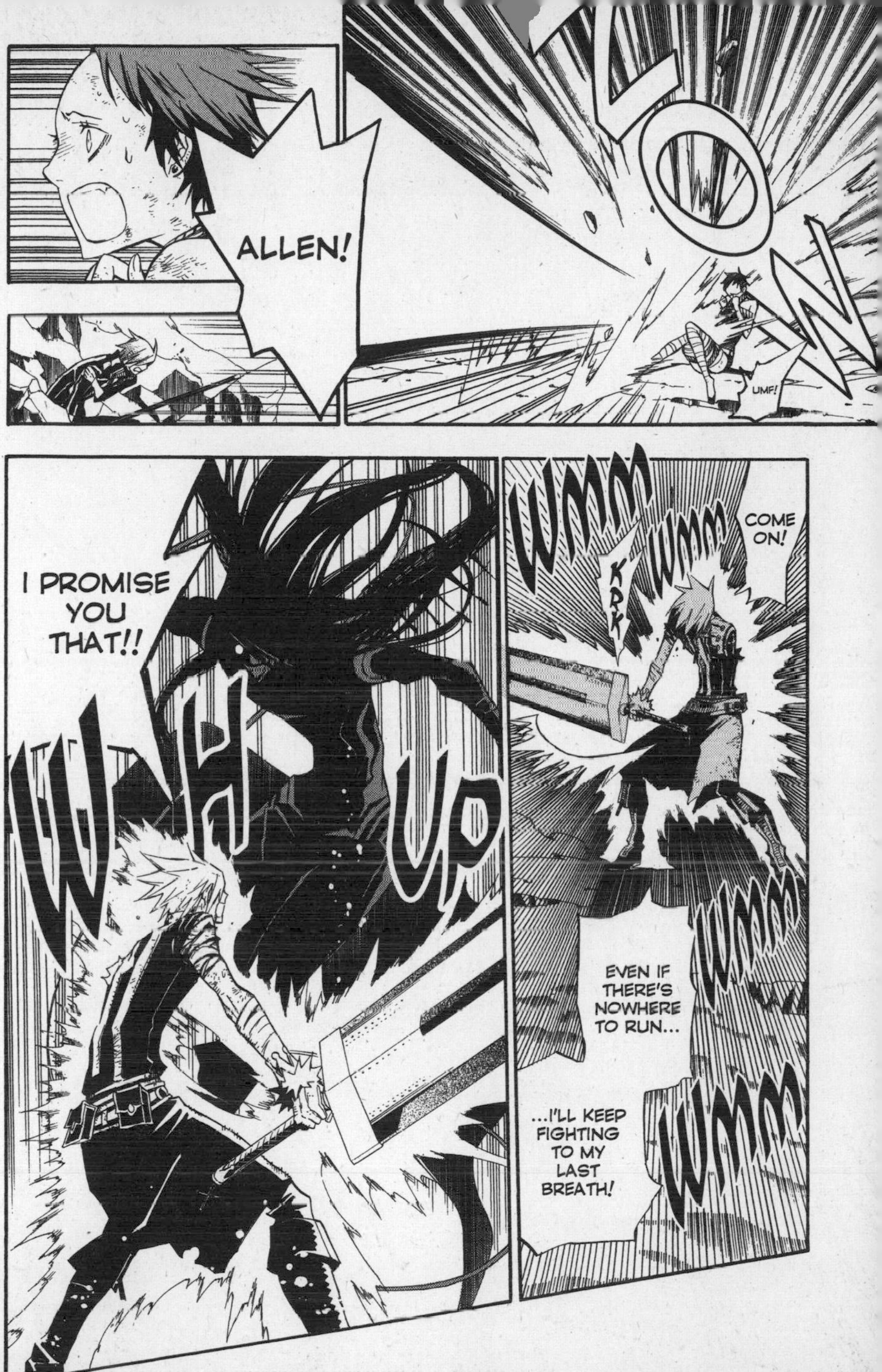
UMF!
ALLEN!
WMM
WMM
KRK
COME ON!
EVEN IF THERE'S NOWHERE TO RUN...
WMM
...I'LL KEEP FIGHTING TO MY LAST BREATH!
WMM
I PROMISE YOU THAT!!
WHUP

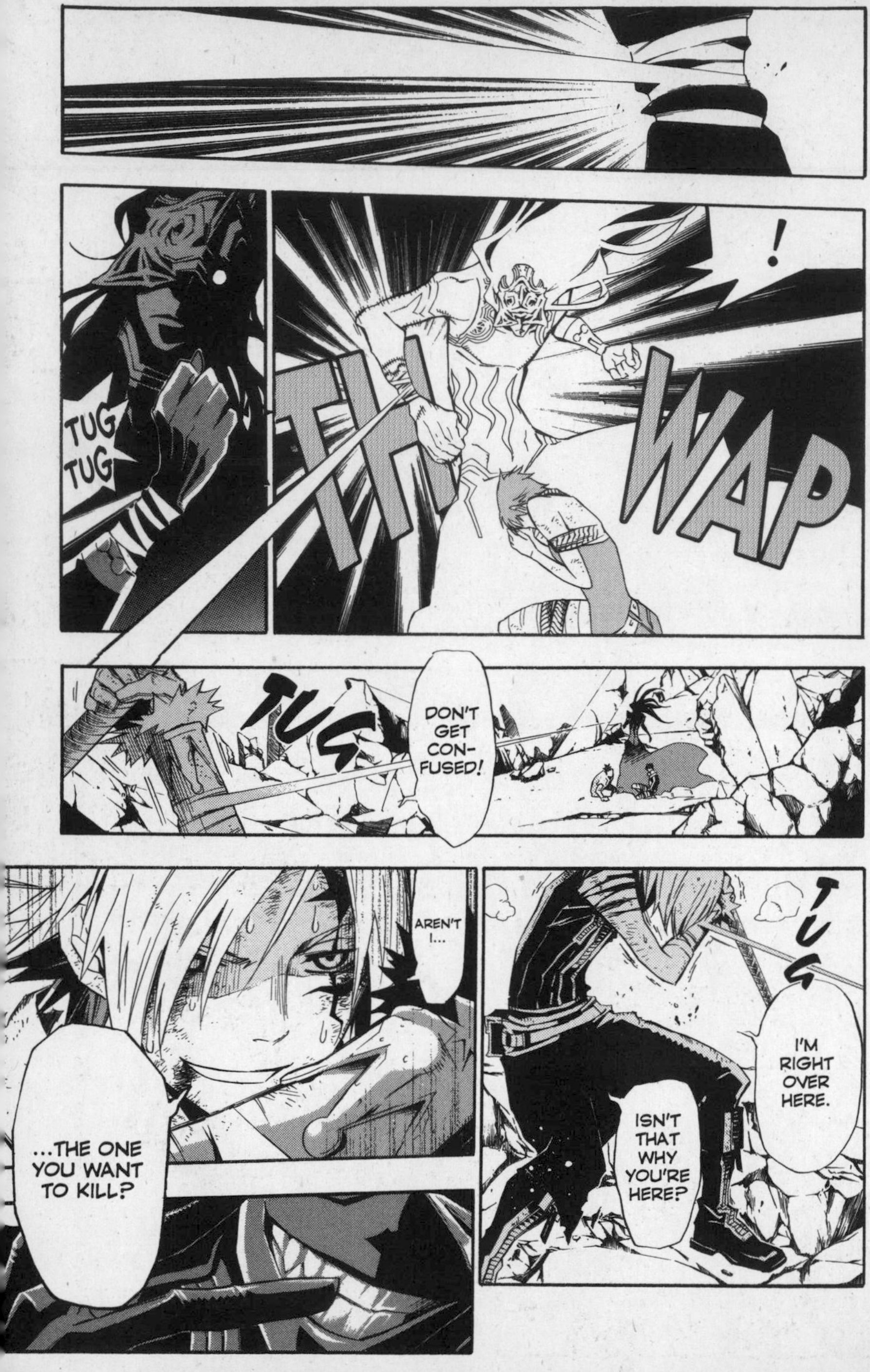
!
THWAP
TUG TUG
DON'T GET CON-FUSED!
TUG
TUG
I'M RIGHT OVER HERE.
ISN'T THAT WHY YOU'RE HERE?
AREN'T I...
...THE ONE YOU WANT TO KILL?

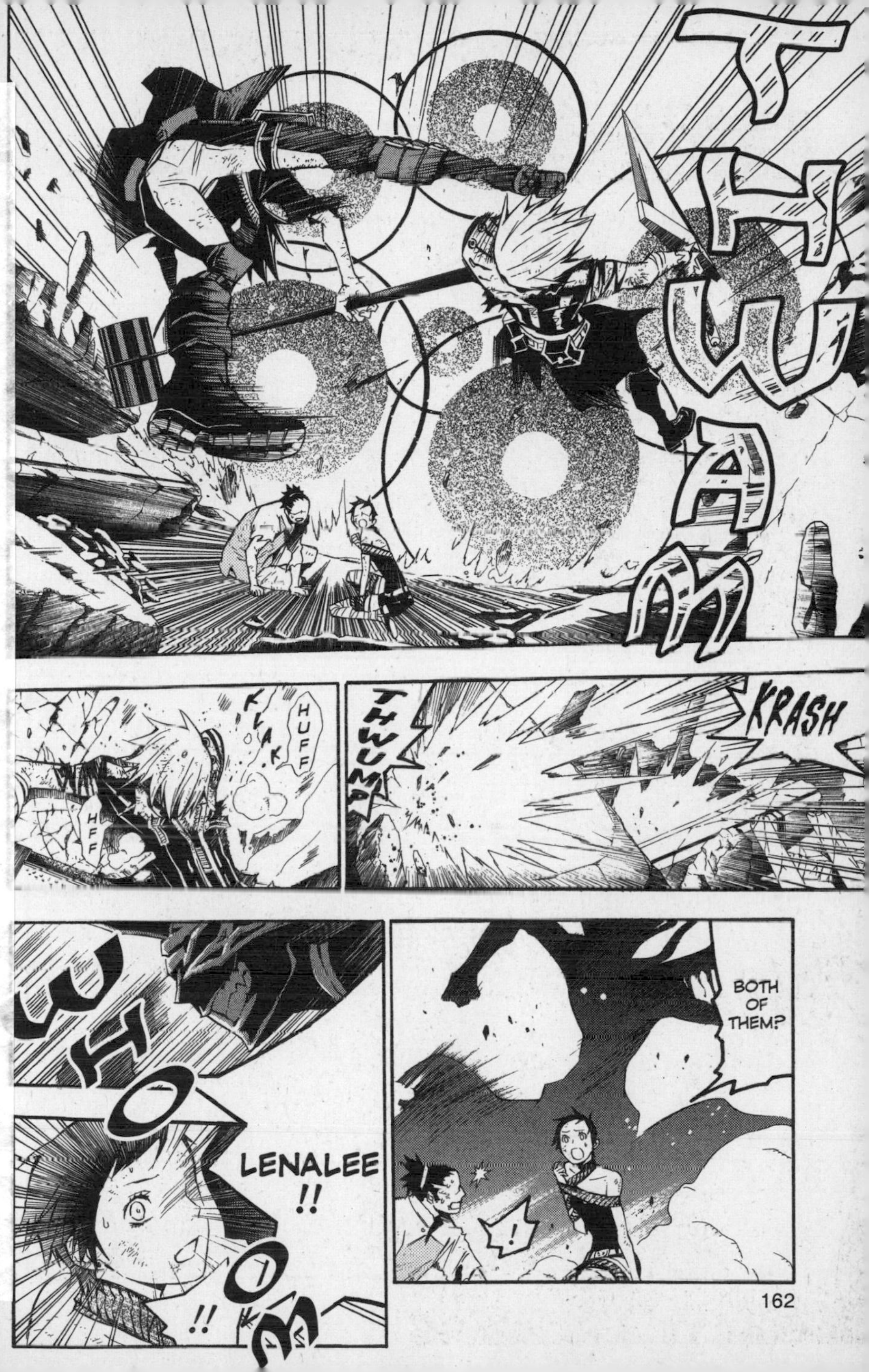
THWAM
KRASH
THWUMP
HUFF
FLAK
HFF
BOTH OF THEM?
!
LENALEE!!
!!

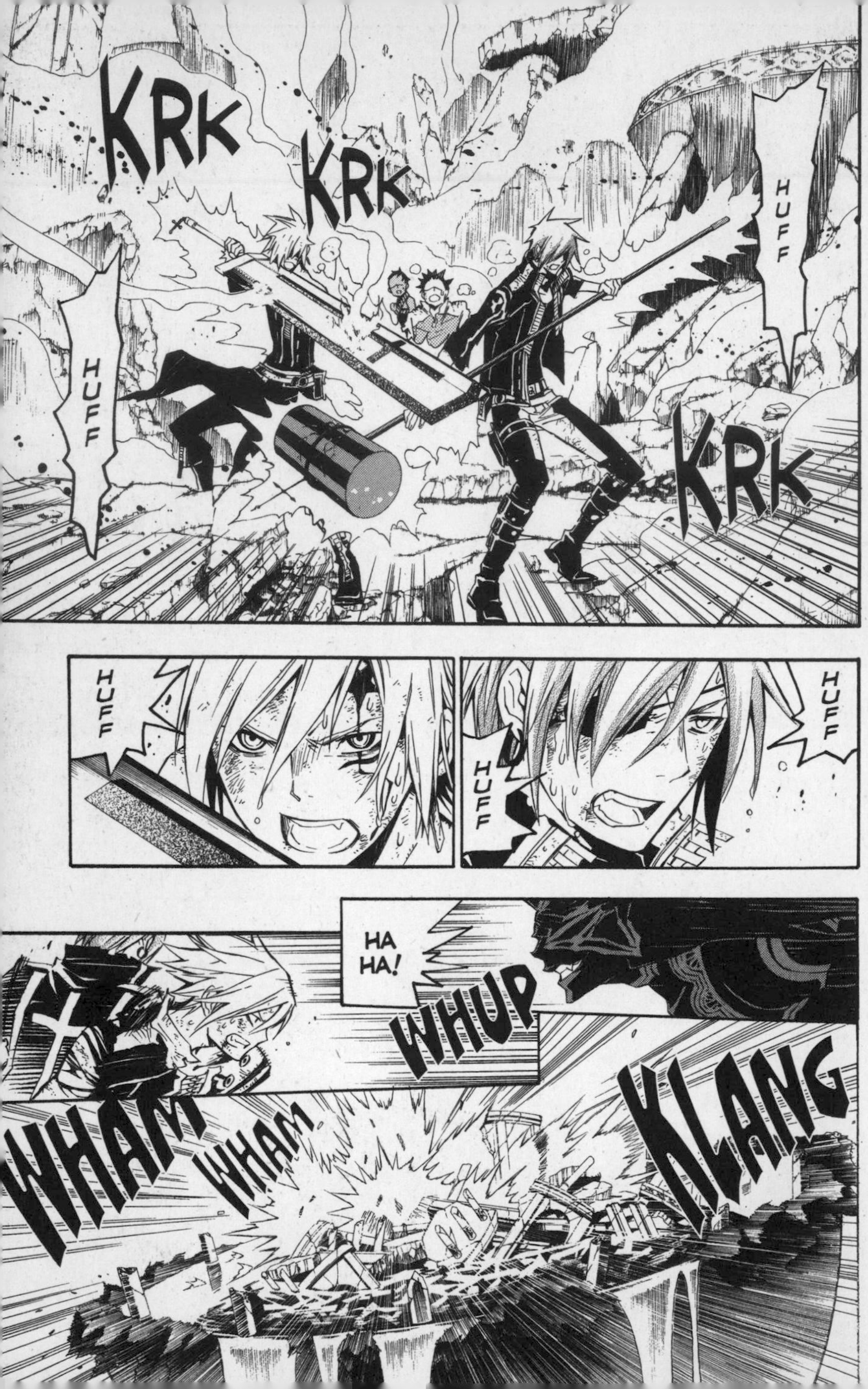
HUFF
KRK
KRK
KRK
HUFF
HUFF
HUFF
HUFF
HA HA!
WHUP
KLANG
WHAM
WHAM

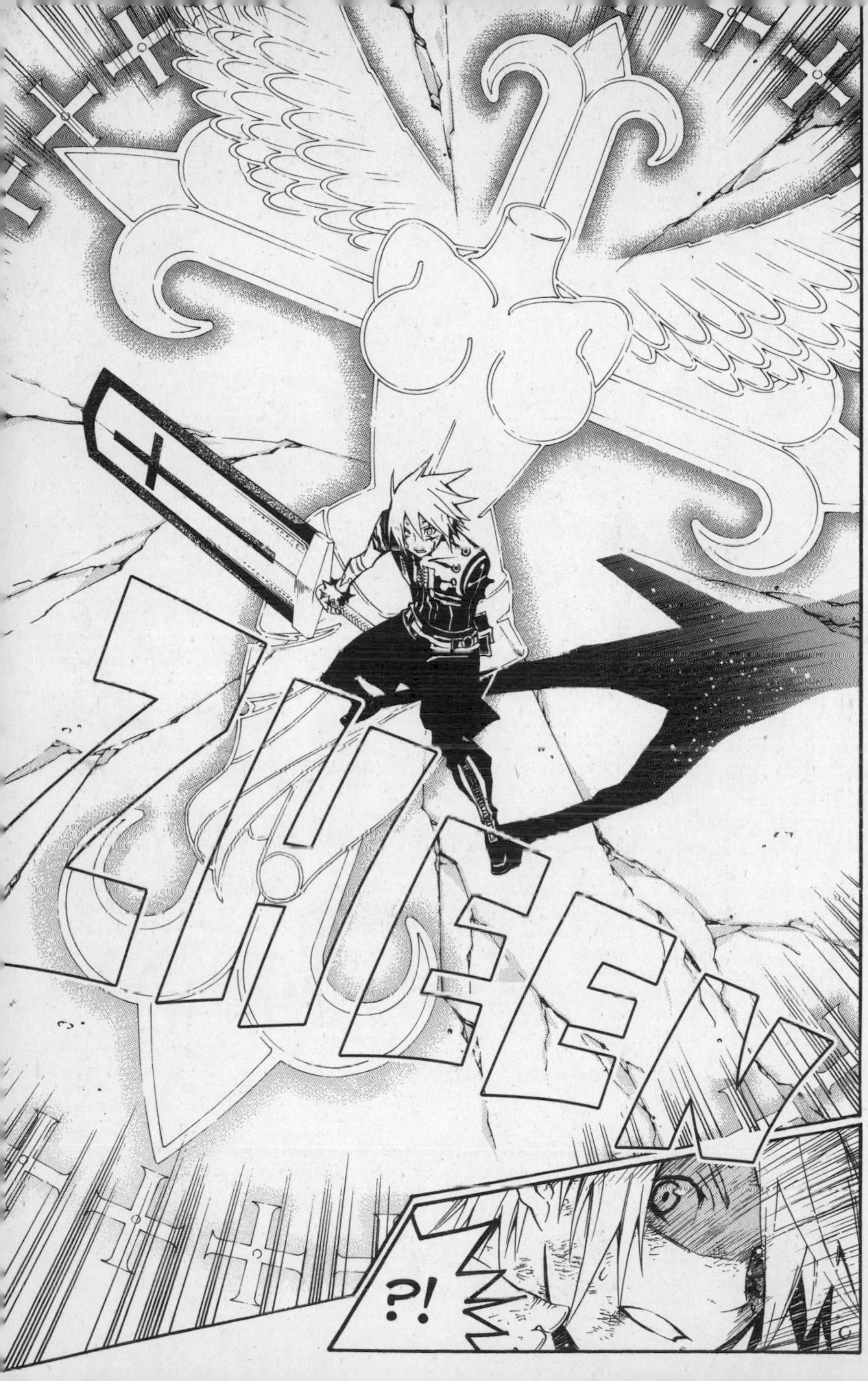
?!

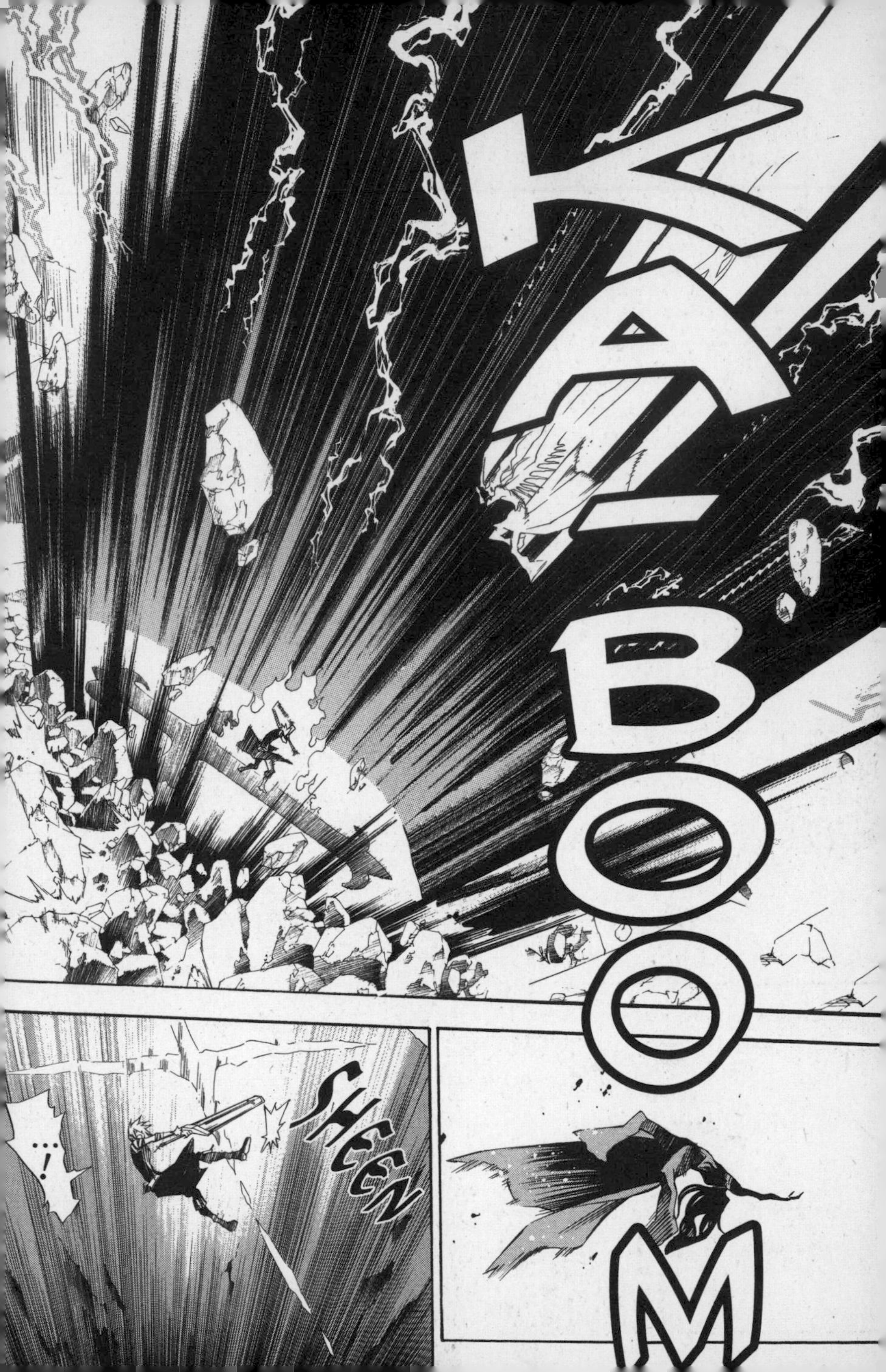
KA-BOOOM
SHEEN
...!

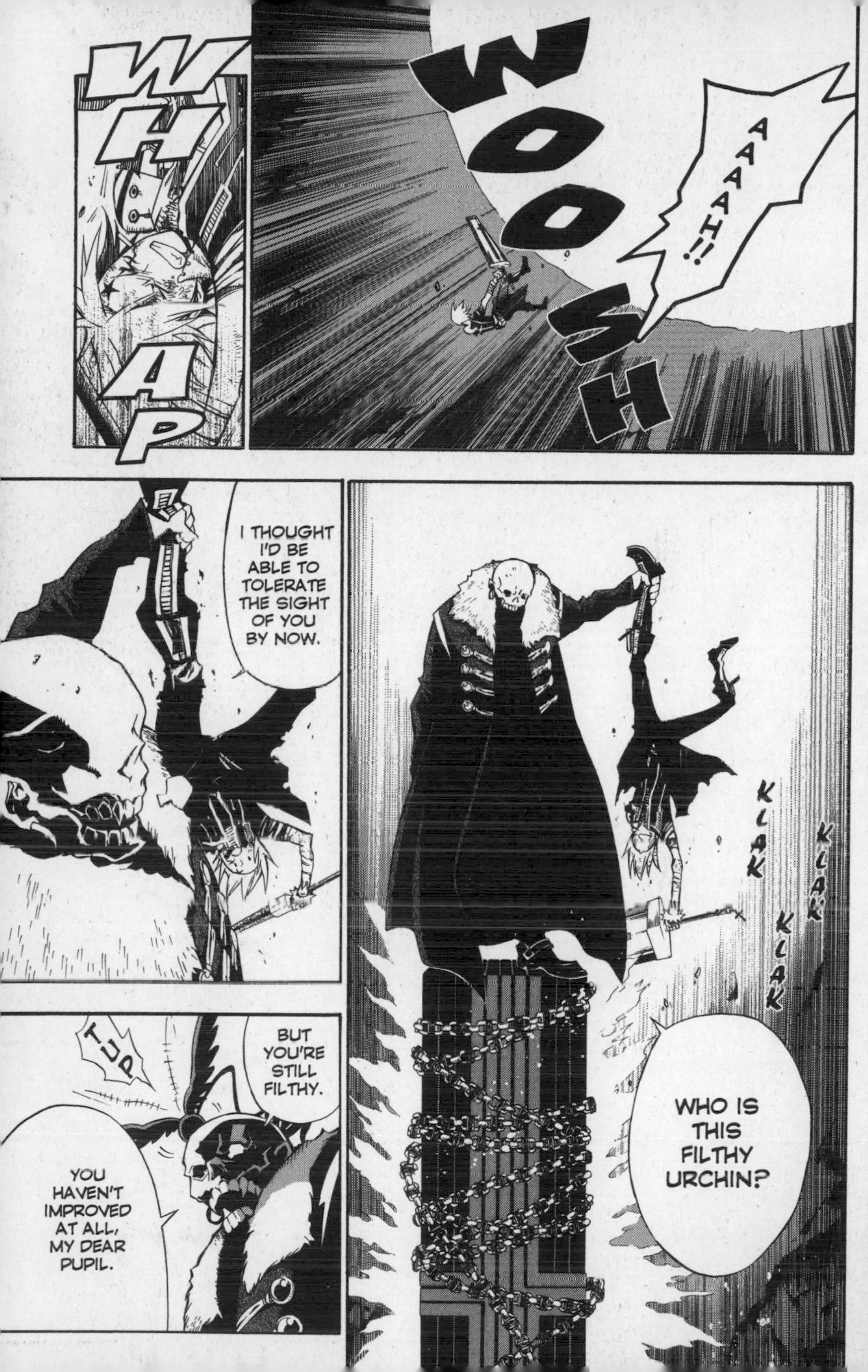
WOOOSH
AAAAAH!!
WHAP
KLAK KLAK KLAK KLAK
WHO IS THIS FILTHY URCHIN?
I THOUGHT I'D BE ABLE TO TOLERATE THE SIGHT OF YOU BY NOW.
BUT YOU'RE STILL FILTHY.
TUP
YOU HAVEN'T IMPROVED AT ALL, MY DEAR PUPIL.

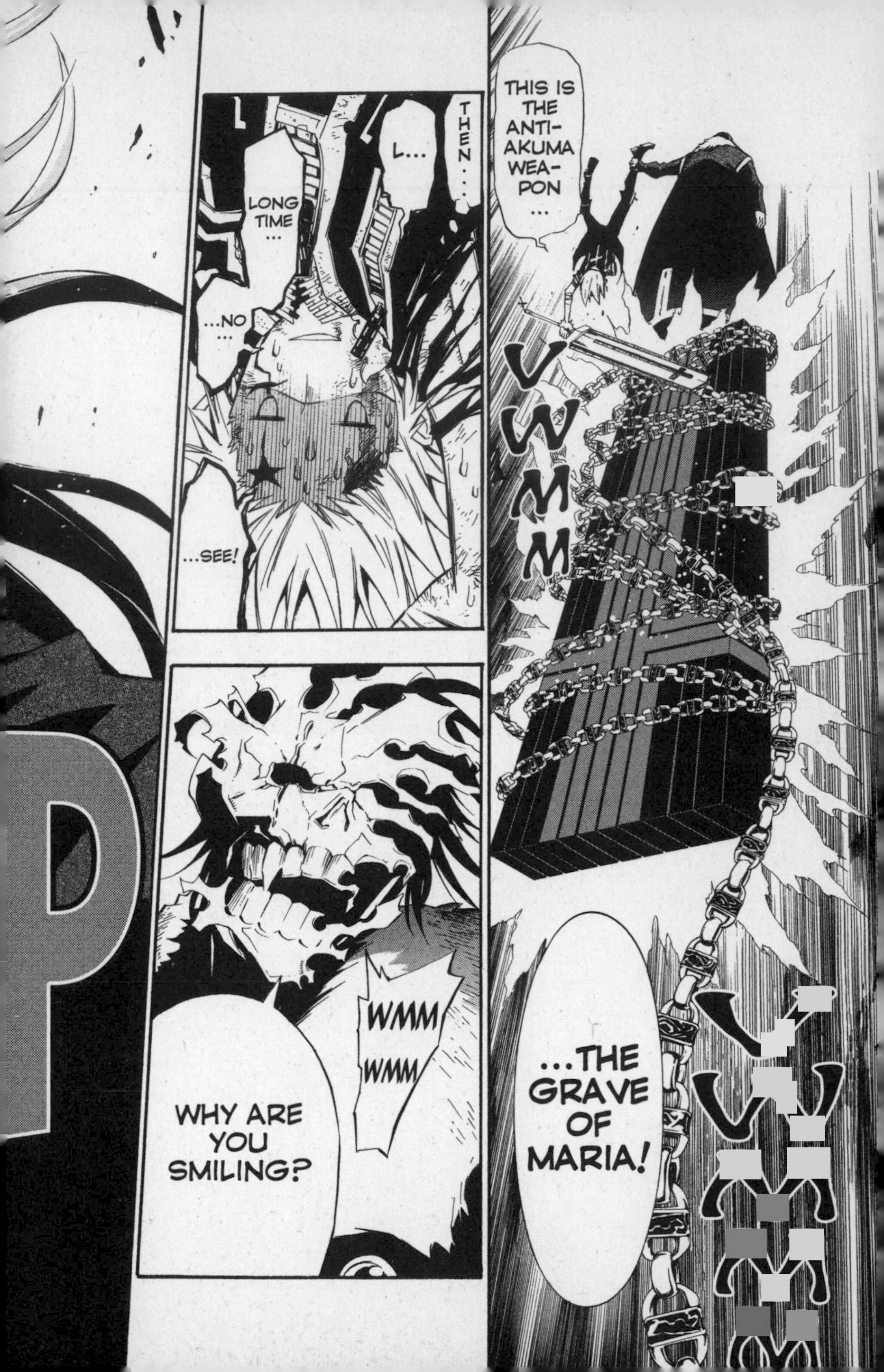
THIS IS THE ANTI-AKUMA WEA-PON...
VWMM
...THE GRAVE OF MARIA!
THEN...
L...
LONG TIME...
...NO...
...SEE!
WMM
WMM
WHY ARE YOU SMILING?

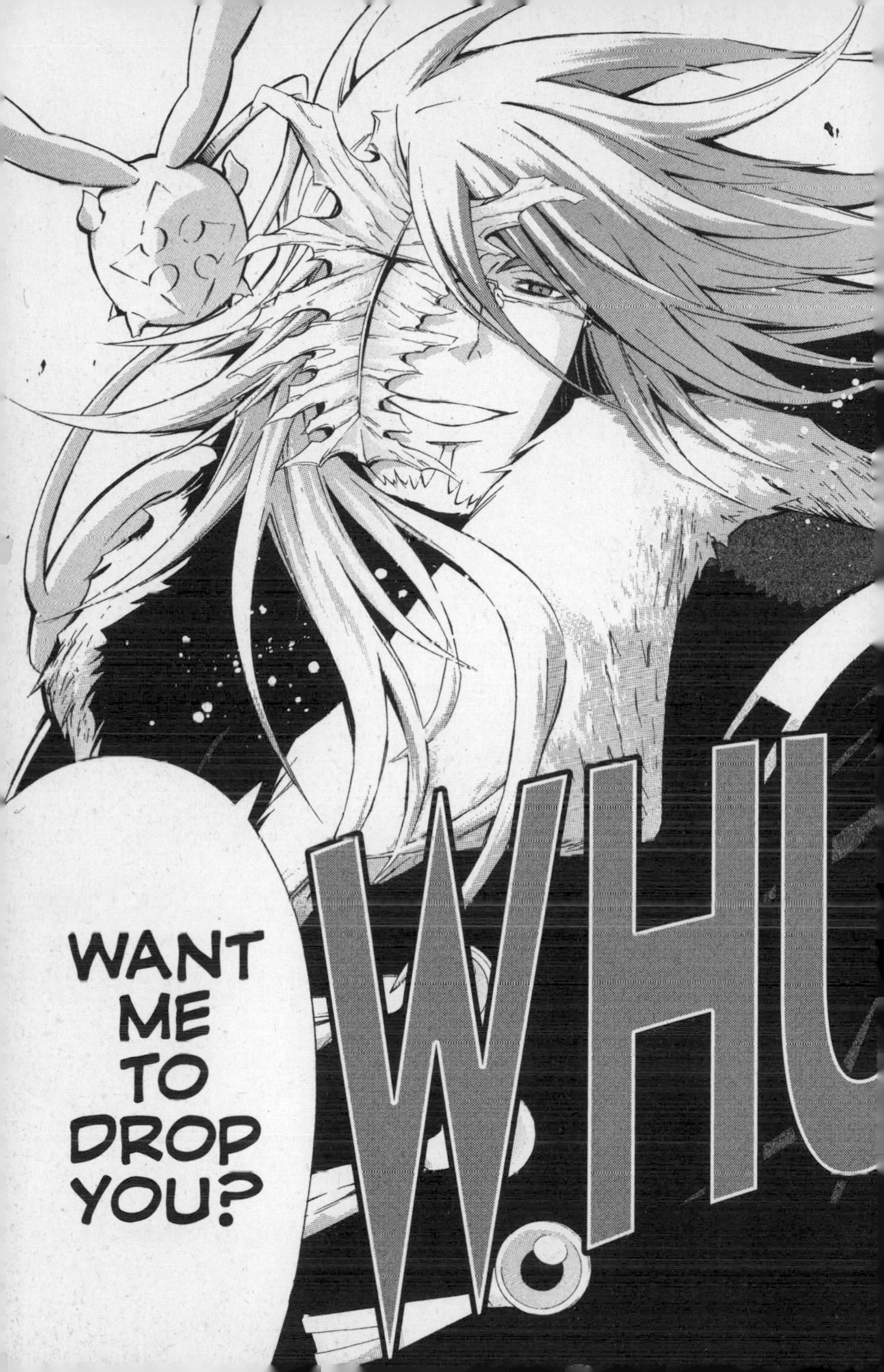
WANT ME TO DROP YOU?
WHU

SWIP

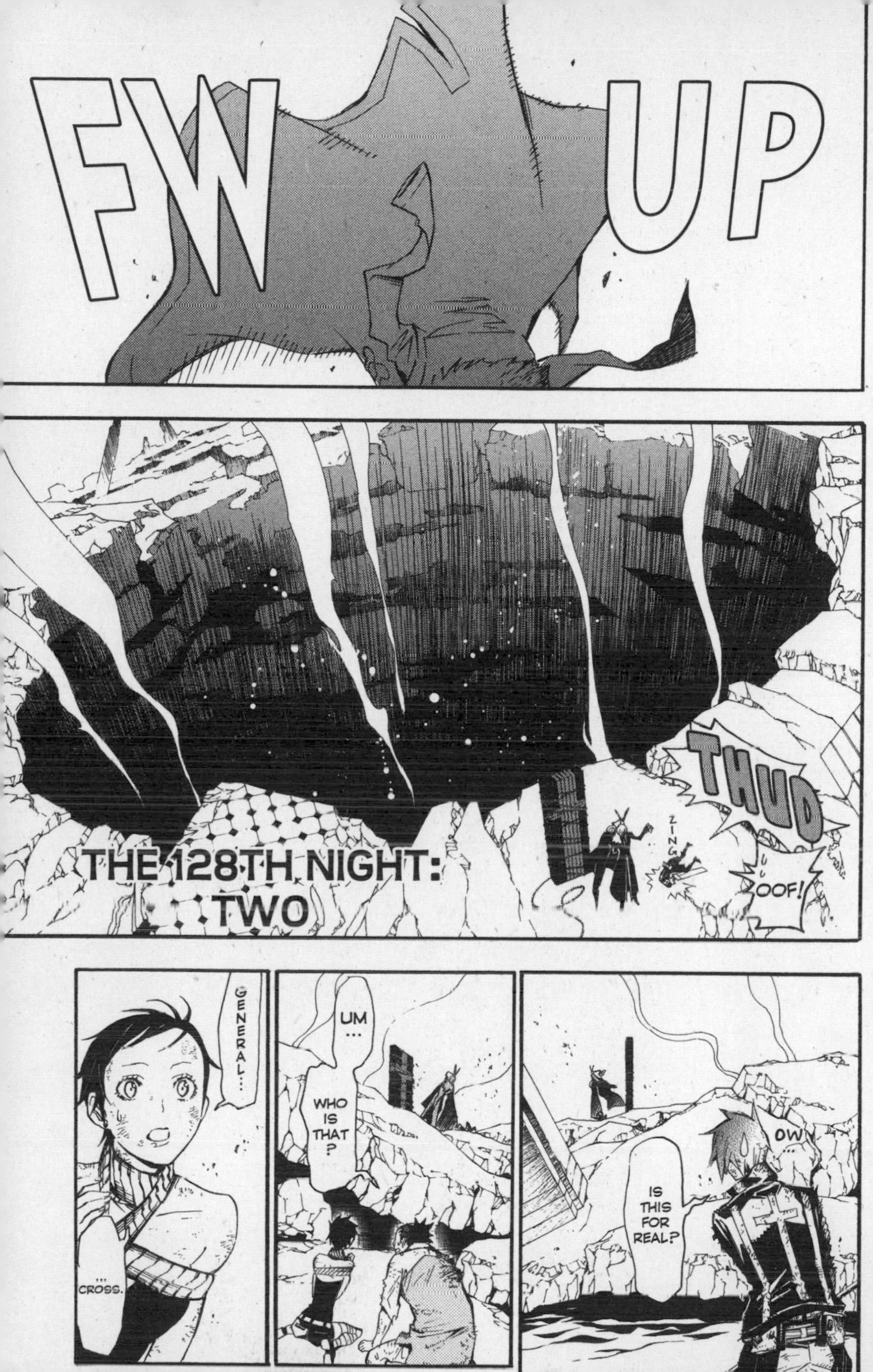
FW UP
THUD
OOF!
ZING
THE 128TH NIGHT: TWO
OW...
IS THIS FOR REAL?
UM...
WHO IS THAT?
GENERAL...
...CROSS.

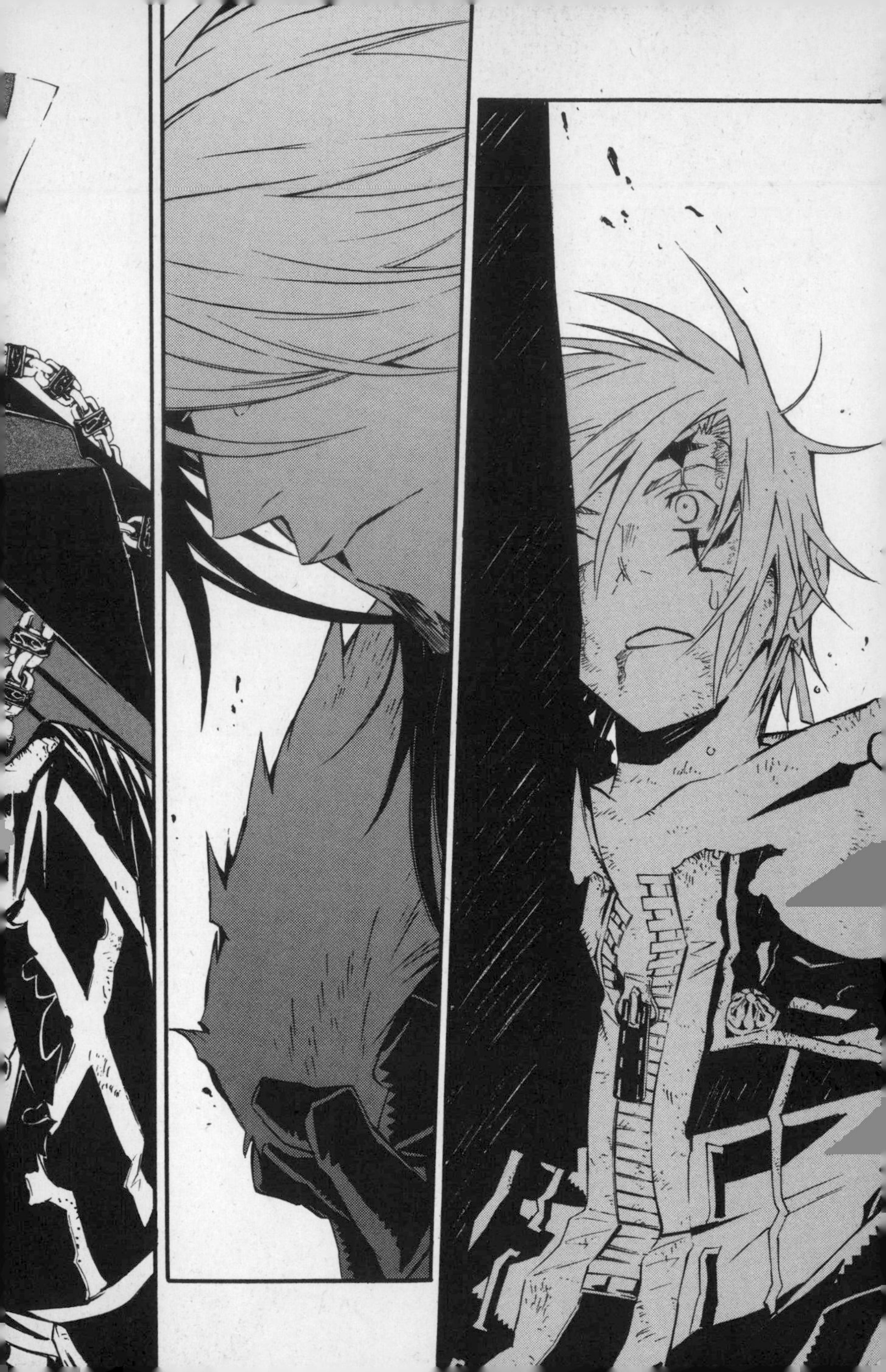

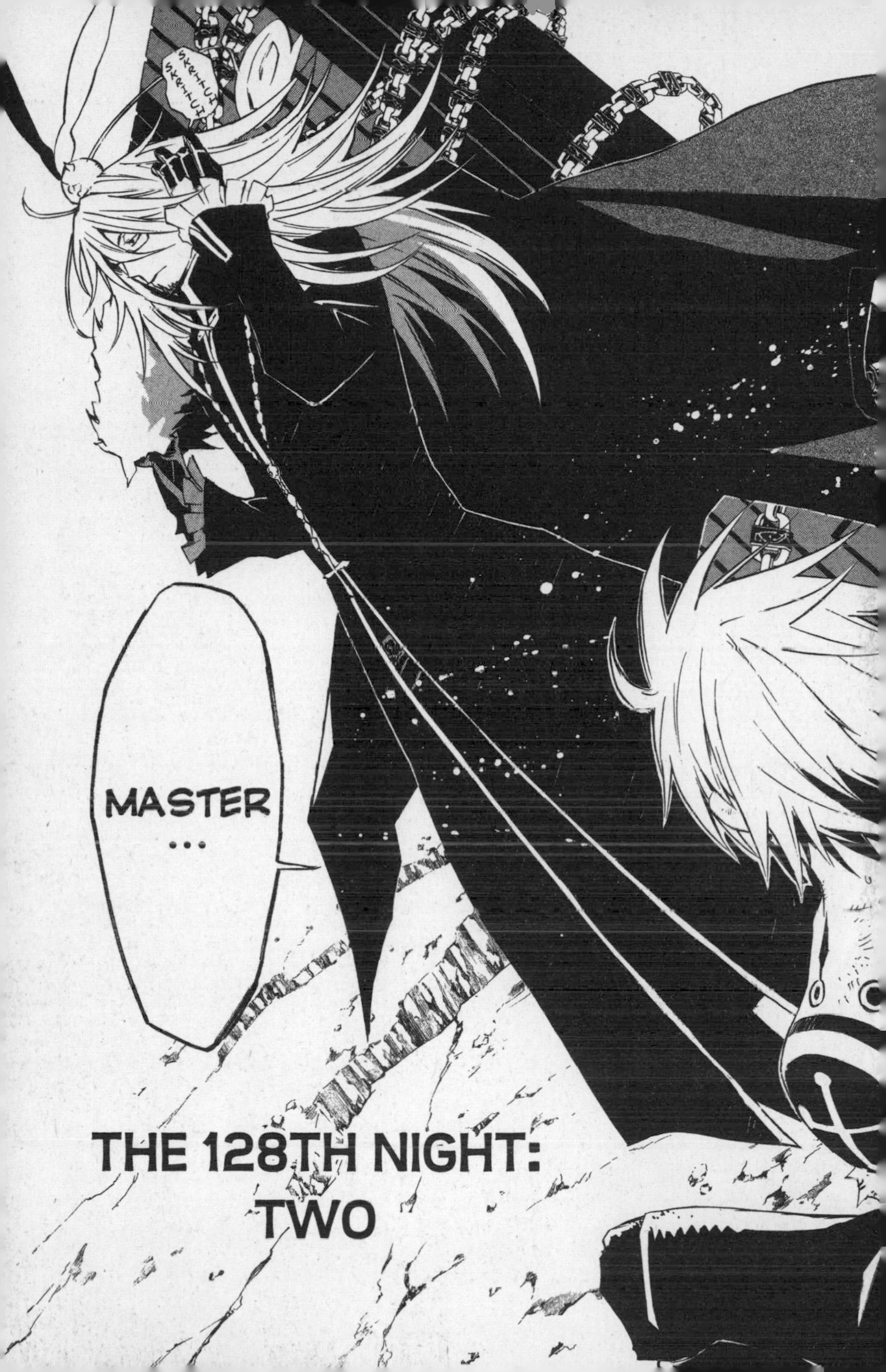
SKRITCH SKRITCH
MASTER ...
THE 128TH NIGHT: TWO

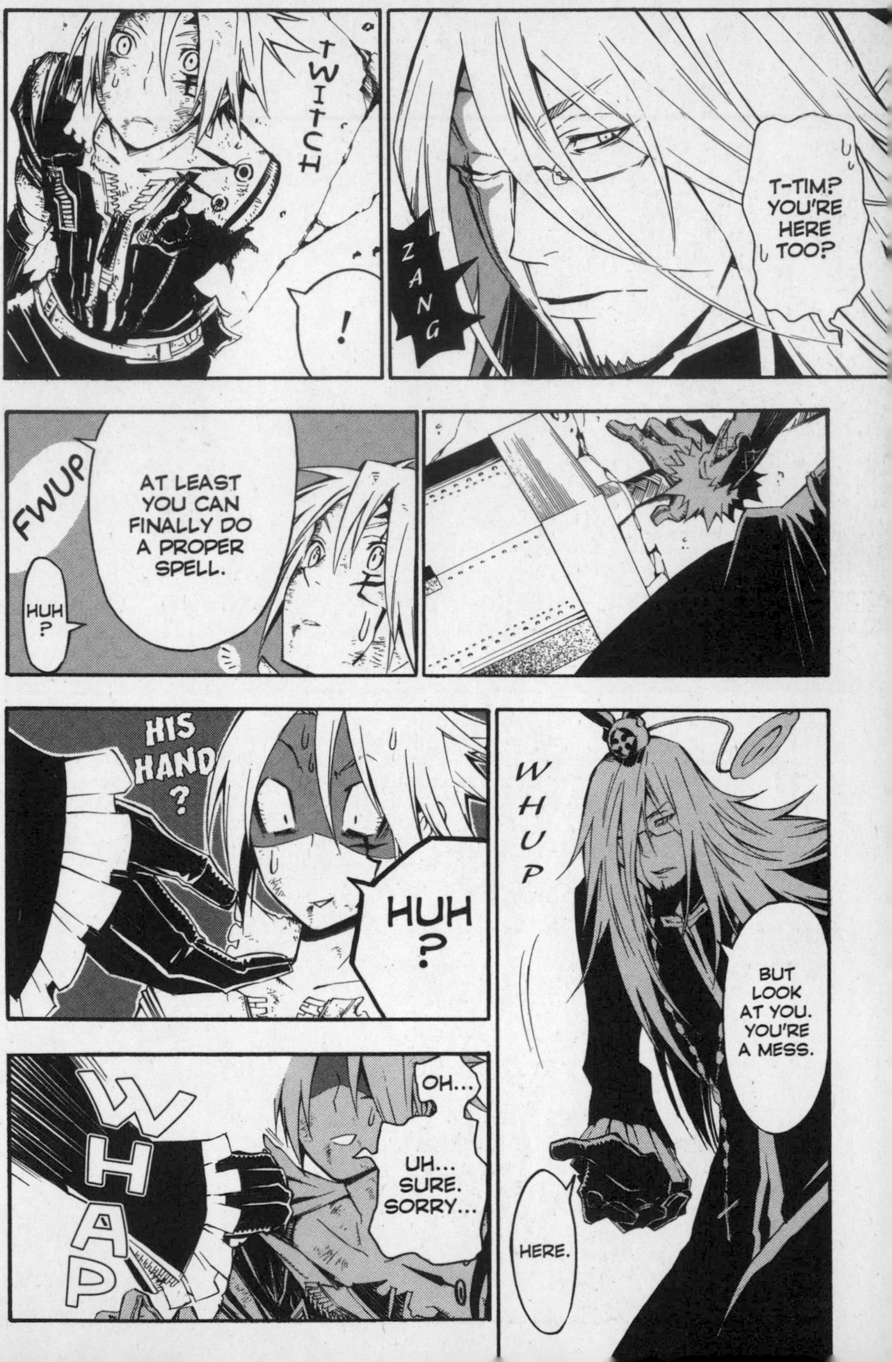
ZANG
T-TIM? YOU'RE HERE TOO?
TWITCH
!
FWUP
AT LEAST YOU CAN FINALLY DO A PROPER SPELL.
HUH?
WHUP
BUT LOOK AT YOU. YOU'RE A MESS.
HERE.
HIS HAND?
HUH?
WHAP
OH...
UH... SURE. SORRY...

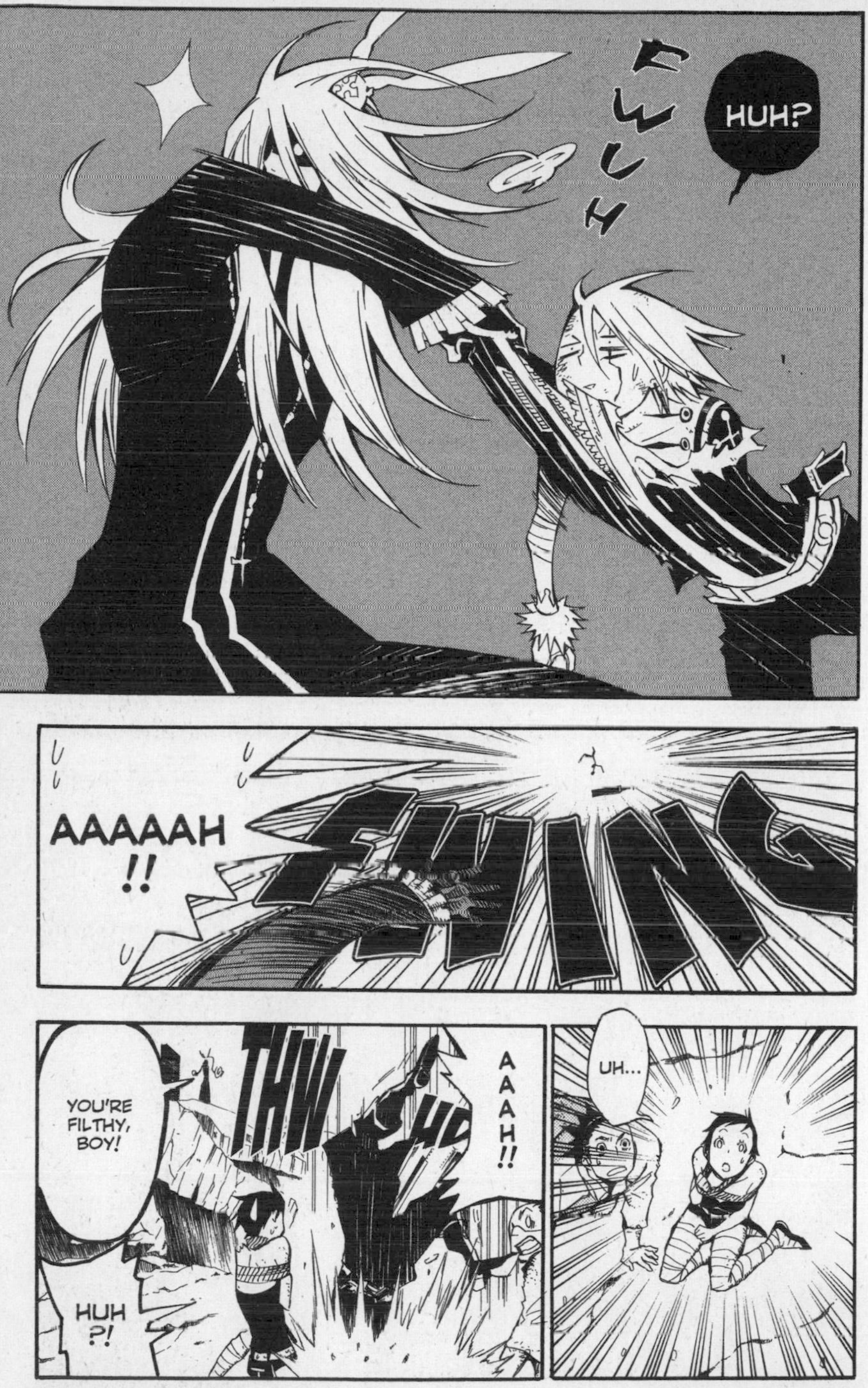
FWUH
HUH?
SHING
AAAAAH!!
UH...
AAAAH!!
THWUD
YOU'RE FILTHY, BOY!
HUH?!

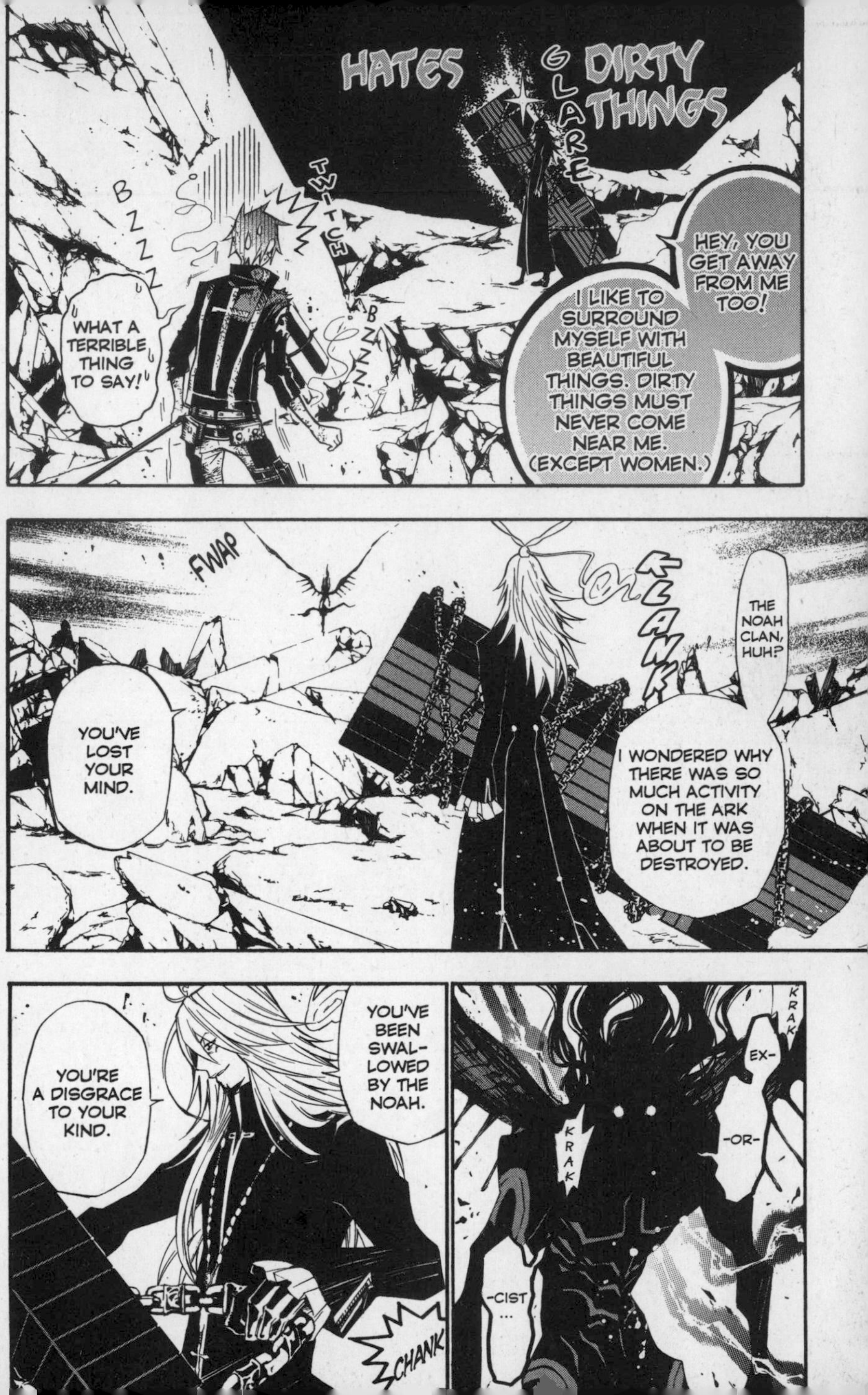
HATES DIRTY THINGS
GLARE
HEY, YOU GET AWAY FROM ME TOO!
I LIKE TO SURROUND MYSELF WITH BEAUTIFUL THINGS. DIRTY THINGS MUST NEVER COME NEAR ME. (EXCEPT WOMEN.)
TWITCH
BZZZ
BZZZ
WHAT A TERRIBLE THING TO SAY!
THE NOAH CLAN, HUH?
KLANK
I WONDERED WHY THERE WAS SO MUCH ACTIVITY ON THE ARK WHEN IT WAS ABOUT TO BE DESTROYED.
FWAP
YOU'VE LOST YOUR MIND.
KRAK
EX-
-OR-
KRAK
-CIST...
YOU'VE BEEN SWAL-LOWED BY THE NOAH.
YOU'RE A DISGRACE TO YOUR KIND.
CHANK

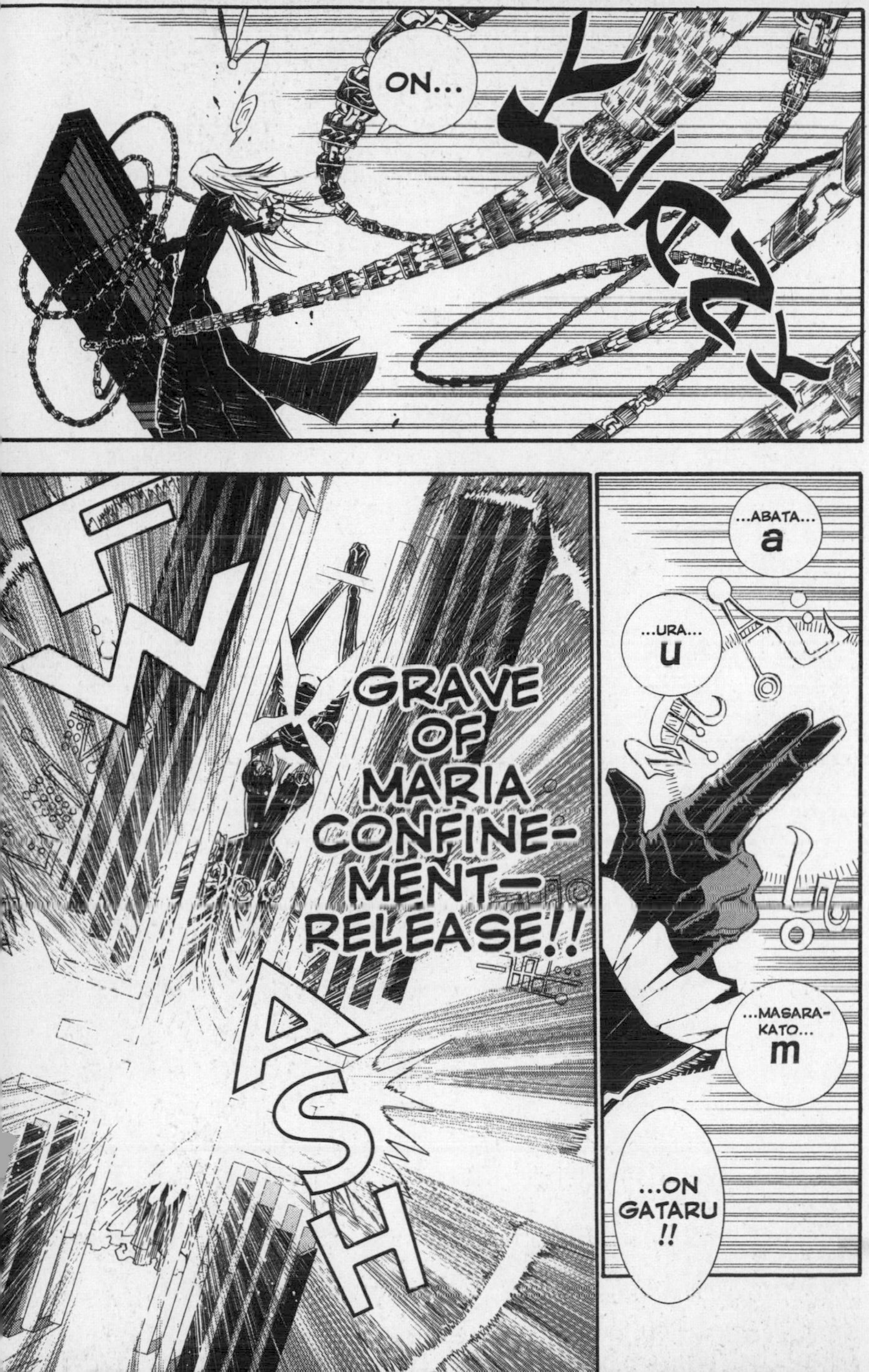
ON...
...ABATA... a
...URA... u
...MASARA-KATO... m
...ON GATARU !!
FWASH
GRAVE OF MARIA CONFINEMENT— RELEASE!!

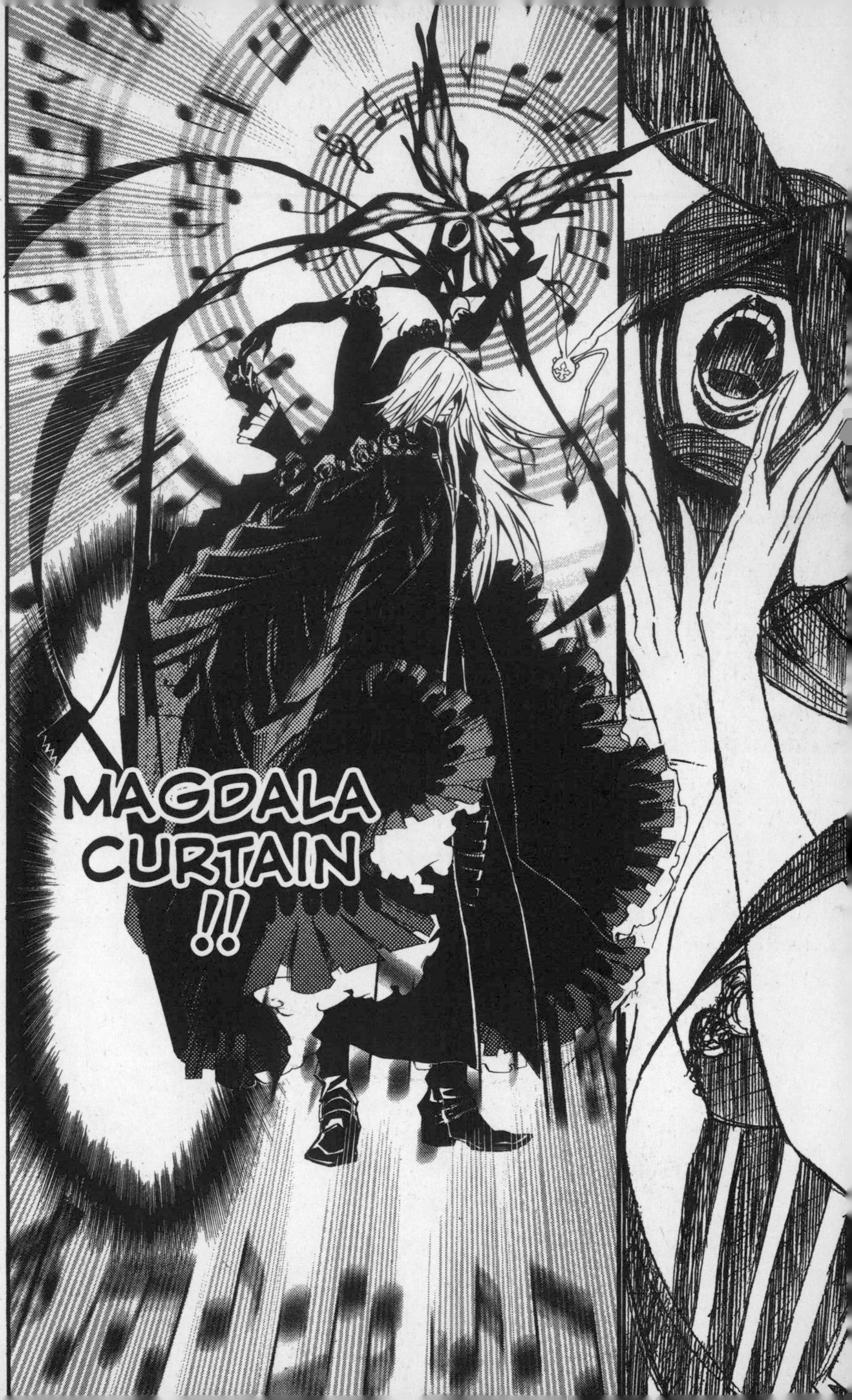
MAGDALA CURTAIN !!

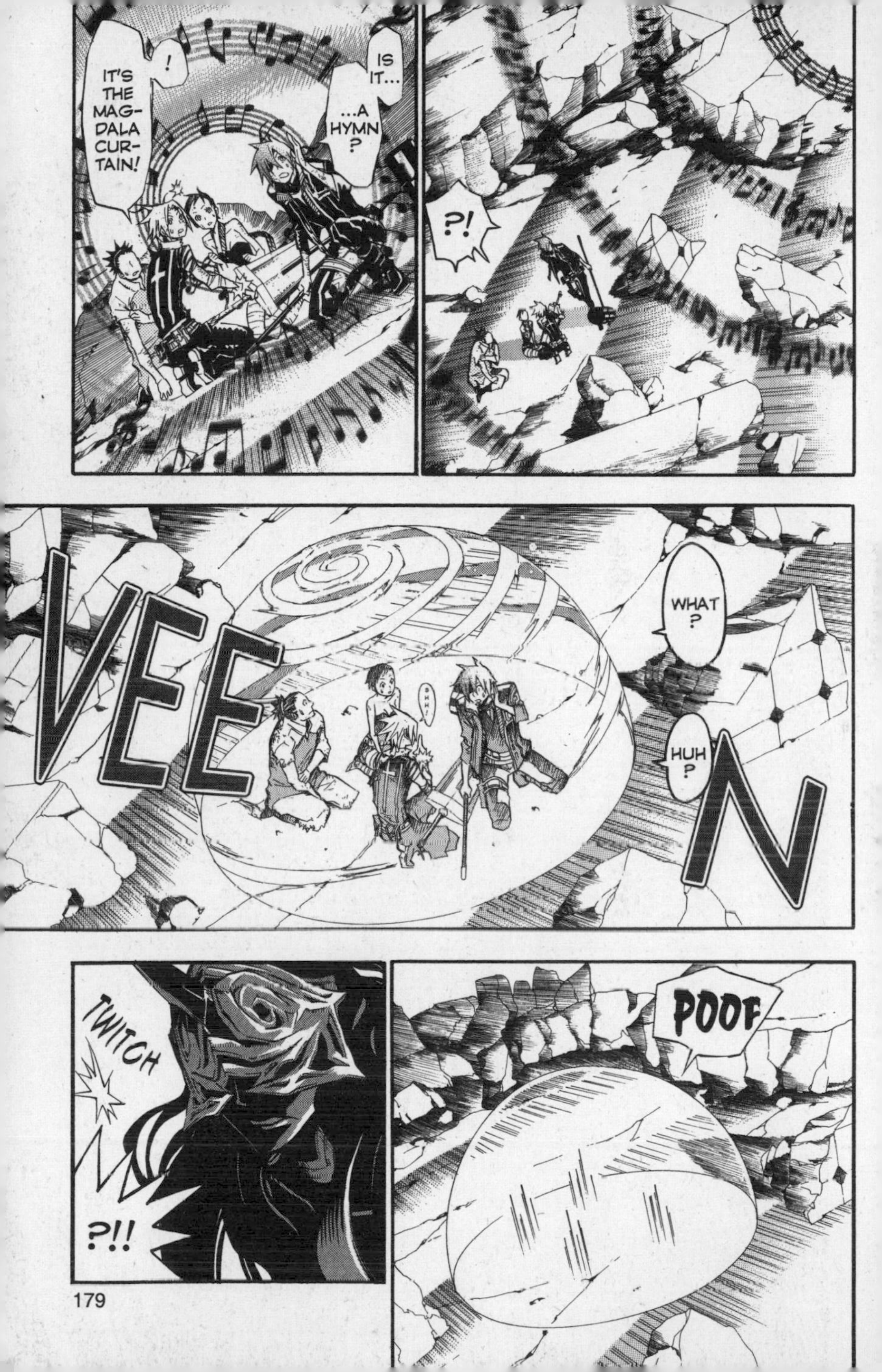
?!
IS IT...
...A HYMN?
!
IT'S THE MAGDALA CURTAIN!
WHAT?
HUH?
VEEN
POOF
TWITCH
?!!

WOOO OO

I'VE REMOVED THE CHILDREN.

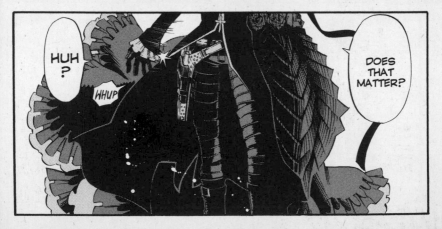

HUH?

WHUP

DOES THAT MATTER?

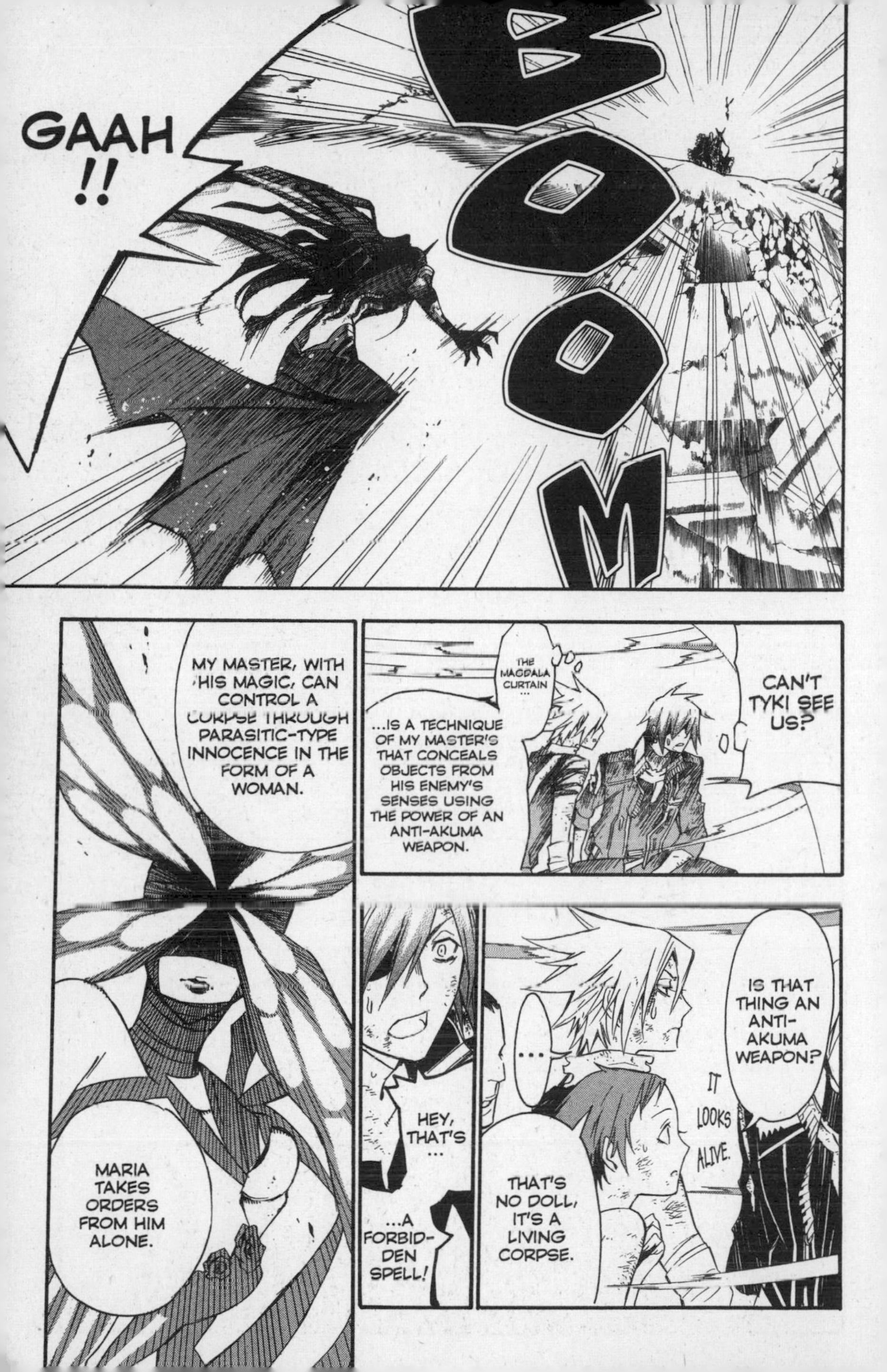
BOOM
GAAH !!
CAN'T TYKI SEE US?
THE MAGDALA CURTAIN ...
...IS A TECHNIQUE OF MY MASTER'S THAT CONCEALS OBJECTS FROM HIS ENEMY'S SENSES USING THE POWER OF AN ANTI-AKUMA WEAPON.
IS THAT THING AN ANTI-AKUMA WEAPON?
IT LOOKS ALIVE.
...
THAT'S NO DOLL, IT'S A LIVING CORPSE.
HEY, THAT'S ...
...A FORBID-DEN SPELL!
MY MASTER, WITH HIS MAGIC, CAN CONTROL A CORPSE THROUGH PARASITIC-TYPE INNOCENCE IN THE FORM OF A WOMAN.
MARIA TAKES ORDERS FROM HIM ALONE.

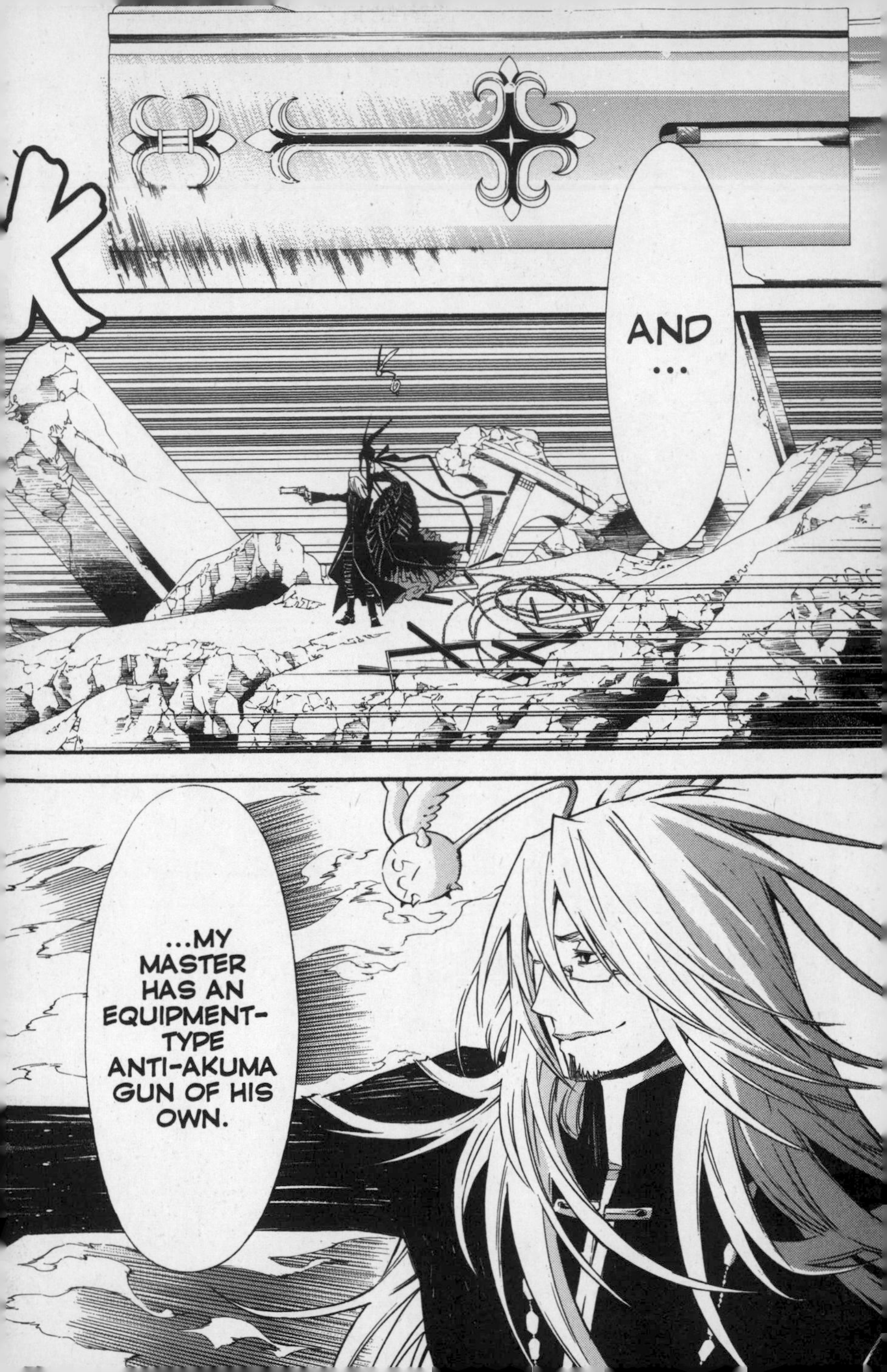
AND ...
...MY MASTER HAS AN EQUIPMENT-TYPE ANTI-AKUMA GUN OF HIS OWN.

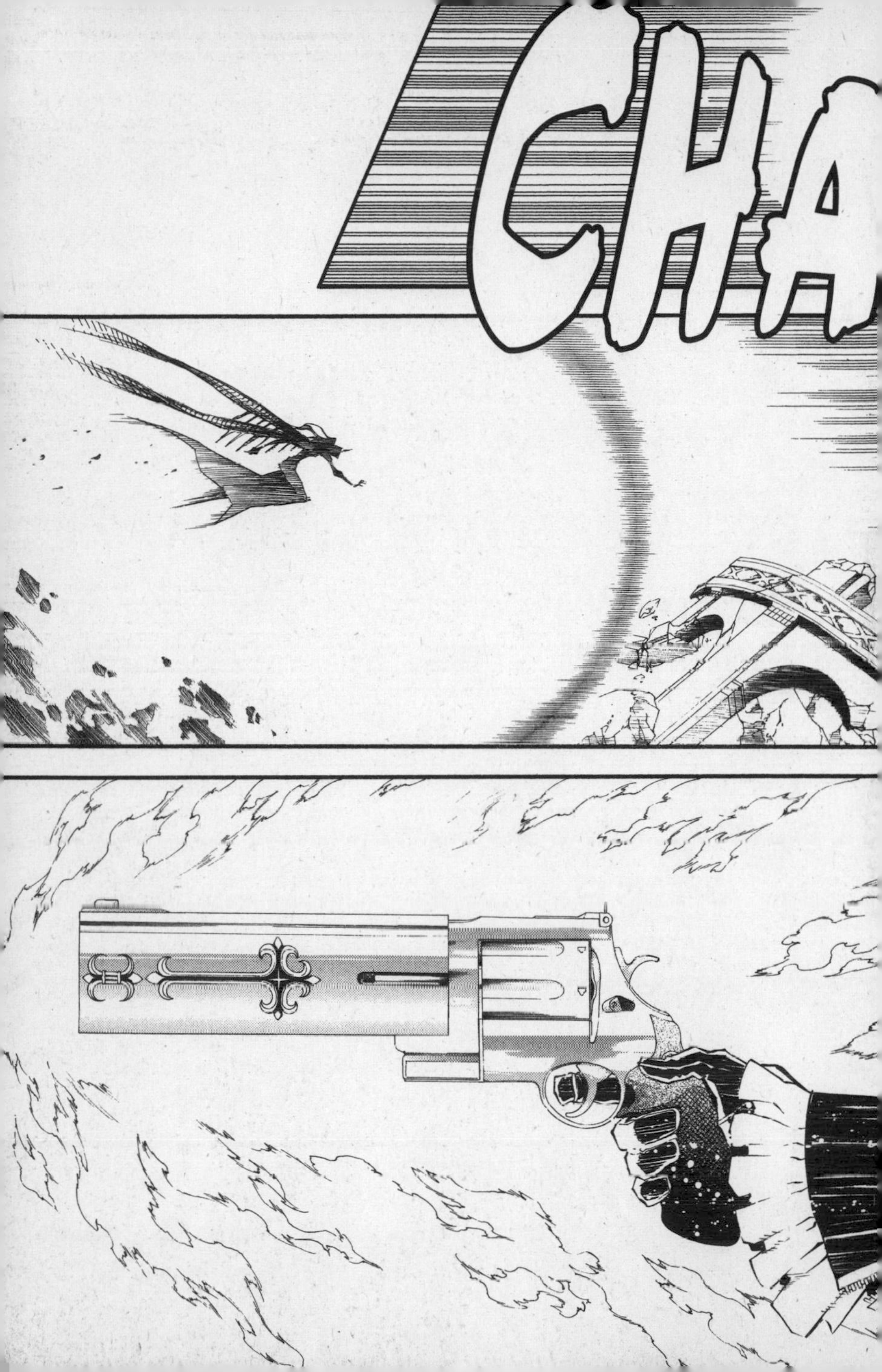
CHA

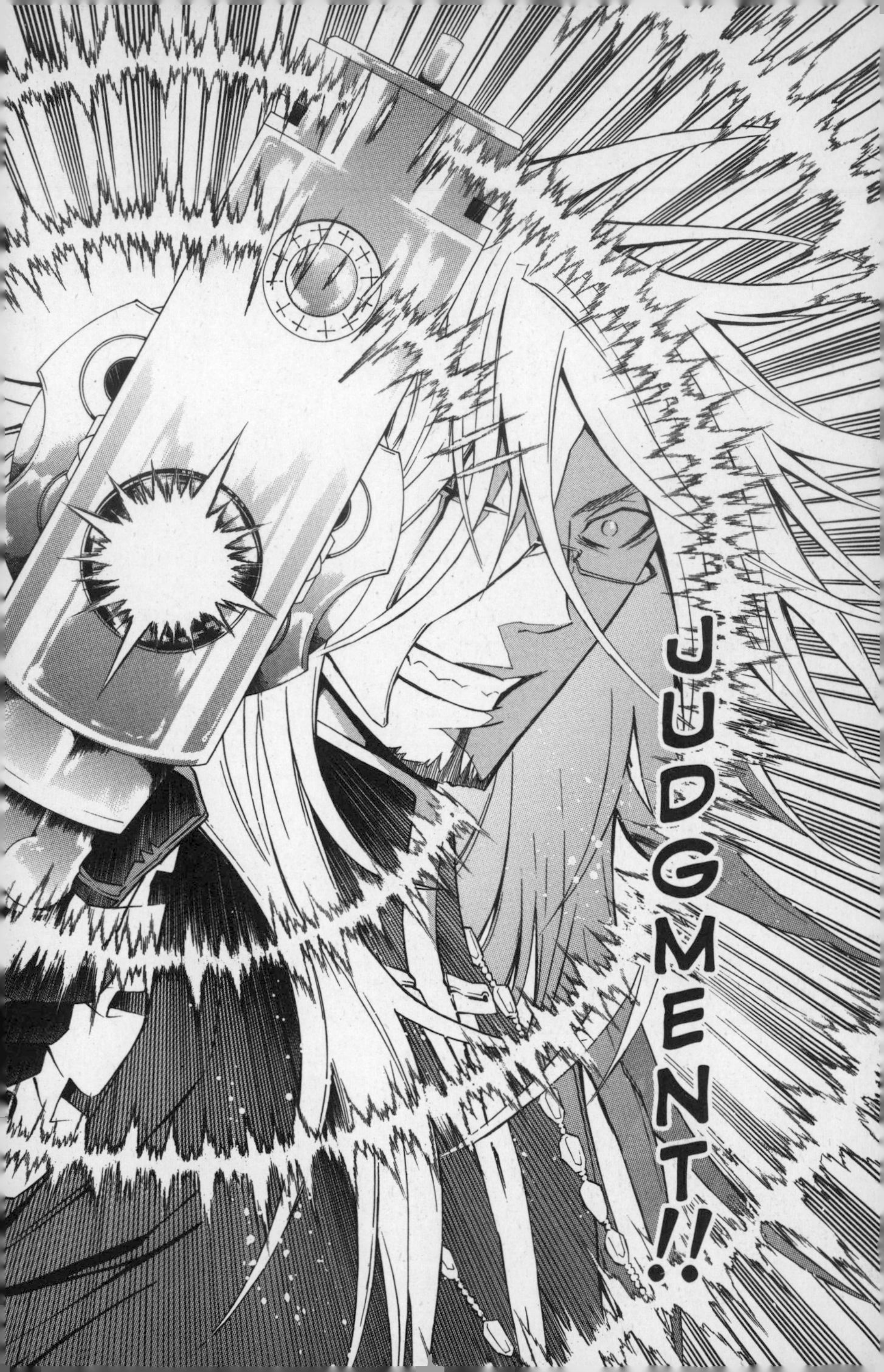
JUDGMENT!!

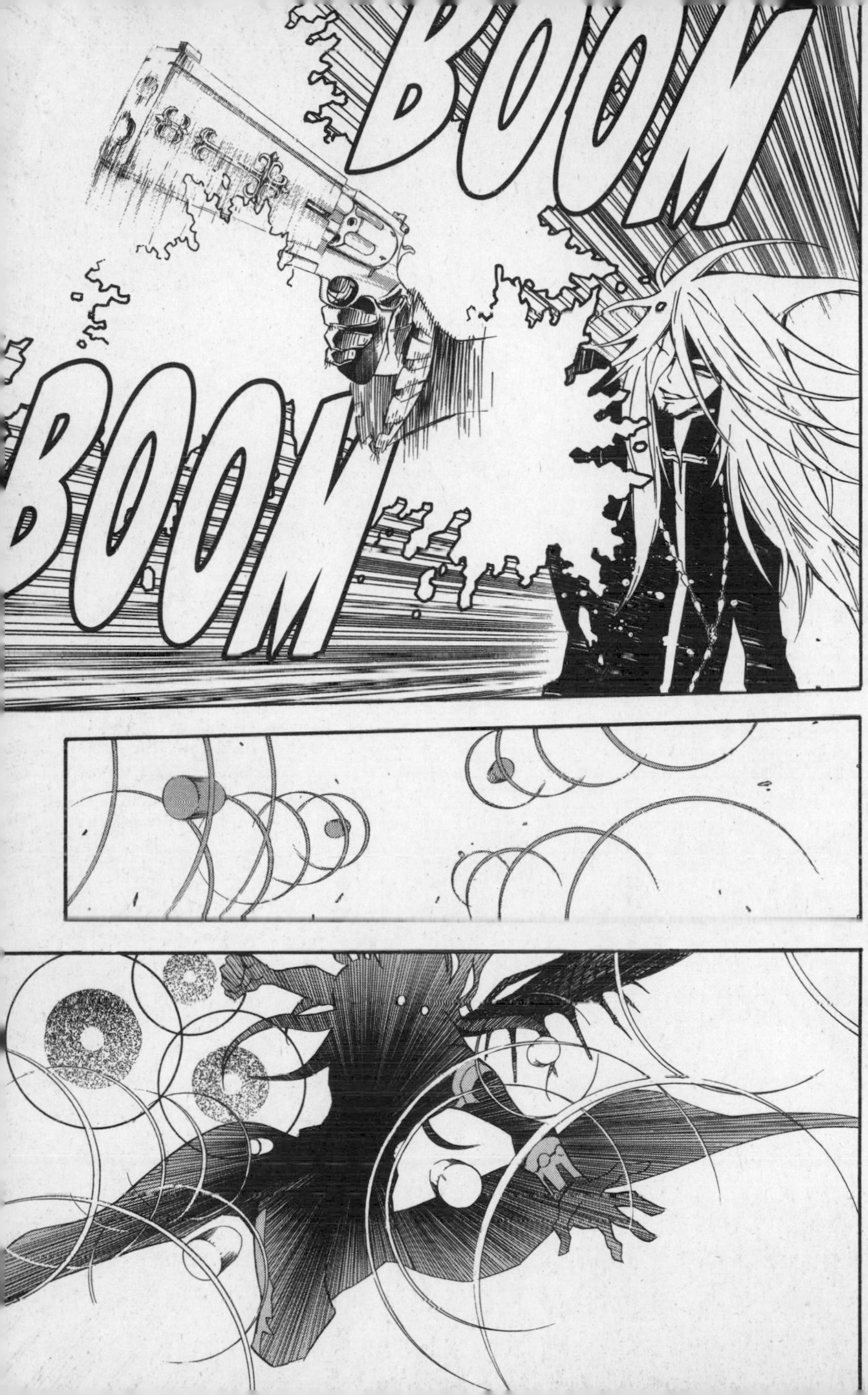
BOOM
BOOM

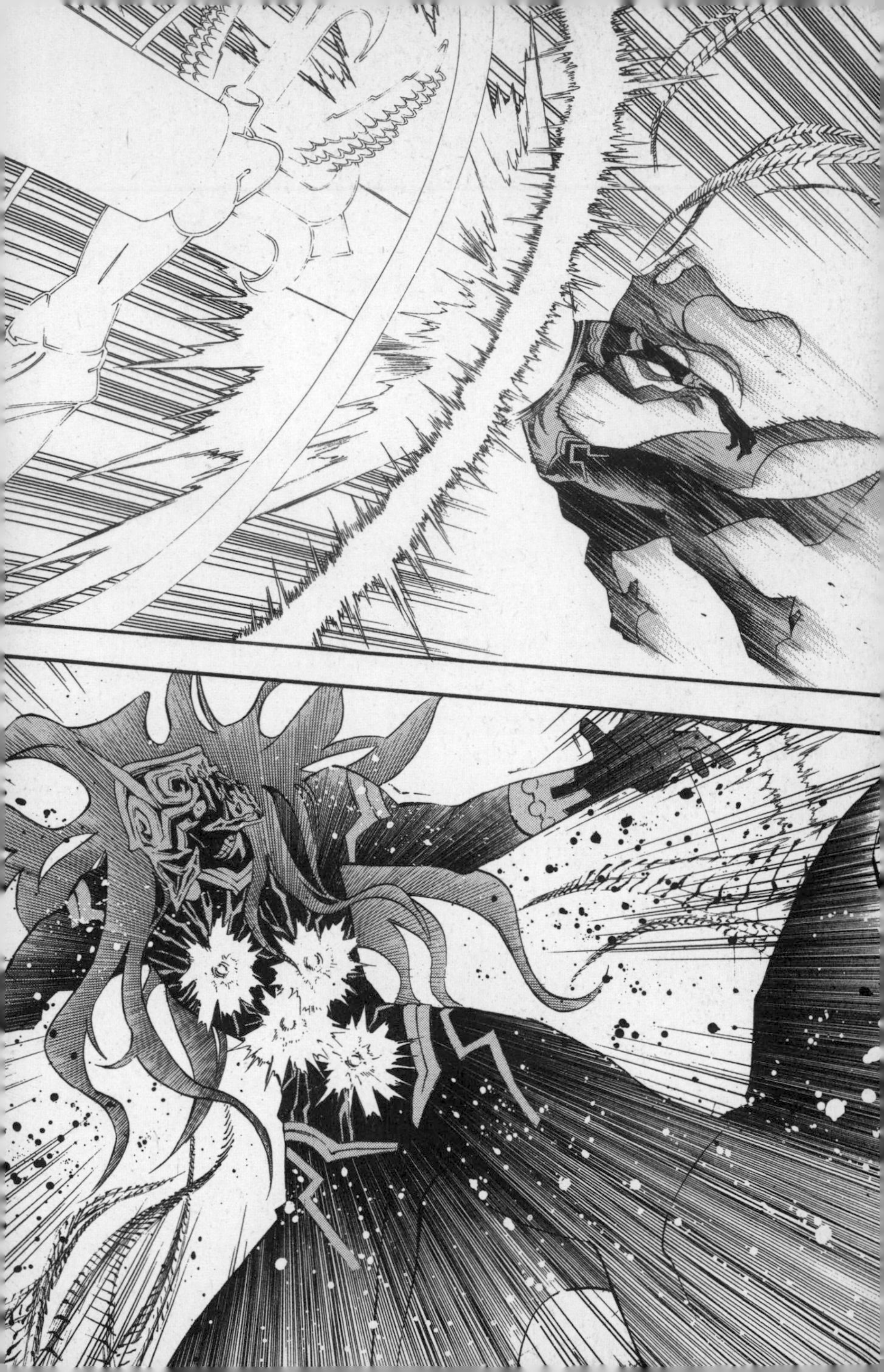

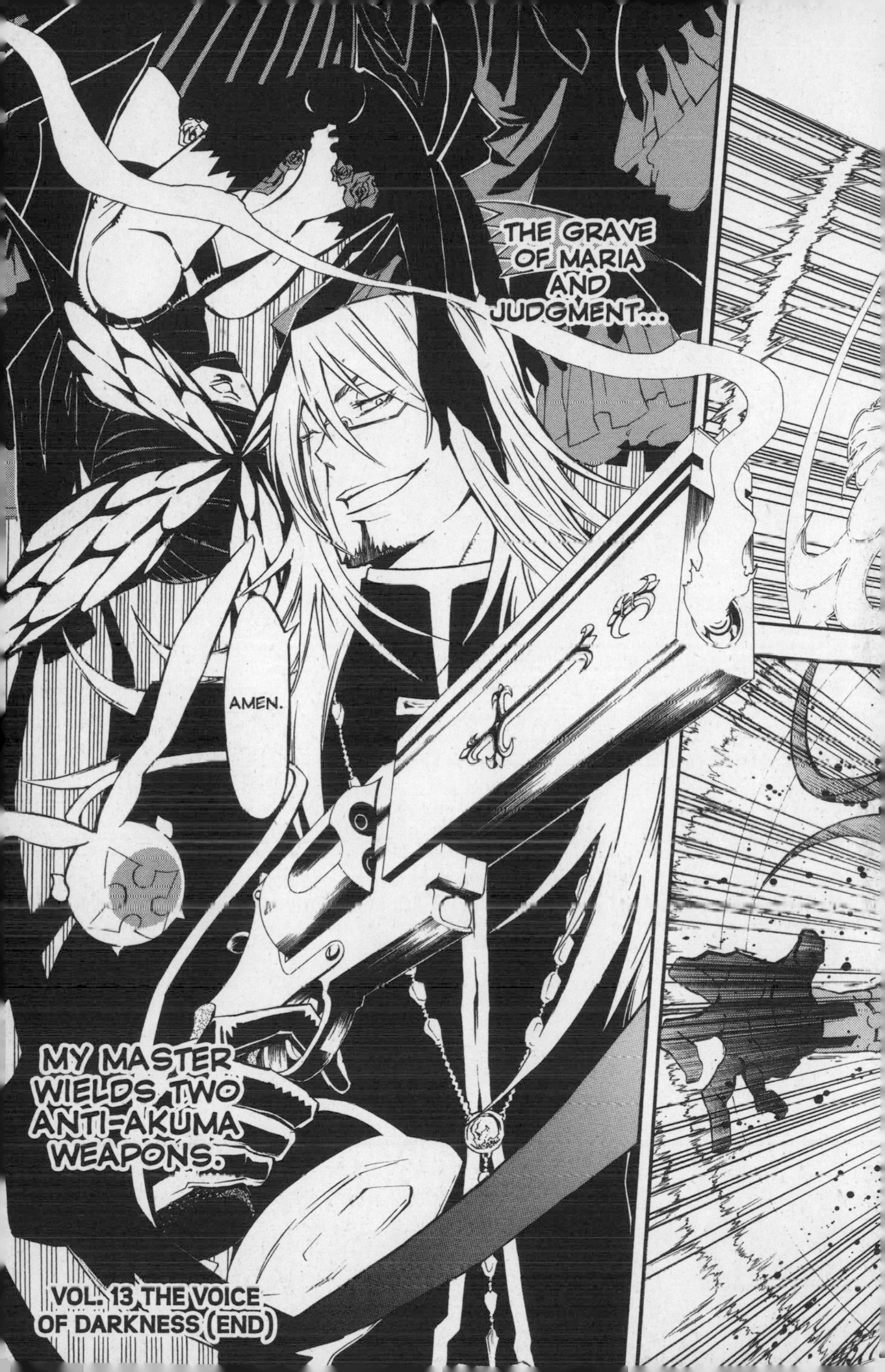
THE GRAVE OF MARIA AND JUDGMENT...
AMEN.
MY MASTER WIELDS TWO ANTI-AKUMA WEAPONS.
VOL. 13 THE VOICE OF DARKNESS (END)

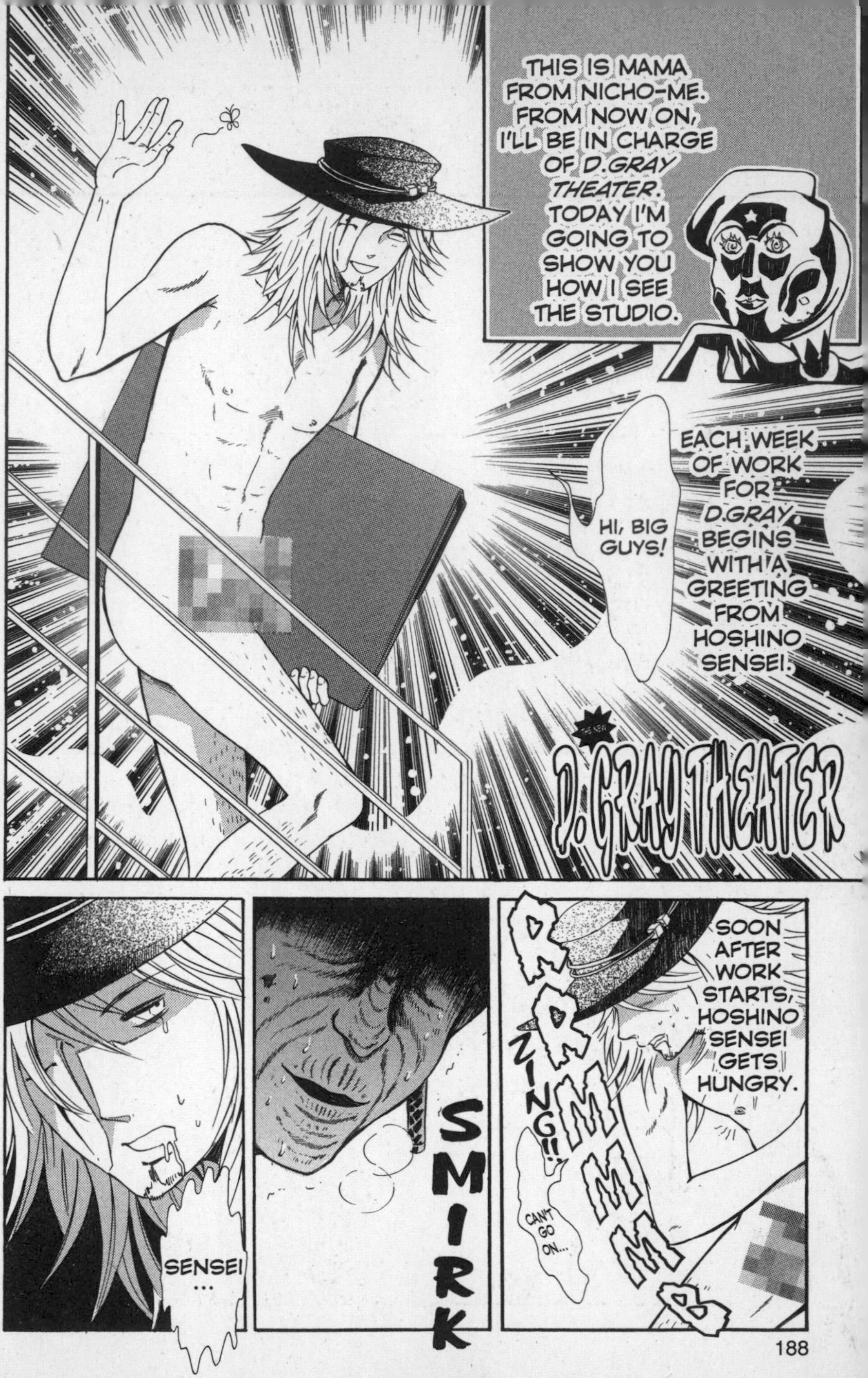
THIS IS MAMA FROM NICHO-ME. FROM NOW ON, I'LL BE IN CHARGE OF *D.GRAY THEATER*. TODAY I'M GOING TO SHOW YOU HOW I SEE THE STUDIO.
EACH WEEK OF WORK FOR *D.GRAY* BEGINS WITH A GREETING FROM HOSHINO SENSEI.
HI, BIG GUYS!
THE NEW
D.GRAY THEATER
SOON AFTER WORK STARTS, HOSHINO SENSEI GETS HUNGRY.
RRRMMMM
ZING!!
CAN'T GO ON...
SMIRK
SENSEI...

READ THIS WAY

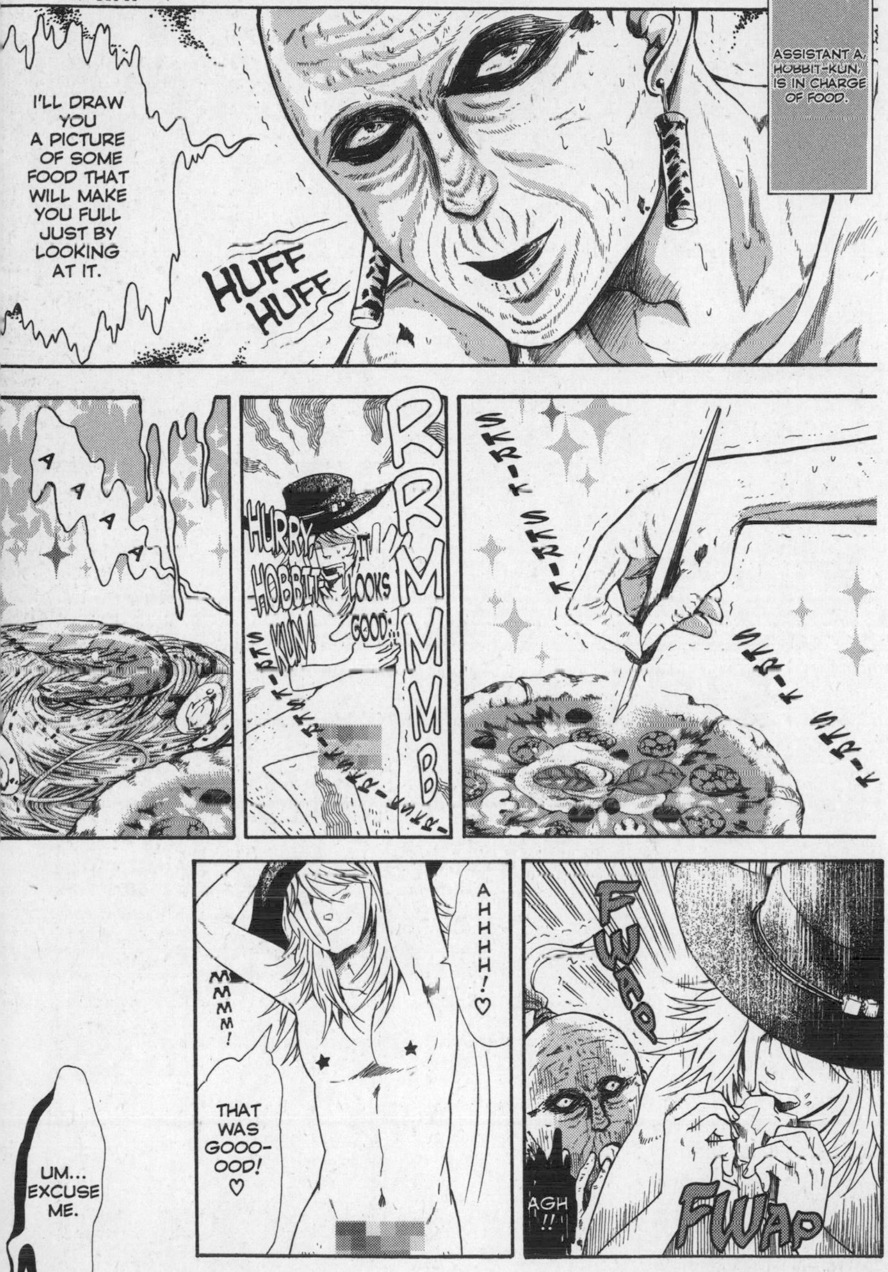

ASSISTANT A, HOBBIT-KUN, IS IN CHARGE OF FOOD.
HUFF HUFF
I'LL DRAW YOU A PICTURE OF SOME FOOD THAT WILL MAKE YOU FULL JUST BY LOOKING AT IT.
SKRIK SKRIK SKRIK
SKRIK SKRIK
RRMMMB
HURRY, HOBBIT-KUN!
IT LOOKS GOOD...
SKRIK SKRIK
AAAAA
FWAP
FWAP
AGH!!
AHHHH!♡
MMMM!
THAT WAS GOOOOOD!♡
UM... EXCUSE ME.

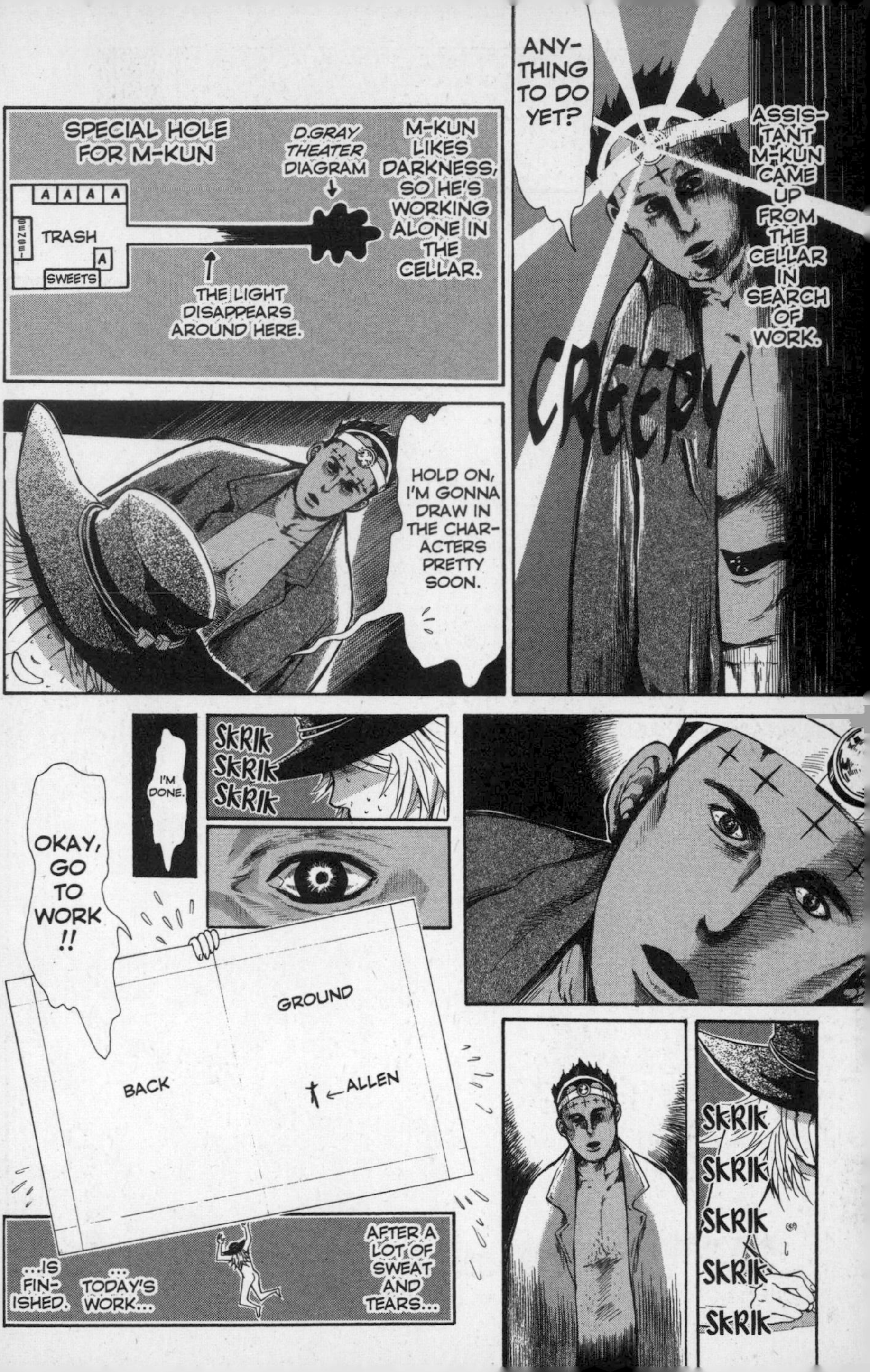
ASSIS-TANT M-KUN CAME UP FROM THE CELLAR IN SEARCH OF WORK.
ANY-THING TO DO YET?
CREEPY
M-KUN LIKES DARKNESS, SO HE'S WORKING ALONE IN THE CELLAR.
D.GRAY THEATER DIAGRAM
SPECIAL HOLE FOR M-KUN
A A A A
SENSEI
TRASH
A
SWEETS
THE LIGHT DISAPPEARS AROUND HERE.
HOLD ON, I'M GONNA DRAW IN THE CHAR-ACTERS PRETTY SOON.
SKRIK SKRIK SKRIK
I'M DONE.
OKAY, GO TO WORK !!
GROUND
BACK
ALLEN
SKRIK
SKRIK
SKRIK
SKRIK
SKRIK
AFTER A LOT OF SWEAT AND TEARS...
...TODAY'S WORK...
...IS FIN-ISHED.

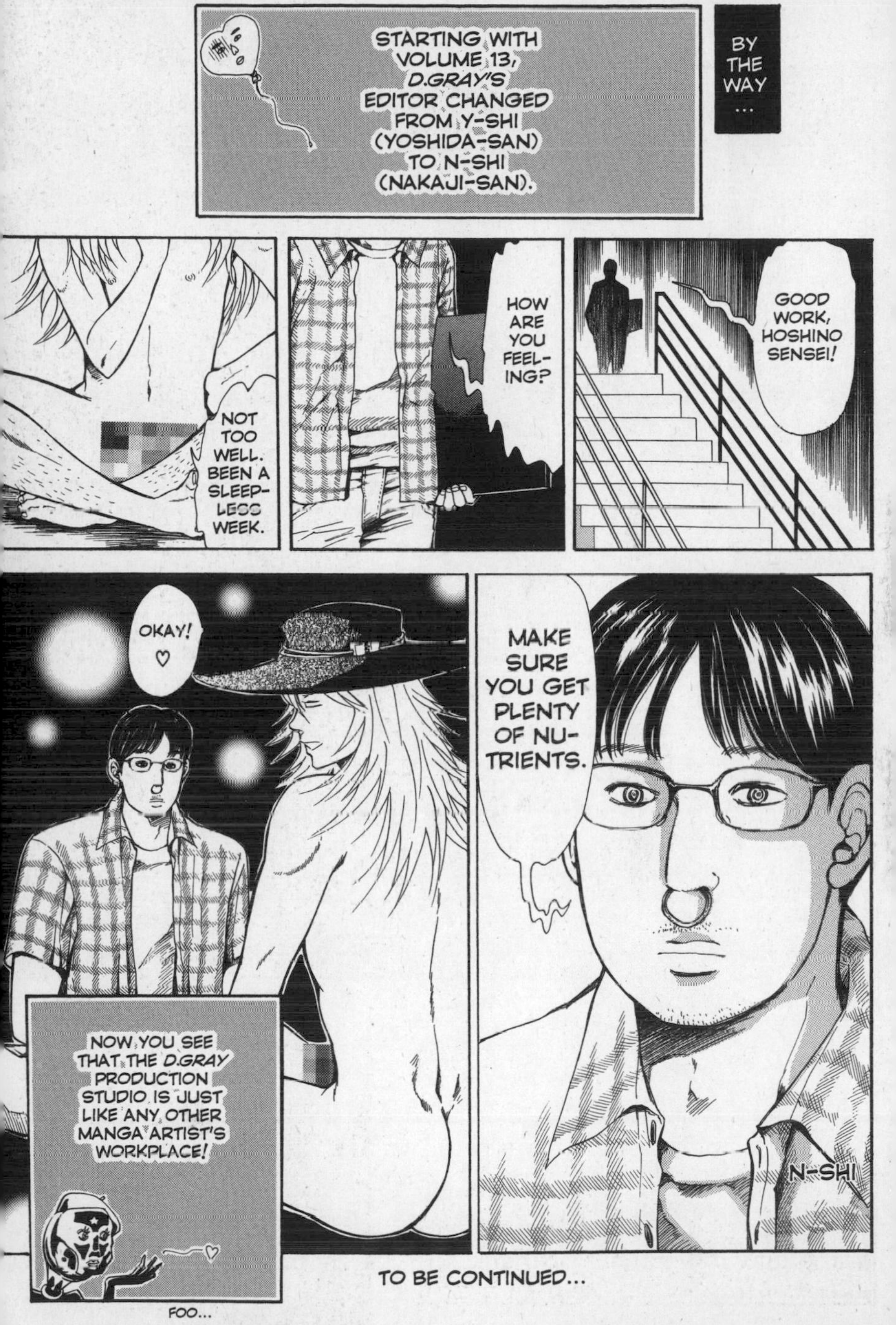
BY THE WAY ...
STARTING WITH VOLUME 13, D.GRAY'S EDITOR CHANGED FROM Y-SHI (YOSHIDA-SAN) TO N-SHI (NAKAJI-SAN).
GOOD WORK, HOSHINO SENSEI!
HOW ARE YOU FEEL-ING?
NOT TOO WELL. BEEN A SLEEP-LESS WEEK.
MAKE SURE YOU GET PLENTY OF NU-TRIENTS.
N-SHI
OKAY! ♡
NOW YOU SEE THAT THE D.GRAY PRODUCTION STUDIO IS JUST LIKE ANY OTHER MANGA ARTIST'S WORKPLACE!
~♡
FOO...
TO BE CONTINUED...

IN THE NEXT VOLUME...

Cross Marian confidently faces off against both the new Tyki Mikk and the newly arrived Millenium Earl, but fighting these menaces is not Cross's primary concern. He's come to deal with the Egg, a unique data transfer device that will allow the Millenium Earl to build a new Ark. Allen, however, holds the key to success or failure—if he can just figure out how to play the piano!

Available August 2009!

NORA
THE LAST CHRONICLE OF DEVILDOM
By Kazunari Kakei

An Exchange Student
From Hell...
LITERALLY!

**MANGA SERIES
ON SALE NOW**

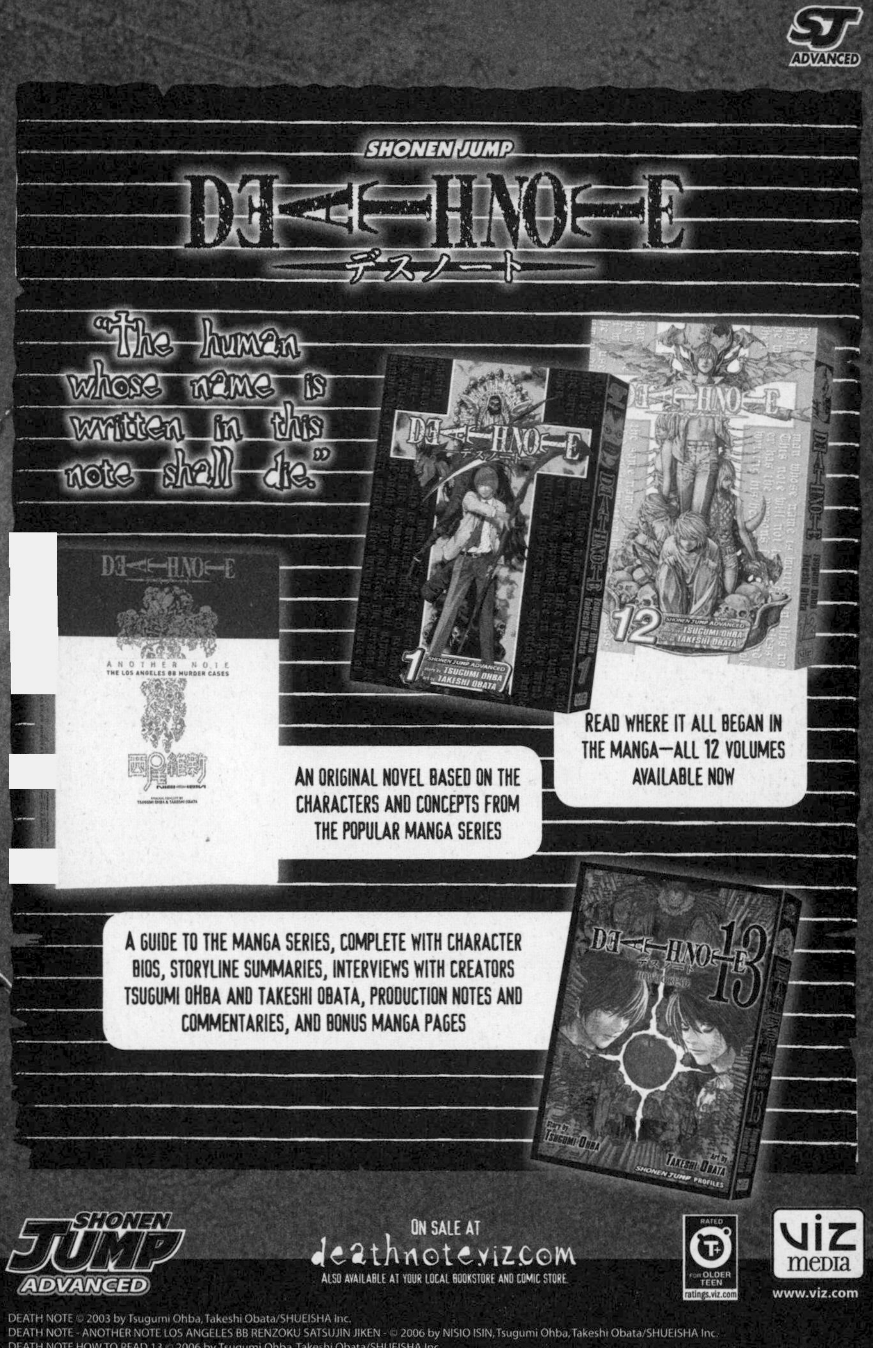
SJ ADVANCED
SHONEN JUMP
DEATH NOTE
デスノート
"The human whose name is written in this note shall die."
AN ORIGINAL NOVEL BASED ON THE CHARACTERS AND CONCEPTS FROM THE POPULAR MANGA SERIES
READ WHERE IT ALL BEGAN IN THE MANGA—ALL 12 VOLUMES AVAILABLE NOW
A GUIDE TO THE MANGA SERIES, COMPLETE WITH CHARACTER BIOS, STORYLINE SUMMARIES, INTERVIEWS WITH CREATORS TSUGUMI OHBA AND TAKESHI OBATA, PRODUCTION NOTES AND COMMENTARIES, AND BONUS MANGA PAGES
SHONEN JUMP ADVANCED
ON SALE AT
deathnote.viz.com
ALSO AVAILABLE AT YOUR LOCAL BOOKSTORE AND COMIC STORE
RATED T+ FOR OLDER TEEN
ratings.viz.com
viz media
www.viz.com

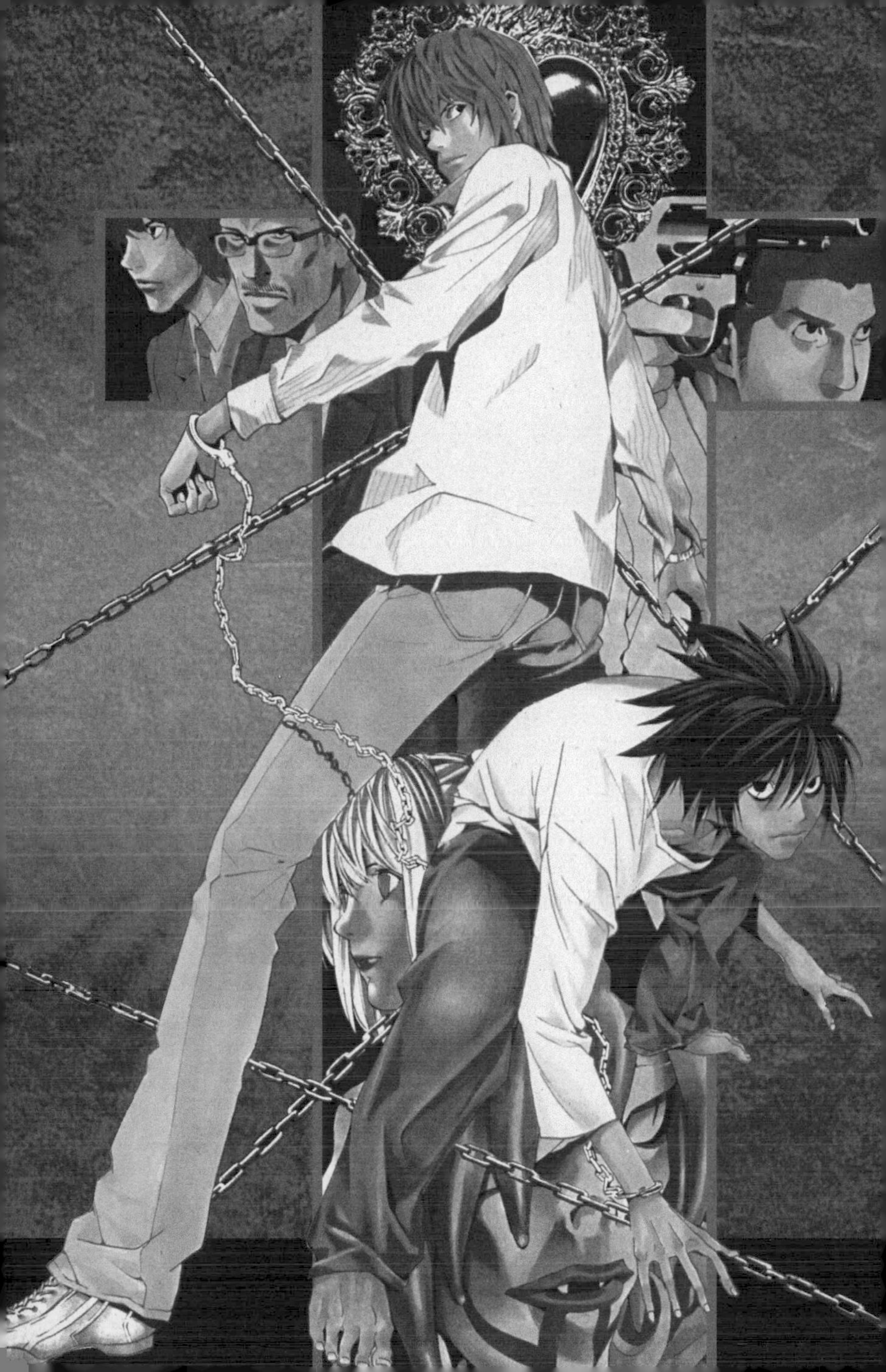

SJ PROFILES

DEATH NOTE 13

デスノート

HOW TO READ

"A god of death has no obligation to completely explain how to use the note or rules which will apply to the human who owns it"

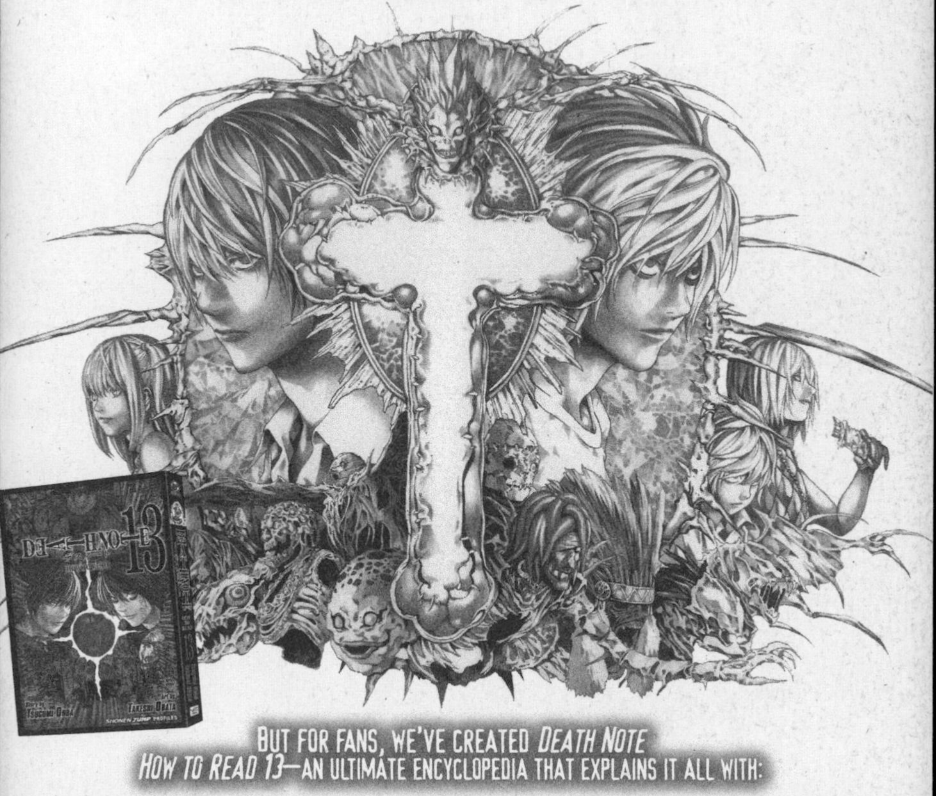

BUT FOR FANS, WE'VE CREATED *DEATH NOTE HOW TO READ 13*—AN ULTIMATE ENCYCLOPEDIA THAT EXPLAINS IT ALL WITH:

PLUS, A BONUS MANGA CHAPTER OF NEVER-BEFORE-TRANSLATED MATERIAL!
•COMPLETE CHARACTER BIOGRAPHIES •DETAILED STORYLINE SUMMARIES •PRODUCTION NOTES •BEHIND-THE-SCENES COMMENTARIES •EXCLUSIVE INTERVIEWS WITH CREATORS TSUGUMI OHBA AND TAKESHI OBATA

GET THE COMPLETE *DEATH NOTE* COLLECTION—BUY THE MANGA, FICTION AND ANIME TODAY!

SHONEN JUMP ADVANCED

ON SALE AT
DEATHNOTE.VIZ.COM
ALSO AVAILABLE AT YOUR LOCAL BOOKSTORE AND COMIC STORE.

RATED T+ FOR OLDER TEEN ratings.viz.com

viz media www.viz.com

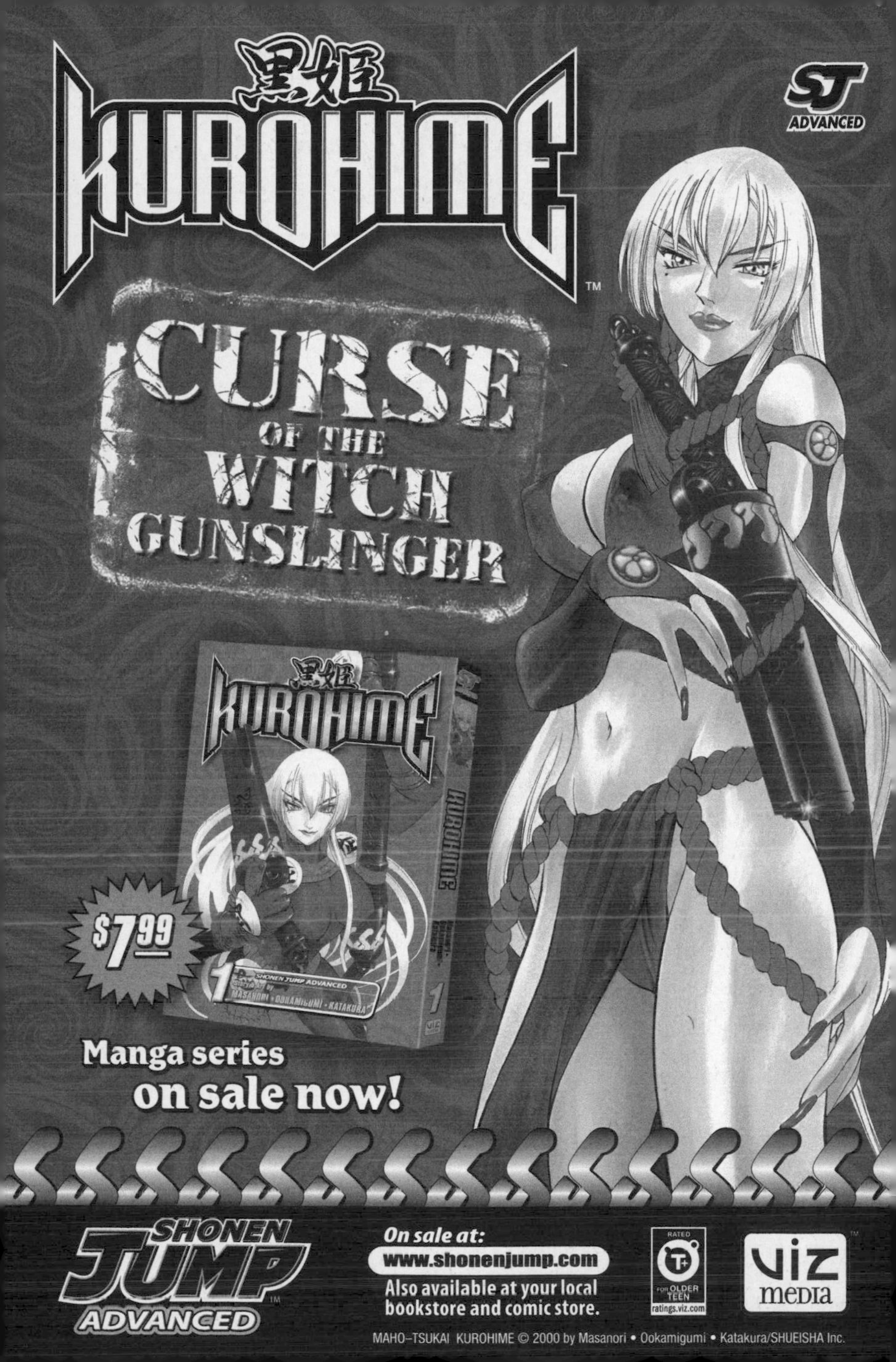

黒姫
KUROHIME™
SJ ADVANCED
CURSE OF THE WITCH GUNSLINGER
KUROHIME
SHONEN JUMP ADVANCED
MASANORI • OOKAMIGUMI • KATAKURA
$7.99
Manga series on sale now!
SHONEN JUMP ADVANCED™
On sale at:
www.shonenjump.com
Also available at your local bookstore and comic store.
RATED T+ FOR OLDER TEEN ratings.viz.com
viz media™
MAHO-TSUKAI KUROHIME © 2000 by Masanori • Ookamigumi • Katakura/SHUEISHA Inc.

Tell us what you think about SHONEN JUMP manga!

Our survey is now available online.
Go to: **www. SHONENJUMP. com/mangasurvey**

Help us make our product offering better!